T. Batista
Japan 1971

J H

New O. Weekly Mammin Ass.

STREET GANGS
AND
STREET WORKERS

STREET GANGS
AND
STREET WORKERS

Malcolm W. Klein
University of Southern California

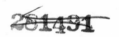

Prentice-Hall, Inc.
Englewood Cliffs, New Jersey

To Terry—
for the very best of reasons

Library of Congress Catalog Card No.:
79-163396

Printed in the United States of America

Current printing (last digit):
10 9 8 7 6 5 4 3 2 1

C 13-851519-0
P 13-851501-8

Prentice-Hall International, Inc., *London*
Prentice-Hall of Canada, Ltd., *Toronto*
Prentice-Hall of Australia, Pty., Ltd., *Sydney*
Prentice-Hall of Japan, Inc., *Tokyo*
Prentice-Hall of India Private Limited, *New Delhi*

Contents

Preface

Gang Worker: "Who you having troubles with?"

Gang
Spokesman: "High Riders, El Lobo, Chieftains, Latins, Pico-Villa."

Worker: "What happened recently?"

Spokesman: "With which one?"

In some ways, this exchange between a street gang member and a street worker speaks directly to both the content of this book and the need for it. The urban gang member is surrounded by opportunities for getting into trouble. By contrast, the gang worker is almost devoid of the resources thought necessary to reduce those opportunities and the gang's penchant for using them. There is still so little known about gangs and so much assumed about gang work that putting the two together is a highly questionable enterprise. But this is what I have attempted in this book.

In committing this material to paper, I have tried to keep three audiences in mind. For the academic community, and particularly students of delinquency, I have tried to provide a summary of the current state of knowledge about juvenile gangs. The emphasis here is upon empirical knowledge rather than theoretical suppositions or attempts at casual explanations. I have become, regrettably, highly sympathetic toward Gresham Sykes' conclusion: "... It is worth raising the possibility that current theories of crime causation are not so much wrong as irrelevant for a large share of criminals."*

---

*Gresham M. Sykes, *Crime and Society*, 2nd ed. (New York: Random House, 1967), p. 136.

The gang theories of Cohen, Miller, Cloward and Ohlin, Bloch and Niederhoffer, and others mentioned throughout the book *each* seem to make so much sense that they have proven—to me, at least—unproductive guideposts. As one becomes familiar with the members of a juvenile gang, he finds that it contains Cohen-type boys, Miller-type boys, Cloward-and-Ohlin-type boys, and perhaps an equal number whose situations seem to refute the core of each theory. I very much fear that the gang has been the theoretician's Rorschach in criminology —one can easily find what he seeks. In the following quotes from two of my favorite gang boys, those readers familiar with gang theory will recognize first the Cloward and Ohlin boy and second the Cohen boy. Both were responding to the same query, "What's it like, living around here?"

> Negroes and Mexican-Americans, we all get the low things in life compared to what the regular white person have ... We don't have that rich envir'ment that we can drive Daddy's car and let him put us through college ... We don't see Daddy in his suit every day and his white tie—we can't go to his office ... Now, you read the statistics and they say the crime rate is higher in the poor neighborhoods ... And why is it high, because we don't have the drive to go to school but we have to have money ... So, if it's crime that get us there, then that's the path that we take to get it. We don't have too many paths to take. (Former President, the Red Raiders)
>
> Man, bein' poor's a motherfucker. (Former President, the Operators)

For my academic friends, then, this book is empirically oriented, quite speculative at points, but atheoretical: it is hard to say—ever—that theory is premature, yet the current status of gang research is such that to build either a single project or a single book around one theoretical approach seems to me terribly confining. We must still build *toward* theory more than from it.

My second audience is the practitioners—the gang worker and, even more importantly, his supervisor and administrator. There are some things this group must hear, lest they continue, inadvertently, to compound the problem of the juvenile gang. It is the clear message of our Los Angeles research and the six years my colleagues and I spent on the streets with gang workers that new approaches must be tried out; the traditional ones range from ineffective to destructive. "It's like working in a factory," one gang worker told me, "but you're not standing at the machine, you know—you can do anything you want to do."

Unfortunately, this "factory" turns out some undesired products and the traditional stance accurately reflected by this worker does nothing to control the output. I hope that my practitioner audience will read these pages without assuming a defensive posture. I know of no gang intervention program which, in the face of the evidence to be presented here, can afford to say "that doesn't apply to us." The tragedy is that it does.

My third audience is that strange breed of cat, the action researcher, or—more properly—the researcher who desires to test his notions in the field setting. I can't claim the research described in this book as a model, but a description of some of the procedures and problems involved can, I trust, be of value to others whose laboratory is the street. I can't imagine why it is that we teach research methods courses as if there were no constraints on the research, or report our research results as if they were simply the end product of a purely logical, efficient, and rational procedure. The action research procedures in particular are so open to uncontrolled and unpredicted events that we might well be grateful for *any* furtherance of knowledge that results. The descriptions of our gang research in Los Angeles are therefore somewhat more personal and more concerned with our failures than may be customary.

The aim of this book is quite simple. I hope to please my three assumed audiences. I hope to do so by providing for each of them materials of value, be they hard data, observations, speculations, or caveats. Secondarily, I think I owe it to all who have worked with me these last few years to communicate their experiences to as wide an audience as possible. Finally, the book allows me to pull together and fulfill in one stroke my obligations to all those who gave financial support to our research projects and to my other related activities since 1962.

The Ford Foundation was the instigator. In 1961, the Foundation awarded a grant of $132,764 to the Los Angeles County Probation Department to carry out a four year program of intensified gang intervention. The program was to be run by the Group Guidance Section of the department, a detached worker operation with an eighteen year history of gang work. To accompany this grant, the County of Los Angeles was to contribute an additional $117,108 in direct services and an estimated $114,936 in indirect services.

At the same time, the Foundation provided a grant of $138,580 to the Youth Studies Center of the University of Southern California to evaluate the impact of the program which came to be known as the Group Guidance Project. After the first year, the need for a full-time research director became apparent and I was asked to fill that position.

Shortly thereafter, we received a grant of $57,852 from the National Institute of Mental Health (#MH07993) to investigate the nature and roles of female gangs. Together, these two research grants permitted the gathering of much of the data presented in Parts I and II.

Upon completion of the Group Guidance Project and as it became quite clear that the results were going to be quite negatively toned, two of my colleagues—Lois Y. Crawford and Richard I. Martin—joined with me in designing a new project which we hoped would be quite distinctive. First, the intervention model was to be fully spelled out in advance and based *solely* on the data from the Group Guidance Project. Second, the intervention procedures were themselves to be based on the model and on constantly updated information from the field setting. Third, as opposed to the Group Guidance Project, the new project was to be under the control of the research team. There would be no administrative separation between research and field operations.

The project, known by the pseudonym The Ladino Hills Project, was supported by a two-year grant of $119,519 from the Office of Juvenile Delinquency and Youth Development, H.E.W. (Grant #66012) and a matching grant of $46,825 from the Ford Foundation. The Los Angeles County Commission on Human Relations contributed an additional $12,694, primarily in "in kind" costs and acted as a partner in the project.

In line with much of the above, the book is divided into three sections. In Part I, I have been concerned primarily with questions of knowledge about gangs—what is known, what has been reported, what are the sources of this knowledge. I have concentrated on matters of gang structure and delinquency, as did our research. Although the Group Guidance and Ladino Hills Projects provided much of the data—especially in Chapters 3 and 4—Part I also serves as a summary on a national level. Much of this summary material is taken from my report on gang violence to the National Commission on the Causes and Prevention of Violence (*Crimes of Violence*, Washington, D.C.: Report of the Task Force on Individual Acts of Violence, U.S.G.P.O., 1970, Appendix 31).

Part II contains the bulk of the material on the workers and the nature of gang programs. But rather than handle this material separately, I have attempted to tie it to the data of Part I, especially those dealing with gang cohesiveness and delinquency.

Part III, being basically a report on the Ladino Hills Project, brings much of the preceding material together since it puts to the test major hypotheses generated out of the preceding projects and literature reviews. This, while each of the three major parts of the book can be read separately and are so designed, I would hope that the serious student would work through all three sections in order, as there is a logical sequence therein. It is a matter of some pride that one is able to progress from an exploratory project which is used to generate hypotheses to a second project designed to test those hypotheses.

It is a bit incongruous that this book is authored by a single individual. Field research and action over a six or seven year period obviously involves many, many people in diverse capacities. In merely listing their names, I do many an injustice, for their contributions were truly valued and often quite unique. I apologize for the coldness of our standard acknowledgment format.

Those who worked on the street or supervised that work included Richard Brown, James Burks, Rex Christensen, Alva T. Collier, Miguel Duran, Sue Eichelsbach, Raul Felix, Evelyn Gaines, Joan Green, Richard Gravelly, Ray Herbert, Frances Hollis, Verne Horn, Bruce Hunter, William Jones, Al Koenig, Gerry Moore, Gwen Moore, Ricardo Munoz, Gwen Murphy, Carole Nusinow, Borden Olive, Donald Porter, Norton Sanders, James Schwab, Fred Scott, Anthony Serrato, Ralph Sterling, Robert Tandy, Dave Torres, Norman Weiss, and Ernest Wilson.

Members of the research and administrative staffs of the L. A. County Probation Department who were particularly involved in the projects were Stuart Adams, Jack Cocks, Karl Holton, Elnoise Jett, Ellen Kanagae, David MacPherson, Harold Muntz, Roger Rice, and Carl Terwilliger.

From the L. A. County Department of Community Services, David Bisno, Jerry Inglis, and Burton Powell of the administrative staff bravely accepted the burdens of interagency collaboration. For the same reasons, thanks are extended to John Buggs and Herbert Carter of the County Commission on Human Relations, C. R. Gross and W. L. Richey of the Los Angeles Police Department, Leonard Herendeen of the Los Angeles County Sheriff's Office, and Fred Schneidewind of the California Youth Authority.

In the Ladino Hills Community, special thanks for opening doors and supporting the staff go to John Badger, Nick Lucero, Stephen Salenger, and John Tutak.

At the University of Southern California's Youth Studies Center (now incorporated into the Public Systems Research Institute), a number of people were associated with the research team, or used project data, or in some other direct way contributed to the projects. Included among these were Herbert Aarons, Elizabeth Alaniz, Vivian Brown, Lois Y. Crawford, Janna Gadden, Albert Gasser, Annette Gromfin, Helen Shimota Gross, LeRoy Gruner, Jean Studt Gunnel, Chung Kwan Ha, Carolyn Johnson, Truman Jolley, Helen Kandel, Jewel Kilgour, Ann Mangum, Wiley Mangum, Richard I. Martin, Kenneth Mitchel, Barbara

Myerhoff, Hooshang Poorkaj, Paul Pope, Rudy Sanfilippo, David Shichor, Neal Snyder, Eileen Ward, Daniel Wilner, Judy Weissman Wilson, and Serrapio Zalba.

Very special appreciation is expressed to LaMar T. Empey, Karl Holton, E. K. Nelson and A. W. McEachern whose administrative skills and valued friendship made every step easier and more worth the taking. LaMar T. Empey, Solomon Kobrin, and Wiley Mangum were particularly helpful in their critical evaluations of this manuscript. I am grateful for their honest appraisals and generous encouragement.

In addition, I am indebted to Anthony Serrato, who could do more with gang boys in five minutes than I ever imagined possible. I sometimes felt that Tony had accepted as his special mission in life teaching me about the realities of both the gang and the gang worker. He was a fine teacher and remains—perhaps to his surprise—a valued colleague.

The boys and girls whom we knew as the Operators, Generals, Red Raiders, Victors and Latins never were asked if we could work with them, around them, or even on occasion against them. But they tolerated us, and this may be the supreme compliment. For their sakes, and in memory of the three who died so violently, I fervently hope we may yet devise effective techniques for the resolution of gang problems. The lesson by now is clear; such resolution starts in research and is clarified only as a solid knowledge base is established. This, I trust, is the contribution of this volume.

Los Angeles, California   Malcolm W. Klein

Special
Acknowledgments

Portions of this manuscript have appeared elsewhere, in part or whole, prior to publication of this volume. In all cases, the publishers and co-authors have graciously permitted their use in the present work so that a more comprehensive picture might result. My gratitude goes to the following:

The Crime Control Council, State of New York, for "Criminological Theories as Seen by Criminologists," a report prepared for the Governor's Special Committee on the Criminal Offender, December, 1967.

Libra Publishers, Inc., for "Impressions of Juvenile Gang Members," *Adolescence* 3, no. 9 (Spring, 1968): 53–78.

National Association of Social Workers, for "The Detached Worker: Uniformities and Variances in Work Style" (with Neal Snyder), *Social Work* 10, no. 4 (October, 1965): 60–68.

National Council on Crime and Delinquency, for "Gang Delinquency, Cohesiveness, and a Street Work Program," *Journal of Research in Crime and Delinquency* 6, no. 2 (July, 1969): 135–66 and "Groups, Gangs, and Cohesiveness" (with Lois Y. Crawford), *Journal of Research in Crime and Delinquency* 4, no. 1 (January, 1967): 63–75.

University of Chicago Press, for "Juvenile Gangs, Police, and Detached Workers: Controversies about Intervention," *Social Service Review* 31, no. 2 (June, 1965): 183–90, copyright © 1965 by the University of Chicago.

University of Southern California, for "Factors Related to Juvenile Gang Membership Patterns," *Sociology and Social Research* 51, no. 1 (October, 1966): 49–62 and "On the Group Context of Delinquency," *Sociology and Social Research* 54, no. 1 (October, 1969): 63–71.

Trans-action, Inc. for portions of "White Gangs" by Walter B. Miller, September, 1969. Copyright © by *Trans-action*, Inc., New Brunswick, New Jersey.

Introduction
and
Epilogue

I've had it with gangs.

From September, 1962, to the beginning of 1968, my research world was the universe of the gang and its setting. This is a very small universe, and while there is much yet to be learned about it, I have personally reached the point of diminishing returns in my own journey through it. This speaks, not to the simplicity of the gang phenomena, but to the conceptual limits of the observer.

There comes a time, six years from the time of the initiation rites in my case, when little seems new. Every gang face, every gang member's statement of fear and bravado, every gang worker's after-the-fact explanation of his actions seems just a bit too familiar, too easily subsumed under a convenient pattern or category. There comes a time when the new seems familiar and the familiar, soporific.

By the time I left Ladino Hills for the last time, it was clear that further field exploration with gangs would be a waste of my limited talents and an affront to my stimulus-seeking nature as a living creature. I had come to the point where all observations were neatly put into a predetermined slot, reinforcing rather than expanding what I felt I had learned. When this point is reached, it is time for the scientist to seek different areas of discovery, lest the discovery process, his primary target, be lost in the redundant documentation of his own biases.

But my decision to move beyond the gang world was not purely rational. In this, I am sure, I am far from unique among investigators whose careers undergo change in target, if not in the investigative weapons employed. At the risk of over-personalizing the nonrational, I ask the reader to follow my steps on one Wednesday evening in which the frustration of action research were joined with the rational decision basis outlined above. It was on this evening that I knew it was time to leave the decreasingly fascinating arena of the street gang.

It was a Wednesday like all the others; home for an early dinner, the plaintive queries from my two young daughters ("Daddy, when can you stop going to Wednesday night meetings?"), the dusk drive along the freeways in the setting sun with the sudden dimming and closing in of the world as the freeway exit led down into the shadow of two-story Ladino Hills.

The scene at the church as I arrived was the same as it had been for several months. Raul and Ricardo were sitting on the steps talking with the first two gang boys to arrive. I parked my car up the street a ways—close enough to keep it under observation, far enough to avoid tampering by Latins looking for diversion. At 7:32 I reached the steps and leaned against the cold concrete railing. After I had shifted my weight from one foot to another for an hour, a half dozen more members had shuffled up to the church where they were joined by the worker and two of the girls.

The evening temperature drops quickly in Los Angeles and invites one to shelter. Our shelter was the basketball court in the basement of the church, so in we went—slowly, aimlessly, bravely searching for conversation which had not been played over and over in the past 18 months. By 9:30 we were 15—4 adults, 8 Latins, and 3 girls sitting on the benches or tinkering with the piano. The atmosphere was relaxed, slightly jovial, and no more fitting the stereotyped image of the fighting gang than it had been for several months. It was boring but also highly satisfying; clearly, Latin was dying as a "hot" gang and that, after all, was the name of the game.

I hope the reader is well bored by this description so that he can appreciate the setting. Remember, in contrast, that I have witnessed (only twice, it is true) gang meetings of 80 and 90 members screaming for revenge against rival groups, flashing weapons and almost coming to blows over the pure mechanics of retaliation. The contrast to this little Wednesday group cannot be overstated. But in the midst of my self-satisfied reveries on the death of Latin, down the steps and into the gym came Mad Man and Narco. Both were high and excited, shouting in street Spanish about the Gaylords and the High Riders in a stream of obscenities that defy the imagination of the uninitiated. Within two minutes the group was hopping around the basketball court, infected by the chronic germ of all gangs—the rumor of the clash between opposing groups.

The immediate change in atmosphere, the susceptibility of my quiet little group to this new input, and the readiness of all to follow Mad Man and Narco into the suddenly electrified night air took me quite by surprise. I had been lulled into a dream world and awakened by a nightmare. Were this not enough, I realized that the worker was doing nothing to intervene. In fact, he seemed to feel it was time to go home. What a fine opportunity for observation of a crisis situation; what an opportunity to watch group process; and what an opportunity to observe the interplay between peer group pressures and the effects of an 18-month intervention project.

I got up from the bench, swept the room for a panoramic, visual inhalation, put on my jacket, and walked out of the room and up the stairs. From the top of the stairs I looked down into the gym through the bars of the balcony, then turned down the long corridor, skipped down those cold outside steps, crossed the street, keys already in hand, and unlocked my car door. Within five minutes, I was changing from the Pasadena to the Harbor Freeway, honking my horn at cars which were in my way even though they were themselves flirting with the informal edges of the speed limits. I was halfway home before my own recklessness became apparent through a shroud of anger and frustration that, had it been captured on tape, I'm sure would have rivaled Mad Man and Narco at their best. The streets are good teachers.

As I realized the state I was in, I eased up on the accelerator and myself, thus undoubtedly saving the lives of some unknown family returning from the movies as well as my own self-image as the cool, detached scientist. The remainder of the trip home was spent in heavy introspection about my own untoward behavior. Why had I felt in such a huff? What was really bothering me? The answer was obvious, of course. I'd seen two pot-heads destroy a valued image. They had no right, I heard myself saying, to do that to us, to pose such an obvious threat—an affront, really—to all we felt we had achieved. We had done in less than a year and a half what Group Guidance had failed to do in four years.

But here's the point. As I considered the matter further, I realized that the scene in the church, frustrating though it was, would not have bothered me in the years before. I would have relished the chance to observe such a potentially critical event. But now I didn't care to be an observer; I was tired of observing. And I began, in my mind, to estimate how many gang meetings, outings, and various informal gatherings I had witnessed since 1962. When the count reached 300, I stopped counting, although I had not reached the end. And as I pulled exhausted into my own driveway, I knew that Mad Man and Narco had done me a personal favor. They had made obvious what I should have known months before, that I was no longer able to see anything new, or even any true variations on established themes. Once you've seen 300 gang meetings, you've seen them all—and you've *felt* them all.

So, whether one adopts the rational stance of the scientist seeking new fields of discovery or the more human stance of the bored and tired observer, one reaches the same conclusion. Old lamps must be traded for new. I've had it with gangs.

Part I

CURRENT
STATUS
OF
KNOWLEDGE
ABOUT
GANGS

Chapter 1: Sources of Information

Definition

A report on street gangs and street workers must live in double jeopardy, for neither the gang nor its worker is a well-defined phenomenon. The problem of the gang worker will be approached in later chapters. First, we must deal with the gang and its character.

Historically, the use of the word *gang* has undergone considerable transition, as outlined elsewhere by Geis.[1] The sources of the definitional problem, in addition to historical changes, are several. Lay usage is based on whim, habit, and example. Three boys lounging outside a suburban movie theater are nothing more than a set of neighborhood friends. Those same three boys molesting a mother and daughter in the ticket line are teases to the daughter but perhaps the nucleus of a gang to the mother.

By the same token, the mass media and the official agencies of the criminal justice system use the term gang more to meet their own ends than to achieve disinterested enlightenment. Depending on the context, the reporter's viewpoint, and the current predispositions of his editor, a slight melee at a rock and roll festival or a "love-in" may be described as youthful exuberance, political protest, or gang hooliganism. When the Los Angeles Police Department maintained a gang intelligence squad during the early 1960's, a gang incident was defined *as any legal infraction involving three or more juveniles* and a gang was *any group of eight or more juveniles.* For most purposes, such arbitrary criteria are patently useless and misleading, yet for police intelligence purposes they served what seemed to be necessary functions for maintaining records and

7

"selling" the notion of the widesperad incidence of gang delinquency.

A third source of definitional inconsistency—discouraging to the lay reader, perhaps, but regrettably familiar among social scientists—is the professional literature on gangs. Practitioners, researchers, and theoreticians alike have used "gang" sometimes inconsistently, sometimes loosely, and sometimes in direct opposition to each other, but never in concert. Thrasher[2] has applied the term to preadolescent play groups and college fraternities, to groups ranging in size from 3 to 2000 members. DeFleur[3] has generalized findings from incarcerated members of neighborhood cliques to delinquent gangs. Rafferty and Bertcher[4] have described as a "gang" a small clique in a boys' institution which formed around a particular therapeutic program. And, if we are to believe Yablonsky's claim[5] to an "intimate" knowledge of over 100 New York gangs, then we must certainly envision these groups as being highly diverse and uncommonly accessible. Intimate knowledge of any one large gang, in my own experience, requires many months of observation for the outsider.

There is the further problem that gangs constitute several forms of an even broader concept, that of the social group. If the gang literature is unclear with respect to what constitutes a gang, the broader delinquency literature is even less clear about what constitutes group delinquency. The belief, or the finding according to some of our most distinguished colleagues, that delinquency is a group phenomenon has been highly dysfunctional to the search for valid generalizations.

The history of the problem starts with the pioneering work of Clifford R. Shaw and Henry D. McKay[6] in Chicago whose data taken from the courts indicated a heavy predominance of delinquent incidents involving more than one youngster. Without meaning to be unduly critical, one might add that criminologists not only started with these data, but have relied upon them ever since with very little independent validation. This history can be briefly summarized as follows:

1. Shaw and McKay reported data that showed multiple involvement in delinquent court cases;

2. The data were derived from urban studies which also showed the preponderance of delinquency to be manifested in the inner city areas;

3. Because the involvement of several persons is more easily stated as group involvement, delinquency seemed primarily an urban, group phenomenon;

4. Frederic M. Thrasher's[7] work in Chicago, and E. H. Sutherland's[8] theoretical emphasis on intimate groups stimulated an abiding interest in urban gangs;

5. Modern theories,[9] especially in sociology, have reflected the traditions of this Chicago work by focusing on *gang* delinquency, thus reinforcing the assumption that most delinquency—and certainly the most interesting form of delinquency—is a group phenomenon.*

If most delinquency is group delinquency, then there might be no need for a separate concept of gang delinquency or gangs as such. But, at least currently, we can't go this far; for although the literature should be full of data testing the validity of the group delinquency statement, this is not the case. In fact, most writers assume the preponderance of group delinquency, as can be seen in the following references:

1. Frank Tannenbaum[10]—". . . most delinquencies are committed in groups." In fact, Tannenbaum makes this assumption the cornerstone of his entire approach in this reference.

2. Joseph Lohman[11]—"Delinquency is, in the main, a group phenomenon. Three-fourths of the delinquent acts are committed with delinquent partners."

3. Rose Giallombardo[12]—"There is considerable evidence that most juvenile delinquency is a group phenomenon."

4. Harry M. Shulman[13]—"There is ample evidence that serious juvenile delinquency is a group phenomenon."

5. Lois DeFleur[14]—in a good example of confusing peer groups with gangs: "Among these sixty-three 'hard core' delinquents, forty-nine claimed to be members of some type of group with regular associations. Two such groups were made up of only two persons and for the present analysis these were eliminated. The remaining forty-seven respondents were questioned at length on a number of aspects of their *gang*** membership." DeFleur then employs the data to throw doubt on cross-national generalities about *gang* structure and the applicability of American subcultural *gang* theories.

6. LaMar T. Empey[15]—"Most studies, including some which use self-reported data, place the incidence of group delinquency somewhere between 60 and 90 per cent of the total." He cites six studies to confirm these figures and adds, "Unpublished data in our possession on self-reported delinquency, both from Utah and California, confirm this figure."

---

*The sociologist might reply that the group is a more appropriate unit of analysis for sociology, leaving nongroup delinquency to other disciplines. However, it is equally "legitimate" for sociologists to study the behavior of many *individuals* if the independent variables are socio-structural in nature. The emphasis on group or gang delinquency thus represents sociologists' preference, rather than a requirement.

**Emphasis mine.

7. Marshall Clinard[16]—"Most delinquents are arrested in company with others, and it can be safely assumed that those who had no companions at the time of their arrest had had at least one in the beginning of their delinquency." He cites Shaw and McKay, Healy and Bronner, and the Gluecks as the sources of evidence.

8. Peter Scott[17]—he describes data on group delinquency in the British Isles, and attempts a categorization of various groups having greater and lesser delinquency involvement. He concludes, "Figures, since at least 1920, consistently show that the great majority of juvenile crime, i.e., between 8 and 17 years, is committed in company of others. In that year the Board of Education estimated that 63 per cent of delinquent boys were 'working in gangs'."

9. LaMar T. Empey and Jerome Rabow[18]—". . . the greater part of delinquent behavior is not that of individuals engaging in highly secretive deviations, but is a group phenomenon—a shared deviation which is the product of differential group experience in a particular subculture. . . ." As a basic assumption underlying their well-known Provo Experiment, they list first among their assumptions: "Delinquent behavior is primarily a group product and demands an approach to treatment far different from that which sees it as characteristic of a 'sick' or 'well-meaning' but 'misguided' person."

Only the Sherifs[19] and Richard Korn and L. W. McCorkle emerge from the review as questioners of the group statement, and the latter only by implication when they report that "In the vast majority of instances delinquency is companionate behavior."[20] *Companionate* is not synonymous with *group*, a term they avoid, thus returning us to the empirical as well as the semantic question.

Let us assume now that the existence of the group statement has been established, at least in the sense that many writers accept the notion that group delinquency is preponderant. Even without empirical evidence to the contrary, the present state of theory would suggest that group delinquency may have been overstated. For example, current emphases on the situational determinants of delinquent behaviors[21] and evidence concerning the spontaneity of such behaviors[22] make the existence of group factors superfluous in many instances. The growing realization of the "accidental" factors leading to the non-uniform detection and reporting of incidents[23] militates against positing group contexts in numerous instances.

The question of delinquency definitions additionally beclouds the issue. If delinquency is defined in any but the narrowest terms, it becomes obvious that some types of incidents are less commonly companionate than others. For example, runaways are usually individual behaviors and sex offenses are ordinarily committed between two individuals, whereas vandalism and assaults are more likely to involve multiple companions. In other words, there are empirical, theoretical, and action dangers in the acceptance of the group statement—dangers of treating all delinquencies and delinquents alike, dangers of ignoring differences in reportability, and dangers of constructing a theory of general delinquency causation on unsupportable assertions.

Definition of "Group" Incidents

At this point in the presentation, it might seem that the logical step would be to report data to destroy the group delinquency assumption. However, this cannot be done in the absence of an agreed-upon definition of the "group" in group delinquency. One might approach the problem by looking at it in a different way—by citing several "group incidents" to raise the question, not of delinquency, but of the *meaning of "group"* as a context within which juvenile offenses are committed and detected.

   1. Two brothers were involved in an assault against a third boy. The first brother struck the first blows, and when the victim attempted to escape into a liquor store, the second brother followed and cut him in the neck with a roofing knife. The assaulters were members of a primary (family) group, and also members of the same clique of a well-established gang.

   2. Three boys were involved in a large-scale department store robbery. One, an older neighborhood boy previously unknown to one of the two other boys, escaped. The other two boys, both arrested, were three and a half years apart in age, and fringe members of different cliques of a large gang. In what sense, then, was this a group incident?

   3. A detached worker was driving several gang members down the street when a patrol car was spotted behind them. Despite a speed of 35 miles per hour, one of the boys panicked, opened the door, and jumped from the car. He was arrested for being drunk by the officers in the patrol car. Was this an instance of group delinquency?

   4. One year, to the day, after a fellow member had been killed by a rival gang, a boy stabbed a 14-year-old resident of the rival gang's neighborhood and also shot to death a 50-year-old neighborhood resident. This "anniversary present" clearly was related to feelings of group identification, as the subject sought revenge. Is this sufficient to claim it as a group incident?

   5. At a supervised teenage party in a fashionable section of town,

one boy sold marijuana cigarettes to a number of other participants. He then left the party, but a disturbing-the-peace complaint brought out a juvenile car in which I was cruising that night. Three of the 50 or 60 party-goers were booked for possession of marijuana. The three were relative strangers and had no known group ties to each other; were they involved in a group incident just because they were booked with each other, or just because they were in the same place at the same time?

The point—probably quite obvious, and certainly not original—is that we may be getting a bit sloppy terminologically when we speak of group delinquency. We slip back and forth in our thinking among sub-culture, reference group, and membership group; between primary and secondary group; among groups, gangs, companions, and legal co-subjects. In writing about and doing research on delinquency, we have been less than careful in specifying the parameters of the relationships between our delinquent subjects. At this point, then, the critical question would seem to be:

What definitions of "group" will encompass various illegal behaviors as "group" incidents?

This phrasing of the question makes several things obvious. One cannot use arrest reports or court records as indices of group delin-quency unless the definition of group is unicriterial; that is, a group is nothing more nor less than two contiguous individuals, or two individuals arrested as co-subjects. No social scientist would be satisfied with such a narrow definition, yet the original Shaw and McKay data are based upon little more than this definition. Nor can one rely on the subjects' reports of their group affiliation, since their definitional criteria would be even more varied than ours:

"Do you guys belong to some kind of group?"

"No, man, he's my brother."

"Sure—we all go to the same school."

"Yeah, we're all Egyptian Cobras, and this is our turf."

"No, we just hang around the same hotdog stand."

"I never saw those cats before last night."

"Yeah, we all hate cops."

It seems that the resolution to the problem must come, not from the official agencies or from the boys, but from the social scientist. Nor will the answer come from a simple percentage, such as that 83.9 per cent of all offenses are group offenses. Rather, one must review the several definitions of group[24] and then determine what percentage of incidents is encompassed within each of these definitions. This will be a difficult task, because most criteria of group definition are dimensional rather than simply dichotomous. Cohesiveness, degree of normative structure, longevity, group identification, commonness of goals and values, and dividing lines between in-group and out-group are all examples of commonly employed definitional criteria which share serious operational problems.

Bernard Cohen has published recent analyses of data in the Philadelphia police files which strongly support the necessity of careful gang and group definition.[25] Although methodologically limited, Cohen's conclusions are worth considering. Comparing incidents committed by known gang groups with incidents involving groups without known gang affiliations, Cohen found that,

a. Gang offenders were more homogeneous with respect to age, race, sex, and residence patterns than nongang group offenders;

b. The victims of gang offenders were more homogeneous in their characteristics than were the victims of the nongang group offenders;

c. The gang offenders had more extensive prior records and were charged with more serious offenses.

Commenting further, Cohen suggests that the gang has a greater sense of territoriality as a result of social isolation and the presence of various external pressures, and concludes, "Gang and group delinquency are different forms of juvenile deviance and should be approached etiologically, as well as for purposes of treatment and prevention, from different starting points." (p. 108)

By way of summary, then, we can see that the professional literature on group delinquency and on gangs must share the "blame" with the usages of the lay public, the media, and the official agencies of the criminal justice system for the definitional problem. Until greater clarity and uniformity of usage is achieved, we will be forced to use the term *gang* in a rather arbitrary fashion.

For our purposes, we shall use the term *gang* to refer to any denotable adolescent group of youngsters who (a) are generally perceived as a distinct aggregation by others in their neighborhood, (b) recognize themselves as a denotable group (almost invariably with a group name) and (c) have been involved in a sufficient number of delinquent incidents to call forth a consistent negative response from neighborhood residents and/or enforcement agencies.

This is not meant as a definitive denotation of the "gang" label. It is merely designed to say that a group is a gang when it is reacted to as a distinctly antisocial group of genuine concern and accepts itself as a group apart. This is nothing more than a confirmation of contemporary lay usage of the term. Thus, this definition does not find us marching down the true and righteous road to conceptual clarity, but at least we may thread our way along a discernible path in temporary agreement that we can remain together for the length of the journey. When I say "gang," you'll know what I mean, and you'll know that I refer to something very akin to modern popular usages of the term.*

When the Philadelphia police department reported a dramatic upsurge in gang killings—30 in 1968 and 24 in the first half of 1969—the Pennsylvania State Crime Commission was instructed by the Governor to investigate the matter. Some were quick to say that there would follow an official vendetta against the black ghetto, since most of the killings occurred there; that the ghetto would be punished, gang and nongang alike.

In such instances, the definition of "gang" loses any trappings of academic or "esoteric" interest. It is necessary to know whether these are indeed *gang* killings, with explanations deriving from analysis of gang phenomena, or whether some more pervasive influences are at work. To make such a determination requires a definition of gang which can be accepted for the initial investigative purposes. By our definition, the Pennsylvania Crime Commission's first three questions should have been (1) were the assailants generally perceived as members of distinct aggregates in their neighborhoods? (2) did they perceive themselves as having such memberships? and (3) have those aggregates been defined as delinquent in a consistent fashion by area residents and/or the police?

With the answers in the affirmative, we could then say that the upsurge in killings is a more or less distinctive gang phenomenon, to be investigated in terms of those variables already believed to be most

_____

*I am hopeful that my approach here *begins*, at least, to deal directly with Leonard Savitz's clear statement of the problem:

> When proposing to construct theories of gang behavior, one should be
> aware of certain problems. First of all, there is yet no commonly used
> definition of a gang nor any general consensus in the field on what constitutes
> a gang. The degree of formal organization necessary, the minimum (and
> maximum?) number of members required (Can there be a two-person gang?),
> and the degree of control that must be exercised over the individual members
> of the group are simply not dealt with. All too often, what is found is an implicit
> assumption that we all somehow know what a gang is and that there is no
> need to try to define it.
> —Leonard Savitz (reference 91), p. 60.

pertinent to gang matters. The gang, in this view, is something special, something more than is implied by such words as delinquent and group. This view is crucial to this entire book, and I will treat it more thoroughly in pages to come.

One further point before moving on. If it is true that the gang can be successfully defined, then it might well follow that the gang is reacted to in the community in ways not characterizing nongang groups or nongang delinquents. Certainly, it has been my experience that this is true. The existence of a gang, labelled as such, calls forth a perceptual distinction, but often a behavioral distinction as well. Admiration leads to recruitment; fear leads to withdrawal and repressive tactics. Perhaps the greatest accolade one can give to the gang worker is that he bucks this trend, that he marches in where others fear to tread. And just as the community shies away from the gang, it often pretends that the gang worker is not there, or that he is somehow "captured" by the gang and is therefore to be overcome rather than supported. For this one reason alone, the gang worker is a community isolate.

In addition, however, gangs are not plentiful.* Gangs do not constitute the greatest source of urban delinquency. The community knows little about gangs. Under these circumstances, mobilizing community resources to "combat" the problem of the gang is, at best, a frustrating exercize, a role best fitted to the masochist. Even those whose jobs *require* dealing with gangs—the police, school officials, probation officers, recreation officials—were found in a survey during the Group Guidance Project to rank gang delinquency ninth in a list of ten social problems in their areas. The only way to get full and consistent community mobilization around gang problems may be to wait for gang killings to increase a hundred-fold. This, at least, would seem to be the lesson of the Philadelphia experience.

The Media

Most juvenile gangs are a component part of ghettoized urban enclaves seldom seen by most Americans. As we will point out later, most victims of gang activities are other gang members and, secondarily, nongang

---

*For instance, in the Group Guidance Project area the census tract with the highest number of gang residents was still relatively "safe"; gang members accounted for only 6 per cent of all gang-age youngsters living in that tract. In Philadelphia, according to the Pennsylvania Crime Commission's 1969 report, *Gang Violence in Philadelphia*, only 6.4 per cent of all juvenile arrests in 1968 were of known gang members.

residents of these same hidden urban areas. Yet, say "gang" to almost any American, urban or rural, and you will get a reaction indicating at least some familiarity with gang matters. Say Blackstone Rangers in Chicago, White Fence in Los Angeles, or Egyptian Kings in New York, and millions who have never seen a gang member will know that you are talking about gangs.

This is made possible, of course, by the reports of our newspapers, radio, and television. Gangs are dramatic and therefore newsworthy. But are the news reports worthy of our attention? Do they tell us about gangs what we should know, or what somebody thinks we want to know?

I yield to no one in my admiration for the makers of "West Side Story," but I have never seen a gang like the Jets in that musical. However, the Jets and other fictional juvenile gangs seem to the general public to epitomize the general run of real gangs. In part, this is because the descriptions of the Jets constitute a more definitive description of gangs than one can ordinarily derive from the media. These descriptions fill a vacuum of information and thereby become accepted as valid.

In addition, the fictional accounts, with their stress on violence, strong leadership, and highly organized group structure make "sense" in terms of the limited information supplied to the public by the mass media—especially the press. Is it any wonder that the Jets are acceptable as gang prototypes when the newspapers supply us with such headlines as these:

'RAT PACKERS' ON RAMPAGE
TEEN GANGS FLARE; TWO LEADERS SHOT
GANG RAMPAGE IN L.A.
POLICE THWART GANG WAR
L.A. GANG LEADER NEAR DEATH—FELLED WITH GUNSHOT[26]

These headlines come from our file of newspaper stories on gangs gathered between October, 1962 and August, 1965. The file contains 41 stories covering 28 incidents during the major part of the Group Guidance Project.* While our search for stories in both "major" and "minor" Los Angeles newspapers was not fully systematic, the collection undoubtedly contains the bulk of printed stories and feature series printed during that period in Los Angeles. A brief content analysis of these materials is highly instructive.

Of the 41 stories, four could be categorized as "positive," that is, they reported positive efforts to deal with gang problems or otherwise steered clear of disapproved gang activity. One of these "positive" arti-

---

*See Preface, p. ix.

cles reported the statement of a public official that street gangs were *not* involved in any organized fashion in the Watts riots of August, 1965.

Another five articles could be categorized as "neutral," reports on issues in which gang activity was not involved in a crucial fashion. Four of these were reports of public statements critical of the police or the probation department for their approach to gang problems. The fifth reported a suit for false arrest revolving around a confrontation between police officers and a large number of youths gathered near a movie theater.

The remaining 32 articles, or 78 per cent of the total, are classified as "negative" in the sense that each reports on gang offenses. Included in the incidents covered are ten shootings, three stabbings, several beatings, and a further assortment of assaults. Every one of these incidents involved violence against persons rather than property. There were no reports about theft, burglary, drugs, vandalism, truancy, and so on. Whatever else newspaper reporting of gang activities may represent, it does *not* represent reality. Contrast this with the data in Table 1-1 summarizing the official charges brought against the gang members involved in the Group Guidance Project between July, 1961 and June, 1965.

Table 1-1 Offense Distributions During G.G. P.

Category	% for Boys	% for Girls
Thefts	26	14
Juvenile Status*	17	47
Auto Theft, Joy-riding	14	5
Assaultive	13	9
Drugs and Alcohol	10	4
Disturbing Peace, Malicious Mischief, etc.	7	6
Traffic	3	1
Sex	2	5
Other	7	10
	99%	101%

*Offenses which can be charged against children only, such as curfew violation, truancy, incorrigibility, and runaway.

It is obvious, then, that news articles concentrate on negative gang behavior—particularly assaults—in almost total disregard for the reality of the streets. And were this not enough, the manner of reporting is inflammatory. Although our collection of stories is almost devoid of headline adjectives ("savage" and "deadly" being the two exceptions), the nouns used to characterize the reported incidents clearly are in the worst traditions of journalism. Even the most minor confrontations, as well as the more serious incidents, are introduced to the reader by the terms "hoodlum band," "war," "battle," "flare-up," "violence," "rumble," "rampage," and "gang war battle."

But this is not the major point. This chapter is concerned primarily with *where* we get our information about gangs and with the *validity* of that information. Certainly it is clear that the news media are highly suspect as sources of accurate gang information, yet by and large the public is restricted to that source. The media, with the apocryphal exceptions, serve both to form and to reinforce dramatic stereotypes of gang structure and behavior.

Gang members often are almost as willing as the general public to accept the exploits attributed to them by the press as being typical of their peers. In fact, the only thing worse than the young reporter's description of a gang incident is his acceptance of the gang participant's statement about it. The gang member is often the worst informant about gang affairs, a fact nicely illustrated by Short and Strodtbeck[27] but too often overlooked by news reporter and social scientist alike.

Clinical Knowledge

The question of the gang member's validity as an informant introduces a second major source of information about the gang, namely those people whose mandate it is to get close to the gang in order to affect their behavior. For instance, what of the police? They are closer to the problem than the media, but they too are exposed to less than the complete picture. Further, their mandate is to "serve and protect" and to gather evidence on legal violations, activities which occasionally lead to distortions of what they see or how it may be interpreted. One highly experienced juvenile officer in Los Angeles told me, quite insistently, that in the Ladino Hills section of East Los Angeles, "Every kid in that area belongs to the Latins gang—they're all involved."

The tendency among many police officers is to draw a caricature of the delinquent gang, emphasizing its internal codes of conduct, its disrespect for authority, its coercive nature in recruiting new members and enforcing its code, and its organization. With respect to organization, the police stress two points. First, they feel that juvenile gangs coalesce around delinquent activities, that they form, at least partly, specifically to commit illegal acts. Second, police see the structure of the gang as revolving around a few central leaders, usually older boys, who "call the shots" on what will and will not be done. This latter premise in turn leads to one of the primary police tactics in dealing with gangs—to "get the leaders!"

Although the Los Angeles Police Department was exceedingly retentive about its gang information during the days of the Group Guidance Project, occasional "infiltrations" were possible for those outsiders who could establish nonthreatening personal relationships with particular officers and supervisory personnel. In one such instance, I was shown the files on the Generals gang kept by one LAPD division. The word most closely approximating my reaction at seeing this material is shock—shock at the inadequacy and incompleteness of the information. Whereas I had the names of over 100 Generals, the police had, as I remember, less than 20 (some of whom were unknown to me). Addresses were out of date, offense histories were incomplete, and pictures of the boys were as much as three and four years old. My understanding of police intelligence operations was drastically revised by this and subsequent experiences. On the other hand, my appreciation for some of the obstacles to good police work was often increased by these exposures.

In a similar vein to the preceding experience was that of one of our street workers who spent as much time in the police station as with his gang members. In the process, he and the station officers played a cat and mouse game of gang intelligence—trading a little information to get a little. In the end, I think the police scored more points, for during this "game," the worker showed them his entire gang roster of almost 150 names, an act which would have been decried by his fellow workers and perhaps more severely punished by a few of the older gang members had it come to light.

The worker reported to us, not without considerable glee, that most of the names on the roster were unfamiliar to the sergeant (to whom the list should have constituted a quick review of his own knowledge). The simple fact is that police knowledge about gang membership is not, and cannot be, very complete nor up to date. This incomplete knowledge, coupled with the almost inevitable stereotyping of gang structure and activity to which police are inclined, points once again to an inadequate source of valid data. The function of police departments almost dictates that this should be the case; their gang data is limited because their needs restrict the type of data to be collected as well as its currency.

As we move even closer to the gang, we come upon the street worker whose job it is to transform the groups, to guide them in prosocial directions using his own personal counseling skills and the often inadequate resources of the community. To accomplish this end, he spends anywhere from one third to two thirds of his highly irregular work day with the gang members and, once accepted by them as a helping adult, is privy to more personal and group data than anyone else.

Typically (if such a word is permissible), his view of the gang differs quite radically from that of the newsman or the policeman (not to mention that of the local businessman, the assault victim, or other concerned individuals).

His is the view of one involved in any complex process; he sees more of trees than of forest. The trees—the individual gang members—become the focus of the gang worker who is more of a rehabilitator than a preventer or enforcer. He views illegal acts more as symptoms or obstacles than as violations. He often loses sight of gang structure in the day to day interactions among gang members and between members and himself. The group is viewed as the last vestige of democracy in which membership is based on friendship rather than power, where the most disadvantaged individuals can be accepted and where the bureaucratic regimens of middle class society hold no sway.

Having spent some five years highly dependent upon gang workers both for information in their possession and for access to their gang members and various adults in the gang neighborhoods, I have great admiration for their ability to penetrate the inner core of this relatively unknown world. Much of the material in this book is in a sense theirs more than mine.

At the same time, my research associates and I have learned with increasing exposure to the ghetto world that independent verification and amplification of even the most first-hand of reports is an absolute necessity. We have learned all too often of fights that never took place, marriages that didn't exist, community support that melted away when put to the test, instances of police brutality that were dreamed up somewhere between the arrest and the first conference with an attorney, and so on.

Further, we learned that the social scientist's concern with gang structure and cohesiveness was something overlaid upon the worker's interest in individual problems. The abstractions for which the scientist strives must be *his,* for the worker will seldom supply them. Rather, the worker's information is more profitably used to test and verify notions, not to formulate them.

At various times in the past few years, I have been asked by both the idly curious and the seriously inquisitive to comment on trends in gang matters. It was assumed, I suppose, that my personal observations and my access to police and to street worker programs would automatically lead to valid generalizations. But one learns to respect one's own ignorance and to question the reliability of his informants. Typical queries include the following:

1. *"Is it true that gangs have changed drastically since the days of Thrasher?"* In general, I have responded in the affirmative, but added

that Thrasher's descriptions were so varied and all-encompassing that it's more a matter of emphasis than structural change. Further, the urban setting of Thrasher's investigation was very different from that of the modern city, and to say that gangs have changed may be more of a comment on urban change than on any "natural history" of gangs as a separate phenomenon. But perhaps most important of all is the fact in the quarter century between Thrasher's Chicago and present day Chicago, New York, Boston or Los Angeles, there appeared almost *no* empirical descriptions of juvenile gangs. The progression from then to now is a matter of almost pure conjecture, illuminating next to nothing about the status of today's gangs. A plausible hypothesis remains, as David Bordua has eloquently noted,[28] that many changes one might list could just as well exist in the attitudes and perceptions of the investigators as in the realities of the gangs.

2. *"Aren't gangs really a training ground for the adult rackets?"* Here again, the older writers including Thrasher presented much gang activity as a racketeering apprenticeship, and juvenile gang structures as a major source of recruitment into adult criminal gangs. How prevalent was this trend in the 1920's and 1930's? We'll never know. How prevalent is it now? We don't know. Most gang workers today report relatively little racket recruitment out of the street gang, but their estimates vary according to city, neighborhood, and the audience for their remarks. The same seems to be true of police spokesmen.

The most vehement deniers of recruitment, at least in my personal and therefore selective experience, are the gang members themselves. Perhaps they are more sophisticated than their brethren of generations past, but their response was summed up by a senior member of the Operators who provided this taped conversation:

Q: What about these older guys in the rackets who hang around the park?

A: See, we don't fool with 'em personally, only to buy marijuana and stuff of that nature from 'em. Other than that, we don't like 'em.

Q: But don't they want you? Isn't there an attempt to enlist you into their system?

A: Yeah, they try to, and that's when they get jumped on. Don't nobody want them kinda jobs, less they are real low, you know. . . . Most of them that's in the rackets, shall we say, they're not big time. We don't look at 'em as bein' big time. They're just little bitty people that's trying to make it and they really don't have that much for themself. You'll only find one or two out of fifty that would succeed.

3. *"Are gangs on the decline?"* This is by far the most frequently posed question. I first heard the question in July of 1962 from a member of a city commission. I last heard it in July of 1969 from the Chairman of the Pennsylvania Crime Commission. The answer remains substantially unchanged; the majority of experts think gangs may be declining, but relevant data are not available. However, one can add this at least, that the frequency of the question suggests the existence of a decline. The reader may draw his own conclusion from a three-city summary, remembering at the same time that these are primarily *anecdotal* summaries, relying as usual on the personal experience of various officials. Solid, empirical data are still lacking.

Los Angeles. From 1960 to 1965, both the police and several street work agencies were consistent in their view that Los Angeles gangs were as plentiful and as violent as ever, perhaps even growing worse. Following the Watts riots in August of 1965, reports began to be heard that Negro gang activity was declining. I was inclined to believe these reports, for I too was hearing increasingly less about Negro gangs. However, the Group Guidance Project ended just a month before the riots and my access to informants decreased immediately. All formal gang work in the area ceased. Was it Negro gangs that were on the decline, or was it the information sources that were on the decline? Suppose that news coverage of Arab-Israeli clashes in the Middle East were to be curtailed suddenly by editorial policy. Would we not soon assume, in the absence of information to the contrary, that Mid-East tensions were easing?

The reader might well say that there are other sources of data on gangs—the police, the schools, other social agencies, and so on. What do they report? Essentially nothing, is the answer. An informal report is heard from time to time. Some of these seem to confirm the continued existence of gang X or gang Y, while others suggest that gang members have been coöpted by civil rights or Black Power groups. The greater number of reports are on the side of a gang decline. We cannot, in all honesty, go beyond this simple level of knowledge.

In East Los Angeles, the home of the traditional Mexican-American gang, just the opposite seems to be the case. The majority of reports stress the continued existence of juvenile gangs, some of which have been a part of the scene for well over 30 years. And once again, I am *personally* inclined to accept the majority reports, since we were running the Ladino Hills Project from 1966 to 1968. We *saw* gang activity; two of our boys were killed; we attended community meetings devoted to the continued rivalry between gangs over a 20-mile expanse. If out of sight means out of mind, then the opposite also may be true. In any case, such coincidence of personal experience and word-of-mouth information makes one suspicious of any nonempirical conclusions about the level of gang activity. In confirmation, I might add that, with the completion of the Ladino Hills Project, I am now hearing more reports of a decline in gang activity in East Los Angeles. I can neither dispute nor confirm these reports.

Chicago. Thrasher and William Foote Whyte[29] made Chicago the gang center of America through their writings. The Hyde Park Project,[30] the Chicago Youth Development Project,[31] and the research of Short and his colleagues[32] have continued the Chicago tradition. Major theoretical approaches, such as those of Albert Cohen[33] and Cloward and Ohlin[34] are heavily dependent upon Chicago observations. Yet, if my contacts with researchers and practitioners in Chicago lead to any conclusion about the decline question, it is that gang activity is highly cyclical—the answer varies with the year in which the question is posed. I have been in Chicago during periods both "hot" and "cold" in gang matters, according to some very knowledgeable informants. But as in Los Angeles, no one has collected data to suggest whether there is an overall trend cutting across the cyclical pattern. Perhaps we can best hypothesize a lack of significant change in the level of gang activity.

New York. The more one hears reports of a national decline in gang activity, the more one tries to pin down their source. Significantly, in most cases they derive primarily from New York. Since New York has both more gangs and more gang workers than any other city, persistent reports of a decline in gangs in that city soon become generalized to the nation as a whole. Although Bernstein's report of a gang decline was based on interviews in several cities,[35] the other decline reports all center on New York City. Samuels,[36] Gannon,[37] and Grosser,[38] have all commented on the New York trend.

Gannon's analysis yields a 40 per cent reduction in conflict incidents in the early 1960's, with the traditional fighting gang adopting a more defensive posture. Geis[39] quotes Kenneth Marshall's observation that conflict is giving way in Harlem to civil rights activism and drug use. In a statement which claims the impossible, and must be taken principally as a public relations pronouncement, Grosser indicates that a decline in gang fighting may not be an unmixed blessing:

> By the early 'sixties, the combined efforts of the New York City Youth Board and Police Department succeeded in eliminating the fighting street gang. The conditions which produced the deviance remained untouched: the youth were involved at best (and rarely)

as clients, and at worst (and frequently) as criminals; the
neighborhood community, not at all. As a result, new, but less
visible forms of deviance developed largely around the use of
narcotics (i.e., Ohlin and Cloward's retreatist model). This new
deviance, by any measure, has proven infinitely more costly than
the old. It was to avoid pitfalls such as these that innovative
comprehensive programs with strong community bases were
evolved.

Recently released data from Philadelphia present an even more
discouraging picture. From 1962 to 1968, that city has manifested a
significant decrease in gang fights and rumbles. But during the same
period there has been a drastic increase in gang-related stabbings,
shootings, and killings.[40] It is quite conceivable that the "japping" pattern of deliberate, planned, small scale assaults, if it is indeed becoming
a new norm, is far more serious in consequences than the old style of
gang fight. Perhaps, as Hayes and Hogrefe[41] have suggested, the gang
contains its own proscriptive norms which serve to mitigate serious violence which might jeopardize its autonomy. Such norms might lose their
effectiveness in the "japping" pattern.
Finally, leaving this city-by-city analysis which seems to defy any
generalization other than that there can as yet be no generalization, we
have Walter Miller's most recent statement on the decline of the fighting
gang:[42]

Today, the one-time devotee of this sort of stuff might be excused
for wondering where they went, the Amboy Dukes and all those
other adolescent warriors and lovers who so excited his fancy a
decade ago. The answer, as we shall see, is quite simple—nowhere.
The street gangs are still there, out on the corner where they
always were. (p. 11)*

Miller continues his analysis by citing the Philadelphia data mentioned earlier, along with recent data from Chicago (33 killings in the first
half of 1969) and Boston (38 gang "incidents" in one 90-minute period),
concluding that ". . . street gangs are not only still widespread in United
States cities, but some of them appear to have again taken up 'gang
warfare' on a scale that is equal to or greater than the phenomenon that
received so much attention from the media in the 1950's" (p. 12). Quite
rightly, I believe, Miller attributes both the reported decline of the fighting gang and the inconsistency of these reports to confusions over gang
definition, inadequate empirical data, and the vagaries of media
reporting.

---

*Copyright © by Trans-action, Inc., New Brunswick, N.J.

The place of the definitional problem and its intricate interplay with perceptions of gang prevalence may sound overly academic, but I think in fact that it can hardly be overstated. Miller illustrates the issue perfectly:

> How then can one account for the widespread conception of gangs as somehow popping up and then disappearing again? One critical reason concerns the way one defines what a gang is. Many observers, both scholars and non-scholars, often use a <u>sine qua non</u> to sort out "real" gangs from near-gangs, pseudo-gangs, and non-gangs. Among the more common of these single criteria are: autocratic one-man leadership, some "absolute" degree of solidarity or stable membership, a predominant involvement in violent conflict with other gangs, claim to a rigidly defined turf, or participation in activities thought to pose a threat to other sectors of the community. Reactions to groups lacking the <u>sine qua non</u> is often expressed with a dismissive "Oh, them. that's not a <u>gang.</u> That's just a bunch of kids out on the corner."
>
> For many people there are no gangs if there is no gang warfare. It's that simple. For them, as for all those who concentrate on the "threatening" nature of the gang, the phenomenon is defined in terms of the degree of "problem" it poses: A group whose "problematic" behavior is hard to ignore is a gang; one less problematic is not. But what some people see as a problem may not appear so to others. In Philadelphia, for example, the police reckoned there were 80 gangs, of which 20 were at war; while social workers estimated there were 200 gangs, of which 80 were "most hostile." Obviously, the social workers' 80 "most hostile" gangs were the same as the 80 "gangs" of the police. The additional 120 groups defined as gangs by the social workers were seen as such because they were thought to be appropriate objects of social work; but to the police they were not sufficiently troublesome to require consistent police attention, and were not therefore defined as gangs. (p. 25)*

Miller's analysis is typical of his unique and often insightful approach to gang matters. Before leaving this general discussion of our clinical knowledge of gangs, I would like to raise one more topic which he has handled quite succinctly—why we *want* to believe in gang violence. We have already shown that gang violence does not approach our assumptions of its prevalence, nor most public reports thereof. The need to portray violence is one side of the story. The need to *believe* in it is another. Miller's statement on this point is very persuasive. He cites several factors in the disproportionate attention paid to violence as

---

*Copyright © by *Trans-action*, Inc., New Brunswick, N.J.

opposed to the far more common theft behaviors of gang members. The first of these is particularly pertinent to our discussion.

> Four reasons for this may be cited: the high emotional shock potential of violence, the low shock potential of non-violent theft, the focus on individuals rather than on behavior, and the confusion of appropriate and aggressive aspects of crime.

> The exaggerated perception of the prevalence of violent crime and the corresponding underestimation of the prevalence of appropriative crime reflect a fundamental human concern with violence and aggression as general forms of behavior. The urgency of human concern with violence strongly influences perceptions of crime prevalence. The principle governing the general perception of crime frequency might be phrased "intensity of concern converts to exaggerated perception of prevalence," or, in simpler language, the more you are concerned about it, the more common you think it is.

> The reasons for this are not hard to understand. Violent or assaultive crimes pose a clear threat to the internal order of a societal unit and to the safety of its members. These are acts which, in the words of Émile Durkheim, "offend very pervasive and intense sentiments" and "shock the common conscience," and which are subject to the most severe punitive sanctions.[43] Violent crimes by youth—gang fights, gang assaults on individuals, sexual attacks—have particular power to evoke feelings of fear, threat, and danger among adults.[44]

Theoretical Knowledge

Our third major source of knowledge about juvenile gangs comes from the theoreticians who have attempted to deduce general abstractions from the specific data and observations available to them. The job of the theoretician is also the source of his frequent failure, for to generalize over many cases is too often to lose sight of the variation in those cases. Thus, Richard Korn and Lloyd McCorkle have noted that ". . . criminology is without parallel in the behavioral sciences for the sheer prevalence of invalidated ideas over positive knowledge"[45] and Eldefonso writes that, "Because of this inadequacy of knowledge, each specialist tends to formulate his theory in terms of his own experiences."[46]

The President's Crime Commission implicitly attributed this state of affairs to the complexity of the crime problem itself, repeating its stand thus:

No single formula, no single theory, no single generalization can explain the vast range of behavior called crime.[47]

Thinking of crime as a whole is futile.[48]

The causes of crime, then, are numerous and mysterious and intertwined. No one way of describing crime describes it well enough.[49]

And while there is certainly much truth in these statements it is discouraging to see their overall message promulgated in the most comprehensive review ever prepared for the public. There is a defeatism in this approach which can only solidify the obvious tendency among criminologists to throw up their hands in despair over the possibility of developing useful theories of crime. The result fits perfectly the broader-targeted complaint of George Homans:

Social geographers speak of a 'hollow frontier'—where waves of adventurers have swept through the backlands looking for quick wealth but leaving behind them no settled territory, consolidated for civilization. We sociologists are adventurers of the same stripe. We get more and more grants for 'exciting' research at the 'growing edge' of the field, but behind the growing edge lies no body of organized knowledge.[50]

Another impression one gets from the literature is that the theorists themselves have been reluctant to expand very far beyond their original formulation. It's as if each said to himself, "I'll take my shot, and then stand back to see what happens." Where expansion does occur, typically it is undertaken by someone other than the originator. When this happens, it is seldom clear whether the originator would go along with the suggested modifications. The result is a watering down of the original directions and a loss of opportunity to push the logical extensions to the point of severe and crucial tests. It may be that in this area the field has not provided sufficient reward to entice the theorist into pursuing his theoretical interest. This is an interesting question for the sociology of knowledge.

If it is true as claimed that gang theory constitutes a "hollow frontier," one might expect the practitioner and researcher alike to view such theory with much skepticism. However, just the opposite has been the case, with theoretical propositions acting to fill the knowledge vacuum in almost total disregard for their empirical status. The fault lies not with the theoreticians, nor with those who would assign them such honorable status. The fault lies with the very existence of the knowledge vacuum.

By way of analogy, we might recall Shakespeare's handling of the events following Caeser's assassination. In his funeral oration, Mark Antony swayed the Roman mobs against Brutus and his fellow plotters by impugning the motives of Brutus even while saying, "But Brutus is an honorable man." In considering the "knowledge" provided by the gang theorist, I would urge that we accept the skepticism applied to the statements of Brutus. Theoretical proposals are to be tested, not accepted out of hand. While I don't wish to turn the mobs against the theoreticians, I do wish to suggest that, as of this writing, many of the theoretical statements about gangs currently so widely accepted as fact are nothing of the sort. Rather, they are either undemonstrated, undemonstrable, or actually demonstrated to be in error. We take the following as examples.

Albert K. Cohen

Published in 1955, Albert K. Cohen's book *Delinquent Boys* set forth a theory of delinquency founded upon social class variables. Limiting his concern primarily to lower class delinquency, Cohen found the lower class boy to be lacking in self-esteem and suffering from a high degree of status frustration as a result of his class position. This was said to lead to an inversion of values, a "reaction formation" against middle class values wherein the lower class boy struck back at the source of his frustration, the middle class and its values, with the adoption of opposite values.

From this inversion developed a "delinquent subculture" as a collective solution to the class-based frustrations. Cohen described this subculture as "nonutilitarian, malicious, and negativistic," stressing versatility, short-run hedonism, and group autonomy. Cohen postulated that it is the *subculture* which serves to transmit delinquent values.

Delinquency, then—primarily a group phenomenon—is the behavioral manifestation of the learned, inverted values. Concerned with the reinforcement of these values, especially their delinquent aspects, Cohen and James F. Short, Jr.[51] hypothesized the existence of a "parent" subculture which serves to spawn and support various types of delinquent subcultures, such as conflict, drug, and semiprofessional subcultures.

The beauty of Cohen's formulation in at least most of its hypotheses can be verified. The existence of the delinquent and parent subcultures represents a problem here, because their verification requires greater specification of substance and contrast to their nondelinquent contexts than Cohen has provided. One initial step has been reported by Cohen and Hodges.[52]

The concept of reaction formation has been tested by Gold[53] and by Rivera and Short,[54] with negative results. Reiss and Rhodes[55] and Berkowitz[56] have reported data throwing doubt on the existence of excessive status frustration in the lower class. Short and Strodtbeck failed to support the class differences in values central to the theory. Finally, while the Myerhoffs[57] and the Schwendingers[58] provide some support for the cognitive class differences implicit in the theory, Matza's and Sykes'[80] deductions go contrary to these findings.

In sum, then, the relatively high verifiability of the theory has led to a distinct lack of verification. Those who accept the gang as a manifestation of the lower class boy's status frustration, or believe the gang boy merely to be striking out against the barriers established by the middle class, had best tread lightly. They walk on unsupported ground.

Cloward and Ohlin

A second approach to gangs, and a widely popular one, is Opportunity Theory (or Opportunity Structure), an attempt by Richard Cloward and Lloyd Ohlin to combine some salient data and propositions from the Chicago School (Shaw, McKay, Thrasher, Sutherland) with Cohen's theory of delinquent subcultures, and to place them within an expanded notion of Merton's analysis of the opportunity structure of western society. The system goes roughly like this:

1. Society has cultural goals (such as material gain) generally accepted and legitimated by the major sectors of the society;

2. Not all persons have equal access to these goals, nor to the accepted means of achieving them;

3. Therefore, those for whom the goals are blocked may turn to illegitimate means;

4. Just as communities differ in the integration of *legitimate* means and goals, so also they differ in the availability and integration of *illegitimate* avenues;

5. The nature of the community's integration of legitimate and illegitimate means will determine the nature of the subcultural (delinquent) accommodation to goal achievement. Three of these are specified by Cloward and Ohlin, and they represent the end product, the dependent variable, predicted from the propositions above:

   a. a *criminal* subculture, and criminal *gangs*, will develop where there is cross-age integration of offenders plus close relations between the "carriers of criminal and conventional values;"

     b. a *conflict* subculture, and conflict *gangs*, will develop in
       neighborhoods not integrated as above, where social con-
       trols are relatively absent, and there is an absence of avail-
       able systematic illegitimate means to material goals. The
       use of violence becomes in this setting an alternate means to
       an alternate goal (status rather than material goals);
     c. a *retreatist* subculture, and retreatist *gangs*, will develop
       among boys locked out of the previous two subcultural adap-
       tations because of the lack of means integration and because
       of "internalized prohibitions" or "socially structured barriers"
       to the use of violence. This "double failure" leaves only
       retreat, through drugs or alcohol most specifically.

In developing this theory, Cloward and Ohlin have successfully
bridged the gap between socio-structural variables (the means–end
model) and behavioral variables (the subcultural adaptations). The
theory depends on the boys, only to the extent that they perceive (in a
manner unspecified by the authors) opportunity blockages, but this perception is a central fulcrum about which the theory is balanced. The
Cloward and Ohlin boys differ from the Cohen boys in that (a) they seem
somewhat more able, less handicapped by personal or social disabilities,
and (b) they are more concerned with material gain and social injustice
than with status and personal dissatisfaction.

While most of the central concepts are rather easily operational-
ized, those dealing with the integration of legitimate and illegitimate
means–ends systems present some difficulties. However, the problem
is not of great concern; the status of these propositions is more that of
assumptions or postulates than of hypotheses to be tested. With this
qualification, the Cloward and Ohlin formulation has proven in just a
few years to be the most tested of all major theories on both minor and
major scales. Elliott[59] failed to confirm class differentials in opportunity
perception, while Short et al.,[60] Vaz,[61] Monod,[62] the Sherifs,[63] DeFleur,[64]
and Downes[65] have had little success in verifying the existence of the
three distinct subcultures hypothesized by the theory. Only Spergel[66]
has provided empirical support for the general theory, at the same time
revealing a necessary modification with regard to age differentials.[67]
Most of the negative evidence has had to do with the purity of the subcultures,[68] but it is counterbalanced by strong support in the area of
objective existence of opportunity differentials in both the legitimate and
illegitimate sectors.[69] In sum, the theory has been sufficiently verified to
warrant continued investigation, but certainly not sufficiently to justify its
current level of acceptance.

It is interesting and by no means inconsequential for its verification that Opportunity Theory has almost become a national policy. The President's Committee on Juvenile Delinquency and Youth Crime* inaugurated a series of large community action programs (many of which later became the cornerstones of the War on Poverty in our largest urban centers) which were explicitly based upon Opportunity Theory. The best known of these was Mobilization for Youth on New York's Lower East Side. These large-scale programs offered a magnificent opportunity to verify the theory and to test the feasibility of its implementation. Unfortunately, program planning was not geared to such theory testing, and we still remain in the dark on the effects of this theory application to major urban concentrations of delinquency. In this connection, the reader may be interested in reading Daniel P. Moynihan's highly critical analysis of the way in which the propositions and ethos of Opportunity Theory were incorporated into both local and national social policy.[70]

Walter Miller

Walter Miller, a cultural anthropologist, has developed a third approach to delinquency that represents quite a departure from the previous theories.[71] The central difference is that Miller sees lower class delinquency—including that among the gangs from which his data are taken—as _not_ deviant or aberrant behavior except from a narrow, middle class viewpoint. From the facts of life among working class citizens, Miller deduces that delinquent forms of behavior are part and parcel of lower class culture and highly functional in preparing the youngster for adult life within that culture. In other words, the delinquent behaviors exhibited by lower class youth are **normal**.

In the cultural content of lower class life, Miller notes certain "focal concerns" which he labels as trouble, toughness, "smartness," excitement, fate, and autonomy. These cultural concerns are determined by the socio-economic setting of lower class citizens and by a singular, structural fact, the predominance of the female-based household. For boys in this setting, the absence of a strong father figure and the dominance of the female role in the home setting creates a need to practice the male role and assert masculinity outside the home. The gang is the opportunity for boys to achieve these goals, and provides in addition a sense of belonging and source of status not otherwise readily available.

---

*Later incorporated in the Welfare Administration as the Office of Juvenile Delinquency and Youth Development.

Thus, lower class gang delinquency is a normal response to the socio-structural and cultural demands of lower class life which prepares one for the dominant themes which he will encounter as an adult. Miller's approach has provided an interesting antidote to the usual view of delinquent behavior (especially the view of Cohen) as either sick or anti-social. Miller says this behavior is anti-social only in the sense that it runs counter to the moral expectations of the institutional carriers of middle class mores. This is a view especially appealing to those practitioners, especially street workers, who feel a strong identity with their delinquent clients. Miller's article in *Trans-action*,[42] written primarily for the practitioner, states his case succinctly:

> The subtle and intricately contrived relations among cliques, leadership and crime ... reveal the gang as an ordered and adaptive form of association, and its members as able and rational human beings ... the gang serves the lower-class adolescent as a flexible and adaptable training instrument for imparting vital knowledge concerning the value of individual competence, the appropriate limits of law-violating behavior, the uses and abuses of authority, and the skills of interpersonal relations. From this perspective, the street gang appears not as a casual or transient manifestation that emerges intermittently in response to unique and passing social conditions, but rather as a stable associational form, coordinate with and complementary to the family, and as an intrinsic part of the way of life of the urban low-status community, (p. 25)*

Miller's theory consists of a series of assumptions, observations, or postulates (the status of the propositions is a bit uncertain) which play into each other in a fashion that has led numerous critics to cry tautology. These critics note that Miller's observations were the source of hypotheses or assumptions which are subsequently used to explain the self-same observations, a form of circular reasoning which defies logic.

If Miller's proposition is, literally, that lower class delinquency is a normal part of lower class life, then the causal connection between the two is inherently untestable—the tautology is complete.

On other matters, some empirical testing does exist. The Cohen and Hodges' data on lower class life styles[52] fit rather well with Miller's description. Tennyson has provided direct support for the family propositions, but was unable to validate the observation that membership in a female-based family is related to gang membership.[72] Equal numbers of nongang lower class boys also come from the same family

---

structure. Tennyson has also demonstrated that Miller's social class emphasis beclouds differences related to racial distinctions. Finally, Short and others[73] have indicated that value differences between lower and middle classes are not sufficiently large to justify the central place accorded them by Miller.

Despite the faults of logic, and despite the failure to confirm the assumptions concerning the place of family structure and the class disparities in values, Miller's propositions are accepted by many as fact. At the same time, Miller's *empirical* data on patterns of gang offenses, gang structure, and so on have found little acceptance as guidelines to action. This is a seemingly strange reversal which characterizes much of the "discipline" of social welfare. Theory, assumption, and doctrine take precedence over demonstrated fact. This is not a formula for success.

The Adolescent Striving Theorists

A fourth approach, which we might label the Adolescent Striving Theory, has been spelled out by Bloch and Niederhoffer[74] and finds strong support in the writings of Erik Erikson[75] and S. N. Eisenstadt.[76] The approach represents an interesting cross-fertilization between neo-Freudian psychology and cultural anthropology.

The basic theme of these writers, restricted to delinquency, is that adolescence is a very special period of development in most societies and provides in its *natural* processes the clues to delinquent behavior. Adolescence is the period of transition between the dependence of childhood and the autonomy of adulthood, a transition which makes great demands on youth. It is in this period that the youngster strives to achieve a self-identity, principally by experimenting with new roles and behaviors. He is often supported in this experimentation by an adult audience which expects and condones it, but frequently fails at the same time to teach its limits.

Thus we have here an approach based on age strivings rather than class strivings, an approach which sees delinquent behavior as delinquent only "by default" or as the normal result of normal behavioral acts of youngsters seeking to find themeslves in an ambiguous role →
structure. The delinquent gang is seen as a collective response to these age-transition problems wherein the individual finds peer support for his temporary strivings.

The major difficulty with the adolescent striving approach, empir-. ically, is that it fails to specify adequately why it is any more pertinent to · gang behavior than to nongang behavior. It gives little clue to the gang

?) For l/c boy must find id. in both role and class structure while m/c boy only in role structure.

worker, other than to say, "help the boy achieve meaningful status and hold your breath." In fact, as the adolescent striving theorist accepts the gang as a potent source of status, he clearly supports the tendency among gang programs to reinforce gang structure. As we shall note later, this can have disastrous results.

Finally, in this selective review of theoretical propositions which have too often been accorded the status of accepted knowledge, we should mention a growing body of speculations which do not, as yet, constitute a systematic approach. There is (as yet) no such animal as the Probabalistic Cognitive Process Theory of delinquency. However, there are several prominent writers who have sought to explain certain aspects of criminology by reference to such notions as self-image, stigmatization, and neutralization on the one hand and drift, risk, and situational determinants on the other. The fit is not a neat one, but the reader familiar with the criminological literature may see some common social psychological directions behind the work of such men as Reckless, Sykes, Matza, the Schwendingers, McIver, Nye, Reiss, Short, and Strodtbeck.

Within criminology, the world of social psychology relates delinquency to the meeting of two sets of variables, (1) the perceptions and cognitive styles of the juvenile and (2) the "chancy" or probabilistic nature of the environment. The hypotheses and explanations offered by these writers are their attempts to come to grips with the *process problem* in particular; they seem relatively unhampered by concerns about disciplinary purity or reductionism. Some of the more prominent conceptions are these:

1. *Self-definitions*—as "good boys" as insulators against delinquency;[77]

2. *Containment theory*—the molding of inner and outer controls in determining conduct norms;[78]

3. *Techniques of neutralization*—(denial of responsibility, denial of injury, denial of victim, condemnation of the condemners, appeal to higher loyalties) as rationalizations employed by the offender before the act which decrease behavioral restraints and therefore maintain criminal patterns;[79]

4. *Subterranean values* — secondary middle-class values which take on primary status in lower class life;[80]

5. *Stigmatization*—the labelling of individuals by societal institutions as "bad," "criminal," or "deviant" thus reinforcing such self-images and creating a self-fulfilling prophecy;[81]

6. *Drift*—the probabilistic nature of exposure to values and restraints often resulting in inconsistency of delinquent patterns;[82]

7. *Aleatory risk*—the inadequate or ineffective perception of the relations between the commission of an illegal act and the odds on consequent negative sanctions;[83]

8. *Triggers of action*—the often unpredictable chance occurrences or cumulative patterns that finally tip the normative balance toward criminality.[84]

The general tenor of these concepts has to do with the individual's interpretation and cognitive response to an environment which is not highly structured. The gaps in the structure permit variations in perception and response, while these in turn provide the structure which—in our case—may perpetuate and reinforce the perceived legitimacy of deviant behavior.

One major distinction between these approaches and the theories covered earlier is that these approaches generally assume less about the offender's having drawn conclusions about the world around him, his chances in that world, the class structure, and so forth. To the cognitive process theorists, the offender—and especially the delinquent—is more of a *reactor* than an interpreter. His actions do not require the accurate perception seemingly demanded by Cohen or Cloward and Ohlin in particular.

For the most part, the speculations of the cognitive process theorists remain just that—speculations—not demonstrated causal variables and propositions. Because of their poor operationalization, the concepts of containment theory and drift represent serious verification problems. Other than this, the major problem, at this stage of concept development, seems to be one of too heavy reliance on after-the-fact explanations of behavior. For instance, almost all of the work on self-image by Reckless[77] and his associates has been of an *ex post facto* nature, while Matza[82] has relied primarily on interpretations of past observations and interviews. In time, we may see the incorporation of concepts and techniques taken from conflict and cognitive dissonance theories, which are rather well established and highly relevant to the approaches being reviewed here. The possibility of controlled experimental verification has been neatly demonstrated by the Schwendingers' work on offenders' stereotyping of victims.[85] To date, however, very little empirical work has been done to validate the utility of the cognitive process concepts.

Some "Popular" Variables

The foregoing discussion has concentrated on theories of causation, rather than on causes *per se*. Still, the reader may well wonder if this has not been too academic an exercise. Isn't delinquency really caused by a few major factors such as inadequate homes, or poverty, or psychological disturbance? The answer, discouragingly enough, seems to be "no." To make the point somewhat more concrete, let us take a few examples.

Constitutional Factors. Numerous investigators over several centuries have noted statistical relationships between crime and certain inherited or at least biologically identifiable characteristics of offenders. These characteristics have included skull formation, body type, chromosomal abnormalities, mental deficiency, glandular or neurological aberrations, and so on. Because of time limits, and because there does not exist a comprehensive "constitutional theory" of delinquency causation, I have arbitrarily excluded consideration of these matters in this book. But several personal judgments may not be out of order.

First, I would hope that we have come too far in our recognition of the complexities of delinquency causation to expect easy answers from *any* single collection of factors. Second, any constitutional explanation raises the question of the *processes* by which constitutional variables result in delinquent behavior. Finally, the references to constitutional factors in the literature suggest quite strongly that each major finding of significant relationships is followed by a set of negative findings or serious methodological criticisms. I feel that we can spend our research funds better in directions other than the biological.

The Family. The family as a source of crime and delinquency is a prominent feature of Miller's lower class culture theory, of the Gluecks' approach,[86] and of psychoanalytic theory.[87] In addition, it is recognized as one of the mediating variable complexes by Sutherland, the adolescent-striving theorists, and certain cognitive process writers. At the same time, family considerations are notably absent in the theories of Cohen and especially Cloward and Ohlin. One could conclude, therefore, that the family is fairly prominent in causation theories, but not so prominent as it is among the implicit causal hypotheses of the lay public.

Obviously, it is not the family *per se* which is important, but various factors or dimensions of the family, such as broken homes, working mothers, criminal experiences and values, supervision, affection, modes of discipline, and so on. Various studies of these aspects of the family situation have produced equivocal results, leading to the general conclusion that family variables, although important, probably attain that importance through combination with many other factors. As single "causes," they do not stand up well.[88]

For the practitioner, there is the additional problem that family variables are among the most difficult to manipulate. His levers of influence are minimal, the most potent being removal of the individual from the family environment. This drastic action runs counter to many of our social values and, in addition, creates the problem of suitable alternative placement for juveniles. For adults, it is too late.

Personality Traits. Another prominent assumption is that delinquency can be attributed primarily to personality traits. After all, offenders are people; offenses are the acts of people; and therefore the answer must lie in the psychological characteristics of the people involved. Once again, however, careful reviews of research into personality variables related to crime fail to yield any consistent result—except that personality and character traits are somewhat involved in the etiology of criminal behavior.[89] Slowly but surely, research into personality characteristics is beginning to take a more promising direction: the development of trait factors or offender typologies (a) which can be related to etiological factors, (b) which can serve as mediators of these factors, and (c) which can then be related to grossly conceptualized situations conducive to various categories of offense behavior. In this context, personality traits may take their proper place in the etiology of delinquency. Taken out of this context and given primary status, they will continue to beguile us but lead us nowhere in our attempts to understand and control delinquent behavior.

The Schools. Outside of the family, the school system has often been cited as the primary socialization mechanism in our society. Naturally then, the schools have been the focus of much attention in the delinquency area. Unfortunately, it is not clear whether schools are contributors to delinquency or insulators against it. School administration, truancy, failure, dropout rates, curriculum, and special services have been reviewed.[90] We can conclude that (a) not enough is yet known and (b) the school system is simply another medium through which other variables may have their effect. There is little to indicate that the school, by itself, is a primary direct cause of delinquency or of conformity.

Poverty. Last in our list of single variable explanations of crime is poverty, with associated unemployment, race and ethnic oppression, slum living, and so on. Remember that many delinquents are neither poor at the time of their offenses nor did they have poverty-stricken childhoods. The poverty variables have to do less with the *overall* incidence of illegal behavior than with disproportionately high crime rates among the poor. Poverty, like other variables, does not act in a consistent fashion. The majority of the poor do not become criminals in the usual sense of that word. The greatest rise in crime rates is currently to be found in suburbia, not in the slums.

Finally, poverty is not a single variable. It is a result of many factors as well as a contributor to many. The complexity of the poverty–delinquency relationship would require a separate treatment of greater length than this entire book, the conclusions of which would probably be that (a) elimination of poverty would reduce crime and delinquency by a small percentage, (b) the elimination of poverty without simultaneous concentration on employment, family stability, educational achievement, and prejudice would be self-defeating, and (c) delinquency is not inherent in poverty; it is merely facilitated by it. There are enough independent reasons for attacking poverty besides the unrealistic hope that reducing poverty levels will proportionately reduce delinquency.

To summarize this discussion very briefly, we need only state three primary conclusions. First, theoretical *attempts* to explain gang delinquency (and delinquency in general) abound. Second, relatively little empirical verification exists for the majority of these attempts. Most important to our discussion is that far too often practitioners as well as the lay public have taken unverified theoretical propositions as fact and have acted accordingly. We can only hope that as more empirical gang research is done there will be less unconsidered acceptance of speculation and more use made of what actually is known. This book is designed to help shift the balance. The chapters to follow will present some of the more recently available empirical data and suggestions as to their practical implications.

References

1. Gilbert Geis, *Juvenile Gangs* (Washington, D.C.: President's Committee on Juvenile Delinquency and Youth Crime, 1965).
2. Frederic Thrasher, *The Gang: A Study of 1,313 Gangs in Chicago,* abridged and with a new introduction by James F. Short, Jr. (Chicago: University of Chicago Press, 1963).
3. Lois DeFleur, "Delinquent Gangs in Cross-Cultural Perspective: The Case of Cordoba," *Journal of Research in Crime and Delinquency* 4, no. 1 (January, 1967): 132–41.
4. Frank T. Rafferty and Harvey Bertcher, "Gang Formations 'in Vitro' " *The Journal of Nervous and Mental Disease* 137, no. 1 (July, 1963): 76–81.
5. Lewis Yablonsky, *The Violent Gang* (New York: The Macmillan Co., 1963).
6. Clifford R. Shaw and Henry D. McKay, *Juvenile Delinquency and Urban Areas* (Chicago: University of Chicago Press, 1942); "Social Factors in Juvenile Delinquency," *Report on the Causes of Crime,* (Washington, D.C.: National Commission of Law Observance and Enforcement, 1937) 11, no. 13.
7. Thrasher, *op. cit.*

8. Edwin H. Sutherland, *Principles of Criminology,* 5th edition, revised by Donald R. Cressey. (New York: J. P. Lippincott Co., 1955).

9. Richard A. Cloward and Lloyd E. Ohlin, *Delinquency and Opportunity: A Theory of Delinquent Gangs* (New York: The Free Press, a division of The Macmillan Co., 1960); and Albert K. Cohen, *Delinquent Boys* (New York: The Free Press, a division of The Macmillan Co., 1955).

10. Frank Tannenbaum, "Point of View," in Rose Giallombardo (ed.), *Juvenile Delinquency: A Book of Readings* (New York: John Wiley & Sons, 1966), pp. 69–79.

11. Joseph Lohman, "County Communities, the City of Pleasant Hill, and the Unincorporated Area of Lafayette," excerpt from a report issued by the School of Criminology, University of California, Berkeley, 1966 (mimeo).

12. Rose Giallombardo, *Juvenile Delinquency: A Book of Readings* (New York: John Wiley & Sons, 1966).

13. Harry Manuel Shulman, *Juvenile Delinquency in American Society* (New York: Harper and Brothers, 1961).

14. DeFleur, *op. cit.*

15. LaMar T. Empey, "Delinquency Theory and Recent Research," *Journal of Research in Crime and Delinquency* 4, no. 1 (January 1967): 28–42.

16. Marshall B. Clinard, *Sociology of Deviant Behavior* (New York: Rinehart and Co., 1952).

17. Peter Scott, "Gangs and Delinquent Groups in London," *British Journal of Delinquency* 7 (July, 1956): 4–26.

18. LaMar T. Empey and Jerome Rabow, "The Provo Experiment in Delinquency Rehabilitation," *American Sociological Review* 26 (October, 1961): 679–95.

19. Muzafer and Carolyn W. Sherif, "Group Process and Collective Interaction in Delinquent Activities," *Journal of Research in Crime and Deliquency* 4, no. 1 (January, 1967): 43–62.

20. Richard R. Korn and Lloyd W. McCorkle, *Criminology and Penology* (New York: Henry Holt and Co., 1959), pp. 350–51.

21. David Matza, *Delinquency and Drift* (New York: John Wiley & Sons, 1964).

22. James F. Short, Jr. and Fred L. Strodtbeck, *Group Process and Gang Delinquency* (Chicago: University of Chicago Press, 1965), especially Chapter 11.

23. Prominent examples of "nonrational" factors affecting delinquency rates can be found in Philip H. Ennis, "Crime, Victims, and the Police," *Trans-Action* 4 (June, 1967): 36–44; A. W. McEachern and Riva Bauzer, "Factors Related to Disposition in Juvenile Police Contracts," in Malcolm W. Klein (ed.), *Juvenile Gangs in Context: Theory, Research, and Action* (Englewood Cliffs: Prentice-Hall, 1967), pp. 148–60; Irving Piliavin and Scott Briar, "Police Encounters with Juveniles," *American Journal of Sociology* 70 (September, 1964): 206–14; Thorsten Sellin and Marvin E. Wolfgang, *The Measurement of Delinquency* (New York: John Wiley & Sons, 1964); Irving Spergel, "Male Young Adult Criminality, Deviant Values, and Differential Opportunities in Two Lower Class Negro Neighborhoods," *Social Problems* 10 (Winter, 1963): 237–50; John M. Wise, *A Comparison of*

Data as Indexes of Delinquent Behavior, unpublished Master's thesis, University of Chicago, 1962.

24. David Horton Smith, "A Parsimonious Definition of 'Group': Toward Conceptual Clarity and Scientific Utility," *Sociological Inquiry* 37 (Spring, 1967): 141–67.

25. Bernard Cohen, "The Delinquency of Gangs and Spontaneous Groups" and "Internecine Conflict: The Offenders," in Thorsten Sellin and Marvin E. Wolfgang (eds.), *Delinquency: Selected Studies* (New York: John Wiley & Sons, 1969), pp. 61–111 and 112–37.

26. In order, these headlines appeared in the *Herald Examiner* (November 29, 1963), *Los Angeles Sentinel* (August 16, 1963), *Herald Examiner* (March 12, 1963), *Los Angeles Sentinel* (November 12, 1964), and *Pasadena Star-News* (September 26, 1963).

27. Short and Strodtbeck, *op. cit.*

28. David J. Bordua, "A Critique of Sociological Interpretations of Gang Delinquency," in Marvin E. Wolfgang, Leonard Savitz, and Norman Johnston (eds.), *The Sociology of Crime and Delinquency* (New York: John Wiley & Sons, 1962); *Sociological Theories and Their Implications for Juvenile Delinquency: A Report of a Children's Bureau Conference* (Washington, D.C.: U.S. Government Printing Office, 1960); "Some Comments on Theories of Group Delinquency," *Sociological Inquiry* 32, no. 2 (Spring, 1962): 245–60.

29. William Foote Whyte, *Street Corner Society* (Chicago: University of Chicago Press, 1943).

30. John M. Gandy, "Preventive Work with Street Corner Groups: The Hyde Park Project, Chicago," *Annals of the American Academy of Political and Social Science* 322 (March, 1959): 107–16.

31. Hans W. Mattick and Nathan S. Caplan, *The Chicago Youth Development Project,* (Ann Arbor: Institute for Social Research, University of Michigan, 1964).

32. Short and Strodtbeck, *op. cit.*

33. Cohen, Albert K., *op. cit.*

34. Cloward and Ohlin, *op. cit.*

35. Saul Bernstein, *Youth on the Streets: Work with Alienated Youth Groups* (New York: Association Press, 1964).

36. Gertrude Samuels, "They No Longer 'Bop,' They 'Jap,' " *New York Times Magazine,* March 7, 1965.

37. Thomas M. Gannon, "Dimensions of Current Gang Delinquency," *Journal of Research in Crime and Delinquency* 4, no. 1 (January, 1967): 119–31; "Emergence of the 'Defensive' Gang," *Federal Probation* 30 (December 1955): 44–48.

38. Charles F. Grosser, *Helping Youth: A Study of Six Community Organization Programs* (Washington D.C.: Office of Juvenile Delinquency and Youth Development, 1968).

39. Geis, *op. cit.,* p. 70.

40. Paul Levy, "Youth-Gang Killings Double 1967 Total," *Philadelphia Bulletin,* October 13, 1968; Pennsylvania Crime Commission, "Gang Violence

in Philadelphia," (Department of Justice, Commonwealth of Pennsylvania, July, 1969).

41. Dorothy M. Hayes and Russell Hogrefe, "Group Sanctions and Restraints Related to Use of Violence by Teenagers," paper delivered at the meetings of the American Orthopsychiatric Association, Chicago, March, 1964 (mimeo).

42. Walter B. Miller, "White Gangs," *Trans-action* 6, no. 10 (September, 1969): 11–26.

43. Émile Durkheim, *The Division of Labor in Society,* trans. George Simpson (New York: The Macmillan Company, 1933).

44. Walter B. Miller, "Theft Behavior in City Gangs," in Malcolm W. Klein (ed.), *op. cit.,* pp. 26–37.

45. Korn and McCorkle, *op. cit.,* 304.

46. Edward Eldefonso, *Law Enforcement and the Youthful Offender: Juvenile Procedures* (New York: John Wiley & Sons, 1967), p. 80.

47. President's Commission on Law Enforcement and the Administration of Justice, *The Challenge of Crime in a Free Society* (Washington D.C.: U.S. Government Printing Office, 1967), p. v.

48. *Ibid.,* p. 3.

49. *Ibid.,* p. 18.

50. George Homans, "Filling the Hollow Frontier," *et al.* 1, no. 1 (Fall, 1967): 2ff.

51. Albert K. Cohen and James F. Short, Jr., "Research in Delinquent Sub-cultures," *Journal of Social Issues* 14 (Summer, 1958): 20–37.

52. Albert K. Cohen and Harold M. Hodges, "Lower-Blue-Collar-Class Characteristics," *Social Problems* 10, no. 4 (Spring, 1963): 303–34.

53. Martin Gold, *Status Forces in Delinquent Boys* (Ann Arbor: Intercenter Program on Children, Youth and Family Life, Institute for Social Research, University of Michigan, 1963).

54. Ramon J. Rivera and James F. Short, Jr., "Occcupational Goals, A Comparative Analysis" in Klein (ed.), *op. cit.,* pp. 70–90.

55. Albert J. Reiss, and A. Lewis Rhodes, "Status Deprivation and Delinquent Behavior," *The Sociological Quarterly* 4, no. 2 (Spring, 1963): 135–49.

56. Leonard Berkowitz, *Aggression: A Social Psychological Analysis* (New York: McGraw-Hill Book Co., 1962), esp. p. 310n.

57. Howard L. and Barbara G. Myerhoff, "Field Observations of Middle Class 'Gangs'," *Social Forces* 42, no. 3 (March, 1964): 328–36.

58. Herman and Julia Schwendinger, "Delinquent Stereotypes of Probable Victims," in Klein (ed.), *op. cit.,* pp. 91–105.

59. Delbert S. Elliott, "Delinquency and Perceived Opportunity," *Sociological Inquiry* 32, no. 2 (Spring, 1962): 216–27.

60. James F. Short, Jr., Ray A. Tennyson, and Kenneth I. Howard, "Behavior Dimensions of Gang Delinquency," *American Sociological Review* 28, no. 3 (June, 1963): 411–28.

61. Edmond W. Vaz, "Juvenile Gang Delinquency in Paris," *Social Problems* 10, no. 1 (Summer, 1962): 23–31.

62. Jean Monod, "Juvenile Gangs in Paris: Toward a Structural Analysis," *Journal of Research in Crime and Delinquency* 4, no. 1 (January, 1967): 142–65.
63. Muzafer and Carolyn W. Sherif, *op. cit.*
64. DeFleur, *op. cit.*
65. David M. Downes, *The Delinquent Solution: A Study in Subcultural Theory* (New York: The Free Press, a division of The Macmillan Co., 1966).
66. Irving Spergel, *Racketville, Slumtown, Haulburg: An Exploratory Study of Delinquent Subcultures* (Chicago: University of Chicago Press, 1964).
67. Irving Spergel, "Deviant Patterns and Opportunities of Pre-Adolescent Negro Boys in Three Chicago Neighborhoods," in Klein, *op. cit.*, pp. 38–54.
68. Clarence Schrag, "Delinquency and Opportunity: Analysis of a Theory," *Sociology and Social Research* 46, no. 2 (January, 1962): 167–75.
69. Short and Strodtbeck, *op. cit.*
70. Daniel P. Moynihan, *Maximum Feasible Misunderstanding: Community Action in the War on Poverty* (New York: The Free Press, a division of The Macmillan Co., 1969).
71. Walter B. Miller, "Implications of Urban Lower-Class Culture for Social Work," *Social Service Review* 33, no. 3 (September, 1959): 219–36; "Lower Class Culture as a Generating Milieu of Gang Delinquency," *Journal of Social Issues* 14, no. 3 (Summer, 1958): 5–19.
72. Ray A. Tennyson, "Family Structure and Delinquent Behavior," in Klein (ed.), *op. cit.*, pp. 57–69.
73. Short and Strodtbeck, *op. cit.*
74. Herbert A. Bloch and Arthur Niederhoffer, *The Gang* (New York: Philosophical Library, 1958).
75. Erik H. Erikson, *Childhood and Society* (New York: W. W. Norton, 1950); "Ego Identity and the Psycho-Social Moratorium," in Helen Witmer and Ruth Kotinsky (eds.), *New Perspectives for Research on Juvenile Delinquency* (Washington, D.C.: Children's Bureau, 1956); also see Helen L. Witmer, "Delinquency and the Adolescent Crisis," (Washington, D.C.: Children's Bureau, 1960) Reprint no. 11.
76. S. N. Eisenstadt, "Archetypal Patterns of Youth," *Daedalus* 91, no. 11 (Winter, 1962): 28–46; *From Generation to Generation: Age Groups and Social Structure* (Glencoe, Ill.: The Free Press, 1956).
77. Walter C. Reckless, Simon Dinitz, and Barbara Kay, "The Self-Component in Potential Delinquency and Potential Non-Delinquency," *American Sociological Review* 22, no. 5 (October, 1957): 566–70; Reckless, Dinitz, and Ellen Murray, "Self Concept as an Insulator Against Delinquency," *American Sociological Review* 21, no. 6 (December, 1956): 744–46.
78. Walter C. Reckless, "A New Theory of Delinquency and Crime," *Federal Probation* 25, no. 4 (December, 1961): 42–46.
79. Gresham M. Sykes, and David Matza, "Techniques of Neutralization: A Theory of Delinquency," *American Sociological Review* 22, no. 6 (December, 1957): 664–70.

80. David Matza and Gresham M. Sykes, "Juvenile Delinquency and Sub-terranean Values," *American Sociological Review* 26, no. 5 (October, 1961): 712–19.

81. Edwin McCarthy Lemert, *Social Pathology: A Systematic Approach to the Theory of Sociopathic Behavior* (New York: McGraw-Hill, 1951); William P. Lentz, "Delinquency as a Stable Role," *Social Work* 11, no. 4 (October, 1966): 66–70; National Council on Crime and Delinquency, "Open Hearings in Juvenile Courts in Montana," November 20, 1964 (mimeo); Richard D. Schwartz, and Jerome H. Skolnick, "Two Studies of Legal Stigma," in Howard S. Becker (ed.), *The Other Side: Perspectives on Deviance* (Glencoe, Ill.: The Free Press, 1964), pp. 103–17; Frank Tannenbaum, *Crime and the Community* (Boston: Ginn and Co., 1938).

82. David Matza, *Delinquency and Drift* (New York: John Wiley & Sons, 1964).

83. Short and Strodtbeck, *op. cit.,* Chapter 11.

84. Robert M. MacIver, *The Prevention and Control of Delinquency* (New York: Atherton Press, 1966).

85. Schwendinger and Schwendinger, *op. cit.*

86. Sheldon and Eleanor Glueck, *Unravelling Juvenile Delinquency,* (Boston: Commonwealth Fund, Harvard University Press, 1957); also "Working Mothers and Delinquency," in Wolfgang et al., *op. cit.*

87. David Abrahamsen, *The Psychology of Crime* (New York: Columbia University Press, 1960); Adelaide M. Johnson, "Juvenile Delinquency," in Silvano Arieti (ed.), *American Handbook of Psychiatry* (New York: Basic Books, 1959); also see Michael Hakeem, "A Critique of the Psychiatric Approach to the Prevention of Juvenile Delinquency," *Social Problems* 5, no. 3 (Winter, 1957–1958): 194–205.

88. Herbert C. Quay, *Juvenile Delinquency: Research and Theory* (Princeton, N.J.: D. Van Nostrand Co., 1965); Richard S. Sterne, *Delinquent Conduct and Broken Homes: A Study of 1,050 Boys* (New Haven: College and University Press, 1964); Barbara Wootton, *Social Science and Social Pathology* (London: G. Allen and Unwin, 1959).

89. Ivan N. Mensh, "Personality Studies of Mentally Ill Offenders," in *The Mentally Ill Offender: Variations in Approaches,* Atascadero (California) State Hospital, October, 1963, pp. 21–31; Quay, *op. cit.;* Short and Strodtbeck, *op. cit.;* Karl F. Schuessler and Donald R. Cressey, "Personality Characteristics of Criminals," *American Journal of Sociology* 55 (March, 1950): 475–85; Gordon P. Waldo and Simon Dinitz, "Personality Attributes of the Criminal: An Analysis of Research Studies, 1950–1965," *Journal of Research in Crime and Delinquency* 4, no. 2 (July, 1967: 185–202.

90. Quay, *op. cit.*

91. Leonard Savitz, *Dilemmas in Criminology* (New York: McGraw-Hill Book Company, 1967).

Chapter 2: Gang Prevention Programs

The preceding chapter has suggested that what we often take as knowledge about gangs is in fact something less; hunches, stereotypes, assumptions and misperceptions abound. Most of our *empirical* knowledge, that derived from field research procedures, comes as a result of gang prevention programs. In several very important instances, detached worker (street work) programs have been carried out in conjunction with research teams, resulting in the accumulation of highly useful data on gangs and gang workers.

At the same time, projects in which the research teams have attempted evaluations of project success have yielded very discouraging findings—suggesting that detached work programs have had little impact on gang delinquency or—even worse—have inadvertently contributed to gang delinquency. As with heart transplants in the late 1960's, we keep losing the patients while learning more about the reasons for our failures.

Approaches to gang intervention have taken many forms, although only one of these has been identified as a "pure" gang approach and as such, has led to careful empirical evaluation. Before turning to this primary approach, generally known as a "detached worker program," we shall consider a few others, which range from the most specific to the most general.

The well-known **Mobilization for Youth** program (MFY) in New York attempted to restructure the social organization of the Lower East Side through community participation and special programs to involve residents in expanded opportunities. Within the comprehensive and diffuse activities of MFY, gang members were the recipients of all the

44

programs initiated, including contracted detached work service, but little special attention was devoted to them specifically *because* of their gang membership.[1] They were expected to benefit in a manner similar to that of other youths in the area. No specific evaluation has been reported.

The Los Angeles Youth Project, similar to others in the nation, was an attempt to coordinate agencies in the delinquency area. It was designed to strengthen existing welfare agency programs and lead to more effective control procedures, including those aimed at gang behavior. No specific evaluation has been reported.

The Chicago Area Projects, developed on the basis of the pioneering work of Clifford Shaw and Henry McKay, were aimed at developing local community organizations to fill in the gaps of social control in inner city areas. Included in the Area Projects were the first detached work services, but the major thrust was in developing indigenous leadership and neighborhood organization. No specific evaluation has been reported.[2]

Youth for Service in San Francisco is basically a detached work program, but with a special twist. The distinctive feature of this program has been the involvement of gang youth in service projects throughout the community—clean-ups, repairs, and so on—which provide status, a sense of community identification, self-esteem, and a good image in the eyes of the residents. An unpublished review of the program by researchers at the Berkeley campus of the University of California questioned the effectiveness of the program; otherwise no specific evaluation has been reported. The same holds true for a recent leadership training program carried out by Youth for Service.

More or less standard detached work programs have been employed throughout the nation in Philadelphia, El Paso, San Antonio, New York, Boston, Chicago, and Los Angeles. Gandy's report on the Hyde Park Project in Chicago[3] suggested a certain level of success with delinquent youngsters, but the evaluation was not methodologically sound.* Evaluations of the enormous program of the New York City Youth Board have been limited to impressionistic accounts[4] and to surveys of the opinions of the workers.[5] This has been an inexcusable waste of an opportunity to develop rational prevention strategies. The detached work program of Chicago's Metropolitan YMCA was the source of the very important research carried on by Short and his colleagues

---

*There were no control or comparison groups and, most important, no age controls in the analysis.

and referred to throughout this book. However, the research program was concerned with "basic" research and made no attempt at evaluating the effectiveness of the program as a whole nor any of its component parts.[6]

Although varying in form, detached work programs are grounded in one basic proposition: Because gang members do not ordinarily respond well to standard agency programs inside the agency walls, it is necessary to take the programs to the gangs. Around this simple base of a worker reaching out to his client, other programmatic thrusts then take form—club meetings, sports activities, tutoring and remedial reading projects, leadership training, family counseling, casework, employment training, job finding, and so on.[7] In addition, a community organization component is often built into the program in the recognition that gangs do not exist in a vacuum, but in a context permeated by adults and adult organizations.[8]

Nevertheless, the common denominator—the supposed primary agent of change—is the detached worker. The primary change mechanism is the rapport established between worker and gang member. The primary goal is to bring gang and society back together into a workable style of life, for there is an obvious isolation between the gang and conventional society because, as Thrasher has noted, of ". . . this barrier of unsympathetic social blindness, this inability of either to enter understandingly into the life of the other."[9]

Both Spergel,[10] and Bernstein,[11] have provided useful discussions of the basic goals and formats of detached work programs. In our major urban areas, especially among various minority groups, large numbers of adolescents exist who have become alienated from societal institutions and, being in mutually disadvantaged positions, have banded together loosely in street gangs. It is to these boys (and less commonly, girls) that detached worker programs are directed. The choice of these alienated youth groups or gangs as program targets has been dictated by three related rationales:

1. Members of street gangs typically fail to make use of existing youth facilities, or are barred from admission because of their disruptive behavior. Such boys can best be reached by individuals—detached workers—who base their activities on the street corner, at the taco stand, or in the empty garage where the boys normally congregate; Muhammed must go to the mountain.

2. Members of the street gangs, through a series of processes both social and economic, develop patterns of delinquent behavior that serve to increase their own level of alienation, to deprive themselves further of legitimate access to social and economic opportunities, and result in

sometimes lasting psychological debilities. A vicious cycle develops in which the troubled youth breaks the law, becomes stigmatized as an enemy of society, is incarcerated, and then returns to an environment conducive to further repetitions of the same pattern—repetitions facilitated by the youth's own reactions (and those of his peers and significant adults) to the judicial processing he has undergone. The existence of this cycle is attested to by the decreasing time intervals between subsequent offenses in a gang member's delinquent career. Data from our own study[12] and from Robin's analysis in Philadelphia[13] show the between-offense intervals decreasing from about 13 months between the first and second offense to less than four months between the ninth and tenth offense. Thus, detached worker programs are justified by their protagonists as interrupters of the cycle, as initiators of movement away from self-destruction and toward maximizing the potential growth and productivity inherent in each gang member.

3. Members of street gangs commit a variety of offenses, each of which, upon detection by official agencies, requires an outlay of funds as the youth is processed by the police, courts, and so forth. The taxpayer is always the victim. In addition, there are more direct victims—those who are robbed or assaulted, those whose property is defaced or whose customers are discouraged, those whose responsibilities to the nondelinquent youngsters are interfered with by the antisocial activities of the gang on the playground and in school. Thus, to the extent that delinquent gangs are destructive to other members of society, there is a rationale for giving special service to them designed to lessen their negative impact.

All detached worker programs of which we are aware justify their existence on the basis of one or more of these rationales: the existence of unserved youth groups, the needs and difficulties of the members, and the societal costs of gang existence. Bernstein's review of gang programs suggests that the most common rationale is the first (gangs exist), followed closely by the second (gangs need help). The cost of gang activity emerges from his review as the least salient rationale, perhaps because of the social service ethic underlying most of these programs. Gang programs carried out by agencies more attuned to the enforcement ethic would certainly present a different picture.

Goals

As would be expected, the goals of detached worker programs are similar to their rationales. Spergel has listed five primary goals as follows:

(a) control (principally of gang fighting)
(b) treatment of individual problems
(c) providing access to opportunities
(d) value change
(e) prevention of delinquency

The difficulty with this list, or any other similar in nature, is in assigning priorities. For instance, a rationale emphasizing the societal costs of gang activity would result in the primacy of the control and prevention goals, reserving treatment, value change, and access to opportunities as subgoals or even techniques. This was the general approach of the Ladino Hills Project, an approach with which some social work practitioners felt uncomfortable because fulfillment of individual needs seemed subservient to delinquency reduction.

The confusion over goals can be illustrated by several instances. When the Group Guidance Section of the Los Angeles County Probation Department launched its special four-year experimental program, it used its past experience of almost 20 years of detached work as the foundation for the experiment. That 20-year period had been oriented primarily toward the control goal or "fire fighting," to use the workers' phrase. This goal was primary because the agency had been established following the "zoot suit" riots of the early 1940's. Control of gang fighting was the original *raison d'etre* of the Group Guidance program.

However, the four-year experiment, launched in 1961, was oriented more toward prevention than mere control; consequently it emphasized subgoals and techniques such as treatment, value change, and access to opportunities, among others. This shift in goals caused much confusion in the experimental project and was undoubtedly one of the several reasons for its failure to become fully implemented.[14]

Another illustration comes from *Reaching the Fighting Gang*,[15] a publication of the New York City Youth Board that is probably the best known treatise on gang work among practitioners of the art. Even a cursory reading of this volume demonstrates the confusion around goal priorities and the hazy distinction between goals and techniques. The authors clearly state that the major goal in gang work is to build a bridge between gang members and their community, yet the emphasis of the volume is clearly *not* on bridging, but on fulfilling the needs of the gang members in such a way that gang membership is no longer "necessary."*

We might summarize these comments on goals by saying that detached worker programs have been rather successful in specifying

---

*Twelve such needs fulfilled by gang affiliation are listed on pp. 18–19 of *Reaching the Fighting Gang*.

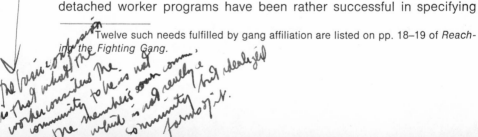

their goals, are highly varied in the emphases applied to the various goals, and are now in a position to clarify goal priorities for themselves. When this latter step has been achieved, the programs will be better able to develop clear and rational means to achieve their goals and to evaluate the level of that achievement. One advantage of the Ladino Hills project in particular was its concentration on the single, primary goal of reduction in gang delinquency, permitting the placing of subgoals and techniques into a conceptual model with clear action imperatives. This project was one of the several listed below which were literally forced into goal specification through the existence of inquiring teams of researchers. Goal specification makes measures of effectiveness possible.

The Roxbury Project. This program, evaluated by Walter B. Miller,[16] took place in Boston between 1954 and 1957. It involved a staff of seven workers assigned principally to seven gangs, Negro and white, male and female. There were four major components: work with local citizen's groups, interagency relations, family casework, and detached work with the gangs. Detached work was the major thrust, involving intensive relations between the workers and 205 gang members. The detached workers' strongest activities were in the employment and education arenas.

Miller describes the project's excellent accomplishments in implementing the detached worker operations, at least as judged by the heavy participation of the gang members with the workers. However, using delinquency data from both the workers and official agencies, he notes no overall impact on delinquent behavior. There was no significant reduction in the number of disapproved acts, in legal violations, or in court appearances among the gang members as compared with "control" gangs not receiving intensified service. In fact, there were a number of increases in delinquency among (a) males as opposed to females, (b) the younger boys as opposed to older boys, and (c) more serious as opposed to less serious offenses. Miller concludes not only that the behaviors of the gang members were resistant to change, but that the adult institutions and agencies in the area acted as major impediments to change.

The Chicago Youth Development Project. This was a six-year program carried out by the Chicago Boys' Clubs between 1960 and 1966 with preliminary evaluation by the Institute for Social Research of the University of Michigan. It differed from the Roxbury project in several aspects: (a) it had far more community organization; (b) it involved more youngsters, including nongang members; and (c) it made greater use of feedback procedures, employing research data about the program in developing and modifying its approach.[17]

Final evaluative statements on the C.Y.D.P. have not been published, but staff members have concluded that, although the project succeeded in implementation, it failed in delinquency reduction.[18] Many employment opportunities were developed, new techniques devised, worker-youth relationships established, and so on, but delinquency rates were not reduced. In fact, they believed that those boys served most intensively manifested the greatest *increase* in delinquency. A dramatic illustration of processes leading to this ultimate failure has been provided by Caplan.[19]

The Group Guidance Project. This was a four-year program carried out under the auspices of the Los Angeles County Probation Department between 1961 and 1965. Similar in form to the Roxbury Project, it involved four Negro gang "clusters" (16 subgroups) with total male and female membership of approximately 800 (see Fig. 3-2 in Chapter 3). Several colleagues and I evaluated the project.

The Group Guidance Project laid heavy stress on group programming: weekly "club" meetings, outings, sports and other special activities, remedial reading and tutoring projects, and parents' clubs. Implementation of group programming was quite successful, but efforts in employment, education, and community organization were minimal. The program was also complicated by a bitter dispute between the action agency and local enforcement agencies.

Our evaluation[20] revealed that the project was clearly associated with a significant *increase* in delinquency among the gang members. This was found to be most true in the gangs most intensively served and, mirroring Miller's findings, among members at the lower age levels. The increase was primarily in those offenses that are ordinarily committed with companions but *not* with offenses more often committed by oneself. The evaluation suggested that the increase in offenses was, at least in part, attributable to the high level of group programming and the gang recruitment to which this led.

The Ladino Hills Project.* Noting that in previous projects intensity of service seemed related to delinquency increases and that group programming seemed to work *against* program goals, colleagues and I mounted an 18-month program (with a six-month follow-up) in 1966 with a Mexican-American gang cluster of approximately 140 members. The project was designed to reduce gang cohesiveness through the cessation of group programming and the provision of alternative activities. We hypothesized that cohesiveness reduction would in turn lead to delinquency reduction.[21]

---

*This is a pseudonym.

Overall project implementation was judged to be reasonably successful: a reduction in cohesiveness of 11 to 40 per cent was achieved,
depending upon the index employed. The entry of new members into the
gang (male, but not female), was completely stopped. Delinquency rates
(number of offenses per member) did not change during the project
period, but the steady reduction in the size of the gang led to an overall
reduction of 35 per cent in the number of offenses. These trends continued through the follow-up period despite the withdrawal of project
staff.

It may seem remarkable to some that the only four projects with
careful evaluations yield such equivocal or even negative findings. This
brief review, of course, does not do justice to the intricacies of the action
and research methods—we have summarized 14 years of work in just
a few pages. But in each of the four cases a determined effort was
mounted and sustained by the project staffs. *Failure to reduce gang
delinquency cannot be explained by lack of program implementation.* In
fact, the very existence of research evaluations, putting the action staffs
"under the gun," probably led to unusually persistent action. There can
be no escaping the conclusion that detached work programs, as constituted in the recent past, are not effective in the reduction of gangs or the
"violent" activities associated with gangs. They may inadvertently *contribute* to gang violence.

Where do we turn now? If programs designed specifically to
reduce gang delinquency and concentrated directly upon gang members do not succeed, what can? Certain hints can be gleaned from these
and other programs. Some alternative suggestions have been offered;
some others may be in order.

We can summarize the present difficulties as falling into five general
areas.

Theoretical Underpinnings

Most gang prevention programs have been either totally atheoretical or blandly eclectic. These approaches have produced inconsistency, random or uncoordinated programming, and uncertainty about
the meaning of seeming program successes or failures. Frequently,
programs have been launched without a clear understanding of their
goals and how to measure their attainments. For instance, the use of
delinquency reduction as the ultimate criterion of success in the four
projects reviewed above was highly acceptable to the researchers, but
not to the workers, who are more concerned with welfare matters and
attitude changes. Until social practice programs are guided by a consistent intervention model with reasonable theoretical bases, they will

continue either to flounder or to add little to our ability to undertake social change.

Enormity of the Problem

By the time 100 boys and girls become affiliated with a juvenile gang, they have experienced 12 to 18 years of formative processes from the family, the neighborhood, and the society. They continue to be bombarded by the contemporary factors of group and social processes even as we work with them. All these factors—and others as well—are acting on the gang member to produce the affiliations and behaviors society decries.

Arrayed against this veritable army of psychological, social, and cultural forces is the detached worker and the few resources at his disposal. David beat Goliath, but at least he had a slingshot. How would he have fared against a hundred Goliaths? How conceited we are to expect one worker, however reinforced, to overcome substantially the combined forces of family, neighborhood, and society. In a gang of 100 boys, the detached worker can reasonably expect to devote 10 to 15 minutes per week per boy on the average, yet from this we expect the twin miracles of fundamental attitudinal and behavioral change. In light of the other problems to be enumerated here, this appears to be an unfair challenge.

Absence of Specific Techniques

Miller reported that, of 14 threatened gang fights in the Roxbury Project, only one took place. The experience in Los Angeles was similar: research observers personally witnessed a number of threatened confrontations that failed to materialize. In the area of intergang conflict, the worker does have specific techniques for avoiding the fight. One of these is his mere physical presence as a witness. Another is his availability as a messenger to enforcement agencies, forewarning them of a fight about which the boys have told him in the hope that he would prevent it. Another technique (of questionable value) is the "truce meeting" between representatives of the warring factions.

But how many other analogous techniques are in the workers' repertoire? There really are none specifically pertinent to burglary, vandalism, statutory rape, curfew violation, drug use, and so on. On a more general level, the previously mentioned Youth for Service program and the Chicago YMCA have mounted carefully designed leadership programs;[22] the YMCA and Group Guidance programs developed extensive tutoring and remedial reading programs; others have attempted civil rights involvement, youth coffee houses and a host of other standard and innovative approaches designed to reform, teach, occupy, involve, or train gang members in nongang behavior.

Unfortunately, these "techniques" are very general, of unknown pertinence to delinquency prevention, and almost invariably undertaken without evaluation of their impact. In the absence of techniques known to be specifically related to delinquency reduction, programs have evolved more and more activities of a less specific nature. If they don't necessarily reduce delinquency, at least these projects appear "morally" good and sound in welfare philosophy. They give the workers a sense of accomplishment and their administrators further justification for agency continuation and expansion. But this is not delinquency prevention.

Inappropriate Techniques

How would a rational worker go about meeting and maintaining rapport with as many as a hundred youngsters—most of whom are street-oriented? Being on the street himself is not sufficient; too many boys are missed that way. The worker has little choice but to encourage *group* gatherings—club meetings, outings, and so on. In this way he can get to know most of the boys, maintain contact with them, and use existing group processes to his own advantage. But the gathering of the group, the reinforcement of gang-as-gang identification, and the solidification of gang structure that may result inadvertently work against the goal of delinquency reduction.

As Spergel has noted, ". . . the presence or absence of the worker on the corner is a powerful stimulus in creating, maintaining, or dissolving the group structure. The worker tends to attract young people and to become an essential person in the organization of the group."[23] Cloward and Ohlin, Miller, and Yablonsky have all commented on the worker as a source of status for the gang. Our own analysis in Los Angeles has gone beyond this—demonstrating that removal of a worker eliminates a major source of gang cohesiveness and may precipitate a partial dissolution of the gang.[24]

Another tendency revealed by the Los Angeles data is for the worker to turn his attention from older boys (who are leaving the gang) to younger boys, whom he sees as the "natural inheritors" of the gang traditions. In working with these younger subgroups, the workers inadvertently create a self-fulfilling prophecy and perpetuate the traditional gang structure.* That this process *can* be interrupted has been demonstrated by the Ladino Hills Project, but it goes against the normal inclination of the worker.

Another inappropriate technique has been revealed by Caplan.[26] He refers to "backsliding"—a serial process in which a given level of worker output brings youngsters up to the brink of important behavioral change, but is then followed by a backing away or reversion to an earlier status. Faced with this setback, the worker redoubles his effort, only to have the youngster revert even further. The process has even been observed by Caplan through three such cycles. The data indicated that whereas 80 per cent of the boys manifested initial desirable change, only 4 per cent "terminated in successful changes that were characterized by postproject autonomy."[27]

Other less dramatic and less destructive practices will be outlined in Part II. The fault, of course, lies not in the lack of concern or dedication of the workers or their programs. These are uniformly laudable. The fault lies, as indicated earlier, in our combined failure to devise, test, and implement workable, theoretical intervention models that could distinguish between helpful and harmful tactics. Lacking such models, we continue to spin our wheels and yet feel the *sense* of progress.

Lack of Leverage

I mentioned earlier that the enormity of the delinquency and gang problems is an overwhelming obstacle to detached work programs. Leverage on the problem depends also on the resources available to these programs. Many operating variables simply cannot be changed by the detached workers: The psychological propensities of gang members, the stresses of adolescence, the opportunity structure of the neighborhood and community, and the normative structure of class and subculture are, for the most part, beyond the reach of the street worker. He has few of the necessary resources; and in many cases he lacks an understanding of which resources would be most useful.

The worker works in a vacuum, detached not only from his own agency but from others concerned with gang prevention. He is often alienated from enforcement officials because of conflicting intervention philosophies. Miller concluded that the greatest resistance to delinquency reduction lay not in the youngsters but in the recalcitrance of the

---

*It may be worth noting, in this regard, that the average age of gang members served by the New York City Youth Board decreased by one and a half years after Youth Board Service was initiated.[25] The Youth Board workers may inadvertently have been providing a funnel into the gang for younger boys in the neighborhood.

adults in community agencies and institutions.[28] Bernstein suggested that "public" delinquencies (fights, vandalism) proved more amenable to change than "private" delinquencies (sex, drug use),[29] and Cooper could report about spontaneous attacks by small groups of boys that "the detached worker's control over these is pretty much limited to the times when he is present, or when one of the youths . . . is willing and able to act as his representative."[30] Too many of the factors which bring boys to the point of gang membership and conflict are not within the capability of a detached worker program to manipulate.

Summary

Although most gang prevention programs remain unevaluated in a proper fashion, it is highly significant that the evaluated programs have proven only slightly successful, ineffective, or even contributory to gang delinquency. They have employed inadequate resources in combating an entrenched foe. Some of their normal and almost necessary practices have acted as boomerangs, effectively increasing gang cohesiveness and delinquency.

Although new, modified approaches to detached work could now be mounted on the basis of the lessons learned from the past, one is inclined to predict that, at best, new programs of this sort could only represent "holding actions." If the data from Philadelphia are at all valid, even the reduction of large scale intergang conflict may have the inadvertent effect of increasing serious violence.[31]

At this point, perhaps, it is anyone's guess as to where we should turn. The accumulated data on levels of gang violence suggest strongly that any new effort will in any case be directed at a relatively minor facet of the urban ills of our nation. Gang violence, it must be admitted, is *not* now a major social problem. In determining future directions we must, as Yablonsky has pointed out, distinguish between "the necessary strategy for broad social change and the practical tactics of local control."[32]

Irving Spergel, who has most successfully bridged the gap between research and action involvements with juvenile gangs, has probably best summarized the present situation.

It is, perhaps, unlikely that social work, through either casework or group work (or street-club work), or combinations of these methods, even on a large scale, will affect substantially the character or reduce the incidence of gang fighting in the

neighborhood containing the conflict subculture. At best, the
social worker's efforts are supplementary.

... social work cannot offer a significant program of intervention.

... only as the larger conventional society opens the floodgates
of opportunity and provides a massive program whereby
adequate schooling, good jobs, better housing, and health and
social services of a broad range and high quality are more fully
available to low-status groups will delinquency of the conflict
variety drastically be eliminated or transformed.[33]

References

1. Marylyn Bibb, "Gang-Related Services of Mobilization for Youth" in Malcolm W. Klein (ed.), *Juvenile Gangs in Context: Theory Research, and
   Action* (Englewood Cliffs, N.J.: Prentice-Hall, 1967), pp. 175–82.
2. Solomon Kobrin, "The Chicago Area Project—A Twenty-five Year Assessment," *The Annals of the American Academy of Political and Social Science* 322 (March, 1959): 1–29.
3. John M. Gandy, "Preventive Work with Street Corner Groups: The Hyde
   Park Youth Project, Chicago," *Ibid*, pp. 107–16.
4. *Dealing with the Conflict Gang in New York*, Interim Report #14 of the
   Juvenile Delinquency Evaluation Project of the City of New York, May,
   1960 (mimeo); *Reaching the Fighting Gang* (New York: New York City
   Youth Board, 1960).
5. Thomas M. Gannon, "Dimensions of Current Gang Delinquency," *Journal
   of Research in Crime and Delinquency* 4, no. 1 (January, 1967): 110–31;
   "Emergence of the 'Defensive' Gang," *Federal Probation* 30 (December,
   1955): 44–48.
6. Charles N. Cooper, "The Chicago YMCA Detached Workers: Current Status
   of an Action Program" in Klein (ed.), *op. cit.*, pp. 183–93.
7. Saul Bernstein, *Youth on the Streets: Work with Alienated Youth Groups*
   (New York: Association Press, 1964); Bibb, *op. cit.*; Nathan S. Caplan,
   Dennis J. Deshaies, Gerald D. Suttles, and Hans W. Mattick, "The Nature,
   Variety, and Patterning of Street Club Work in an Urban Setting" in Klein
   (ed.), *op. cit.*, pp. 195–202; Cooper, *op. cit.*; *Dealing with the Conflict
   Gang, op. cit.*; Buford E. Farris and William N. Hale, "Mexican-American
   Conflict Gangs: Observations and Theoretical Implications," *Research
   and Educational Reports*, no. 1, Wesley Community Centers, San Antonio,
   (undated); Malcolm W. Klein, *From Association to Guilt: The Group Guid-
   ance Project in Gang Intervention* (Los Angeles: Youth Studies Center,
   University of Southern California, 1968); Malcolm W. Klein, *The Ladino
   Hills Project* (Los Angeles: Youth Studies Center, University of Southern
   California, 1968); Hans W. Mattick, and Nathan S. Caplan, *The Chicago
   Youth Development Project* (Ann Arbor: Institute for Social Research, Uni-
   versity of Michigan, 1964); Walter B. Miller, "The Impact of a 'Total-

Community' Delinquency Control Project," *Social Problems* 10, no. 2 (Fall, 1962): 168–91; Walter B. Miller, Rainer C. Blum, and Rosetta McNeil, "Delinquency Prevention and Organizational Relations" in Stanton Wheeler (ed.), *Controlling Delinquents* (New York: John Wiley & Sons, 1968), pp. 61–100; *Reaching the Fighting Gang, op. cit.*; Irving Spergel, *Street Gang Work: Theory and Practice* (Reading, Mass.: Addison-Wesley Publishing Co., 1966); Gerald D. Suttles *The Social Order of the Slum: Ethnicity and Territory in the Inner City* (Chicago: University of Chicago Press, 1968).

8. Bibb, *op. cit.*; Klein, *From Association to Guilt, op. cit.*; Mattick and Caplan, *op. cit.*; Walter B. Miller, "Inter-Institutional Conflict as a Major Impediment to Delinquency Prevention," *Human Organization* 17, no. 3 (Fall, 1958): 20–23; Miller, Blum, and McNeil, *op. cit.*; Spergel, *op. cit.*

9. Frederic Thrasher, *The Gang: A Study of 1,313 Gangs in Chicago,* Abridged and with a new Introduction by James F. Short, Jr. (Chicago: University of Chicago Press, 1963), p. 180.

10. Spergel, *op. cit.*

11. Bernstein, *op. cit.*

12. Klein, *From Association to Guilt*, pp. 263–64.

13. Gerald Robin, "Gang Member Delinquency in Philadelphia," in Klein (ed.), *Juvenile Gangs in Context*, pp. 15–24.

14. Klein, *From Association to Guilt.*

15. *Reaching the Fighting Gang* (see ref. #4).

16. Miller, "The Impact . . ." *op. cit.*

17. Mattick and Caplan, *op. cit.*

18. Frank Carney, "Comments on Youth Gangs," in Sol Tax (ed.), *The People vs. the System: A Dialogue in Urban Conflict* (Chicago: Acme Press, 1968), pp. 352–53; Carney, Hans W. Mattick, and John D. Callaway, *Action on the Streets* (New York: Association Press, 1969), esp. the Introduction.

19. Nathan Caplan, "Treatment Intervention and Reciprocal Interaction Effects," *Journal of Social Issues* 24, no. 1 (January, 1968): 63–88; "Motivation and Behavior Change," *Proceedings of the Industrial Relations Research Association* (Winter, 1967), pp. 229–35.

20. Malcolm W. Klein, "Gang Cohesiveness, Delinquency, and a Street Work Program," *Journal of Research in Crime and Delinquency* 6, no. 2 (July, 1969): 135–66.

21. Klein, *The Ladino Hills Project, op. cit.*

22. Cooper, *op. cit.*

23. Spergel, *op. cit., p. 33.*

24. Klein, "Gang Cohesiveness . . . ," *op. cit.*

25. *Reaching the Fighting Gang*, p. 29.

26. Caplan, *op. cit.*

27. Caplan, "Motivation and Behavior Change," p. 231.

28. Miller, "Inter-Institutional Conflict . . . ," *op. cit.*

29. Bernstein, *op. cit.*

30. Cooper, *op. cit., p. 188.*

31. Paul F. Levy, "Youth-Gang Killings Double 1967 Total." *Philadelphia Bulletin*, October 13, 1968; Pennsylvania Crime Commission, "Gang Violence in Philadelphia," Department of Justice, Commonwealth of Pennsylvania, July, 1969.

32. Lewis Yablonsky, *The Violent Gang* (New York: The Macmillan Company, 1963), p. 237.

33. Irving Spergel, "An Exploratory Research in Delinquent Subcultures," *Social Service Review* 35 (March, 1961): 33–47, 45.

conceive

Chapter 3: The Gang

e
m

working class

Locations

↑

Although there are a few descriptions of juvenile gangs in middle class settings,[1] it is clear that the gang problem is primarily an urban, lower-class phenomenon. The middle-class groups described to date are generally short-lived aggregations with a minimal orientation to delinquent values. +

Two types of urban areas have emerged as the primary spawning grounds of gangs. The first was described 40 years ago by Thrasher, but the description is still appropriate in the 1960's:

> "In nature foreign matter tends to collect and cake in every crack, crevice, and cranny-interstices. There are also fissures and breaks in the structure of social organizations. The gang may be regarded as an interstitial region in the layout of the city."[2]

The second gang area is the "stable slum" in which population shifts of the past have slowed, permitting the development of neighborhood patterns and traditions over a span of years. Most typical of these areas are the Negro and Puerto Rican slums of the East and the Mexican-American "barrios" of the Southwest and California cities. As Bernstein[3] and others have suggested, the shifting, interstitial or transitional areas spawn the more spontaneous gang structures, often pitting groups of different ethnic backgrounds against each other. The stable slum, on the other hand, more often produces the large, vertically structured gang cluster which has proven most resistant to intervention attempts. These two types of urban, lower-class areas—transitional and stable slum—do

though the neighborhood remains the same, the population changes

...it for all gangs in the city, but the evidence to date strongly ...ests that they do contain a large majority of them.

Although the sociological literature is filled with descriptions of lower class communities, only recently has concentration on specific gang areas by Cartwright and Howard[4] updated Thrasher's original descriptions. Among the most useful aspects of this recent work is its demonstration that the gang arena, far from being homogeneous, is in fact highly variable along many dimensions; that gang neighborhoods differ from nongang neighborhoods in the same city, but not so much as many are led to believe; that the relationship between neighborhood characteristics and gang behavior is measurable but neither strong nor direct.

Suttles' ethnographic description of the Addams area in Chicago emphasizes varieties of intricate social relations and sense of territoriality.[5] Miller's analysis of the neighborhoods of two white gangs, the Outlaws and the Bandits, illustrates not only variety in setting, but also hints at possible relationships between the particular settings and the approach to delinquent behavior in each.[6] Even more pointedly, Spergel has demonstrated the very close, and perhaps causal, ties between neighborhood characteristics and distinct differences in gang styles.[7]

These authors have made it clear that it is not sufficient to characterize a gang neighborhood (as I shall do in the next paragraph) in terms of median family incomes, types of housing, educational levels, or population density. A life style—a *subculture*—can be distinguished that helps to spawn particular varieties of gangs.

Because the Group Guidance and Ladino Hills Projects have contributed much to the data in this book and have shaped my viewpoints, I will summarize here very briefly the nature of the geographical areas in which these projects were carried out. It was not our purpose to delve substantively into the ethnography of these areas; hence I hope the reader will find occasion to read the descriptions cited above. I need only add that, as I consider the Los Angeles areas of our own gang experience, the differences noted by these other authors ring true more in spirit than in fact.

Lower-class areas in Los Angeles, as has so often been noted about its vast suburban sprawl, have a "washed out" appearance and feeling. I suspect that the lower population density has much to do with this, but in any case—as a research team—we were often far more impressed by neighborhood similarities than by differences.

Test Areas

Early in the planning stages of the Group Guidance Project, the decision was made to place the program "where the action is" or, more specifically, to place it in an area which would truly provide a test of its efficacy. Two sorts of areas would have provided such a test, a traditional Mexican-American gang community or a developing Negro gang community. Because the Group Guidance staff wanted to generalize techniques originally developed for Mexican-American gangs, and because the Negro supervisor of the workers was concerned about the community immediately adjacent to his own residence, the final decision was to place the project in that section of the primarily Negro community in which large-scale gang activity threatened to take on massive proportions in the near future.

A "test area" for program implementation was chosen in the south-central district of Los Angeles—an area most likely to show an increase in gang activity in the ensuing years. Following the workers' best judgments, the test area boundaries were fixed so as to include the bulk of the residences and gathering spots of the boys and girls in the four gangs to be served. Final data indicates that 59 per cent of the residences fell within the boundaries, with most of the remainder within a half-mile radius. Almost all of the facilities used by the gang members, including schools, playgrounds, and "hangouts," were included within the test area.

Demographically, the test area was typical of the widespread minority ghettos of Los Angeles. Land use was about 80 per cent residential and 20 per cent commercial. Residences usually consisted of single family units interspersed with duplexes and two-story apartment dwellings. Often one house hid a second dwelling in what would otherwise have been the backyard. There were no housing developments in the area.

The commercial enterprises consisted primarily of retail trade and services. Little manufacturing existed; during the period of the project the War on Poverty hardly touched the area. Thus, not only was unemployment high among the gang youngsters, but the resources for reducing it were rather low. Table 3-1 summarizes other pertinent data for the two segments of the test area.

Several points are obvious from the data in Table 3-1: The test area compared rather poorly with the city as a whole with respect both to socio-economic conditions and delinquency arrest rates.

However, it is also clear that matters could have been worse. The test area, especially the northwest segment, was not a full ghetto strictly speaking; nor was it a fully qualified poverty area. Much of it could have been characterized as lower middle class, lying as it did in the area of ghetto expansion and "escape."

Finally, the two segments of the test area were not equally deprived. This difference may have affected the impact of the project on the gangs in the area: the impact was more positive in the northwest than in the

Table 3-1:   Selected Demographic Characteristics of Test
             Area,* G.G.P.

	Northwest Segment	Southeast Segment	Total	City
Population	49,180	42,832	92,012	2,479,015
% Aged 10-17	9.7	10.1	9.9	11.5
Median family income	$5,608	$4,894	$5,306	$6,896
Median school years completed	11.9	9.8	11.0	12.1
% Negro	70.0	75.6	72.4	13.5
Household crowding (% 1.01 + persons per room)	7.7	11.2	9.2	8.2
Delinquency arrests, 1961	420	485	905	17,270
Delinquency arrest rates per 1,000 persons 10-17	87.6	111.6	99.0	60.3

*The first items are taken from the U.S. Census for 1960. The arrest data are taken from quarterly reports published by the Los Angeles Police Department.

southeast segment. Guests from eastern cities are seldom surprised by the housing situation in the latter when told that gang activity is prevalent there; but in the northwest segment we often encountered disbelief at the disparity between the visible appearance of the area and our description of its gang activity. A cruise of these areas, in fact, was one of the favorite "games" we played with "visiting firemen" from Chicago, Boston, and New York. We tried to teach the lesson that social problems are as much a function of *relative* as of absolute deprivation. The lesson is hard to learn, but it is crucial to an understanding of the Los Angeles poverty areas.

The second project was located in an area of East Los Angeles that I shall call Ladino Hills. To the east and north, low hills provided an effective boundary marker; to the northwest, a major freeway separated Ladino Hills from a major recreation area; to the west lay a dry river bed; to the southwest, south and southeast, major arteries provided informal definers of the area.

In local gang terminology, the area was called "Latin," the generic term for the delinquent gang cluster that has claimed the Ladino Hills territory as its own for the past 30 years.** The heart of this project target area was comprised of seven census tracts with a total population of 24,187. It was one of perhaps a dozen or so areas in Los Angeles

**A gang "cluster," as we will use the term, consists of from two to five age- and sex-related groups that are somewhat distinct in structure but are clearly aligned as *subgroups* of a larger whole. In using the term "cluster" for this confederation of groups, we achieve a more comprehensive and accurate terminology than those who merely enumerate all the subgroups and speak of "five gangs." At the same time, our definitional approach sacrifices some of the drama inherent in gang descriptions.

which were possible sites for the project, each being the locus of a large, traditional juvenile gang that had failed to respond significantly to traditional gang intervention techniques. As such, it was a locale from which project procedures and results might be generalized toward considerably broader application. The project was placed here because (1) the research team was curious about comparisons between Mexican-American gangs and the Negro gangs of the Group Guidance Project, (2) the Latin gang met certain prerequisites of the intervention model, and (3) the detached worker assigned to the Latins was willing to participate in the project.

Ladino Hills was a primarily Mexican-American community located northeast of the Civic Center. While predominately residential, it also included a large railroad yard and numerous industrial properties. It was an older section of the city currently populated by working-class families. Table 3-2 presents comparative figures for Ladino Hills and the City of Los Angeles, based on the 1960 census. Little change has taken place since that date.

Table 3-2: Census Data, Los Angeles and Ladino Hills

		Los Angeles	Ladino Hills
Total Population	% Sound housing	91%	65%
	% Owner occupied	46%	30%
	% 1.01 or more persons per room	8.2%	18%
	Population per household	2.77	3.04
	Median school years completed	12.1	8.6
	Median family income	$6,896	$5,100
	% Males unemployed	6.7%	7.0%
	Ratio, broken to united families (male)	1.6:10	4:10
Spanish Surname Population	% Born in Mexico	20%	30%
	Median school years completed	8.9	7.9
	Median family income	$5,564	$5,097
	% Males unemployed	8.3%	7.1%
	Ratio, broken to united families (male)	1.4:10	2.8:10

The figures in Table 3-2 tell the same old story of minority areas: population disadvantage in housing, family unity, education, income, and employment. In an economic survey of 100 areas, the Welfare Planning Council found the Ladino Hills area to be the 88th.

The community resources available to Ladino Hills residents, and especially to members of the delinquent population, were more apparent than real. The police, probation, and public assistance agencies had inadequate staffs assigned to the area. Recreational facilities included one playground in the center of the area and two others on the periphery.

Several churches and schools represented at best only potential extra-curricular resources. The Ladino Hills Boys' Club was located within the project area, but at the beginning of the project it had been found unacceptable by gang members older than 12 or 13, and the feeling was reciprocated by the club staff.

The County Department of Community Services had initiated a Ladino Hills Coordinating Council in the early 1960's, but this group was just beginning to undertake a survey of area needs when the project began. The Department's consultant in the area was a new man; he was assigned to four other areas as well. Businessmen's groups in the area —Kiwanis, Optimists, and Chamber of Commerce—had not as yet been solicited for aid in gang intervention. Finally, programs funded by the Office of Economic Opportunity, such as the Teen Posts, NYC and NAPP, were just beginning to penetrate the Ladino Hills community.

In sum then, the project area was—like all Los Angeles minority areas—relatively disadvantaged while containing the potential for good resource allocation. As such, it was a perfect target for the sort of pro-gram being proposed. In many ways it was typical of the stable slum areas of many cities in which traditional gangs tend to develop and persevere.

Structure

Because of its variability and the several dimensions which comprise it, the structure of the juvenile gang is perhaps the most difficult aspect to describe. Among researchers, there is less than unanimity on the typical gang structure. When I presented a diagram of the structure of traditional Los Angeles juvenile gangs to one colleague in Chicago, I was told that this structure was either a wild distortion or a Los Angeles peculiarity. When I then presented the same diagram to a second colleague doing gang research less than a mile away from the location of the first, I was told that it represented Chicago gang structures quite perfectly.

The major dimensions along which gang structure has been de-scribed are age, size, subgrouping, level of involvement, leadership and role differentiation, and sex. Leaving aside for the moment the question of leadership and role differentiation, one can discern two *modal* patterns of structure, and several variations deriving from these.

Spontaneous

The first structural pattern is that of the *spontaneous*[8] or *self-contained*[9] gang. It may include from 10 to 30 members within a two- or three-year age range and is more likely to appear in areas of transition.

It is not a permanent grouping, seldom lasting more than a year or two. Sometimes it is a splinter group, having broken off from a larger gang cluster to pursue a particular interest pattern (social or criminal). Members know each other on a personal basis, although core and fringe levels of involvement can be distinguished. Bernstein's nine-city survey suggests that these gangs are predominant, and perhaps increasingly so.[10]

Traditional

The second pattern, variously termed *vertical, area, traditional,* or *cluster,* is far more complex. Examples have been cited by Hardman,[11] Miller,[12] Thrasher,[13] Kantor and Bennett,[14] MacIver,[15] Bernstein,[16] the New York City Youth Board,[17] Spergel,[18] Cohen and Short,[19] and Short and Strodtbeck.[20] The essential feature of this pattern is the inclusion of from two to five age-graded subgroups within an overall cluster. Thus there may be a small group of 12- and 13-year-olds, a larger group of 14- and 15-year-olds, a still larger group in the 16- to 18-year-old bracket, and a smaller disintegrating group of older boys. Each subgroup has a sense of self-identity and a specific name as well as a strong identification with the overall cluster as a superordinate structure.

Such a structure may include as many as 100 or 200 boys over a period of only two years. Cliques form within the larger subgroups, and the observer can differentiate between these cliques, a more inclusive "core" membership, and an even larger fringe membership. Nor does this three-or-four-"generation" description conclude the picture, for the gang cluster often has a neighborhood tradition that goes back from 10 to 40 or even 50 years.[21] Figure 3-1 illustrates the general pattern of relationships and levels of involvement of a typical gang cluster—the Latins.

Figure 3-1 is a compact illustration of several points. The age range of the cluster goes from 11 or 12 to the early 20's. Over 100 boys are identified as members (girls are omitted from the illustration). Core and fringe members are about equal in number, according to worker definitions of core and fringe. Core members comprise the majority of clique membership, although some fringe members also fall into cliques. The ages from 15 to 18 constitute the period of greatest activity and tightest clique structuring. Cliques and major subdivisions of the cluster are highly age-related, although some crossing of age boundaries is also evident. In sum, the traditional gang cluster is a complex arrangement of companionship patterns in which one can distinguish groupings by age and by degrees of involvement (clique, core, and fringe). Remembering that Fig. 3-1 represents a single time slice, it is important to add

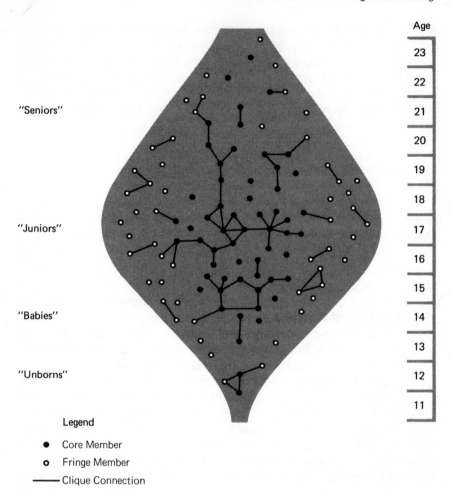

Fig. 3-1: The structure of a traditional gang
cluster—The Latins.

that the companionship patterns are quite flexible. Substantial shifts
take place, sometimes weekly and sometimes monthly.

Now, if the reader will look once more at Fig. 3-1 for its *general
configuration* according to age and number of members, he will see
the symmetrical pattern of a child's top, or perhaps a skinny turnip.
Yablonsky has suggested the analogue of an artichoke, with a smaller
core membership constituting the heart.[22] Just how generalizable this
configuration is can be seen in Fig. 3-2, containing the patterns found in
the four gang clusters involved in the Group Guidance Project.

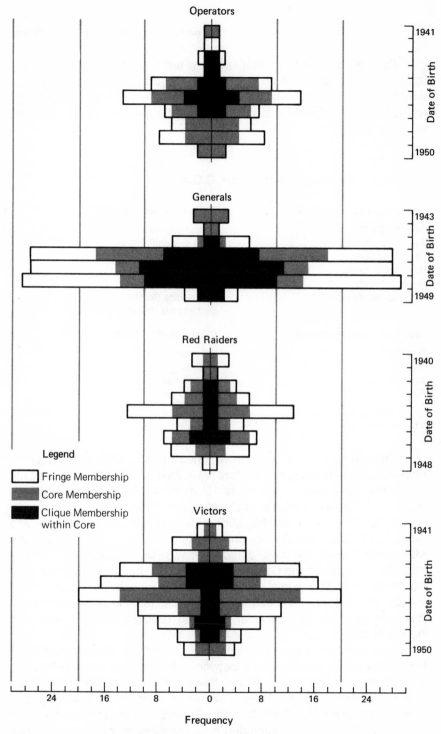

Fig. 3-2: Gang structures of four clusters
separately, G. G. P.

For any one gang cluster, the top-turnip-artichoke analogy only roughly fits the data, yet an average representation of all four clusters would indeed approach that in Fig. 3-1. The pattern of named subgroups as well shows the empirical variety within the overall pattern, as noted in Table 3-3.

Table 3-3: Clusters and Subgroups, G.G.P.

Cluster A—The Operators*

Senior Operators
Junior Operators
Baby Operators
Unborn Operators
Belles (female)
Lady Operators (female)

Cluster B—The Generals

Senior Generals
Baby Generals
El Hunters
Diplomats
Generalettes (female)
Huntresses (female)
Diplomettes (female)

Cluster C—The Red Raiders

Red Bluff
Red Raiders
Junior Raiders
Raidettes (female)

Cluster D—The Victors

Valiants
Victors
Baby Victors
Vicettes (female)

*All names of gangs, gang members, adults, and places used in this book are pseudonyms.

The Latins were a Mexican-American gang, while the Operators, Generals, Red Raiders, and Victors were Negro. But the pattern of the traditional gang cluster has no racial or ethnic connotations. Miller's most recent analysis of two white gangs in Boston lists the Brigands, Senior Bandits, Junior Bandits, Midget Bandits, Bandettes (female), and Little Bandettes (female), in one cluster. The second includes the Marauders, Senior Outlaws, Junior Outlaws, Midget Outlaws, Outlawettes (female), and Little Outlawettes (female). The age ranges are from 10 to 25, with approximately 200 members in a cluster.[23] As noted earlier, this pattern of the traditional gang cluster is to be found in most cities which have experienced the gang problem over an extended period of time.

One should not overemphasize the similarity of the pattern without looking carefully at differences between clusters. Miller, in describing the Bandits and Outlaws, indicates that the former were far more delinquently oriented than the latter. Among the four clusters in the Group Guidance Project, the Operators and Generals were far more cohesive and resistant to change, recruited new members at a higher rate, and maintained higher offense rates than the Red Raiders and Victors. Only the Generals showed an improvement in offense rates over the bulk of the project period. Only the Red Raiders threatened to split into two opposing factions. Such differences have both theoretical and practical implications which might be lost were one to overstate the generalizations associated with the overall cluster pattern.

Other Structures

The Specialty Clique. Three other gang structures deserve mention here. The first is the small clique of from three to a dozen boys, sometimes part of a larger structure and sometimes an independent unit, which evolves into a *patterned* delinquent group around criminal or retreatist (drug use) interests. These boys have abandoned the adolescent pattern in favor of a concentrated involvement in adult crime patterns. Such groups, fortunately, are relatively uncommon.[24]

The Horizontal Pattern. In contrast, many writers have noted a second, "horizontal" pattern consisting of temporary alliances across neighborhoods between normally independent gangs.[25] A good description of this pattern has been provided by Mattick and Caplan:

> For the most part, however, the youngsters of the area, aside from a few isolates, are aggregated into cliques or loose local groups having tenuous and transitory relations with one another. On occasion several of these local groups combine in temporary and informal federations for purposes of socialization or athletics, or for purposes of defense or attack, and then dissolve again into their original local groupings.[26]

Mattick and Caplan provide examples of a core group of 15-to-20 boys which might, in the above pattern, expand to 150-to-200 boys at particularly critical times. Often, however, such federations exist more in fantasy than in fact.[27]

The Violent Gang. The final pattern—from its name one might judge it to be the critical one in this book—is the "violent gang" described by Yablonsky.[28] Although Yablonsky does not report any of his data, he distinguishes the violent gang from other forms (social and delinquent) on the basis of size, cohesiveness, normative structure and leadership. The violent gang, he says, is a "near-group" characterized by diffuse role differentiation, limited cohesion, impermanence, minimal consensus on

norms, shifting membership, emotionally disturbed leadership, and limited definition of membership expectations. This account is in many
ways a caricature of the descriptions of other investigators with a strong
additional emphasis on psychopathic behavior, especially among gang
leaders whom he describes as megalomaniac, delusional, and self-
appointed.

Yablonsky claims that his analysis is based upon "direct appraisal
of over 100 gangs."[29] Aside from the disbelief which this claim has
engendered among other researchers, there is the additional problem
that no one else has observed the violent gang as described by Yablonsky. Rather than describing a typical pattern as he suggests, Yablonsky
may have generalized far too much from two groups he studied in depth,
the Egyptian Kings and the Balkans. The former had a "brief but intense
life history of a few weeks," although their roots went back two years.
The latter were studied "over the eight-month period of their existence."
Yablonsky notes further that one major gang fight seems enough to break
up these groups. Jansyn,[30] Klein and Crawford,[31] Short and Strodtbeck,[32]
Thrasher,[33] and Gordon[34] among many others have noted the contrary
tendency—for intergang conflict to *solidify* the gang. In addition, most
practitioners and researchers alike have found that the gang psychopath
seldom exerts genuine leadership, that gang leaders are far more often
relatively stable youngsters known for "holding their cool."

In summary, then, the "violent" gang is seldom seen and is in any
case of short duration. It contributes little to the overall level of gang
violence and its description therefore contributes minimally to a rea-
soned analysis of violence in gangs.

Core and Fringe Memberships

Another approach to the investigation of gang structure is the distinction between *core* and *fringe* members of the gangs. This distinction
is almost universally employed by gang workers the country over. In fact,
the core-fringe distinction and the role of the leader are the only structural variables consistently employed by practitioners in the gang world.
Accordingly, these concepts may provide excellent points of entry for
the researcher interested in gang structures. We will concentrate here
on the *membership* dichotomy, leaving leadership for a later analysis.

There are gang workers, of course, who make finer distinctions
within the categories of core and fringe membership, using such terms
as *hard core, inner core, outer fringe,* or *fringe-fringe,* but the underlying
dimension of degree of involvement is accepted by all, as is the core

and fringe dichotomy. On this basis alone (and knowing that workers respond differentially to core and fringe members) this distinction merits investigation. Another justification lies in the differences in delinquency involvement between the two member types, as indicated later in this section.

To investigate the meaning of core and fringe membership in the Group Guidance Project, the question of criteria was put to five gang workers, four male and one female. They were asked to respond in terms of the gangs to which they were assigned.

The interview responses were highly varied, yielding 18 suggested criteria for discriminating between core and fringe members. One worker steadfastly refused to offer more than one criterion, namely, the member's commitment to his group. It is interesting that at a later date this worker was released by his superiors because of overidentification with his gangs. Another worker supplied three criteria: emotional dependence on the group, level of participation, and the ability to manipulate the other members verbally. The other three workers contributed five, eight, and nine criteria. Of the 26 suggested criteria, only eight were verbalized by more than one worker, and only one—level of participation—by more than two of the five workers. Thus, with eight repetitions, the interviews yielded 18 quite disparate criteria.

For a researcher seeking common factors, such data contain the threat of pure chaos. We were not in a position to say much more than that these workers, as judges of a presumably important and common phenomenon, were unable to verbalize common themes independently. Therefore, we adopted a second procedure: we added to the 18 criteria another 36. These were derived from our own hunches and field observations, yielding the list of 54 items in Table A-1 of the appendix. Then two separate operations took place. Six workers, including four of those mentioned earlier, went down their gang rosters and labeled each member *core* or *fringe*. Then 10 core members and 10 fringe members were randomly selected from each list, yielding altogether 60 core and 60 fringe members (along with some substitutes in case the workers were not sufficiently familiar with some of the boys originally chosen).

Each of the 54 criteria was framed as an item. The workers then applied the 54 items to each of the core and 10 fringe members on their lists. The workers were told that the selection of names was purely random, and were given a cover story for the exercise. Upon questioning later, it became clear that none suspected the judgments were in any way related to the core-fringe distinctions they had previously made.

Most of the items contained a four-point response scale. For example:

"As compared with the average member, to what extent does (this boy) seem to prefer following the leadership of other members?"
a. much more than the average member
b. somewhat more than the average member
c. somewhat less than the average member
d. much less than the average member

A few items had only two response categories if so dictated by the item content. For example, "Does he know how to drive a car or not?"

Responses to each item were dichotomized around the median and chi-squares performed on the data relating item responses to the core-fringe distinction. Thirty of the 54 items differentiated between core and fringe members at the .05 level, another 4 at the .10 level, and 4 at the .20 level. That is, 38 of the 54 items looked promising. Eight of these were included as reliability checks, leaving 30 others for further analysis. Phi and phi/phi max coefficients were computed for each pair of items, the phi/phi max coefficients were entered into a 30 × 30 matrix, and this matrix was then subjected to principal-axis factor analysis with Kaiser's Varimax rotation. (Table A-2 in the appendix presents the results of the factor analysis.)

The first nine factors to emerge account for 80 per cent of the total variance, but seven of them contain only 1, 2, or 3 items, and none of these 7 accounts for more than 6 per cent of the total variance. The two *major* factors are listed in Table 3-4, and are labeled the *Deficient-Aggressive* factor and the *Group Involvement* factor.

The Deficient-Aggressive factor, accounting for 34 per cent of the variance, is of particular interest. It reveals a relationship between delinquency or aggressiveness and personal deficiency. The Group Involvement factor, which accounts for another 13 per cent of the variance, does not include any acting out behavior items. Thus, to judge from the workers' use of these items, delinquency is more related to individual characteristics than to group characteristics.

Since the Deficient-Aggressive and Group Involvement factors together account for more of the total variance than the remaining seven factors taken together, the bulk of our discussion will be concerned only with these first two factors. However, factors III, IV, and VI taken together (see Table A-2 in the appendix) suggest a dimension that is not revealed by the various factors taken separately, the dimension of the *worker-member relationship*. It must be remembered that our analysis is of worker judgments about member characteristics, not of member traits independently assessed. Thus we should not be surprised that the nature or quality of the worker-member affective relationships should

[handwritten annotation at top: "...the splendid cooperation of my colleague, ..."]

Table 3-4: Two Major Factors in Core-Fringe Membership

[handwritten: "from workers' statements"]

Original Item # (see Appendix)	Content*	Factor Loadings I	II
24	Lower school performance	.86	.07
33	Lower intelligence	.83	.11
48	Lower impulse control	.81	.12
39	More likely to get others in trouble	.80	.30
8	Higher recorded delinquency	.80	.07
26	More often truant	.79	.01
49	Lower desire for rehabilitation	.77	.14
42	More psycho-, sociopathic	.76	.21
54	Needs more help	.70	.15
25	More dependent on group	.65	.41
14	Fewer outside interests	.61	.03
7	More willing to fight	.58	.48
15	More often participates in spontaneous activities	.13	.78
22	More clique involvement	.14	.76
3	Greater total contribution to group	.03	.60
32	Greater desire to lead	.22	.52
20	More accepted by core members	.01	.48

I Deficient-Aggressive *[handwritten: "34% variance"]*

II Group Involvement *[handwritten: "13%"]*

*For illustrative purposes, the content is phrased in the direction of high core responses.

emerge as a meaningful dimension in our analysis. Our operational definition of core and fringe status is the worker's label for each member—a judgment of one human being about the status of another. The current analysis relates judgments of individual characteristics to judgments of individual statuses in groups, leaving the judge himself as a common denominator. If this is, as we suspect, a significant component of the responses and their analysis, then future investigations of this sort must attempt to "parcel out" or otherwise account for this judgmental dimension when judges have established affective relationships with the judged.

Of course, this analysis does nothing to determine to what extent the major factors mirror reality, or merely the conceptual perspectives of the judgers. However, other data *do* support the notion that core and fringe members differ on the two major factors.

Clique membership, as determined by frequency of mutual contacts, is almost entirely restricted to the core members of gangs. We also know that participation in group activities such as club meetings and outings is higher for core than fringe members. Thus, the Group Involvement factor receives independent validation from several sources on its ability to differentiate between core and fringe members.

During the four years of the Group Guidance Project, core members were charged with 70 per cent more offenses than fringe members; they committed their first offenses five months earlier on the average; less time elapsed between offenses of core members; core members "terminated" their delinquent careers at a later age. In other words, we can independently validate the delinquency component of the Deficient-Aggressive factor.

The assaultive offenses* of these boys—those presumably most closely related to aggressiveness—comprise a small portion of their total recorded offenses. Nevertheless, the core members' assaultive offenses were proportionally greater—35 per cent higher than fringe members' assaultive offenses. This helps to validate the specifically *aggressive* component of factor I, over and above greater overall delinquency involvement.

The deficiency component must await further data collection, and we cannot as yet deal with the judges' implied hypothesis that delinquency involvement is more closely related to *intra*personal than to the *inter*personal dynamics. The relevant differences between core and fringe members are summarized in Table 3-5.

Table 3-5 : Validating Comparisons of Core and Fringe Involvements**

Behavioral Index	Comparison
1. Attendance at gang meetings:	
a. average number of boys	Core, 2½ times as many as fringe
b. average number of meetings per boy	Core, 1¾ more than fringe
2. Number of recorded offenses	Core, 70% more than fringe
3. Proportion, assaultive/all offenses	Core, 35% greater than fringe
4. Time lapse between offenses	Core, 15% shorter time period
5. Date of first offense (career onset)	Core, five months earlier
6. Date of last offense (career termination)	Core, nine months later

---

**An unexpected further validation of the core-fringe distinction emerged from the "Watts riots" in August of 1965. Nineteen members of the gangs under study are known to have been arrested as riot participants. Of these, 18 were core members, only one a fringe member. Since the workers divide gang membership almost equally into core and fringe categories, this 18:1 ratio again suggests that the factor analysis has isolated "a difference that makes a difference."

With the differences noted above being so substantial, it would seem reasonable to expect that background and demographic charac-

---

*These include murder, manslaughter, assault and battery, aggravated assault, forcible rape, and weapons violations.

teristics of core and fringe members would also differ very noticeably, even to the point of suggesting why some boys become core members and others fringe. That such is not the case is a bit surprising, but very clear from the data in Table 3-6.

Table 3-6: Background Data on Core and Fringe Members

Item	Core	Fringe
Born in county (%)	43	46
Year came to county (median)	1955	1955
United, original parents (%)	31	24
Single parent family (%)	40	45
Number of children in family (mean)	4.2	3.8
Number of people in home (mean)	5.0	4.7
Mothers' education (median)	10th grade	10th grade
Fathers' education (median)	10th grade	10th grade
Annual family income (median)	$4,500	$4,500
Intelligence test scores (mean)	85	86

Although the differences favor the fringe members, they are slight differences at best and certainly of no predictive value. As a sample of presumably relevant background characteristics, the items in Table 3-6 explain nothing. It would seem, on this basis, that an understanding of causal factors relating to the observed core-fringe differences will have to come from other sorts of data—a sort not collected during the project. We can describe core-fringe differences, but we cannot explain them.

Our data shed some light on a commonly employed structural dimension of delinquent gangs—the core-fringe dimension, suggesting that members' position on this dimension is related to a Deficient-Aggressive factor and a Group Involvement factor. These data are generally in accord with independently collected information on gang behavior. It would be convenient to assume that the core-fringe dichotomy employed by gang workers corresponds to distinctions made by the gang members themselves. However, for the moment this is an untenable assumption. Some boys do talk about the "ins" and the "outs," and many have derogatory terms for boys who might be classified as fringe members—"They just a bunch of poop-butts," "Them rooty-poots are square, man, they got no cool." On the other hand, persistent questioning of the boys often leads to denial of differences in membership status—"We all equal," "That kind o' leadership take hold of everybody. Everybody mostly get in that position at one chance or another."

Both Yablonsky[35] and Short and Strodtbeck[36] have reported tangentially on the characteristics of core members, but their descriptions are anecdotal and confuse core membership with leadership. The present findings clearly indicate that a separation between these two concepts must be maintained in the mind of the researcher, if not of the gang member. Core membership is a status applied by our workers to fully one-half of the entire membership. Gang leaders are usually a few individuals singled out from among the core members.

Aside from these two recent writings, only one other paper, that by Gerrard, speaks directly to the core-fringe distinction.[37] Gerrard overlooks the fringe member, but characterizes the core member as "marked by a generalized feeling that others are hostile or indifferent to his welfare" and as having "marked inferiority feelings with regard to conventional activities outside the home." He identifies the cause of these two sets of feelings as the home and parental setting, but reports no data to support his positions. Thus, so far as can be determined, the present findings represent the first empirical description upon which more refined analyses of gang membership structure may be built.

Finally, we are now in a better position than before to deal with the cohesiveness of these groups. As practical examples, it seems reasonable to hypothesize that attempts at gang dissolution will be more effective among boys with low Group Involvement scores. A second hypothesis might be that attempts to provide adult role models as alternative opportunities for gang members are more likely to succeed with low Group-Involved, high Deficient-Aggressive boys. If the factor analysis is to receive further empirical validation, this may best be accomplished through the testing of such hypotheses in the action arena.

Gang Composition

Race: Mirroring the urban distribution of gangs is the racial and ethnic composition of most gangs. The gang is primarily a minority group phenomenon which reflects the population of the ghetto. While Yablonsky reported his "violent gangs" to be racially mixed, the majority of writers have described relatively "pure" groups—all-Negro, all-Mexican, or all-white along lines of national or religious origin.[38] By the same token, most (but by no means all) intergang fights are between groups of the same type. Gang conflict is typically among groups of like background. Our Los Angeles observations confirm these findings.

Age: Thrasher included in his descriptions groups of prepubertal boys as well as adult criminals. Whyte[39] and Kobrin[40] have also reported on young adult gangs. However, most gangs under study have consisted primarily of teenagers. Some of the age ranges reported have been 10 to 25,[41] 12 to 22,[42] 11 to 25,[43] and 12 to the early 20's in the Los Angeles Projects. However, this range within *one* gang structure is only applicable to the age-graded vertical gang cluster; smaller gangs typically encompass only a two-or-three-year age span. It seems fair to say, overall, that entry into gang life is a postpubertal act; withdrawal occurs as the member approaches the age of majority.

Sex: Of over 1000 groups included in Thrasher's monumental survey, only half a dozen were female groups. If this was a valid estimate for the 1920's, then a dramatic change has taken place. While it is still true that female gangs as independent, self-originating, and self-perpetuating units are highly unusual, female "auxiliaries" to boys' groups seem quite common in all major cities. One or two such groups were associated with each of the five male gang clusters under study in Los Angeles. Miller[44] cited two of seven groups in Boston as female. Geis[45] cites a New York City Youth Board estimate of three female members for every eight male gang members—an increase over the period of the Youth Board's existence.

Evidence from an independent study of ours in Los Angeles suggested that these girls' groups usually consist at first of the sisters and girl friends of male gang members, but that they soon take on a more diverse membership as the girls recruit new members among their own friends. The female gang is smaller (from 5 to 25 members), less seriously delinquent, and less stable than its male counterpart. It forms in response to the male structure and dissolves as the boys' group loses cohesion. While it is a common myth that girls are at the root of much (some say most) male gang fighting and delinquency, preliminary analyses of the Los Angeles data suggest that this is *not* the case. In fact, in many ways girls are the most effective instruments of positive intervention currently available. An unpublished report by Helen Shimota Gross of interviews with 207 boys detained in Juvenile Hall, 40 per cent of whom were gang affiliated, yields the following conclusions:

> If others, in addition to the reporter, were involved in the event, they are the reporter's peers. Nongang youth rarely (5.7%) report that gang members are involved in their incidents, but 53.2% of the gang members report nongang youth as co-participants ($p < .001$). Adults are rarely involved as co-participants, either in planning or the actual event. Girls are also infrequently involved; they participated directly or indirectly in the planning of 2% of the incidents and in only 10.8% of the actual events. When involved, the offense was most often one of assault ($p < .001$), and the girl's role was that of an observer, on the fringe of the event.

In only 5 incidents (1 theft, 1 runaway, 2 drug offenses, and
1 lynching) were girls viewed as primary participants; in 5 others
(2 assaults, 2 thefts, 1 rape) they were seen as having a secondary
role.

. . . The reporters were also asked for certain post hoc speculations
about alternative outcomes. What effect was predicted had girls
happened onto the scene? In only 4.7% of the incidents (primarily
auto thefts) would the girls have been included in the event.
Reporters in 26.2% of the incidents said that girls had or would
have had no real effect on the action itself. Another 44.6% would
have been postponed or prevented by the accidental presence of
girls. Their effect on the remaining 24.5% could not be predicted by
the reporter. Differences in the estimated effect of girls' presence is
significantly related to gang membership (p < .001), to the type
of offense (p < .001), and to the age of the reporter (p < .05).
More gang members report "no change," while nongang
members "don't know." Thefts of all sorts could be prevented or
postponed by the mere appearance of girls, but those reporting
runaways feel that either the outcome would be unchanged or
is indefinite. Age of the reporter has the same effect: either the
preadolescent would be undeterred by the girls, or he cannot
predict their potential effect. As the reporter's age increases, so
does the likelihood that girls would postpone or prevent the offense.

Detention for the offense, the penalty for getting caught, is rarely
seen as enhancing girls' opinion of the reporter (2.7%). Others,
41.8%, say no change in opinion will result, and 22.7% are unsure
of its effect. A decrease, however, in what girls think of them is
forecast by 32.8% of the reporters. Nongang members are more
likely to expect a damaged public image than are gang members
(p < .02). As the reporter's age increases, so also does the
likelihood of his viewing his detention as having no effect on
what girls think of him (p < .05).

But does it really matter what girls think of him? It does, at least
to a moderate extent, to 50.5% of the reporters. Caring about
girls' opinions is not related to gang membership or to the type
of offense. However, it is significantly related to the reporter's
age (p < .001); only 14.3% of the preadolescents, but 53% of the
15-year-olds, and 77% of the 17–18-year-olds are concerned with
what girls think of them.

Although the predicted change in opinion because of one's
detention is not related to the predicted change in behavior
resulting from girls' presence, if the reporter values girls' opinions
of him, he reports that their appearance would postpone or
prevent the delinquent behavior (p < .01). Apparently one can
take chances with being apprehended and detained without

worrying about one's image, but the behavior cannot be denied or disclaimed when girls actually witness it.

Certainly the opinions and reports obtained in these interviews cast serious doubt on the opinions of those who attribute to girls much of the responsibility for the delinquencies of boys. If girls are the instigators and encouragers of gang boys, either their effect is so subtle that the boys are unaware of it, or the boys are ashamed and unwilling to report their influence.

Perhaps Riccio and Slocum's comments in <u>All the Way Down</u>,[46] a story of gang life in the New York slums, are made more meaningful by this study: "Gang members all want a nice girl. There are two kinds, nice and bad .... Good girls in (the) neighborhood (are the) only ones that effect dramatic changes in gang membership ... Only rehabilitation I saw was the result of a good girl."

Size: As with most of the preceding structural dimensions, gang size is highly variable, both within and between gangs. Spontaneous gangs have been cited with memberships of 35,[47] 30,[48] 6 to 15[49] and 25[50] as averages. Vertical gang clusters are generally larger when the sub-groups are taken together, with maximums variously set at 92,[51] 100,[52] and 118 for the Latins in Los Angeles. Over a period of two or three years, as many as 200 boys and 50 girls may reasonably be said to have affiliated with such a group.

On the relatively rare occasions when several groups coalesce across neighborhoods, it may be fair to suggest a total membership of several hundred active members. Thrasher's figure of 2,000 members, or the figure in the thousands currently projected for the Blackstone Rangers and Disciples in Chicago, suggest that the interest in large numbers has been acquired at a sacrifice to any meaningful definition of the term *gang*.[53]

Type of Gangs

This final descriptive category can be highly confusing. It has been the understandable practice of writers in the gang arena to derive meaningful typologies of gangs. Among these have been the following:

a. Social, delinquent, and violent[54]
b. Diffuse, solidified, conventionalized, criminal, and 'secret society'[55]
c. Criminal, conflict, and retreatist[56]

d. Theft, conflict, and addict[57]

e. Nonproblem, problem, and conflict[58]

f. Area and spontaneous[59]

g. Vertical, horizontal, self-contained, and disintegrative[60]

As can be seen, there is much in common among these typologies, but also there are many differences as the various writers have employed different dimensions in their typologies; for instance, group structure (f. and g.), type of behavior (a., c., d., and e.), or a combination (b.). Numerous empirical attempts to verify the existence of gangs with separate delinquent orientations have proven fruitless for the most part,[61] revealing that gang members engage in a wide variety of offenses in cafeteria style. A factor analysis of all offenses recorded against members of the four gang clusters in the Group Guidance Project revealed a totally chance distribution of correlations between offense categories. By and large, gang boys are patternless offenders.

Because the so-called *conflict* gangs have been the usual targets of intervention programs, even these have been dissected into different types. Spergel[62] has found conflict gangs to manifest the structural differentiation between vertical, horizontal, and small, independent forms. The New York City Youth Board[63] has described conflict gangs as active aggressive, passive aggressive, and defensive gangs. Gannon,[64] describing these same New York groups, has divided them simply into fighting and defensive gangs. What is not clear is whether these typological differences actually mirror qualitative differences between the gangs themselves or merely nominal distinctions for the convenience of the typologists. The paucity of data available on gang structure and behavior makes such clarification difficult, but the best guess would be that structural differences between gangs may be greater than differences in delinquency patterns.

Summary

The foregoing materials make it abundantly clear that *the* gang does not exist; rather, gangs come in a wide variety of forms. While there is said to be a relationship between gang form and the level and type of gang delinquency, this relationship is somewhat ephemeral. Delinquency and violence, in one form or another, can be expected from any gang, but because some gangs are more permanent than others, it may be crucial to concentrate efforts on those gangs with established traditions—in which delinquency is a matter not of weeks or months, but of decades. The vertical or traditional gang, being a cluster of subgroups that perpetuates itself for many years, is the most important target for intervention. Fortunately, its general structure is now sufficiently described that intervention efforts can perhaps be more rationally designed than they have previously been.

Gang Members

The accepted publication mores within social science seldom provide the opportunity for investigators to loosen the bonds of scientific rigor sufficiently to say "This is what I *think* I saw, even though I can't document it with hard data." We already know from the foregoing materials that gangs appear primarily in lower-class neighborhoods, so there is no point in repeating here the various financial, familial, educational, and "cultural" disadvantages which surround them. Good materials on values and perceptions of gang members have been reported by Short and others.[65] Research into psychological differences between delinquents and nondelinquents has yet to prove particularly enlightening. Therefore, after one cautionary note, I will concentrate on impressions of gang members, rather than on hard empirical data.

The cautionary note is simply this: gang members come in all shapes. They are short and tall, bright and dull, aggressive and passive, easy to know and practically unreachable. They manifest, in short, the very same range of biological, psychological, and sociological characteristics as any large collection of self-selected youngsters in our society, except perhaps as noted below. This is not to say that the "average" gang member is just like the "average" teenager. Obviously, this is not true. But the *variety* of boys one finds in the gang is considerable—so considerable that to attempt finite descriptions is to defeat the point. With this point firmly in mind, then, we can attempt some shaky generalizations.

Adolescence

If there is one overall impression of the gang boys that most strikes one at first acquaintance and remains uppermost in the mind, it is a *caricature of adolescence*. All those behavioral manifestations which allow one to say of a person's behavior that it is adolescent can be seen in the gang members—usually in excess. It is adolescence overplayed. The pattern shows first, perhaps, in their approach to humor, especially in a group setting.

The boy who tells a joke or makes a clever crack looks for the response even more quickly than the response can be given. He seeks out the reaction—how many are laughing, and how loud; how are the adults reacting; how can he build on the first crack to maintain the reaction? Humor is used less for its value *per se* than for the approbation and momentary status it might bring to its user. Humor is attention-getting and is used consciously for that purpose. The behavioral clue here is neither the joke nor the reaction to it, but the search for the reaction.

In the same way, the boys do a great deal of boasting about their individual exploits. But more often than not the exploits are imaginary; simple events are elaborated to sound dangerous and exciting. Continual observation suggests, as one would expect, that boasting serves the purpose of ego-building where few objective qualities or accomplishments are available for the task. More than their nongang age peers, these boys feel little confidence in themselves. They tend to be insecure both with respect to their own abilities and with respect to social relationships.[66] The pattern is illustrated in these descriptions given by the workers:

> Eddie, in spite of his boasting, appears to be one of the main catalytic agents in the Victors-Vampires conflict and is actively seeking a following to enhance his own need for security and acceptance.

> He is a nice looking boy, but he has the problem of not believing in people.

> Those who have not broken away hang around in the park with Junior Operators. They are not strong leaders. They are guys who have not grown up, and who cannot cope with problems of everyday life. They seem to be in limbo.

> This is one guy that I know I'll spend more time with, jacking him up and building confidence within him. He's somewhat introverted. I think . . . he . . . would drop pills or sit in a corner and shoot junk.

> The day of the trip they all found excuses not to go. Later they admitted that they were scared to go out of their environment. They might have confidence in me, but not in themselves.

How can this be? How is it that the associating together of such youngsters can lead so directly to involvement in delinquency? This is a question the worker *must* deal with if he is to intervene positively. He must understand the dynamics by which association leads to guilt: guilt *through* association rather than *by* it.

At first, it might appear (as some people believe) that gang boys come together to commit delinquent acts, much in the fashion of the Capone mob or the Cosa Nostra. But this is a naïve view of adolescent relations. Juvenile gang members tend to float toward each other as they reject and are rejected by the other opportunities in a lower-class community.

> They find strength in numbers. There are, for example, very few of these kids in organized sports. To play by the rules, to take the frustration of not winning is too much for many of them. In my opinion, they are deficient in all aspects of what we value, but I don't think their relationships among themselves are deficient. I mean, I think . . . that they are wholesome.

Perhaps, as Caplan[67] has suggested with regard to Chicago's inner-city youth, gang development is in part the result of many "floaters" coming together in their search for noninstitutionalized activity that will fill the empty hours.

> This youth can often be seen . . . wandering up and down the streets. He appears to be the kind of person that is psychologically dependent on the Victors, and does not admit that there has been any diminishing of the Victors' cohesiveness.

From this point of view, the gang is seen as an aggregate of individuals held together more by their own shared incapacities than by mutual goals. Primarily, group identification is important as it serves individual needs; it leads to delinquent group activity only secondarily and only in the absence of prosocial alternatives:

> Now, all winter long, you take a guy like Perry. He's just done nothing because there was nothing for him to do. But now he carries the wine; he comes to the park with the wine . . . and so he gets five of these guys coming behind him with the wine and so (they) go out and hustle some dimes, get some wine. . . . So he becomes a big deal, which is everybody laying around in the park and drinking wine.

Thus a gang boy is, first and foremost, an adolescent with all of the problems and advantages accruing to that age group in our society. But he tends to be a *caricature* of the adolescent—more shy, more dependent on his peers, more ambivalent about appropriate role behaviors—exhibiting the features of a well-cataloged age group, and yet showing significant departures from the norm.

A boy named Manny is a good example, though a tragic one. The son of a convict, he was a boy at loose ends described by a staff member as a "happy follower." He returned from a juvenile institution with little notion of what he wanted to do, and immediately melted back into the group. We observed him on the street 45 times in the month following his return, and he was alone in only three of those situations. The group was his life and, as it happened, his death.

Manny

9/08:   Returned from probation camp. Seen immediately in the company of various core members.

9/22:   Enrolled in high school with staff help.

9/23:   With three others, attacked member of a rival gang.

10/04: Recommended to Boys' Club as youth aid under Neighborhood Youth Corps program.

10/10: Though considered a bad risk, Manny was accepted for the job at the Boys' Club.

10/13: Job held up because of N.Y.C. regulations.

10/15: During raid by rival gang, Manny ran up the back stairs of a house only to find the door locked. Trapped there, and with his pals scattering in all directions, he was shot and killed.

Manny was not the particular target of this raid. But his heavy dependence on the group, and staff inabilities to come up with alternate activities soon enough, placed him at that place at that time. His death, in this sense, was purely accidental—an accident brought about by the personal inadequacies which led him to be with the group whenever he could, including the time of the attack.

Individual Deficiencies

There is no need to dwell on the family background of gang members. Although there is much variance, the situation of the average member is not good; poverty, broken homes, inadequate educational and vocational role models, family members with criminal histories, and similar features are common enough in the world of the gang member to ring a familiar bell.

On the other hand *physical* handicaps are exceptional. The gang is not a very tolerant group. Exclusion of the malformed is common.

The presence of an identity that is reasonably whole, or more than viable elsewhere.

Those who *are* accepted must overcome the stigma of physical defects. For example, two boys in our Los Angeles gangs with severe skin problems were known as "Cornflakes" and "Potato Face"; a boy with glasses was called "Goggles"; and a Mexican boy given a mascot role in a Negro gang was called "Taco." The desire for membership must be strong to overcome these verbal insults.

But if these youngsters are not physically handicapped, are they intellectually deficient? Restricting ourselves to performance on intelligence tests, the data are discouraging. Out of 243 available records containing test scores, 8 per cent show scores below 70, and only 8 per cent show scores of 100 or better. The median score is 84. Fully one third of the boys have scores that would dictate their placement in special education classes according to the overall guidelines employed by the Los Angeles city schools.

Does this mean that the boys are stupid? No, it clearly does not. What it does mean is that they are not well prepared to take advantage of the educational system as it exists, or to prepare themselves for remunerative employment beyond school. It means, in the words of a physician familiar with the situation, that "in the absence of adequate *capability*, they develop *cope*-ability." They become "street wise," learn to handle many problems with a style of their own. They also learn to avoid those which present difficulty or a threat to the self-image.

Perhaps the only major exception to this pattern is the handling of impulse control. *Lack* of impulse control is certainly a most common characteristic of many of these boys and, of course, those who habitually act on impulse stand out to the observer. The lack of restraint in the expression of hostility, greed, and status needs—restraint ordinarily present in the form of guilt, or anticipation of negative consequences—makes one wary of pushing these boys too far. Although violence is not their way of life it is a predominant "myth system" among them, and the line between myth and reality is often thin indeed. Aggression, verbal or physical, is a coping mechanism that receives constant reinforcement within the gang. It is this reinforcement in the presence of low impulse control that often stands as the public hallmark of gang behavior:

> . . . a guy like Frisco, that likes to get high and raise a lot of hell and fight and argue . . . .
>
> Carlos does not seem too rational. He likes to agitate and fight . . . the others use him to start fights. He reported later that they became abusive and tried to fight him. Corky broke a bottle and tried to attack him with it. Both boys have been in Juvenile Hall repeatedly, but were released. Both are considered gang psychopaths, and are only 14 years old.

But we may become lost in a morass of speculation if we attempt to explain these behavior patterns in terms of "types"of boys; there are as many types as there are boys. To understand better the situation of the worker it is perhaps more valuable to think in terms of types of *behavior*, any one of which may be exhibited by any number of gang members. In fact the seeming behavioral inconsistency *within each boy*, and the fact that he seems to exhibit the full range of behaviors in cafeteria style prevent the worker from developing consistent intervention approaches for individuals: he must have a repertoire fully as broad as that of the boys.

One of these patterns, if it can be called that, is the potential for truly dangerous behavior to which the worker must *always* be alert. The danger is well described by the workers:

> JoJo was observed walking . . . with a .22 caliber rifle in his hands, chamber loaded and cocked, and bullet between his teeth. He was looking for Robert Simmons in order to kill him because, according to JoJo, Robert had beaten him unfairly in a fight. This boy seems to be in need of psychiatric help. These are the comments made by his peers, who are uneasy in his presence. He does not seem to have a conscience.

> Big Mambo is somewhat unbalanced. He can be dangerous since he is large.

> Randy's status about his part as originator of these chains of violence was not said with too much modesty . . . . One of his problems is apparently an attempt to find a suitable platform in which to give vent to his aggressiveness. . . . Randy can be extremely dangerous when provoked. He's positive in meetings, but he's a gang psychopath.

Attempts to intervene in the lives of such youngsters are highly frustrating. In the following case one can sense the dedication of the workers in their dogged pursuit of rehabilitative resources, and, in the final analysis, the waste of professional time with a boy who invariably retreats or acts out in the face of progress.

Richard

One of five siblings, Richard lived alternately with his grandmother and with his mother and stepfather. His father's family lived in New Mexico, and Richard went there occasionally. His mother was said to be a prostitute; his stepfather was of a different racial stock. Family dissension ruled the home, and no one was willing to put up with Richard for very long.

Richard was a core member of the gang but not ordinarily an initiator of activities. He used money and marijuana to "buy in" to the group, being personally insecure and visibly torn by a negative and destructive self-image. He admitted that fighting was the one activity that made him feel good. Prior to the project he was lucky in having been arrested only three times on minor charges. He was expelled from tenth grade for drug use.

1st month: (a) Working in hardware store out of the area.
            (b) Plans to join Marines after release from probation.
            (c) Going steady with Ginger.

2nd month: (a) Lost job because of transportation problems.
            (b) Given N.Y.C. job by staff. Job #2.
            (c) Pressured by Ginger to return to school.
            (d) Finds a second girl friend, Anna, in rival gang area.
            (e) Fight at work over racial epithets.
            (f) In possession of a gun; alternately carries it or loans it out.
            (g) Escape from police, avoiding arrest for possession of marijuana with three companions.
            (h) Staff confirms Richard is pushing marijuana.

3rd month: (a) Registered for school by staff.
            (b) Dropped course after attending drunk.
            (c) Quit N.Y.C. job.
            (d) Has finished off his marijuana supply.
            (e) Arrested for attempt to rifle public phone.
            (f) Drops Ginger in favor of Anna.
            (g) Job at Boys' Club arranged by staff. Job #3.
            (h) Job offer rescinded when Richard announces plans to enter Marines soon.
            (i) Fight with gang friend over use of car.

4th month: (a) With two companions, attacked by rival gang.
            (b) Flunked Marine exam, but will be given second chance.
            (c) Failed to appear for second Marine exam.
            (d) Arrested for interfering with police in aftermath of intragang fight.
            (e) Secured job in plant opened to members by staff: Job #4.

              (f) Arrested for possession of marijuana.

              (g) Received Job Corps notice.

              (h) Departed for Job Corps through staff help.

6th month: (a) Letters from Job Corps report depression, fighting, and town jail.

              (b) Quit Job Corps.

              (c) Hit on head by tire iron in attack by rival gang results in chronic dizziness.

              (d) Started job, via stepfather, out of the area at $1.87. Job #5.

              (e) Reported by other boys to be experimenting with heroin.

7th month: Arrested for joy-riding.

8th month: (a) Admits recent gas station robbery to staff; gave money to newsboy who had no shoes.

              (b) Admits heroin use to staff.

              (c) Taken by staff to narcotics rehabilitation center.

              (d) Refused to return to rehabilitation center.

9th month: (a) Laid off work through stepfather's influence.

              (b) Given job in clothing plant by staff. Job #6.

              (c) Laid off by foreman.

              (d) Family strife reported increasing.

              (e) Got away with pursesnatch and housebreak.

10th month: Rehired at clothing plant. Job #7.

11th month: (a) Quit job.

              (b) Reported involved in raid on rival gang area.

              (c) Complaints of severe headaches.

12th month: (a) Attacked at party.

              (b) Unable to make psychiatric appointment arranged by staff.

              (c) Arrested for possession of marijuana.

              (d) Family evicted from home.

              (e) While blind drunk, beat up unknown boy, attacked fellow member, and collapsed.

              (f) Having impregnated Stella (another girl from rival area), announces marriage plans.

              (g) Given Job #8 by staff.

13th month: (a) Failed to appear for job.

              (b) Runaway, with Stella. Sleeping in garage.

              (c) Beaten up by rivals at hot dog stand.

              (d) Detained for failure to appear in court.

14th month:	In solitary confinement twice for fighting with fellow prisoners.

15th month:	(a) Given suspended sentence and probation.
	(b) Beat up Stella, who has had miscarriage.
	(c) In fight with fellow member.

16th month:	(a) Given job training spot by staff. Job #9.
	(b) Fired for absenteeism.
	(c) Arrested for riot and disturbing the peace. Five days in jail.

17th month:	(a) Family moves again.
	(b) Admits more heroin use to staff.
	(c) Taken to psychiatric ward of County Hospital by staff; refuses self-commitment to Narcotics Center.
	(d) Receives knife wound in fight.
	(e) Refuses visit to Narcotics Center.

18th month:	(a) Wrecked car.
	(b) Beaten up in fight with fellow member.
	(c) Given Job #10 at $2.00 an hour by staff.
	(d) Dislocated wrist in job accident.
	(e) Kicked out of the house by grandmother.
	(f) On anniversary of Manny's killing, went with companion to rival area and stabbed a 14-year-old boy (in critical condition), and shot two other people, one of whom died. Arrested, expected to be put away for a long time. Age, 18.

A more self-destructive pattern would be hard to find. Here is a boy—an extreme example, but an example nevertheless—whose every behavior was a call for help, and yet sufficient help was not forthcoming. So often it is true that the helpers are helpless for lack of resources, lack of knowledge, lack of ability to crack the bureaucratic structures of the welfare and criminal justice systems.

So far, we have described the negative patterns; but there are others, equally important, which allow a worker to maintain a modicum of optimism. The first of these—the "righteous defender" pattern—is in fact one in which the workers almost take pride, for it combines manliness with coolness: two highly valued characteristics of the ghetto boy. Every gang we have seen reacted to the accusation of being a fighting gang with the same phrase, "No, man, we a defensive club." This was the group version of the individual pattern:

For some reason, he is the epitome of the gang aggressor, don't take no stuff type . . . .

These were the cool heads—they would fight. But according to them they didn't look for trouble, but they took care of trouble.

Benny expresses some fear for his personal safety by saying, "I think I ought to move from this area. But if anybody comes up on the porch, I'm ready for them."

And finally, the pattern to which everything points—the "reformation." When a worker speaks of his success, almost invariably he turns to the description of individuals who have "seen the light"; the more individuals and the brighter the light, the greater the success. In essence, then, the workers—and gang programs generally—rely on testimonials as evidence of success. The difficulty in assessing this pattern lies in several directions. First, does the *statement* of progress equal progress itself? Second, what level of progress and over what period of time can be taken as success? Third, how do we separate those elements of progress or reformation attributable to the worker's intervention from those which would have occurred anyway? And finally, how many cases of reform constitute overall success? There is, of course, the understandable tendency to remember the successes but not the failures. One success experience can wipe out a score of failures in the mind, if not in the street. When a worker really "glows," it is while reporting individual cases like these:

He finally found out that all he was doing was drinking wine out at the park, so . . . when a kid arrives at this point, I think it's pretty good.

He has insight into his problems, and likes to counsel at length. "I know I'm bad. I want to change . . . but I've been bad for so long that changing is hard. I wish I didn't have a reputation, then I wouldn't have to worry."

Reno is beginning to show real positive attitudes toward himself, the club, and myself . . . at one point he confided in me that he had had a fight . . . and had not appreciated the blows he had received . . . . He is beginning to articulate a little bit more about himself and race problems.

He told me that . . . he was tired of foolish gang life, and was expecting to do the right thing.

I know people who knew him in forestry camp, and other people, and they say they just can't get over the change that's come over him. It's wonderful, his ability to behave.

The foregoing represents a sampling of salient observations of juvenile gang members in the 1960's. The general tenor of our observations is in many ways similar to that of other recent writers,[68] but considerably different from that of investigators writing in an earlier period.[69] It has become standard in the gang literature of the 1960's to note that the historical differences have to do with gang structure, offense behavior, and the "style" of a gang member's life.

Formerly, gang structure was conceived of as tight and cohesive, with well defined leadership and other role structures. Current analyses emphasize low cohesiveness and shifting role structures. Earlier studies found strong relationships, sometimes of a master-apprentice nature, between adult criminal systems and gang members; but the gang of the 1960's seems to be more divorced from the adult criminal system. Finally, the gangs of earlier years (best exemplified by Thrasher's descriptions) were described as happy-go-lucky collections of healthy youngsters who enjoyed their experiences together as adventurers in the great game of cops and robbers. Today gang members are seen as "driven" toward the group: dissatisfied, deprived, and making the best of an essentially unhappy situation.

Whether the gangs have changed or the researchers have changed is difficult to assess. Today's data are more reliable because of improved methods; but this does not necessarily invalidate past findings.

Our own observations place us in agreement with current research. Our gang member is thrown into his group. He is frustrated, insecure, and trapped in his environment. He is not having much fun, although he makes much of the enjoyments he finds. He is a rationalizer and a self-deceiver in his attempt to get through his adolescence with as few psychological scars as possible. He is not the man he would like to be, and his search for peer status is seldom adequately rewarded. Sad to say, society's most effective mechanism for transforming him—sheer maturity—is not under its control. Getting older is still the gang member's best hope and will be until social theorists and practitioners are able to translate their observations into theory, and their theory into action *more* powerful than the natural variables of urban society.

Leadership

With the major exception of Yablonsky, most researchers have described gang leaders as relatively stable, "cool" youngsters who have earned their group status through a variety of abilities—fighting prowess, cool-headedness, verbal facility, athletic abilities, or inheritance from older brothers.[70] Additionally, some have emphasized that gang leadership does not reside wholly within one or two individuals but is in fact shared by many depending upon the group's activities and the context of the moment.[71] Leadership, in this view, is a group function: the arrest and incarceration of known gang leaders does not often lead to gang disintegration because the leadership functions are then assumed by other members. Leadership is not the primary clue either to gang organization or to gang dissolution.

My own impressions of gang leadership derive from two sources: direct observation (over 400 gang meetings, outings, tutoring sessions, sports activities, and so forth), and reports from staff members and detached workers assigned to the groups. It may be that my conclusions are in part erroneous; but the notoriety and special attention given to gang leadership, both in the professional literature and in the public media, make it important that we attempt a description of what has been observed. In addition, the importance of dealing with gang leaders is given heavy weight by detached workers. To understand their program, one must listen to the way they see and deal with gang leaders.

1. Leadership in these gangs is not a *position*, a structured set of rights and duties to which a few individuals are assigned. In the gang setting, leadership is best defined as a collection of *functions* that may be undertaken at various times by a number of members. Miller goes so far, in analyzing the Senior Bandits, as to identify "six standby leaders—boys prepared to step into leadership positions when key leaders were institutionalized."[72]

Leadership also varies with particular activities. The "big man" in fighting may be a failure as an athlete or a ladies' man. One cannot come to grips with a gang by dealing with *the* leader but only by dealing with *leadership* as a distributed and often shifting phenomenon. Leadership cannot be considered merely as a personal quality of an individual because it is also a product of group interaction and a response to the context in which the group finds itself. Traditional gangs often have been denuded of their acknowledged leaders, and yet they have continued to survive and thrive. A leadership vacuum does not exist for long.

2. In contrast to Yablonsky's stance,[73] I maintain that most gang leaders are *not* sociopaths or psychopaths. The respected member with lasting ability to influence others is often indistinguishable at first glance, whereas the psychopathic gang member is visible immediately.

"He wants what he wants when he wants it," to use one worker's phrase. There are some very sick boys in every large gang. If they are fighters, their exploits are part of the gang's mythology; these boys live in a world of partial fantasy. But seldom can they exert genuine influence—their reputation does not spill over into leadership.* Below is a brief summary of intervention steps with one such boy in the Ladino Hills Project, a boy of considerable notoriety but little group influence.

Curley

The detached worker has known Curley for over four years, and described him as a gang psychopath and a respected member of the "Veteranos." His father is dead, and for ten years his mother has had a common-law husband. There is constant verbal and physical fighting between all family members, and financial resources are inadequate. Curley has a serious hearing loss in both ears and very poor eyesight. As a juvenile, he was known to be a frequent user of drugs and alcohol and had seven arrests. He has been involved in gang fighting, both as assailant and as victim, and was expelled from school in ninth grade. At the beginning of the project he was legitimately considered an almost impossible case.

1st month:	Given job with recreation department at $1.26 an hour.
4th month:	Called police to report a gang fight in which his friends were being attacked.
5th month:	(a) Laid off from his job.
	(b) Failed to meet court date.
	(c) Recruited younger members into "Veteranos."
6th month:	Taken by staff to State Service Center for processing. Assigned to stockman's job at $1.35 an hour.
8th month:	(a) Quit job because of low pay.
	(b) Began heroin use.
9th month:	(a) Offered second job by staff, but turned it down because it was too far from the neighborhood.

---

*Our favorite example occurred during a "hassle" between the Red Raiders and the Victors. In a Red Raider meeting attended by about 80 members, one of these older psychopaths strongly condemned the notion of a truce meeting, and insisted that the gang's reputation was at stake. When he saw that the membership was opposed to his approach, he stalked out of the room declaring, "Ya win the last fight, then ya conversate!" Not a single boy followed him.

(b) Stabbed in hand by agitated female member while seeking out members of rival gang.

10th month: (a) Offered third job by staff at $1.50 an hour. He accepted.
(b) Foreman gives excellent work report on Curley.

12th month: (a) Received raise to $1.75 an hour.
(b) Staff arranged medical appointments for hearing aid and speech class.
(c) Follow-up appointment kept!

16th month: (a) Returned to using heroin.
(b) Foreman threatened firing for absenteeism.
(c) Ear impression taken for hearing aid through State Service Center.

17th month: (a) Hearing aid obtained, and Curley extremely pleased with the results. Off heroin, and settling into good work habits again.
(b) Assigned as acting foreman during boss' vacation.
(c) Job attendance slipping again; reported back on heroin.

18th month: (a) More absentee reports; continued using heroin.

The up-and-down story of Curley illustrates several points for us. Acknowledged by the boys as a high status member he is nevertheless an addict, physically handicapped, and unstable.

What does a gang leader look like? There is no general pattern. He may be large or small, loud or quiet, strong or weak, attractive or homely. In describing one leader the worker said, "He's illiterate, and doesn't play the tough guy." Another is described as "very quiet and level-headed."

We have found that the only way to distinguish leadership is to observe the actions of the other boys. By their behavior, they provide the clues as to who will be followed and who won't and in what context.

I noticed that where Booker sat, the rest of the boys would sit; where Booker went, the rest of the boys would go.

A good leader has to make the group look like victims when trouble develops. If they get busted because of him he can't keep his leadership.

One particularly interesting pattern revolves around verbal abilities. "This is an exceptionally valued ability among Negro teen-agers, especially gang kids. It doesn't matter too much if what he says is correct or incorrect, but mainly *how* he says it." In this case, then, style rather than substance is paramount.

I have witnessed a beautiful example of this pattern. In a meeting of the Red Raiders, their president gave a partly incoherent but truly moving and impassioned speech about getting a job, finishing school ("You gotta go back and get your smarts, man."), and generally following what he called the "righteous way." No more convincing or effective statement could ever be made by an adult than was put forth by this very sincere young man. At the end of his oration, a thoughtful silence fell over the room until a voice from the rear queried, "Yeah, man, that's all right. But what if them Victors come over into our set [territory, neighborhood, turf] again?"

The response from the orator was immediate and perfect: "If they come down on us, we gonna go through them like a hot knife through butter!" The room was filled with joyous approval—handclapping, floor thumping, and shouts of glee. The orator had played the roles perfectly; first positive leadership, then fighting leadership, and both expressed with style and vigor. Leadership is not just a personal quality; it is also a response to group needs.

3. Leadership is age-related. Although it is true that younger members often idolize the older "veterans" and bask in the reflected glory of past exploits, it is also true that each age level and each clique has defined leadership within it.

> Nobody speaks for an area. I don't gave a damn who he is. Nobody. Or for a gang.

This fact is acknowledged by the boys themselves. One worker quotes an older leader's comments about members of the younger group in the cluster:

> Well, we can tell them, you know, to hold it down to a trot. But the little rooty-poots have got to get experiences; they got to get knocked on their asses so they can understand what we're talking about. We can only tell them, and after that if they don't want to believe what we're saying, it's up to them. I'm not their father.

So although the older gang member may have a great "rep" (high status) in the eyes of the younger boys, he does not automatically have the ability or the desire to wield influence. The younger member or the clique member has his own leadership closer at hand; he has a dual allegiance to the subgroup and to the cluster. What we are saying, then, is that leadership is related directly to the overall structure of the gang cluster; or, on a more abstract level, structure and function are part and parcel of the same phenomenon—a lesson too often overlooked by social scientist and practitioner alike.

4. An interesting corollary to the foregoing comments is the existence of what might be called "hesitant leadership." When we first noticed this phenomenon, we thought it was peculiar to the gang context, but continued exposure to the Negro and Mexican-American ghettoes has suggested that its roots and existence stem more generally from the culture of poverty as it exists in the disorganized minority ghetto.

Briefly stated, "hesitant leadership" refers to reluctance to assume an identifiable leadership *position.* Sometimes this takes the form of active *denial* of leadership: "We got no leaders, man. Everybody's a leader, and nobody can talk for nobody else."

But, in addition, often there is a strong flavor of ambivalence about the pattern. Many youngsters have started to assert leadership only to pull back at crucial moments. This can be seen in intergang truce meetings during which selected "leaders" verbalize group feeling and assume a spokesman's role, only to pull back when challenged or requested to take some action on behalf of the group: "Y'understand, I can't talk for them other dudes. I'm saying it for me."

This is an extremely frustrating pattern with which the gang worker has to deal. He cannot physically influence 100 boys at a time and is therefore forced to select a few pivotal members through whom to attempt his interventions. But when the time of crisis comes these selected "leaders" may either deny their own influence, or refuse to stick their necks out for fear of interfering with other and equally ambivalent leaders. None is sure of his following, and each has seen rival leaders "cut down to size" by other peers. Leadership, then, as a *position,* is aspired to but withdrawn from for fear of losing status; and status is extremely important and must be preserved at all costs.*

Given these few descriptive notions of gang leadership, what route does the gang worker follow? As might be expected, he treads his way very cautiously, trying out different approaches, alternately depending upon and circumventing the ephemeral leadership structure of his gang. He too becomes ambivalent about leadership and its uses, as can be

*One acknowledged leader of the Senior Operators wrote it this way: "There are no leaders . . . and this is caused by the different groups or cliques inside the subgroups. Those that are popular inside these cliques are usually the leaders, except for the Seniors. If you ask a member of the Seniors why they don't have a leader, he would probably say, 'I don't believe in no one giving me orders.' Or if there is a leader, 'Why shouldn't it be me?' "

seen in the different philosophies underlying the following three state-ments:

> There haven't been any more incidents at the theater since they hired two leaders as ushers.
>
> Albert Houston, the president of the El Hunters, is home from camp and could solidify the group. However, (I've) encouraged Albert to remain close to home for a while.
>
> I feel I made a mistake in relegating coaching responsibilities to Frisco, one of the older Operators. He was too excitable, transmitting this to the Baby Operators. He used poor judgment throughout the game. He swore at the Baby Operators and exhorted them to play a rougher type of game.

The result, during many projects, is an inconsistent approch to the use of gang leadership; inconsistent both within a cluster and between workers. Until a conceptual scheme exists[74] to which workers can turn for guidance, loosely supervised gang programs will always be featured by a "seat-of-the-pants" approach to leadership utilization, much to the detriment of the programs and youths.

As an example, rather than as a solution to the problem of utilizing gang leadership, consider one facet of the Ladino Hills Project. We were faced—as all practitioners with heavy caseloads are faced—with the problem of maximizing the benefits of a few interventions among over 100 boys. A scheme was developed for identifying four categories of "primary targets" among the boys. One of these categories we termed "clique leaders," although in fact a more accurate term would have been "central clique members," avoiding the issue of leadership. The clique leaders were identified by weekly analyses of the companionship data collected by our cruising field observer, who noted down each day which boys he observed in the company of which other boys. Figure 3-3 reports the composite clique structures which emerged from the companionship data collected during the first seven weeks of the project.

Figure 3-3 is similar to a sociogram, but based on *behavioral* data. It omits many boys who were not observed sufficiently often to be assigned clearly to one of the three clique structures. Boys #1, #2, and particularly #9 emerge as prime intervention targets, with the assumption that success among them will have the greatest likelihood of spreading to others. It is important to note here that the Latins' detached worker cited #10, #12, #13, and #6 as also being gang leaders. One advantage of the clique structure analysis is that it allows one to focus one's attention a bit, and on the basis of observed behavioral patterns rather than possibly idiosyncratic intuitions and observations.

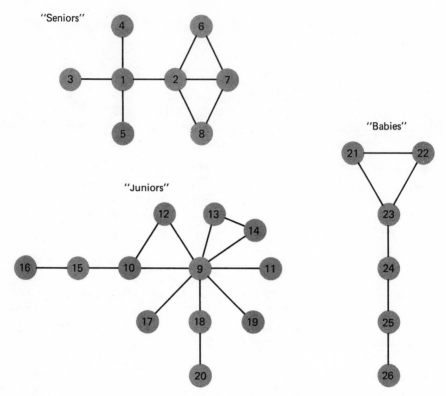

Fig. 3-3: Clique structures of the Latins,
May-June, 1966.

The concentration on the three clique leaders, with other interventions of a secondary nature, was in our opinion quite instrumental in bringing about significant changes in the clique structures of the "Seniors" and the "Juniors" over a six-month period. Figures 3-4 and 3-5 present the "before" and "after" pictures.

Obviously, a rather substantial shakeup of these two major cliques took place. To what extent staff interventions were responsible is of course a matter of conjecture, although the *processes* of change carefully documented in the project "log" suggest a strong partial relationship between intervention and clique changes.

One further point is of interest. The original "Juniors" clique seemed to us at the time a rather inexplicable amalgam of friendship patterns. The two factions evident in the "after" illustration were clearly connected on different bases: the three-man faction served as the hard core of the most delinquently oriented boys, while the five-man faction was based on residence, all five living close to each other at the time. This suggests that the original clique was in a sense "unnatural" and, as

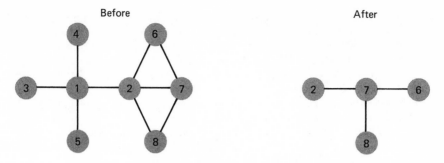

Fig. 3-4: Six-month clique modifications—"Seniors."

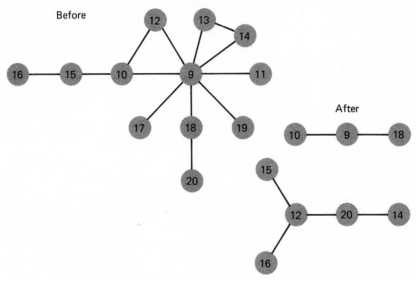

Fig. 3-5: Six-month clique modifications—"Juniors."

we shall suggest later, typical of the gang situation in which alternative activities are either unavailable or unattractive. One might well conjecture, then, that leadership in these "unnatural," forced cliques is equally "unnatural" and subject to positive change by carefully diagnosed intervention strategies.

References

1. Andrew Greeley and James Carey, "An Upper Middle Class Deviant Gang," *The American Catholic Sociological Review* 24, no. 1 (1963): 33–41; Larry Karacki and Jackson Toby, "The Uncommitted Adolescent:

Candidate for Gang Socialization," *Sociological Inquiry* 32, no. 2 (Spring, 1962): 203–15; Howard L. and Barbara G. Myerhoff, "Field Observations of Middle Class Gangs," *Social Forces* 42, no. 3 (March, 1964): 328–36.

2. Frederic Thrasher, *The Gang: A Study of 1,313 Gangs in Chicago,* abridged and with a new Introduction by James F. Short, Jr. (Chicago: University of Chicago Press, 1963), p. 20.

3. Saul Bernstein, *Youth on the Streets: Work with Alienated Youth Groups* (New York, Association Press, 1964).

4. Desmond S. Cartwright and Kenneth I. Howard, "Multivariate Analysis of Gang Delinquency: I. Ecologic Influences," *Multivariate Behavioral Research* 1 (July, 1966): 321–71.

5. Gerald D. Suttles, *The Social Order of the Slum: Ethnicity and Territory in the Inner City* (Chicago: University of Chicago Press, 1968).

6. Walter B. Miller, "White Gangs," *Trans-action* 6, no. 10 (September, 1969): 11–26.

7. Irving Spergel, *Racketville, Slumtown, Haulburg: An Exploratory Study of Delinquent Subcultures* (Chicago: University of Chicago Press, 1964).

8. Bernstein, *op. cit.*

9. *Reaching the Fighting Gang* (New York: New York City Youth Board, 1960).

10. Bernstein, *op. cit.*

11. Dale G. Hardman, "Historical Perspectives of Gang Research," *Journal of Research in Crime and Delinquency* 4, no. 1 (January, 1967): 5–27.

12. Walter B. Miller, *op. cit.* and "The Impact of a 'Total-Community' Delinquency Control Project," *Social Problems* 10, no. 2 (Fall, 1962): 168–91.

13. Thrasher, *op. cit.*

14. David Kantor and William Ira Bennett, "Orientation of Street-Corner Workers and Their Effect on Gangs," in Stanton Wheeler (ed.), *Controlling Delinquents* (New York: John Wiley & Sons, 1968), pp. 271–86.

15. *Dealing with the Conflict Gang in New York*, Interim Report no. 14 of the Juvenile Delinquency Evaluation Project of the City of New York, May, 1960 (Mimeo).

16. Bernstein, *op. cit.*

17. *Reaching the Fighting Gang, op. cit.*

18. Irving Spergel, *Street Gang Work: Theory and Practice* (Reading, Mass.: Addison-Wesley Publishing Co., 1966).

19. Albert K. Cohen, and James F. Short, Jr., "Research in Delinquent Subcultures," *Journal of Social Issues* 14 (Summer, 1958): 20–37.

20. James F. Short, Jr. and Fred L. Strodtbeck, *Group Process and Gang Delinquency* (Chicago: University of Chicago Press, 1965).

21. Miller, *op. cit.;* Thrasher, *op. cit.*

22. Lewis Yablonsky, *The Violent Gang* (New York: The Macmillan Co., 1963).

23. Miller, "White Gangs," *op. cit.*

24. Short and Strodtbeck, *op. cit.*

25. Hans W. Mattick, and Nathan S. Caplan, *The Chicago Youth Development Project* (Ann Arbor: Institute for Social Research, University of Michigan,

1964); *Reaching the Fighting Gang, op. cit.*; James F. Short, Jr. and Fred L. Strodtbeck, "Why Gangs Fight," *Trans-action* 1, no. 6 (September–October, 1964): 25–29; Spergel, *Street Gang Work, op. cit.;* Yablonsky, *op. cit.*

26. Mattick and Caplan, *op. cit.*, pp. 26–28.

27. Yablonsky, *op. cit.*

28. Lewis Yablonsky, "The Organization and Behavior of Violent Gangs," paper delivered at the A.A.A.S. meetings, New York, December, 1960 (mimeo); *op. cit.*

29. Yablonsky, *The Violent Gang, op. cit.*, p. 147.

30. Leon Jansyn, "Solidarity and Delinquency in a Street Corner Group," *American Sociological Review* 31, no. 5 (October, 1966): 600–614.

31. Malcolm W. Klein and Lois Y. Crawford, "Groups, Gangs, and Cohesiveness," *Journal of Research in Crime and Delinquency* 4, no. 1 (January, 1967): 63–75.

32. Short and Strodtbeck, "Why Gangs Fight," *op. cit.*

33. Thrasher, *op. cit.*

34. Robert A. Gordon, "Social Level, Social Disability, and Gang Interaction," *The American Journal of Sociology* 73, no. 1 (July, 1967): 42–62.

35. Yablonsky, *op. cit.*

36. Short and Strodtbeck, *Group Process and Gang Delinquency, op. cit.*

37. Nathan L. Gerrard, "The Core Member of the Gang," *British Journal of Criminology* 4, no. 4 (April, 1964): 361–71.

38. *Dealing With the Conflict Gang in New York, op. cit.;* Miller, *op. cit.;* Short and Strodtbeck, *op. cit.;* Spergel, *Racketville . . . , op. cit.;* Thrasher, *op. cit.*

39. William Foote Whyte, *Street Corner Society: The Social Structure of an Italian Slum* (Chicago: University of Chicago Press, 2nd ed., 1955).

40. Solomon Kobrin, Joseph Puntil, and Emil Peluso, "Criteria of Status Among Street Groups," *Journal of Research in Crime and Delinquency* 4, no. 1 (January, 1967): 98–118.

41. Kantor and Bennett, *op. cit.*

42. *Reaching the Fighting Gang, op. cit.*

43. Charles N. Cooper, "The Chicago YMCA Detached Workers: Current Status of an Action Program," in Malcolm W. Klein (ed.), *Juvenile Gangs in Context: Theory, Research, and Action,* (Englewood Cliffs, N.J.: Prentice-Hall, 1967), pp. 183–93.

44. Walter B. Miller, "The Impact of a 'Total-Community' Delinquency Control Project," *op. cit.*

45. Gilbert Geis, *Juvenile Gangs* (Washington, D.C.: President's Committee on Juvenile Delinquency and Youth Crime, 1965).

46. Victor Riccio, and W. Slocum, *All the Way Down* (New York: Simon & Schuster, Inc., 1962).

47. Thomas M. Gannon, "Dimensions of Current Gang Delinquency," *Journal of Research in Crime and Delinquency* 4, no. 1 (January, 1967): 119–31.

48. Miller, *op. cit.*

49. Spergel, *Street Gang Work, op. cit.*

50. Yablonsky, *op. cit.*
51. Cooper, *op. cit.*
52. Walter B. Miller, Hildred Geertz, and Henry S. G. Cutter, "Aggression in a Boys' Street Corner Group," *Psychiatry* 24 (November, 1961): 283–98.
53. Jonathan R. Laing, "The 'Black Disciples,' " *Wall Street Journal,* September 12, 1969, p. 1.
54. Yablonsky, *op. cit.*
55. Thrasher, *op. cit.*
56. Richard A. Cloward and Lloyd E. Ohlin, *Delinquency and Opportunity: A Theory of Delinquent Gangs* (Glencoe, Ill.: The Free Press, 1960).
57. Cohen and Short, *op. cit.*
58. *Dealing With the Conflict Gang in New York, op. cit.*
59. Bernstein, *op. cit.*
60. *Reaching the Fighting Gang, op. cit.*
61. Malcolm W. Klein, *Criminological Theories as Seen by Criminologists: An Evaluative Review of Approaches to the Causation of Crime and Delinquency* (Albany, N.Y.: Governor's Special Committee on the Criminal Offender, 1967).
62. Spergel, *op. cit.*
63. *Reaching the Fighting Gang, op. cit.*
64. Thomas M. Gannon, "Emergence of the 'Defensive' Gang," *Federal Probation* 30 (December, 1955): 44–48.
65. Short and Strodtbeck, *op. cit.*
66. Short and Strodtbeck, *op. cit.,* Chapter 12; Gordon, *op. cit.*
67. Nathan Caplan, from a seminar presentation at the Youth Studies Center, University of Southern California, 1967.
68. Albert K. Cohen, *Delinquent Boys,* (Glencoe: The Free Press, 1955); Short and Strodtbeck, *op. cit.*
69. Hardman, *op. cit.;* Thrasher, *op. cit.*
70. *Dealing With the Conflict Gang in New York, op. cit.; Reaching the Fighting Gang, op. cit.;* Short and Strodtbeck, *op. cit.;* Thrasher, *op. cit.*
71. Miller, "White Gangs," *op. cit.; Reaching the Fighting Gang, op. cit.*
72. Miller, *op. cit.,* p. 18.
73. Yablonsky, *op. cit.*
74. Hans W. Mattick, and Nathan S. Caplan, "Stake Animals, Loud Talking and Leadership in Do-Nothing and Do-Something Situations," in Klein (ed.), *Juvenile Gangs in Context, op. cit.,* pp. 116–19.

Chapter 4: Cohesiveness and Delinquency

Cohesiveness

There have been two major concerns with respect to cohesiveness; (a) how cohesive the gang is and (b) how cohesiveness is related to delinquency. With respect to the first, earlier writers[1] stressed the *esprit de corps,* face-to-face relations, and general camaraderie to be found in juvenile gangs. More recently, however, gangs—including the Los Angeles groups—are found to be rather loosely structured with varying but generally low cohesiveness.[2] A recent analysis by Gordon[3] suggests that cohesiveness is not only a function of neighborhood factors but also a function of, *and limited by*, the very social disabilities that help produce gangs in the first place.

It is clear that the size and subgrouping of the vertical gang cluster militates against high cohesiveness. Many of the members know each other only by sight, and sometimes even this is lacking. At a gathering of the Latins, a girl new to us came with a boy named Gregory Sanhueza, whose nickname was Cornflakes. We had heard about this girl, and knew that she had been dating Sanhueza for several weeks. Attempting to strike up a conversation, a staff member asked, "Did you come with Gregory Sanhueza?" "No," the girl responded, "I came with Cornflakes."

It is also generally agreed that cohesiveness and delinquency go hand in hand, but the nature of the relationship is still unclear. While my associates and I see increased cohesiveness leading to increased delinquency, the opposite relationship has been suggested by Jansyn[4] and by Gordon.[5] Although the effects are obviously interactive, the predominant direction may indicate the most fruitful approach for intervention programs. Shall we concentrate our efforts directly on reducing cohesiveness or on reducing delinquency?

Internal Sources

Most nongang groups may be said to derive their cohesiveness primarily from "internal" sources—with respect both to origination and to perpetuation of the group. In identifying these sources of cohesiveness as "internal" I recognize a certain semantic looseness, but the meaning may become clear as major sources are examined.

I contend that internal sources operate with far *less* impact among gangs than among other groups, and that, in contrast to other groups, gang cohesiveness derives from and is perpetuated by sources primarily external to the group. This contention is not new; Cohen's[6] "reaction formation" analysis and Yinger's[7] discussion of "contraculture" are in the same tradition. I believe in addition, however, that elimination of external sources of cohesiveness of gangs, in most cases, would be followed by dissolution of a relatively large proportion of the gang membership. That is, only rarely does a gang develop enough internally-oriented systems to perpetuate itself in the absence of external pressures. This is the result of two characteristics: (a) internal sources of gang cohesion are weak and (b) external pressures are strong. These two characteristics of delinquent groups provide an explanation for what Gerrard has described as "the intense but fragile quality of gang cohesion."[8]

More specific aspects of the weak internal sources of cohesiveness can be listed.

1. *Group goals* as such are usually minimal. The most commonly expressed group goal is the protection of members against rival gangs. Clearly this goal is what we have termed an *external* source of cohesion. Gangs assigned a detached worker sometimes learn to speak of goals such as self-betterment, improving their group image, and "holding their cool." However, such goals are far more easily verbalized than internalized and their general acceptance, when it does take place, is more often associated with gang dissolution than with solidification.

2. *Membership stability* in gangs is relatively low. We have observed large groups in which the combined subgroup members have totaled more than 200 over a two- to three-year period, yet at any given point of time there may be only 30 or 40 active members. In other words, turnover is high; many members affiliate with the group for brief periods of from a few days to a few months, while others move out of the neigh-

[handwritten annotation: are gangs the only permanent ties in this situation, i.e., normalized?]

borhood or are incarcerated for periods sometimes exceeding a year. Intragang suspicions make the bonds of member relationship even more transitory. Under these circumstances, it is hard to *conceive* of, much less observe, a continuing cohesive group. Even within gangs which have existed over several generations, the mobility factors mentioned above reduce the stability of active membership, in spite of the fact that allegiance to a given group may persist for many years.

3. *Group norms* among gang members have received much attention in the literature, but few have been found which are distinguishable in kind from those of the social class from which gang members generally are drawn. Group norms as such are relatively nonexistent in the gang world except as myths which explode upon test. For instance, gang members often say that they are loyal, will not inform ("fink") on each other, and will come to each other's aid in time of threat, attack, or retaliation; yet most gang researchers report numerous occasions in which such behavior does not occur, or does so only among selected members. The one norm that *does* seem to be shared is that of acceptance of a wide variety of illegal acts. Again, however, this may be more class or subculture related than specifically gang related.

4. *Role differentiation* is difficult to observe in gangs. There are often official positions, such as president, vice-president, or war counselor, but the influence of the position incumbents is nebulous at best. Functional leadership in different categories of activity is often present but this leadership is unstable and tends to shift from one person to another during various phases of group development. A most illuminating experience in this regard is to question several members of a group about the respective roles which they expect others to assume during various anticipated future activities. Uniformity of expectation is *not* the standard finding. The members agree on status, not on role. In fact, the boys can seldom differentiate beyond the status dimension.

5. *Group names*—Gladiators, Vice Lords, Egyptian Kings—are assumed by many to indicate a common "we-feeling" among gang members. In fact, however, these names often change within a group and derive their greatest effect during conflict periods when cohesiveness is increased by external threat. Many gang names derive from street or neighborhood labels—Ochenta, Parks, White Fence—suggesting again an external rather than internal base for identification.

Thus, minimal group goals, membership instability, a paucity of unique group norms, little group role differentiation, and a lack of lasting identity with group names all militate against the formation of delinquent gangs based on internal sources of cohesion.

An exception is to be found among gangs with a long history, for gang tradition does seem to be a major internal source of cohesiveness. These traditions in Los Angeles extend over 30 or 40 years. A boy growing up in the Clover, Hazard, or White Fence areas of East Los Angeles knows at an early age that gang membership is a highly visible opportunity. This perception is continually reinforced on the street, in school, and even in his home. In this sense, a boy living in such a neighborhood is initiated into the gang culture before he has any opportunity to make an independent decision.

External Sources

In contrast to relatively weak internal sources, strong external sources of cohesion are apparent everywhere. Any informed layman can discourse on the perils of poverty, low educational performance, few job skills, disrupted family relations, social disability, and so on. It needs to be added only that these facts of urban life lead to withdrawal symptoms, as documented by Cohen and Hodges.[9] When a number of boys in a neighborhood withdraw from similar sets of environmental frustrations and interact with one another enough to recognize, and perhaps generate, common attitudes, the group has begun to form. Added to threats of rival groups are the many ways in which society reinforces this tendency —police behavior, teacher reactions, lack of acceptance by adults on playgrounds and in local business establishments, and so on. Adolescent behavior and adult and rival group reactions thus reinforce each other, and the alternatives open to these youngsters are few. The result— however tenuous—is delinquent group cohesiveness.

The Delinquent Product

Thus far little reference has been made to the deviant behavior associated with the gang. The *delinquent product* of gang interaction is the second factor that distinguishes the juvenile gang from groups that have provided the bulk of social science knowledge of group behavior.

Society does not disapprove of gangs because their membership is adolescent, nor because they are urban, nor because of their normal, urban, adolescent group behavior. Gangs share all of these attributes with many nondelinquent youth groups. Many other youth groups also originate in opposition to adult expectations for their behavior. However, while all the activities of these spontaneous adolescent groups may not be condoned by society, such groups are not likely to engage in behavior which produces social rejection. Society disapproves of juvenile gangs

voluminous

specifically because of their occasionally "delinquent" member behavior. It is this delinquent product of the group that causes the reaction. Society knows this; its agents know it; the boys know it.*

Gangs are distinguishable from most groups on the basis of (a) a disproportionate measure of *external* sources of cohesion and (b) a socially disapproved group "product." But gangs are not the only such groups in existence. Consider other extremist groups, for example— motorcycle clubs, beatniks, the Black Muslims, the KKK, and some inmate cultures. The difference is that in most of these cases there are specifiable common goals for which the groups originated. These goals and sometimes other internal sources of cohesion disinguish them from the gang. The closest parallels to the juvenile gang may in fact be inmate cultures and San Francisco's now defunct North Beach beatnik colony.[10]

Traditional Approaches

In relating gang cohesiveness to gang-connected delinquency, one must choose among available conceptions and measures of cohesiveness or create new ones. A review of the literature strongly suggests that we should create new measures of cohesiveness to fit this particular problem.

Like patient care in medical sociology or morale in industrial psychology, cohesiveness proves on examination to be a complex concept. It has been used as independent variable,[11] dependent variable,[12] intervening variable,[13] and hypothetical construct.[14] It has been used as an experimental device, induced so that relationships between other variables might be illuminated.[15]

Cohesiveness, nominally, has referred to mutual liking or acceptance,[16] attraction to group,[17] degree of shared norms or values,[18] and resistance to disruptive forces.[19] Operationally, it has been measured by coordination of efforts,[20] summated attractiveness scores,[21] reaction to threat,[22] choice of group over other alternatives,[23] ratio of in-group to out-group choices or contacts,[24] and so on.

So many dimensions of cohesiveness run through the literature that cohesiveness can hardly be considered a definitive concept. This problem is perhaps best solved with reference to one's particular theoretical interests.

---

*Parenthetically, it is often the failure to separate specific delinquent acts from the offender which makes for the inefficiency of many of our delinquency prevention programs. Perhaps due to stimulus generalization, it is the whole boy and the whole group which is condemned, rather than their delinquent behavior alone.

We have said that the delinquent product of the gang makes it a special case. Further, it is generally acknowledged that gang membership *increases* delinquency involvement. The question is, how much and why? "Why" is in part a function of cohesiveness; "how much" is ultimately an empirical question. Why should high cohesiveness lead to high delinquency in the gang? It is not just the external sources of cohesiveness that bring this about; these have to do with gang formation before reinforcement. Most gang theorists presently concur that, if one's offenses vary with gang membership, it is because the antecedent deviant values, the requisite skills, and the opportunities for misbehavior are learned and reinforced through association with other members. Status forces are also operative. We would add only that these processes can occur and persist because the external sources of cohesiveness continually throw gang members together, forcing the kinds of interaction which are preliminary to increased gang-related offenses. These interactions become secondary sources of cohesion in conjunction with offense behavior, each reinforcing the other as the members mingle and verbalize the deviance which labels them as different.

Some of the jargon, the "tough" talk, and the recounting of delinquent exploits engaged in by gang members probably serve the function of reinforcing the weak affiliative bonds within the group. Several writers have analyzed both individual and group offenses at critical points in gang development—points of low status and low cohesiveness—to indicate how these offenses revitalize failing groups.[25]

To relate most directly to gang delinquency, a measure of cohesiveness must involve *membership interaction.* It should not rely on members' verbal responses to an investigator, however; those willing to respond are not likely to constitute a representative sample of the membership. Interviewing and questionnaire responses are of limited value for the task at hand.

Group measures as such are also inappropriate, for they reflect only *indirectly* a presumed summation of member interaction. This eliminates retaliations against rival groups as a measure—an infrequent occurrence.

Index measures that are based on the attractiveness of gang participation (as opposed to various alternative activities) are suspect because the researcher cannot adequately assess these alternatives. We attempted one such analysis, using average distance from member homes to evening meeting sites as representing a summation of barriers overcome to join group activities. This measure yields findings that are highly gang-specific, rather than generalizable. In some groups it is related to attendance figures; in others it is not. The variance seems more a function of core than of fringe members in the analysis of differences between gangs, and variance is far greater between gang clusters than within subgroups of the same cluster. All in all, I see little advantage in continuing to use this approach. Readers with an interest in this kind of index may wish to refer to the discussion of gang "dispersion" by Cartwright *et al.*,[26] although that measure as well did not correlate significantly with delinquent behavior.

Companionship

Another approach seems more promising. This method is not dependent upon member responses. It presents fewer sampling problems and is a direct measure of member interaction, our primary criterion. It requires the presence of an observer or a detached worker who keeps an accurate record of youth observations. These observations, recorded and tabulated in terms of companionship patterns, yield various possible indices of cohesiveness, including the clique patterns used in Chapter 3 describing the Senior and Junior Latins (Figs. 3-3, 3-4, and 3-5). Employing this behavioral approach during the Group Guidance Project proved very enlightening; in the Ladino Hills Project, it was almost indispensable.

From many sources in the Group Guidance Project, we knew that gang Clusters *A* and *B* continued the gang pattern far longer than did Clusters *C* and *D*.* Further, we knew from structural premises that cohesiveness declines with age beyond a certain point. In comparing the indices of cohesiveness taken from the workers, we found the following (see Table 4-1):

1. The number of identifiable cliques within a cluster seems unrelated to delinquency patterns, but the proportion of boys identifiable as clique members *is* related.

Table 4-1: Cohesiveness Measures in Four Gang Clusters

	Higher Delinquency Clusters		Lower Delinquency Clusters	
	A	*B*	*C*	*D*
a. Clique members ÷ all members	.42	.43	.16	.15
b. Mutual contacts ÷ $n(n-1)$	.81	.72	.20	.32
c. Single contacts ÷ all contacts	.54	.35	.73	.77
d. In-clique contacts ÷ all clique contacts	.82	.73	.47	.40

---

*Operators (*A*), Generals (*B*), Red Raiders (*C*), and Victors (*D*).

2. The index based on the number of mutual contacts between members divided by the number of boys contacted, squared (actually $n \times [n - 1]$), clearly differentiates between clusters.

3. Similarly, the number of single, mutual contact situations (two boys see each other just once during a standard period of time) over the number of all mutual contact situations yields large differences.

4. Among clique members, the proportion of in-clique contacts to all clique member contacts is related to the cluster patterns.

That these indices refer to more than differences between clusters is revealed by a pilot analysis carried out on Cluster A. The older and younger members were compared on two indices over three consecutive six-month periods, with the results shown in Table 4-2.

Table 4-2: Cohesiveness Index Changes Among Older
and Younger Members of Cluster A

Index	Age Group	July-Dec. 1963	Jan.-June 1964	July-Dec. 1964
Number of contacts ÷	Older	.25	.25	.16
$n(n - 1)$	Younger	.21	.25	.29
Number of nonsingle contacts ÷	Older	.65	.54	.51
total contacts	Younger	.60	.57	.70

As expected, both indices of cohesiveness show an increase with time for younger members and a decrease for older members. This represents a capsule summary of gang perpetuation: As older boys reduce their involvement, they are replaced by increased involvement among their younger peers.

Nor is age the only determining factor. For instance, what effect might a special program for gang members have on gang cohesiveness? During the third year of the Group Guidance Project, the staff initiated a remedial reading program with 72 adults in the community volunteering their time as teachers over a 15-month period. A total of 115 youngsters were involved in the program, drawn from various sources as indicated in Table 4-3.

Although the remedial reading program proved to be a fascinating experience and yielded some very interesting data about both the enrollees and their teachers, our concern here is with its effect on cohesiveness. The analysis is limited to male gang members who attended the program more than once, yielding an n of 39 boys.

Table 4-3: Gang and Sex of Program Attenders

	Male	Female	Total
Operators cluster	21	0	21
Generals cluster	10	36	46
Raiders cluster	8	0	8
Victors cluster	12	0	12
Other gang	3	0	3
Nongang*	20	5	25
Total	74	41	115

*A few of these were specially referred to the program by their probation officers but most appeared on their own. Some claimed to be gang members or friends thereof, but most were never questioned concerning their eligibility.

The analysis procedure was relatively simple: The duration of each boy's participation in the program was determined, and then an equal period immediately prior to and following this participation was analyzed. For example, if a boy participated in the program for 72 days, three sets of contact reports were analyzed: the 72 days prior to his first program session, the 72 days during which he participated, and the 72 days following his last program session.** Treating the program period as the independent variable, comparisons were then made between the pre-program and postprogram periods.

Overall, the number of worker-youth contacts per day went up by 58 per cent and, as a corollary to this, the amount of total contact time rose by 24 per cent. At the same time, number of youths per contact situation decreased by 14 per cent and length of contact dropped by 21 per cent. In other words, as judged by activity following each boy's participation, the effect of the program seems to have been to increase worker-youth contacts in numbers while decreasing the length of the contacts. More boys were seen, but for shorter lengths of time and on a more individual basis. Two factors were observed to bring about these effects. First, the reading program drew out a number of boys who had previously been in only occasional, if any, contact with the workers. Second, the twice-weekly opportunity for contact provided by the program "spilled over" into the postprogram period as particular workers "captured," or were captured by, particular gang members. The reading program, then, provided for the workers a new access to gang members, but at the same time *drew more boys into contact with the gang.*

As with other analyses in this book, a comparison was made be-

** In 17 of the 39 cases, the last period had to be prorated because the project concluded not long after the end of the reading program.

tween core and fringe gang members. The data revealed that program impact on worker-youth contacts had an opposite effect on core and fringe members in five of six areas of analysis. This fact by itself is more significant than the specific nature of the differential effects: It confirms the importance of *distinguishing between types* in understanding their involvement in intervention programs. These data constitute but one of several instances in which the core-fringe distinction, gross as it is, provides important clues both to program strategies and to useful theoretical hypotheses.

Specifically, we found that after the program workers *increased* their contact with fringe members but *decreased* it with core members. This is in direct opposition to the aims of a program designed to wean away fringe members, leaving greater freedom to concentrate on the more intractable core group. However, counseling topics increased with core members as opposed to fringe members, suggesting that the workers (or perhaps the youngsters) took better advantage of their contacts. This *is* in line with project objectives. Perhaps reduced contact time forces a more direct counseling approach.

Finally we come to the category labelled "number of youths per contact," which can be viewed as an index of cohesiveness. Taking it as such (that is, the more youths seen together at a time, the more cohesive the group), it would appear that *the reading program helped to separate the fringe members—a desired effect—but also increased the group affiliation among core members.* Under ordinary circumstances, this would be considered a positive effect by group workers because it increases their opportunity to "use the group on itself" to effect changes in values and attitudes. However, gang workers are seldom in a good position to take advantage of such a strategy. In pages to follow, we will question the place of cohesiveness in gang intervention strategies. For the moment, it is sufficient to suggest, as many other writers have, that increased cohesiveness among gang members will lead to more detrimental than beneficial results. Thus, any tendency for a program to increase grouping phenomena, as in the case of the remedial reading program, may be viewed as inadvertent negative impact. Although it is based on a small number of cases, one conclusion of our analysis nevertheless is that the remedial reading program drew in new members and reinforced the cohesiveness of core members.

Recruitment

This hint that programming activities can increase gang size—and perhaps cohesiveness as well—can be further investigated using a greater mass of data from the Group Guidance Project. It seems reasonable to suggest that more cohesive groups will add new members at a faster rate than will less cohesive groups—as a means of replacing older members who depart. Since the Victors and Red Raiders clusters were known to be less cohesive than the Operators and Generals clusters, we would expect them to show a slower recruitment rate. Furthermore, if cohesiveness *is* related to program levels in a positive fashion, a change in program levels should bring about a change in recruitment—younger average age levels, or more members of "gang age" at various ensuing points of time.

To perform this analysis, we have chosen the age range from 13 to 20 as the effective "gang age" in the four clusters. Using the project period of four years and including all boys for whom we have birthdates, we have totalled the number of gang-age boys in the four clusters separately in Table 4-4.

Table 4-4: Number of "Gang-Age" Boys During the Project Period (By Three-month Periods)

Year	1961		1962				1963				1964				1965	
Quarter	3	4	1	2	3	4	1	2	3	4	1	2	3	4	1	2
Victors	95	97	100	99	102	106	105	107	107	104	104	100	99	99	99	97
Red Raiders	76	75	76	76	76	77	76	76	74	72	72	68	67	65	65	61
Generals	107	116	119	122	123	125	128	130	131	131	132	129	131	130	129	128
Operators	67	72	73	77	82	87	92	94	97	99	100	105	106	108	107	106
Total	345	360	368	374	383	395	401	407	409	406	408	402	403	402	400	392
V. + R.R.	171	172	176	175	178	183	181	183	181	176	176	168	166	164	164	158
G. + O.	174	188	192	199	205	212	220	224	228	230	232	234	237	238	236	234

Summarizing Table 4-4 briefly, it can be seen that:

(1) The Victors increase in size very slowly until the summer of 1963, and then decline at about the same rate

(2) The Red Raiders remain stable until 1963, and then decline

(3) The Generals increase steadily into 1964, and then drop very slightly

(4) The Operators continue to increase until 1965

The significance of this table, however, rests in the last two rows in which the Victors have been combined with the Red Raiders, and the Generals have been combined with the Operators. The period around the summer of 1963 stands as a watershed for the first two clusters, while the pattern of the other two clusters continues to rise.

Figure 4-1 shows the pattern of the two sets of clusters, the significance of which lies in this: In the summer of 1963, the workers assigned

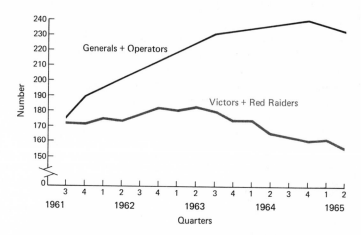

Fig. 4-1: Size of "gang-age" membership over time—
Victors and Red Raiders vs. Generals and Operators.

to the Red Raiders and Victors were transferred and replaced by new workers. It is at just this time that recruitment reverses, cohesiveness begins a significant decline, and offense rates begin to improve. We believe these workers had themselves become major sources of gang cohesiveness. Their removal signalled the decline of both clusters.

Although this graph visually overdramatizes the difference in the two sets of groups, it does illustrate the different times at which the peaks are reached. Together with the previous findings and the data yet to come, it allows us to speculate seriously about the relationship between group programming and gang cohesiveness.

It may be obvious by now that the direction of this section is changing. From a straightforward report of the data, we have been moving slowly toward an attempt to account for some of the findings from the Group Guidance Project by combining several notions. This would be a good point to review the situation.

We will show later that the project period was clearly associated with an increase in offense rates well beyond what would have been expected. We found that core members are charged with offenses significantly more often than fringe members are.

In addition, we can show that the project had its worst effect on the offenses committed at earlier age levels rather than later age levels. For the ages 12 through 15, significantly more offenses were recorded during the project than before it. Ages 16 and 17 showed no such trend. Another way of saying this would be that the period of gang *entry* is more often associated with project failure. With this finding we have the intercluster comparisons which suggest that offense *rates* are related to group programming levels and that recruitment rates dropped precisely *because* of the worker transfers.

Taken together, these analyses suggest that program impact, as measured in this section, is related to programming, worker style, and cohesiveness, with cohesiveness emerging as the core variable. This, at least, is the tentative hypothesis: Increases and decreases in cohesiveness are positively related to increases and decreases in gang offense behavior. Corollary hypotheses would include (a) that higher levels of group programming lead to higher levels of cohesiveness, (b) that cohesiveness is increased, through recruitment, by focusing program efforts on younger age levels, and (c) that the effect of worker transfers is to eliminate one major contributor to gang cohesiveness. Finally we have also suggested, in contrasting the Operators and Generals with the Victors and Red Raiders, that factors affecting cohesiveness (and thus delinquency) are more pronounced in their effects among the relatively lower cohesive clusters.

These are not hypotheses which can be tested with our data, since they are derived from those data. The tests must await future projects.* However, we can seek more support for the hypotheses through analyses of other data available to us—in the hopes that these new analyses will at least confirm the explanatory direction we have taken as a fruitful one. We turn now to the analysis of *types of offenses*, or dimensions of the offenses committed by project boys.

Intergang Incidents

Under this heading we include gang fights,** retaliations, one-on-one fair fights, sneak attacks, "jumpings" (several against one), and so on. These sorts of incidents, while they are dramatic, highly publicized, and form the core of many stereotypes of gang activity, are actually relatively infrequent; they seldom result in serious physical harm.

---

*Even then, the crucial issue may be the *definition* of cohesiveness. Miller's approach is essentially attitudinal, and he includes that his gangs were often highly cohesive. My approach has been *behavioral*, and has led me to the conclusion that high cohesion is not common among the gangs in Los Angeles. Independently, Cartwright *et al.* (see reference 26) have pointed to this distinction in attempting to explain why their attitudinally measured cohesion was not positively related to behavioral patterns among Chicago gangs.

**During the four years of the Group Guidance Project, only one clash approached the classic or journalistic dimensions of a gang fight or "rumble." This one case was the precipitating event which brought about the police controversy reported in a later section. Similarly, the Chicago Youth Development Project saw only one major gang fight over a six-year period beginning in 1960. See Frank J. Carney *et al.* (reference 64), p. 60.

We take our data for this analysis from worker reports, research observations, police reports, reports in the media, and research interviews. Since the research program was not in full swing until 1963, the data cover only the last two and a half years of the project, during which time 55 separate intergang incidents were recorded. Because some of these were between members of our four clusters, we shall speak instead of the 71 *involvements* and analyze these (for instance, if 3 Generals beat up one Red Raider in a fight, we count this as two involvements among our clusters; if 3 Generals beat up one member of a nonproject gang, we are concerned with only one involvement).

Of the total of 71 involvements, the Operators committed 20 (28 per cent), the Generals committed 17 (24 per cent), the Red Raiders committed 19 (27 per cent), and the Victors committed 15 (21 per cent). Thus the four clusters contributed almost equally to the overall total. But if we again compare the Operators and Generals with the Red Raiders and Victors over time, a striking difference appears. In 1963, the Red Raiders and Victors accounted for 68 per cent of the intergang involvements. In 1964, the level fell to 42 per cent, and in 1965, it reached only 27 per cent. The qualitative nature of the change is equally significant. For instance, even at the end of the project the Operators consistently retaliated against other groups if one of the Operators was attacked. By contrast, one of the Victors was openly stabbed to death by a notorious General, yet not only was there no attempt at retaliation, there was practically no discussion of it.

For the theorist, the significance of data on gang fights and assaults lies in the relationship between gang fighting and gang cohesiveness. If there is any one value which lies at the core of gang mythology in the traditional gang, it is that of the gang's fighting reputation. A cohesive gang, one in which there is constant mutual reinforcement of fighting values, can be expected to engage in numerous intergang incidents. And most assuredly, the cohesive gang will more often retaliate for any raid on its members or territory.

Thus, we can take the decline in intergang involvements among the Victors and Red Raiders as a validation of the cohesiveness hypotheses. During the latter part of the project, these two clusters were slowly but surely disintegrating (as later did the Generals at a slower rate). They were losing cohesiveness and causing less trouble in the community.

Companionship Offenses

Our case could be strengthened by another approach, which would connect cohesiveness to offense rate. If the nature of programming is related to gang cohesiveness, is there in turn some way to test the hypothesis that this will be manifested in some fashion by the offense patterns?

Suppose one were to ask what sorts of offenses would be most affected by differences in cohesiveness? Logically, there does seem to be an answer to this question. Some offenses tend to be committed in the company of other youths more than other offenses. In other words, one should be able to distinguish between high-companion offenses and low-companion offenses. For example, arrests for school trespassing tend to be individual events whereas arrests for assaults more often involve more than one boy.

To determine which types of offenses might be considered high-companion and which low-companion, we used two sources. First, we turned to our own anecdotal information from the four clusters. For example, a worker might have reported that five of his boys were picked up for an assault, or one of the boys might have told us that he was arrested for throwing a brick at an empty house. Ninety-six such reports were in our files.

Our second, independent source was the probation records of the Latins, the gang cluster in the Ladino Hills Project. Sometimes these records included names of companions in delinquent incidents. A search of 69 such records yielded 430 incidents.

For each incident, we merely recorded whether or not companions were indicated. After grouping the offenses by "logical" connections, we computed for each major category the proportion of cases in which companions were reported to have been present. The rank-order correlation between the figures from the two sources was +.67, so the data were combined to yield the categories and figures in Table 4-5.

Table 4-5: Proportion of Incidents With Companions Reported

High Companion Offenses		Low Companion Offenses	
Assault	.53	Disturbing the Peace	.22
Grand Theft, Auto	.52	Alcohol	.22
Burglary	.41	Malicious Mischief	.11
Drugs	.33	School Violations	.11
Curfew	.32	Home (e.g. runaway, incorrigible)	.06
Weapons	.27	Ineffective Rehabilitation	.05
Theft or Robbery	.24	Traffic	.00

Although these data are not terribly refined, being drawn from anecdotal reports and inconsistently available probation data, they do afford an opportunity to test the cohesiveness material. If cohesiveness is manifested in delinquent incidents, it should be in such a way that higher cohesiveness is associated with a greater proportion of high-companion offenses than would be the case with lower cohesiveness; birds of a feather who flock together are more likely to be arrested together. This is the basic assumption underlying the test.

The two sets of data from the Group Guidance Project were compared during comparable preproject and project periods, and a statistically significant difference was obtained in the direction expected on the basis of our general cohesiveness notion.* *As compared with the control period, the project period manifested an increase in high-companion offenses and no change in low-companion offenses.* Putting this more directly, but less cautiously, the suggestion is that the project— that is, the workers—may have contributed to *more* group-related offenses, while offenses more often associated with individual offenders remained constant.

However, no differences were found before and after the worker transfers mentioned earlier. Such a difference would have acted as secondary confirmation, but we must settle for what we have, a reliable *indication* that the program served to increase offenses assocated with heavier *group* involvement.

Before moving on in our discussion, we must dispense with one seeming complication in the above analysis. As we do so, a new unexpected finding will be revealed. If the reader will return to Table 4-5 and compare the two sets of offenses listed there, it may seem that they differ not only in companionship, but also in qualitative seriousness. And, indeed, this is the case. Application of the McEachern and Bauzer seriousness index[27] yields an average index score of .38 for high-companion offenses and .22 for low-companion offenses. Thus, it is highly conceivable that the findings concerning companionship are *really* findings about seriousness. To check this out, an identical analysis was performed on high- versus low-seriouness offenses. The results were negative.** Overall impact was not significantly different on high- and low-seriousness, and the companionship analysis holds up.

A reanalysis of Miller's† Roxbury Project data reveals a very similar pattern. The offense increases (11.2 per cent) among Miller's boys were in the areas of assault, theft, and alcohol offenses. Under theft, Miller

---

*Chi Square for high-companion offenses equals 30.86 ($p < .01$); Chi Square for low-companion offenses equals 1.11 ($p > .30$).

**Chi Square for the difference between high- and low-seriousness offenses is 1.52 ($p > .20$).

†These data are reported in Walter B. Miller (reference 65), pp. 168–91.

includes burglary, robbery, and auto theft. Reference to Table 4-5 reveals that all of these categories except for alcohol offenses comprise high companionship offenses. Thus, the offense increases reported by Miller were almost exclusively among high companionship offenses. Our findings in Los Angeles is no anomaly.

The significance of the companionship analysis lies in two directions. First, as with the analysis of intergang incidents, it strengthens the case for attributing a substantial portion of the project's increase in delinquent offenses to the factor of inadvertently increased gang cohesiveness. Second, it yields an impact finding of importance for its own sake, to the effect that group-oriented gang intervention programs may serve to increase the very types of offenses of most concern to the public and to enforcement agencies—those offenses more often committed in groups.

When this latter implication is combined with the finding that the most deleterious effect is among the younger boys, when these are put together with the hypothesis (now having received further support) that group progamming for gang boys serves to increase gang size and cohesiveness, it becomes clear that there is good reason to doubt the desirability of continuing such programs or mounting new ones.

Earlier in this report, differences between the four gang clusters in the Group Guidance Project were outlined, but the question of cluster-specific differences in project impact was omitted. Looking at this matter now reinforces the conclusions just reached about the relationship between programming and cohesiveness if one assumes that increased cohesiveness leads to an increase in gang delinquency.

When a month-by-month analysis of offenses is undertaken, it reveals the following:

1. The Operators exhibited a "success" pattern for the first 18 months, or until January of 1963—the very month in which a worker was permanently assigned to them. In only 8 of the remaining 30 months were Operator offenses below statistically determined expected levels. Thus, the "success" pattern coincided with lack of service, the "failure" pattern with adoption of service and very heavy group programming.

2. The Generals exhibited an overall "success" pattern during the project period, with offense levels generally below expected levels. However, this was *least* true during the period of heaviest group programming and *most* true during the initial and latter stages of the project period when lighter programming was most prominent.

3. The Red Raiders showed a generally negative pattern throughout the project period, with only 4 of 48 months yielding lower than expected offense levels. However, a slight but steadily worsening pattern

of offenses was reversed in the summer of 1963 after which offense levels decreased slowly and erratically. The summer of 1963 saw the transfer of the detached worker just prior to this shift in offense patterns.

4. The Victors also manifested an overall negative pattern, with 10 of 48 months yielding offense levels below expectation. Again, as in the case of the Red Raiders, a definite improvement was initiated in the latter half of 1963, following the transfer of the gang worker.

Thus all four clusters yield evidence that group programming levels are associated with delinquency, and we already know from the earlier recruitment and offense analyses that increased programming is associated with an increase in gang cohesiveness. Admittedly, these data do not *prove* our case, but they do add strong evidence to the attribution of an increase in gang cohesiveness to higher levels of group programming and higher gang delinquency to higher gang cohesiveness. There is now much evidence to support this progression from group activity to cohesiveness to delinquency. There is little to disconfirm the hypothesis.

Further comments on cohesiveness and delinquency will be made later when the test of the major hypothesis is explored—the Ladino Hills Project was designed as such a test. At this point, I want to cite a few additional, almost random, observations which, taken together, provide a better "feel" for the nature of gang cohesiveness and some of the dynamics involved.

So far as gang delinquency is concerned, the preceding materials have suggested that cohesiveness serves as an intervening, mediating, or process variable; that is, causal factors are transmitted and transmuted through group process variables, such as cohesiveness, and thereby result in group-related behaviors of which delinquency is one form. Let's take a few examples of this process.

1. Just as the gang is properly considered a part of the community's social structure, so its cohesiveness is related to general, community-wide change. Changes in housing patterns, demographic in- and out-migrations, freeway construction, employment opportunities, and so on can all affect gang structure. But as the epitome of the community-gang relationship, consider the following: *gang cohesiveness, as measured by levels of interaction between gang members in the Ladino Hills Project, rises and falls in direct relationship to school activity.* Every holiday, every vacation, every return following vacation is accompanied by a clear rise in gang cohesiveness.

There are two mild surprises in this simple statement. First, these school-related increases in cohesiveness take place *even when fewer gang members than one in five* is enrolled in school. Second, the rise in cohesiveness occurs during the time period immediately *preceding* the break in the school routine: the week *prior* to Christmas, Easter, and summer vacations, fall return, and semester breaks; the days *prior* to Thanksgiving and Cinco de Mayo. The increase in activity is anticipatory, suggesting an anxiety or tension base, at least in part. And with so few gang members in school, we are clearly dealing with a community phenomenon—the school pattern affects community life styles independently of school attendance. Thus the gang is indeed involved in its community, and its cohesiveness is a reaction, in part, to the anticipation of forthcoming events in the community.

2. If this latter statement is true, that a rise in cohesiveness is anticipatory, can we use such a rise as a predictor of trouble? Gang workers often "sense" trouble brewing even before being told that intergang tension is mounting. Perhaps these workers note changes in companionship patterns. Figure 4-2 shows the average number of boys seen each month during the 18 months of the Ladino Hills Project. Assuming that the rise from May to June of 1966 is primarily the result of the field observer's increasing recognition of gang members, we can see that *number of boys seen*, as an index of changes in cohesiveness, is rather insensitive to periodic fluctuations.

However, when we look at a measure of gang member interactions, as in Figure 4-3, we see that cohesiveness can change quite radically. There are eight rises in cohesiveness, as measured by the intensity of interactions. Numbers 1 and 6 precede summer vacations; numbers 2 and 7 precede the beginning of the Fall semester; number 4 precedes Christmas vacation; numbers 3 and 8 precede gang killings (one of "ours," one of "theirs"); number 5 precedes both the January semester break and a series of intergang fights. Note that the two low points occur in the summer of each year. This is typical of Los Angeles gangs—contrary to patterns reported for Eastern cities in which the summers see heightened gang activity.

Yes, to some extent increased grouping among gang members can be predictive of serious trouble. It is quite likely that, in the anticipation of trouble and/or excitement, gang members will exhibit a major anxiety reaction immediately *available to them because they are gang members*—they will coalesce, seeking both safety in numbers and mutual reinforcement of challenged group identities. The best reinforcer of gang cohesiveness is the threat—real or merely rumored—of the rival gang. Further, our data suggest that intergang hostilities are most likely to take place soon after major breaks in the school pattern. It is worth considering that the rise in cohesiveness occasioned by anticipation of patterned school changes leads to greater gang visibility among gangs,

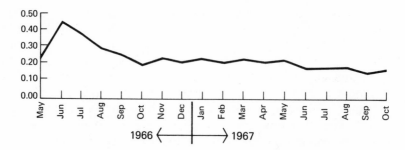

*It should be recalled that "number of boys" in this context means the number of boys sighted at least once, not the number of sightings. This is a measure of how many are visible, rather than how visible each boy is. Each monthly figure is a composite of its own weekly figures.

Fig. 4-2: **Number of boys seen per mile of cruising.** *

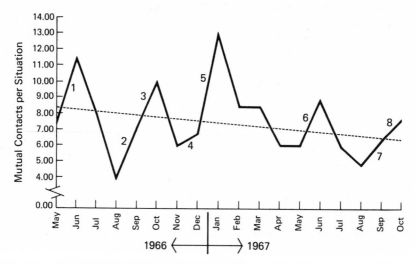

Fig. 4-3: **Number of contacts per contact situation.**

that each reacts to the other's increased visibility by an exaggerated cohesiveness, and that this in turn leads to the confrontation which, in the absence of countervailing forces, may result in the kind of "gang warfare" we eventually see in our local headlines.

3. Although our data are insufficient to provide solid support (there simply aren't enough good gang fights), our observations suggest two cohesiveness reactions to a serious intergang confrontation ("serious" meaning someone *really* got hurt or killed). Some gang members virtually disappear from view; they are not to be found on the street, at the

local hanging-out spot, or near any location easily marked by the rival gang. Usually, they simply stay home, a pattern which for them is somewhat bizarre.

Others group tightly together, or around their gang worker (or even their friendly researcher); they are even friendly with cruising police officers. Let there be no mistake about it; gang boys get scared, very scared, for they have seen or heard the results of gang fighting.

With these preceding three items, I hope to have added some "feeling" for the nature of gang cohesiveness. Contrary to much popular thought, it seems fair to suggest that the traditional gang, while obviously more stable and cohesive than the spontaneous gang (by definition), is far from a compact, autonomous behemoth. It is, in fact, a somewhat fragile, reactive phenomenon. Gang cohesiveness is highly variable and subject to equally variable interpretations by different observers. Jansyn's hypothesis reported earlier, that a drop in cohesiveness leads to delinquent episodes designed to reassert a higher level of cohesiveness, receives little support from our own data and observations.

But Jansyn was in Chicago, not Los Angeles. His observations were based on intensive coverage of one small gang, not comprehensive (or gross) analyses of large, traditional gang clusters. Perhaps the cities differ in gang dynamics, although I doubt it. Perhaps Jansyn picked an unusual group. Or perhaps what appears in microcosm becomes obscured in macrocosm. This much is clear: gang cohesiveness is a potentially fruitful variable for study, and gang cohesiveness and delinquency are not independent phenomena. There is plenty of room here for further study.

Patterns of Delinquency

What do gang boys do—how do they spend their time? Offhand, I can think of few categories of people who are less exciting to observe than gang members simply because, by and large, they just stand around and do nothing! Certainly, their involvement in delinquent episodes is so infrequent that one must wait many months before sufficient offenses have taken place to provide the grist for the statistician's mill. This is perhaps the most important fact about gang behavior—most of it is nondelinquent. In studying gang delinquency, then, it is well to remember that one is studying a very minor sample of daily behavior, that this sample remains primarily undetected, and therefore that detected delinquent behavior is a *lousy* base from which to draw generalizations.

We must also note that the difficulties normally associated with criminal statistics[28] apply equally well to those on gang offenses. Gang statistics are usually taken from one of two sources, the police or the reports of detached workers assigned to work with gangs. Occasionally, court or probation data are also employed.

In Los Angeles, analysis of our workers' reports of delinquency involvement proved highly unreliable, while comparisons of police and probation data revealed considerable comparability despite only an approximate 60 per cent overlap between the two sources. In Chicago, a study of police and worker reports by Wise[29] disclosed serious differences, with the workers being far more aware of gang offenses than the police. Thus the data to be reported below must be taken as more suggestive than conclusive.

Size of the Problem. It is virtually impossible to know how many gangs are active at any point in time nationally. The larger cities consistently yield reports in the hundreds, with total membership amounting to several thousand per city. Yet in some large cities, police officials report a virtual absence of teenage gangs. In Los Angeles, the census tract in the Group Guidance Project with the highest number of gang member addresses yielded an estimate that only 6 per cent of the 10-to-17-year-old bracket were gang affiliated. Cloward and Ohlin, in one of their very infrequent data statements, report, "there is no evidence to suggest that the conflict subculture is more widespread than the other subcultures. . . ."[30]

Thus, without meaning to belittle a vexing problem, one is led to conclude that gang delinquency constitutes a minor portion even of big city delinquency—which in turn is only one of many serious problems of urban America. The place of the gang in the professional literature and in the mass media is exaggerated way out of proportion to its contribution to our social ills.

Types of Offenses. Perhaps the most impressive fact about gang members' delinquency involvement is the "cafeteria style" which it exhibits. Rather than specializing in specific kinds or even broad categories of offenses, gang members tend to get themselves into a wide variety of difficulties. This finding holds for studies in New York,[31] Boston,[32] Philadelphia,[33] Chicago,[34] and Los Angeles.

This variety was forcibly brought to our attention during the analysis of the Group Guidance Project data. We wanted to measure project impact on meaningful *categories* of delinquent offenses. Several writers had suggested systems of offense categorization that seemed potentially useful, but no rational basis for selection among the systems could be found. Therefore, we began a factor analysis of the official offense records in the project, hoping that an empirical base for categorization might be revealed. Inspection of the resulting factors indicated clearly that they should be questioned. The difficulty was soon discovered in the table of intercorrelations yielded in the printout. Using the 0.05 level of significance as a criterion, it was found that only 5.4 per cent of the intercorrelations attained statistical significance. Simply stated, this means that the relationships between the various categories of offenses were randomly determined, that in fact there seems to be no systematic ordering of the offenses. Knowing one offense charged against a boy provides no empirical clue to the type of offense he will commit on other occasions.*

Here is an empirically surprising state of affairs. Contrary to intuition and the experience of most correctional personnel, the data have told us that gang members do not commit *patterned* offenses, that petty theft and rape are as likely to be committed by the same boy as are petty theft and grand theft (or any other such combination, the only limitation being provided by the overall frequency of occurrence of each offense). Why this should be so cannot be determined with our data. It may be simply because the data accurately reflect existing unpatterned offense behavior. But since only a small portion of all offense behavior gets officially reported and recorded by enforcement agencies, it may also be that existing patterns are covered over by the many selective and accidental factors which lead to the recording of an offense in an agency file. Personal observation and field experience suggest that both explanations are pertinent; that gang members engage in a wide variety of offenses, rather than being "specialists," and that the degree of offense behavior patterning which does exist is not transmitted into official records because of the often accidental contingencies which lead to apprehension for that small proportion of offenses known to the police.

How common are the various kinds of offenses? Thrasher[35] found theft to be most common, followed by burglary and robbery. Vandalism was merely a secondary companion to these offenses, while personal violence is hardly mentioned. Robin,[36] while noting that 67 per cent of the gang members known to the Philadelphia police had at least one assaultive charge against them, found only 23 per cent of all the charges to be against persons (that is, assaultive or violent in some way).

---

*Shannon's extensive analysis in Wisconsin yields precisely the same conclusion for all juvenile offenders in two cities, suggesting that the lack of offense patterning among gang members is part of a more general phenomenon. See Lyle W. Shannon (reference 66), pp. 40–41, 47, 52, 96, 106–9, 120.

In Boston, Miller's data[37] revealed assaultive behaviors to be one half to one third as common as theft, and only 14 per cent of the thefts were directly from persons. Property damage was one quarter as common. If court charges were used, these proportions were even lower. Several sets of Los Angeles data, reported in Table 4-6, indicate similar patterns, yet with sufficient variation to remind us that we are not dealing with a totally uniform phenomenon.

Table 4-6: Offenses Charged Against Los Angeles Gang Members

Offense Categories	Four Negro Gang Clusters		One Mexican-American Cluster	
	Prior to Project (%)	During Project (%)	Prior to Project (%)	During Project (%)
Thefts, burglary, robbery	32	26	18	15
Juvenile status*	24	17	23	14
Auto theft	12	14	14	12
Assaults, weapons	10	13	9	9
Malicious mischief, disturbing the peace	6	7	10	3
Drugs & alcohol	3	10	11	20
Sex	2	2	1	0
Traffic	1	3	3	8
Other	8	7	10	20
	98 + %	99 + %	99 + %	101 − %

*Juvenile status offenses are those which are not criminal acts if committed by adults (such as truancy, curfew violations, incorrigibility, runaway, and so forth).

In Los Angeles, as in other cities, the most common recorded offenses are thefts of various kinds and the so-called *juvenile status* offenses. Assault charges, including the display or carrying of weapons, constitute about 10 per cent of the total. Some ethnic differences exist; for example, the boys in the Ladino Hills Project seem less theft oriented and more involved with drugs and alcohol. It also appears that the existence of special projects may affect the apportioning of charges; there was in each case in Table 4-6 a drop in theft and juvenile status offenses, along with an increase in retreatist (drugs and alcohol) involvement.

The data in Table 4-6 should not be taken to represent the *actual* offense behavior of gang boys, but only the detected and recorded offense behavior. Some kinds of offenses—assaults, for instance—are more commonly reported to the police than are others, leading to a greater apprehension rate for such offenses. But for observed and recorded offenses—those which lead to enforcement, judicial, and correctional processes—these data seem in substantial agreement with those reported elsewhere. Gang boys are "caught" most often for minor stealing and strictly juvenile offenses. Gangs are *not* primarily assaultive or violent in their delinquent behavior and, what is more, the greatest part of their time is spent in nondelinquent activity.

   Seriousness. How *qualitatively* serious are the offenses of gang members? The Myerhoffs' middle class groups[38] were found to be very low in violence and destruction. Short[39] reports for Chicago gangs, ". . . we find very little vandalism or destructiveness except in cases where a reasonably specific motivation is close at hand," and ". . . malicious and negativistic behavior [is] relatively rare among our groups" (p. 27). Spergel[40] reports, as a further example, that armed robbery was very uncommon in all three areas in his study.

   Miller's analysis of the Boston data is the most complete yet undertaken and seems to typify the observations of other observers. In the intensely studied gang, the Junior Outlaws, Miller and his associates[41] report that most aggressive acts were verbal—*physical* attacks on persons and property constituted only 7 per cent of these. Miller concludes that gangs ". . . provide an arena in which aggression is played out, its force dissipated in a continuing, persistent, low-level flow, directed at members of the group itself."[42]

   Within all of the gangs under study by Miller, there were no murder or manslaughter charges. Weapon use was unusual; a gun was never used. (This statement is unusual—other cities report higher incidence of weapon use. In two years the Ladino Hills Project saw three deaths by gunfire.) There were very few instances of property damage, and in each case only minor damage resulted. "The average weekend of highway driving in and around Port City produces more serious bodily injuries than two years of violent crimes by Midcity gangs."[43]

   In two years, Miller's project witnessed only one full scale gang fight while in 14 other instances the gangs found a way out (in Los Angeles, the Group Guidance Project also witnessed only one large group conflict in four years). As Miller noted, "the fact is that genuine gang fights, collective assaults on adults, and similar types of gang crime are relatively rare in any given city in any given year."[44]

   Noting that most aggression is verbal rather than physical, that there is far more smoke than fire, Miller concludes:

   While members of slum street gangs engaged in violent crime to a greater degree than middle-class adolescents, violence was not a central preoccupation of the gangs, and most "violent" crimes were of the less serious variety. Cruel or sadistic violence was rare; violence was seldom "senseless" or irrational. Property damage was relatively uncommon.[45]

Miller's findings and conclusions generally fit with the impressions of other careful observers, although usually one does witness more weapons involvement. As noted earlier, several gang members were killed during the Los Angeles studies. One of my associates had to "hit the deck" when a group she was with was fired upon by a rival gang. I have twice been threatened with physical attack, and one of my workers had a gun pointed between his eyes. Miller may have been a bit lucky, but the relative rarity of the truly violent act can easily account for these minor discrepancies.

One other significant set of findings with respect to offense seriousness should be reported. In Los Angeles, we undertook a statistical analysis of offense seriousness over time. Because this analysis has not appeared elsewhere and has, I believe, some value for future research in delinquency measurement, a somewhat detailed description will be undertaken here. Attempts at *qualitative* measurement which would assess the relative seriousness of particular delinquent behaviors have been rather limited in number and value. The history of these efforts has been well summarized by Sellin and Wolfgang in their recently published volume, *The Measurement of Delinquency.*[46]

With the growth in the number of and sophistication of action programs designed to ameliorate the problem of juvenile delinquency, the lack of sensitive measuring devices has become more acute. As Empey and Erickson point out, "At present most control decisions are [made] without the benefit of answers to important questions. Most people are left in a quandary as to whether official records understate or overstate the problem."[47] A strongly felt need now exists for indices which go beyond the mere summation of police or court contacts to the assessment of the *relative gravity* or seriousness of individual acts or of group and geographical patterns of juvenile misconduct. In response to this need, we analyzed four potentially useful indices of delinquency seriousness, each of which assigns differential weights to various categories of delinquent behavior. Our method was to compare the effectiveness of the four indices in differentiating between the delinquent behavior patterns of core and fringe members of the four gang clusters in the Group Guidance Project. Justification for this criterion rests upon the following:

1. Gang membership is commonly dichotomized into core and fringe segments by social workers and enforcement officers across the nation.

2. Gang workers can reliably make the distinction between core and fringe membership. In our studies, the gang workers' nomination was the operational definition of membership status.

3. This nomination is consistently related to obtained judgments about differential member characteristics. As noted earlier, our detached workers consistently distinguished between core and fringe members on nine factors, including the two we labelled "Deficient Aggressive" and "Group Involvement."

4. The core-fringe distinction is significantly related to a *quantitative* measure of delinquency involvement, number of recorded delinquency charges.

Since the analysis rests heavily upon this criterion, I will repeat that the distinction between core and fringe gang segments is a reliable distinction, and that it is related both to magnitude of official delinquency and to independently assessed judgmental factors. Thus we are seeking the best means for measuring yet another factor—seriousness of offenses—by employing a criterion which already seems to "stand on its own two feet."

The sample consisted of 154 core and 120 fringe members of our four clusters. This represents almost half of the 576 members identified in the project. Of the remainder, 149 (26 per cent of the total) were over 18 and their records had been destroyed, while the rest had either not obtained records, could not then be identified because of faulty or insufficient identifying information, or had not then been labelled as *core* or *fringe* by the gang worker.

For the 274 members with records, 1753 recorded charges were analyzed, 635 for fringe members and 1118 for core members. Multiple counts and dependency referrals were included. Also, contrary to many recording systems, the data source records all offenses allegedly committed in a single event rather than just the "most serious" one of them.

The data were taken from the Central Juvenile Index (CJI), a filing system maintained by the Los Angeles County Sheriff's Department. State, county, and local agencies report juvenile contacts to CJI, thus providing a centralized depository of information available to all members.

We selected CJI as the data source for this particular analysis for three reasons: First, as a centralized system for the entire county it included information from over 50 agencies in a standard format. Second, it was easily accessible. Third, it provided the most logical alternative to official police records, which, in Los Angeles, are not available to private research organizations, including universities. This means that one can report the offense as it is officially recorded (that is, the legal definition or the subdivision of the law violated), but one cannot report the nature of the event which led to the charge. Unfortunately—for research purposes—each boy's CJI record is destroyed on his 18th birthday.

The Indices

The first index of seriousness employed in the analysis is based on the Uniform Crime Reports classification (UCR).[48] It is the simplest index and, with 27 broad offense categories, the most inclusive of the four systems. Twenty-four of the 27 categories were included in the present analysis, omitting driving violations, parking violations, and suspicion, most of which are not recorded in CJI.

The second index is taken from the work of McEachern and Bauzer.[49] Their analysis was performed on 1117 delinquent incidents drawn from a random sample of one thousand and ten CJI records. The relative seriousness of an index event is equal to the proportion of each offense type for which a "petition" is requested. A petition request is the means by which the police department initiates consideration of probation, parole, or court action against a juvenile. Thus "seriousness" is here operationally defined by police initiation of further adjudication. The McEachern and Bauzer system contains 32 offense categories (more numerous, but less comprehensive than the UCR categories) and includes juvenile status offenses (offenses which cannot be charged against adults, such as curfew violation and incorrigibility). The McEachern and Bauzer system omits traffic violations and dependency referrals.

The third system was employed by Gerald Robin in his analysis of 3939 offenses committed by gang members known to the Juvenile Aid Bureau of the Philadelphia Police Department.[50] Seriousness of index events is here operationally defined as the proportion arrested for each offense type. Omitted as index events are offenses that were not recorded for Robin's population, and curfew violations that were subject to a nonarrest policy. Robin's system includes 16 offense categories.

The fourth system is taken from Sellin and Wolfgang. The 15 offense categories included here are determined primarily by Sellin and Wolfgang's very extended analysis of delinquent *events* as recorded in Philadelphia police reports. Index offenses are limited to those involving theft, damage, or bodily harm, and omit many offenses which are primarily discovered and reported by the police, rather than by the victim or another private party. Juvenile status offenses are uniformly omitted as well.

Our use of this index to interpret CJI data does not coincide with the dicta put forth by Sellin and Wolfgang. Their procedure makes access to *original* police reports necessary to measure number of victims, dollar value of property stolen or damaged, and so on. Because Los Angeles researchers unfortunately do not have access to these records, we have been forced to fall back on the Sellin and Wolfgang weights reported on page 317 of *The Measurement of Delinquency*.[51] These weights were determined by scale analysis of the ratings of police officers, juvenile court judges, and university students. Table 4-7 reports the offenses and the seriousness weightings in the four systems outlined above.

In the ensuing analyses, offenses excluded from an index were also excluded from the analysis involving that index. For example, Sellin and Wolfgang exclude juvenile status offenses. Such offenses were therefore omitted when employing this index, rather than being assigned a numerical score of zero. Similarly, the analysis of any index includes in its data only those boys who would receive a score greater than zero.

Results

Several points deserve mention prior to a presentation of the major analysis. The first of these is that the four indices do *not* include the same base data. Because of the omission of various offenses, the indices are not equated in the number of offenses nor in the number of boys to be included. Reference to Table 4-8 reveals that the loss of original (CJI) information is least severe for Uniform Crime Reports, followed by McEachern and Bauzer, Robin, and Sellin and Wolfgang in that order. The magnitude of the information loss, in a sense, provides one measure of the adequacy of the four systems.

A second point is that each index is designed to be sensitive to differences above and beyond those due merely to number of offenses charged. All but the UCR index involve interval scales. The entire weighting and scaling process is designed for greater sensitivity than could be obtained by data suited only for nonparametric analysis procedures. Yet parametric procedures are not appropriate, because delinquency seriousness is *not* a normally distributed phenomenon. For the present the nonparametric median test has been employed, with the unfortunate result that some of the power presumably built into the indices gets lost in the process, thus possibly reducing their utility.

Finally, we might note that sex, race, and socio-economic environment are automatically controlled in our differential analyses of core and

Table 4-7: Comparison of Weights for Four Seriousness Indices*

Base Offense Category	UCR	McEachern-Bauzer	Robin	Sellin-Wolfgang
Murder & nonnegligent manslaughter	2	1.00	100.0	26.0
Manslaughter by negligence	2	1.00	100.0	26.0
Forcible rape	2	1.00	92.3	18.0
Robbery	2	.43	92.7	5.0
Aggravated assault	2	.72	83.3	5.4
Burglary: breaking & entering	2	.36	87.4	2.4
Larceny: grand theft ($50+)	2	1.00	72.1	2.2
Larceny: petty theft, shoplifting	2	.25	72.1	2.1
Larceny: all other theft	2	.06	72.1	2.1
Auto theft, joyriding	2	.61	72.1	2.9
Assault & battery, other assaults	1	.41	53.3	4.5
Forgery	1	1.00	—	3.4
Stolen property: buying, receiving, possessing	1	.06	—	3.4
Weapons: carrying, possessing, etc.	1	.00	84.4	—
Commercialized vice	1	.74	—	—
Rape (specified as not forcible)	1	.50	88.2	—
Illegitimate sex relations	1	.74	88.2	—
Other sex delinquencies	1	.62	88.2	—
Marijuana: possession, use of	1	.67	—	—
Narcotics & drugs: possession, use of	1	.67	—	—
Liquor laws (except drunkenness & drunk driving)	1	.19	43.1	—
Drunkenness	1	.19	43.1	—
Disorderly conduct, gang activities	1	.09	39.8	2.0
Malicious mischief	1	.06	23.7	2.0
Vagrancy	1	.14	—	—
Trespassing	1	.17	25.4	2.0
Gambling	1	.17	29.0	3.4
Driving while intoxicated	1	.25	43.1	2.0
Hit and run	1	.60	—	2.0
Arson	1	.10	—	3.4
Municipal code violations	1	—	—	—
Incorrigible	1	.77	23.7	—
Probation violations	1	.50	—	—
Association with narcotics users	1	.44	—	—
Truancy	1	.33	—	—
Curfew violation	1	.07	—	—
Runaway	1	.07	23.7	—
Other school violations	1	.00	—	—
Improper companions	1	.00	—	—
Lack of supervision or control	1	—	—	—
All other (except traffic)	1	.17	44.7	3.4

*The number of categories shown in each index is larger than the actual number of categories employed by the index because CJI offenses were classified as specifically as the most specific categories in each index. For example, larceny appears in three separate categories in the McEachern-Bauzer index, but all are grouped together with auto theft in the Robin index.

Table 4-8: Amount of Information Loss (In Per Cent)

	% Members		% Offense Charges	
	Core	Fringe	Core	Fringe
UCR	0%	0%	1%	1 + %
M & B	1 + %	5%	17%	19%
Robin	4%	13%	42%	41%
S & W	6.5%	16%	50%	50%

fringe members of the same gangs. To this we can add that the core members are an average of only two months older than their fringe counterparts.

The first step in the analysis was to assign a total Delinquency Career Score (DCS) to each boy by summing the index weights for each charge. Application of the median test yields differences between core and fringe groups significant beyond the .01 level using the UCR and McEachern and Bauzer indices. The Robin index yields a probability level between .10 and .05, while the Sellin and Wolfgang measure does not reach the .10 level. Each of these is a one-tailed test, and we seem provisionally justified in accepting only the UCR system and the McEachern and Bauzer system as being sensitive to the group differences.

However, these Delinquency Career Scores are a function both of the number of charges and the weights assigned to them. To eliminate number of charges, already known to be greater for core than for fringe members, we obtained an average seriousness score by dividing the DCS by number of scorable charges. A median test revealed that average seriousness is *totally unrelated* to the core-fringe distinction *except* in the case of the Robin index.

This raises the distinct and obvious possibility that the significance of the Delinquency Career Score differences between core and fringe groups might be attributable solely to total number of charges. If this were the case, then average seriousness and number of charges should be unrelated. Analysis indicates that this is true for all but the Robin index. Since Robin's average seriousness *is* related to total number of charges, and since the purpose of a seriousness index is to add an *independent* measure of delinquency seriousness, it seems clear that the Robin index is the least appropriate of the four.

As for the other three indices, their average seriousness scores seem to be unrelated to the core-fringe distinction, and the inclusion of the average seriousness scores in a Delinquency Career Score *does not increase* the differences attributable to number of charges. From a strictly practical point of view, there seems to be no advantage to employing these seriousness indices for intragang distinctions. There are also some considerable disadvantages through loss of data, as illustrated in Table 4-8.

One final set of data—the most important of all—should be reported here. McEachern and Bauzer, in their report, included data showing that seriousness increased early in one's career (over the first 3 CJI entries), and then levelled off. Robin also indicated a trend, though a weak one, for gang members to progress to more serious offenses. *Analysis of our data shows no such trend, either for core or fringe members, as judged by any of the four measures of average seriousness.* In fact, the Robin index shows an early *decline* in seriousness. It has been common among both agency officials and some social scientists to assume a progression in seriousness as a juvenile grows older. However, our data do not support this assumption (see Figs. A-1 through A-5 in the Appendix). This finding suggests as a practical matter that seriousness progression is an inappropriate baseline for the evaluation of the success of action programs. This point is particularly important because it demands a considerable shift in emphasis for both action and research in a delinquency prevention program. One such shift is suggested by an additional finding that the time period between subsequent offenses declines steadily, as confirmed by Robin with his Philadelphia police data; we can conclude that gang members get into trouble more rapidly, but not into more serious trouble, as their offense career develops.

Victims

Although newspaper reports suggest that gangs prey on innocent victims, those who have observed gangs at first hand find this largely a myth. Bernstein[52] cites a report by the Group Guidance agency in Los Angeles which indicates that 88 per cent of assaults by gang members were against other juveniles and 80 per cent against gang members. For Chicago gangs, Short reports, "It is probably true that most aggressive behavior on the part of even the most conflict-oriented gangs takes place within the gang rather than between gangs."[53] The 1969 report of the Pennsylvania Crime Commission, *Gang Violence in Philadelphia,* indicates that from 1963 to 1969 some 70 per cent (70/101) of all gang-killing victims were themselves known to be gang members. An analysis of nonlethal gang assaults during the first five months of 1969 showed the victims to be gang members in 81 per cent (66/81) of shooting incidents and 80 per cent (49/61) of stabbing incidents.

Miller's Junior Outlaws committed 70 per cent of their aggressive acts within the gang, with very few against adults.[54] Among all of Miller's gangs, 73 per cent of all assault participants were age peers of the same sex and 71 per cent were of the same race. "These data," concludes Miller, "thus grant virtually no support to the notion that favored targets of gang attacks are the weak, the solitary, the defenseless, and the innocent."[55] Through experience, the author has learned that when he receives a report of an assault by a gang member under study, *the "victim" is usually equally at fault* in precipitating the event.

Variations by Gang

Just as gang structures were found to be quite variable, so is the level of gang violence. Wise[56] has reported large differences in delinquency involvement among 14 Chicago gangs. Miller reported his Senior Bandits to have nearly three times as many court charges as the average for his five male gangs. Within the Outlaws, a "bad boy" faction accounted for over eight times as many known illegal acts per boy as in the "good boy" faction.[57] Short and Strodtbeck[58] found conflict behavior to be more variable than any other behavior category among the gangs in their study. Spergel[59] reported gang fights to be four times as frequent in Slumtown as in the second highest area in his study.

In Los Angeles, differences in assaultive offenses between four Negro gang clusters were found by the author to be almost nonexistent, but the resort to violence was much more "effective" among Mexican-American gang members. In the four-year Group Guidance Project, with Negro boys, there was one killing (half accidental) and a number of assaults. In the year and a half of the Ladino Hills Project, with Mexican-American boys, we had three killings and more serious injuries than in the four years of the earlier project. Queried on this, one of our Negro gang informants with a highly respected fighting reputation explained a critical distinction between "Bloods" (Negroes) and "S.A."s (Mexican- or Spanish-Americans):

> The Bloods, they know better than to mix with the S.A.'s. They're not totally crazy. Them S.A.'s are just bad. They don't be jivin'. Bloods don't care too much for fightin' the S.A.'s .... If you want to see a righteous ol' fight, you watch two S.A.'s fight, man. Everything goes. A Blood tends to have a little sympathy for the underdog, you know, but a S.A. don't give you no kinda chance.
>
> The S.A.'s is the ones that do all the shooting. The Blood tends to want to fight it out with chains, tire irons, and bumper jacks.

While the Chicago data reveal more assaultive offenses among Negro than among white groups, Miller found just the opposite in Boston.

Both sets of data reveal more assaultive acts at lower-class levels, although the Los Angeles data do not provide confirmation. All agree, however, that violence is a male problem; female gang members rarely become involved in assaultive behavior. Overall, we must conclude that the more important finding is not the consistency according to member characteristics but the variability over all gangs.*

Progression to Adulthood

Although the need is great, there has been no truly careful study of gang members as they move on into adult status. How many settle down and how many continue into "careers" of crime is unknown. Robin concludes from his work that ". . . these individuals were persistent and dangerous offenders, . . . a large proportion of them became even more serious adult offenders."[61] Miller has disputed this finding,[62] which does not generally fit with the fact that delinquency rates peak several years prior to adulthood. Elsewhere, Miller remarked, ". . . involvement in violent crimes was a relatively transient phenomenon of adolescence and did not presage a continuing pattern of similar involvement in adulthood."[63]

The fact that Robin's data were taken from police files and would therefore reflect the pattern of core members out of proportion to their numbers in the gang may explain part of this conflict. However, until a good follow-up study is undertaken, the question of the future criminal and conventional career patterns of gang members will remain a matter of speculation. Just following local newspaper reports in Los Angeles, I get indications that reaching the age of majority is no sure signal of graduation from a criminal subculture. Among our former subjects of observation we can now count a number of convicted burglars, robbers, and murderers. Some of these, we would have bet, would have stayed clean.

Project Failure

On a slightly personal note, it is interesting to speculate on whether some of these postproject "failures" would have occurred had there been no project. There is no way of knowing of course, although one

---

*We may consider ourselves lucky in America. Jocano's description of criminal activities among young adult gangs in Manila is far more chilling than the lowest grade Hollywood murder film.[60]

can legitimately extropolate from the project itself. Perhaps it is opportune, then, to examine the effectiveness of the Group Guidance Project, for here is where gang offenses and gang cohesiveness so clearly were meshed.

Appendix B (p. 321) contains a brief description of the analysis procedures employed in the Group Guidance Project, procedures which permit a comparison of the levels of recorded gang delinquency before the project with those during the project. As determined by our analyses, *it can be concluded that the Group Guidance Project had the overall effect of increasing the number of recorded offenses committed by the gangs included in its program.* While some qualifications to this statement can be made, they are not sufficient to change this overall conclusion. As judged by the criteria we selected, the project inadvertently led to *greater* gang delinquency, rather than to a reduction in gang delinquency.

Figure B-1 in Appendix B graphs the expected minus the actual offense frequencies for the control and project periods. Visual inspection of Figure B-1 shows that during the control period the number of expected offenses are greater than the number of actual offenses in 39 out of 48 months, while in the project period the figure is 13 out of 48.*

With the exception of the latter half of 1960 and early 1961, the control period looks good. However, the project period, as it must by the logic of our analysis procedure, looks bad. Although the variance is high and a smooth trend difficult to discern, there is a general decline through 1963 followed by a gentler incline starting early in 1964 and continuing through the remainder of the project. This decline and rise very roughly parallels the programming activity during the project, with the decline occurring during periods of heavier programming and the rise occurring when programming was lighter. This pattern mirrors gang recruitment, suggesting that programming may lead to recruitment and greater cohesiveness, and that these in turn may contribute to higher offense rates.

A police Inspector stated his version of this relationship very succinctly in a radio interview:

> The problem is this, that when the Group Guidance worker moves into the area to take over a gang that heretofore had not been organized, the size of the gang increases, the police problem increases, and it is nearly impossible from that time, then, to disperse the group. They're held together by this cohesiveness, by this structure, that is provided by the . . . worker.

*Chi Square equals 26.2, $p < .01$.

Occasionally, one of the older gang members also detected the unintentional role of the detached worker. One of the Operators was asked about providing opportunities for the gang:

A: If you build a center or somethin', that's just gonna attract more people.

Q: What if you pulled all the ... workers out?

A: I doubt, you know, if they could hold together. They feel like some kind of sponsor or somethin' gives them that extra drive.

In the interest of forcing considerations of the issue both theoretically and as a problem for practitioners, I will state the position clearly and unequivocally: The level of group programming provided for gangs is directly related to the level of gang delinquency—*higher programming levels will produce an increase in delinquent activities.* The corollary is also true: *a diminishing of group programming levels will be followed by a decrease in gang delinquency.* How this happens—the particular form of this decrease—will be suggested later in the analysis of the Ladino Hills Project.

Since these preceding statements constitute the heart of my argument, let me summarize the evidence briefly before moving on to the topic of the detached workers and their program.

1. A gross positive correlation exists between programming levels and delinquency levels.

2. Intercluster comparisons revealed more direct relationships, including the decrease in gang activity following removal of workers.

3. Intergang incidents changed in accordance with changes in cohesiveness.

4. High-companionship offenses, specifically, were increased by project efforts.

5. Recruitment patterns paralleled programming levels.

6. Data from the remedial reading program suggested an increase in core-member cohesiveness and greater involvement of workers with fringe members as a result of initiation of the program.

7. The greatest increase of actual over expected offenses took place at the earlier age levels, those at which boys *become* involved in gang activities and are drawn even more closely to their peers by the workers' efforts. The data reveal *negative* impact at ages twelve and thirteen ($X^2 = 11.1$, $p < .01$) and *negative* impact at ages fourteen and fifteen ($X^2 = 15.4$, $p < .01$), but there was no significant difference be-

tween control and project periods at ages 16 and 17. A similar trend was reported by Miller[65] for the Roxbury Project in which the offense increases among younger boys is almost 5 times that among older boys. As boys are drawn into activities in association with the program, they become involved in a higher level of offense behavior. As they become disenchanted at higher age levels, their participation in gang activities, including offense behavior, decreases. It may also be that receptiveness to counseling from the workers is higher at the older age levels, higher because of better understanding and a growing realization of the negative effects of arrest and adjudication.

The Group Guidance Project was first and foremost an *experiment;* its ultimate value, as with any experiment, resides in what it tells us about possible future operations. Three factors of particular importance are (a) levels of programming, (b) the worker transfers which resulted indirectly from the 1963 police controversy [see pp. 211–13], and (c) gang cohesiveness. If we take the data as suggestive rather than demonstrative, we can hypothesize that:

a. Group programming—especially in the absence of activities designed to "wean away" gang members—leads to greater levels of gang member delinquency.
b. Group programming leads to recruitment.
c. Detached workers inadvertently become sources or foci of gang cohesiveness, and their removal following achievement of this focal status will lead to a reduction in gang cohesiveness.
d. These effects will apply in particular to gangs of lower initial cohesiveness.
e. The effects on offense behavior will be particularly manifest among high-companionship offenses and among younger boys.

Finally, a quick summary would be that factors increasing gang cohesiveness, of which worker emphasis on group programming is one, will lead to increased gang recruitment and delinquency. This conclusion from the Group Guidance Project, when taken together with the findings of the few other detached worker programs to receive independent evaluation, suggests that the detached worker approach should be severely modified or abandoned. We must develop *alternative* activities to gang participation. The well-entrenched practice of using *group* process to transform group values and behaviors is simply not suited to the juvenile gang, or at least to established traditional gangs. The result of these processes damages both the members of the gang and society.

References

1. Frederic Thrasher, *The Gang: A Study of 1,313 Gangs in Chicago,* abridged and with a new Introduction by James F. Short, Jr. (Chicago: University of Chicago Press, 1963); William Foote Whyte, *Street Corner Society: The Social Structure of an Italian Slum* (Chicago: University of Chicago Press, 2nd ed., 1955).

2. Barbara G. and Howard L. Myerhoff, "Field Observations of Middle Class Gangs," *Social Forces* 42, no. 3 (March, 1964): 328–36; Irving Spergel, *Street Gang Work: Theory and Practice* (Reading, Mass.: Addison-Wesley Publishing Co., 1966); Lewis Yablonsky, *The Violent Gang* (New York: The Macmillan Co., 1963).

3. Robert A. Gordon, "Social Level, Social Disability, and Gang Interactions," *American Journal of Sociology* 73, no. 1 (July, 1967): 42–62.

4. Leon Jansyn, "Solidarity and Delinquency in a Street Corner Group," *American Sociological Review* 31, no. 5 (October, 1966): 600–614.

5. Gordon, *op. cit.*

6. Albert K. Cohen, *Delinquent Boys: The Culture of the Gang,* (Glencoe, Ill.: The Free Press, 1955).

7. J. Milton Yinger, "Contraculture and Subculture," *American Sociological Review* 25, no. 5 (October, 1960): 625–35.

8. Nathan L. Gerrard, "The Core Member of the Gang," *British Journal of Criminology* 4, no. 4 (April, 1964): 361–71.

9. Albert K. Cohen and Harold M. Hodges, "Lower-Blue-Collar-Class Characteristics," *Social Problems* 10, no. 4 (Spring, 1963): 303–34.

10. Francis J. Rigney and L. Douglas Smith, *The Real Bohemia: A Sociological and Psychological Study of the "Beats"* (New York: Basic Books, 1961).

11. J. Downing, "Cohesiveness, Perceptions, and Values," *Human Relations* (May 1958), pp. 157–66; A. Pepitone and G. Reichling, "Group Cohesiveness and the Expression of Hostility," *Human Relations* (August 1955), pp. 327–37; S. Schacter, N. Ellertson, Dorothy McBride, and Doris Gregory, "An Experimental Study of Cohesiveness and Productivity," *Human Relations* (August 1951), pp. 229–38.

12. B. N. Phillips and L. A. D'Amico, "Effects of Cooperation and Competition on the Cohesiveness of Small Face-to-Face Groups," *Journal of Educational Psychology* (February 1956), pp. 65–70; H. P. Shelley, "Focused Leadership and Cohesiveness in Small Groups," *Sociometry* (June 1960), pp. 209–16; J. W. Thibaut, "An Experimental Study of the Cohesiveness of Underprivileged Groups," *Human Relations* (August 1950), pp. 251–78.

13. R. S. Albert, "Comments on the Scientific Function of the Concept of Cohesiveness," *American Journal of Sociology* (November 1953), pp. 231–34.

14. A. J. and Bernice E. Lott, "Group Cohesiveness, Communication Level and Conformity," *Journal of Abnormal and Social Psychology* (March 1961), pp. 408–12.

15. L. Berkowitz, "Group Standards, Cohesiveness, and Productivity," *Human Relations* (November 1954), pp. 509–19.

16. B. N. Phillips and L. A. D'Amico, *op. cit. supra* note 19; Bernice Eisman, "Some Operational Measures of Cohesiveness and their Interrelations," *Human Relations* (May 1959), pp. 183–89; Warren O. Hagstrom and Hanan C. Selvin, "Two Dimensions of Cohesiveness in Small Groups," *Sociometry* (March 1965), p. 1, 30–43.

17. Leon Festinger, "Group Attraction and Membership," *Group Dynamics, Research and Theory,* Dorwin Cartwright and Alvin Zander (eds.), (Evanston, Ill.: Row, Peterson and Company, 1953), pp. 92–101; Annie Van Bergen and J. Koskebakker, "Group Cohesiveness in Laboratory Experiments," *Acta Psychologica* 2 (1959): 81–98; Hagstrom and Selvin, *op. cit.*; Eisman, *op. cit.*

18. Eisman, *op. cit.;* Hagstrom and Selvin, *op. cit.*

19. Neal Gross and William E. Martin, "On Group Cohesiveness," *American Journal of Sociology* (May 1952), pp. 546–54.

20. Cartwright and Zander, *op. cit.,* p. 76.

21. Lott and Lott, *op. cit.*

22. A. Pepitone and R. Kleiner, "The Effects of Threat and Frustration on Group Cohesiveness," *Journal of Abnormal and Social Psychology* (March 1957), pp. 192–99.

23. Sherif and Sherif, *op. cit.,* p. 242.

24. Gross and Martin, *op. cit.;* Sherif and Sherif, *op. cit.;* Leon Festinger, Stanley Schacter and Kurt Back, *Social Pressures in Informal Groups* (New York: Harper & Row, 1950); P. R. Hofstaetter, "A Note on Group Cohesiveness," *American Journal of Sociology* (September 1952), pp. 198–200.

25. Jansyn, *op. cit.;* James F. Short, Jr. and Fred P. Strodtbeck, *Group Process and Gang Delinquency* (Chicago: University of Chicago Press, 1965), especially Chapters 8 and 9.

26. Desmond S. Cartwright, Kenneth I. Howard, and Nicholas A. Reuterman, "Multivariate Analysis of Gang Delinquency: II. Structural and Dynamic Properties of Gangs," *Multivariate Behavioral Research* 5, no. 3 (July, 1970): 303–23.

27. A. W. McEachern and Riva Bauzer, "Factors Related to Disposition in Juvenile Police Contacts," in Malcolm W. Klein (ed.), *Juvenile Gangs in Context: Theory, Research, and Action* (Englewood Cliffs, N.J.: Prentice-Hall, 1967), pp. 148–60.

28. William J. Chambliss and Richard H. Nagasawa, "On the Validity of Official Statistics: A Comparative Study of White, Black, and Japanese High-School Boys," *Journal of Research in Crime and Delinquency* 6, no. 1 (January 1969): 71–77; Peter P. Lejins, "Uniform Crime Reports," *The Michigan Law Review* 64, no. 6 (April 1966): 1011–30; Marvin E. Wolfgang, "Uniform Crime Reports: A Critical Appraisal," *University of Pennsylvania Law Review* (1963): 708–38.

29. John M. Wise, *A Comparison of Sources of Data as Indexes of Delinquent Behavior,* unpublished Master's thesis, University of Chicago, 1962.

30. Richard A. Cloward and Lloyd E. Ohlin, *Delinquency and Opportunity: A Theory of Delinquent Gangs* (Glencoe, Ill.: The Free Press, 1960), p. 171.
31. *Reaching the Fighting Gang* (New York: New York City Youth Board, 1960).
32. Walter B. Miller, "Violent Crimes in City Gangs," *The Annals of the American Academy of Political and Social Science* 364 (March, 1966): 96–112.
33. Gerald Robin, "Gang Member Delinquency in Philadelphia," in M. W. Klein (ed.), *op. cit.,* pp. 15–24.
34. James F. Short, Jr. and Fred L. Strodtbeck, *Group Process and Gang Delinquency* (Chicago: University of Chicago Press, 1965); Wise, *op. cit.*
35. Thrasher, *op. cit.*
36. Robin, *op. cit.*
37. Miller, *op. cit.;* "Theft Behavior in City Gangs" in M. W. Klein (ed.), *op. cit.,* pp. 26–37.
38. Howard L. and Barbara G. Myerhoff, "Field Observations of Middle Class Gangs," *Social Forces* 42, no. 3 (March, 1964): 328–36.
39. James F. Short, Jr., "Street Corner Groups and Patterns of Delinquency: A Progress Report," *American Catholic Sociological Review* 28, no. 2 (March, 1963): 27.
40. Irving Spergel, *Racketville, Slumtown, Haulburg: An Exploratory Study of Delinquent Subcultures* (Chicago: University of Chicago Press, 1964).
41. Walter B. Miller, Hildred Geertz, and Henry S. G. Cutter, "Aggression in a Boys' Street Corner Group," *Psychiatry* 24 (November, 1961): 283–98.
42. *Ibid.*
43. Miller, "Violent Crimes in City Gangs," *op. cit.,* p. 108.
44. Miller, "Theft Behavior in City Gangs," *op. cit.,* p. 29.
45. Miller, "Violent Crimes in City Gangs," *op. cit.,* p. 96.
46. Thorsten Sellin and Marvin E. Wolfgang, *The Measurement of Delinquency* (New York: John Wiley & Sons, 1964).
47. Maynard L. Erickson and LaMar T. Empey, "Court Records, Undetected Delinquency and Decision-Making," *Journal of Criminal Law, Criminology, and Police Science* 4 (1963): 456–69.
48. *Uniform Crime Reporting Handbook,* (Washington, D.C.: U. S. Department of Justice [F.B.I.], 1962).
49. McEachern and Bauzer, *op. cit.*
50. Robin, *op. cit.*
51. Sellin and Wolfgang, *op. cit.*
52. Saul Bernstein, *Youth on the Streets: Work with Alienated Youth Groups* (New York: Association Press, 1964).
53. James F. Short, Jr. (ed.), "Introduction to Part I," *Gang Delinquency and Delinquent Subcultures* (New York: Harper & Row, 1968), p. 19.
54. Miller, Geertz, and Cutter, *op. cit.*
55. Miller, "Violent Crimes in City Gangs," *op. cit.,* pp. 109–10.
56. Wise, *op. cit.*

57. Walter B. Miller, "White Gangs," *Trans-action* 6, no. 10 (September, 1969): 11–26.
58. Short and Strodtbeck, *op. cit.*
59. Spergel, *op. cit.*
60. F. Landa Jocano, "Youth in a Changing Society: A Case Study from the Philippines," *Youth and Society* 1, no. 1 (September, 1969): 73–89.
61. Robin, *op. cit.,* p. 24.
62. Miller, "Theft Behavior in City Gangs," *op. cit.*
63. Miller, "Violent Behavior in City Gangs," *op. cit.*, p. 105.
64. Frank J. Carney, Hans W. Mattick, and John D. Calloway, *Action on the Streets* (New York: Association Press, 1969).
65. Walter B. Miller, "The Impact of a 'Total Community' Delinquency Control Project," *Social Problems* 10, no. 2 (Fall, 1962).
66. Lyle W. Shannon, *Juvenile Delinquency in Madison and Racine* (Iowa City: University of Iowa Press, 1968).

Part II

OBSERVATIONS ABOUT PROGRAMS AND WORKERS

Chapter 5: Basic Assumptions in Street Work

In succeeding chapters, I will report on detached workers as I have seen them—more personally and less authoritatively than might be expected of an academician, but more enjoyably from a writer's point of view. To set the stage, we need first to review what detached work is all about. What workers do and how they look at their world takes on some very special meanings when placed in the context of what the agency brochures claim.

Detached Worker Programs

The rationales and goals of gang programs were laid out in Chapter 2 as we described major programs of the past. Three major rationales were suggested:

(a) detached work is the only effective way to maintain contact with the "hard-to-reach" gang membership
(b) left to their own devices, gang members manage to mire themselves ever more deeply into a self-defeating nether world of alienation and deprivation
(c) the societal costs of gang activity, physical and financial, require that special attention be paid to procedures that might reasonably be expected to decrease that activity

Like most publicly financed delinquency programs, the Group Guidance operation was ordinarily justified on the basis of this third rationale of societal costs. The workers themselves however, justified their activities

147

on the basis of the second rationale—the status and needs of the boys—
while the "hard-to-reach" rationale usually emerged most clearly when
the program was under attack, at which time the rationale was restated
as a *strategy* in the service of the other two rationales.

These rationales unfortunately provide little direction as to useful
procedures to be adopted except as they suggest the need for a basically
active rather than reactive program. The five goals listed by Spergel[1] go
farther in this direction. As discussed in Chapter 2, these were

    (a) control (principally of gang fighting)
    (b) treatment of individual problems
    (c) providing access to opportunities
    (d) value change
    (e) prevention of delinquency

It is in these goals and their inconsistent status as goals or strategies
that we begin to get a real feeling for detached worker programs. In
the materials to follow—in fact, throughout Part II—I will be depending
heavily on our Los Angeles experience, especially that of the Group
Guidance Project. I hasten to assure the reader, however, that from what
I have seen and heard on visits to gang programs in other cities, much
of what follows is easily generalized to these other programs.

Strengths

The major strengths of detached worker programs derive from the
very fact that they exist to fill a service vacuum. These programs reach
out and contact youths who otherwise tend to slip through our social
service network relatively untouched and unaffected. Among those
youths who are potential targets, it is the core, the most delinquent and
most alienated, who are the primary targets of the detached worker. He
takes pride in reaching the "unreachable," in being able to maintain
contact with the boy who represents inherent failure for almost all other
social agencies. While close inspection reveals that detached work
has its own sieve through which various youths escape, it is nonetheless
true that the core gang member is far more accessible to this type of
program *than to any other* outside of an institution.

Other advantages derive from the general flexibility of detached
worker programs. Because the workers are street-based and privy to
confidential information prior to actual or planned street behavior, they
are in a unique position to shift gears as the occasion demands. Workers

are given a great deal of discretion in decision-making so that they can take advantage of their position.

A fine example of the use of such discretion was provided by worker H. After several days of "hassling" between the Generals and the Red Raiders, it was clear that the Generals would be waiting for the Red Raiders at 3:15 near a local school. At the Red Raiders club meeting on the eve of the promised clash, approximately 80 members appeared in an unusual show of strength. One might have thought there would be no avoiding of an all out gang fight, but I watched worker H. put together his counseling skills with his knowledge that most members were fearful and would accept a face-saving alternative.

It took two hours of discussion and harangue but H. convinced the boys that they should all gather at *3:30* the next day at a playground some *six blocks* away from the school. I went to the school at 3:00 the next day, and saw some of the Generals waiting. I then went to the playground and counted over 40 Red Raiders making *a show of strength which could not lead to a dangerous fight.* They were in "the wrong place at the right time," with some even claiming that the Generals were "chicken" and "poop-butts" because of their failure to make an appearance. No one, of course, had informed the Generals that the Red Raiders would be at the playground. The Red Raiders were thus able to convince themselves that they had acted nobly by being visible and available, but they had also avoided a serious fight. Worker H. had played a tricky game, and he had won.

There usually exists a similar level of flexibility with respect to intervention techniques, and especially with respect to the targets of intervention. Anybody whose activities might or actually do affect the behavior of gang members becomes the legitimate focus of worker activity in most gang programs. Thus, an observer who spends a few days cruising with a detached worker will find himself in contact not only with youths and their families, but also with local businessmen and politicians, police and correctional officers, teachers and recreation workers, caseworkers, local racketeers, rival gang members, employers and employment counselors, and so on. These contacts are made both on the individual level and in groups, in formal and informal settings. Sometimes a division of labor develops within programs in which certain workers may be assigned to employment, or community organization, but the overall pattern remains one of multitargeted flexibility.

Finally, although some programs may officially stress their preference for psychological or sociological or social welfare theory, most of them are theoretically quite eclectic. They borrow as the occasion demands from Freud, Parsons, Cloward and Ohlin, or any other theorist who can be readily translated into action alternatives. The theoretical parochialism that often hampers other welfare agencies is seldom manifest in a detached worker group.

Weaknesses

Some of the weaknesses of detached worker programs are just as endemic to their nature as their strengths are; they merely represent the other side of the coin. For example, flexibility with respect to client targets, intervention techniques, and theoretical postures often becomes extreme—to the point of lack of focus and inconsistency. Combined with lack of adequate field supervision,[2] this weakness often produces uncoordinated, unplanned responses to field situations. The detached worker becomes an independent entrepreneur who represents himself rather than an agency with a policy and philosophy.

In a similar vein, one finds very often that primary goals, subgoals, and techniques become confused, leading to a diffusion of energies and an unwarranted satisfaction with outcomes which are in reality the achievement of subgoals with ill-defined relationships to such primary agency goals as control or prevention. For example, one hears workers and administrators claim program success on the basis of numbers of youths contacted or number of group activities carried out. These are important achievements but they are hardly valid indices of attitudinal or behavioral changes.

Another weakness derives from the general lack of knowledge in the entire field of delinquency prevention, and the worker is the unfortunate bearer of this burden. I refer here to the lack of specific techniques for dealing with specific forms of delinquent behavior. An exception is the control of gang fighting in which worker visibility, the provision of face-saving alternatives, and truce meetings are accepted procedures for avoiding territorial raids and retaliations.[3]

Unfortunately, few techniques exist that are comparably effective with theft, rape, malicious mischief, auto theft, truancy, and so on. This lack of specific behavior-related techniques forces the worker to fall back upon general intervention procedures such as individual and family counseling, group activities, job development, and so on, procedures which at best have only an indirect relationship to delinquency producing situations.

These problems, plus the inaccessibility of environmental factors spawning delinquent behavior, give the worker little leverage on the delinquency problem. Gang delinquency is an entrenched problem in the urban slum, a function of the life histories of the gang members and the multiple reinforcing factors present in the gang neighborhood. This is no reason to stop trying, but it does suggest that our reasonable expectation for change should be quite low.

Another weakness might be termed the *paradox of programming.* To make significant contact with as many of the gang members as possible, a worker comes to depend to varying degrees on *group* programming, especially in large, traditional gang clusters. This programming may take various forms; club meetings, sports activities, dances, remedial education classes, group counseling sessions, and trips out of the city are common. The paradox, of course, is that these procedures designed for maximizing contact and employing group variables may have the deleterious side effect of increasing group cohesiveness and attracting new boys into gang activities. Most theorists agree that an increase in gang cohesiveness can be expected to lead to increased gang delinquency.

In reviewing this issue, Bernstein[4] has suggested that the burden of proof is upon those who would attempt to *decrease* gang cohesiveness, rather than use it to transform gang attitudes and behavior. Data described in Chapters 3 and 4 suggested that this situation has now been reversed; there is now good reason to believe that program activities that build up cohesiveness in the delinquent gang should be minimized by detached workers, even at the expense of some contacts with gang members.

The Group Need Assumption

There is a widespread belief that there is a *group need* among teenagers. In the gang area, this assumption is used to justify group programming or to defend it against those who attempt to diminish gang cohesiveness: "But these boys need a group—that's why they're in the gang in the first place."

Certainly there is much evidence in the psychological literature relating to affiliative needs of people. However, it is not a necessary logical deduction that there is therefore a strong *group need.* Even if there were, it would not follow that the particular variety of group referred to as a *gang* was a necessary, to say nothing of healthy, opportunity for youngsters. Those who are familiar with the structure of large, traditional gangs will recognize that they represent a *caricature* of adolescent peer groups; there is nothing "normal" about them in the usual sense of the word, normal. Yet the assumption that gang members need their gang is a prevalent one among detached workers and its acceptance leads to the unnecessary perpetuation of gang structures.

When the Ladino Hills Project was initiated, there existed a large central clique of the Latin gang that closely resembled the active cores of the groups we had seen in the Group Guidance Project. After a few months (and as staff interventions began to be highly visible), this central clique showed a rough division: the most delinquently oriented boys in one section and the boys who related more easily to staff in the second.* By the end of the sixth month, three rather distinct subcliques had developed: a residence-based group of a half-dozen boys, a group of boys attending school together, along with residence-based friends, and a "left-over" conglomerate of the more alienated or delinquently oriented core members.

I would maintain that such a tripartite arrangement is just as "normal" as the original larger clique was—perhaps more so, since we can specify some of the bases for the companionship patterns in the later development. Instead of saying that one *breaks up* a natural grouping, it can be said that one changes the context to one which *permits* smaller common-interest groups to exist without the pressure of external factors forcing an unholy alliance. If there *is* such a thing as a group need—and the point is debatable—there is certainly nothing in that "need" which specifies the type of group which will satisfy it. To assume the normality of a particular group form simply because that is the form of the moment is, at best, lazy thinking and perhaps more accurately, pseudoprofessional chauvinism.

The Transformation Assumption

There are two major avenues by which a project can reduce gang delinquency: decreasing offense rates per member and decreasing gang size. Impact of the first variety seems in most cases to have been negative. Impact of the second variety has not been fully tested to date, although I suggested some possibilities in Chapters 3 and 4 and in Part III I will report one highly pertinent field experiment.

It is clear at this point that in our gang programs we may have been barking up the wrong tree, placing our emphasis on offense rates per member without the tools necessary for the job (and without knowing which tools are adequate). Whereas enforcement agencies have traditionally approached this problem with equal blindness through such techniques as surveillance, visibility, and detention, the prevention and rehabilitation agencies have adopted the "transformation" approach. In this approach, several assumptions are involved.

---

*The reader may find a parallel in Miller's description of the two segments of the Junior Outlaws (see reference 5).

First, delinquent behavior is assumed, at least in part, to be the consequence of predisposing attitudes, values and perceptions. Second, it is assumed that these attitudes, values, and perceptions can be *transformed* into variations *not* predisposing toward antisocial conduct. It is thought to follow, therefore, that the primary task is to reduce delinquency rates through attitudinal transformations within the gang. The same reasoning is applied to the community agents: their isolation from and reactions to delinquent boys can be changed, and this change will lead to an integration of youths and adults in prosocial enterprises.

I suggest that this logical train of thought is fraught with pitfalls, primarily because the assumptions involved are partly invalid. The assumption of the behavior-directing strength of the underlying attitudes is a weak one—more of an American social science bias than a demonstrated fact. We don't even know *which* attitudes, values, and perceptions act as causes. We merely *think* we know.

Even if we did have such knowledge, it would be questionable to assume that these predispositions contributed more to gang delinquency than such factors as cohesiveness, poverty, educational and skills levels, police patrol practices, school practices, community attitudes, and so on. No study of which I am aware has successfully been able to separate the relative contributions to delinquency of these various assumed factors. If it is fair to consider that gang delinquency is affected by factors external to the gang, we must honestly admit that our control on these factors is at best minimal.

Perhaps even more questionable is the assumption that we can bring about a significant change in the cognitive structures of these youngsters, that we can change attitudes, values, and perceptions which (a) have been a decade and a half in the making and (b) receive constant reinforcement from the current environment. We place one adult in the gang setting, arrange matters in such a way that he has an average of only a few minutes of contact per week with each boy, and expect him to perform miracles.

The gang worker, no more nor less than the teacher or the psychiatrist, knows too little about factors related to attitude change. He has few demonstrably effective tools for change, and little time to use them. Yet when he observes change after three years, he is as likely to claim success as he is to grant the influence of other maturational processes. Thus he perpetuates the myth of effectiveness through transformation.

How can we finally demonstrate that general worker effectiveness is more myth than fact? How can we overcome our intense desire to say, in effect, "We are here, and therefore there must be change"?

First, we can look at the impact data. The Los Angeles data confirm those from the Cambridge-Sommerville study,[6] the Roxbury Project,[7] and the Chicago Youth Development Project[8]—equivocal or negative impact.

Second, we can look at the data on contact time between worker and youth and make a fair assumption that so little potential for influence exists that we don't even need impact data. Third, we could consider the worker's main stock in trade—*rapport.* The workers generally feel that their ability to induce change is directly proportional to the level of rapport established with the individual boy. A great deal of contact time is therefore devoted to the establishment and maintenance of rapport.

The Rapport Assumption

Two points are of interest here. The first is that the workers often *underestimate* their level of rapport in the particular sense that they overstate its tenuous nature. They back off from any action—especially in regard to their own police contacts—that *might* be interpreted by the boys as being on the side of the police or giving information to the police.

But second, and even more important, is our belief that rapport— whatever that word is assumed to mean—is neither so comprehensive nor so crucial as the workers usually maintain. They overemphasize *affect,* the feeling level, and do not understand well enough the implicit bargain relationship between worker and boy. The emotional bonds between the two individuals may in fact be quite strong, but this does not necessarily spill over into action—"I'm nice to you and I like you, so you should stay in school and keep out of trouble." If rapport is taken to mean a good emotional relationship, then we would accept the belief that good rapport is often established. But if rapport is *operationally* defined and judged by the degree to which it can lead to important behavioral change, then one would have to conclude that it is seldom strong. Too often I have seen a worker fail to counsel on a sensitive subject for fear of weakening or losing rapport. I am suggesting, very simply, that this reveals both an overestimation of the tenuousness of this relationship to the youngster and a miscalculation of the crucial status of rapport.

We can tie this discussion together by citing Caplan's findings in the Chicago Youth Development Program.[9] Caplan followed the parallel development of the worker-youth relationship over a 12-month period along with the level of worker "output." He found that a medium level of output brought boys up to the level of behavioral action or change, at which point the boys manifested "back-sliding" to a prior relationship level. The workers in turn increased their output or effort; this increase was followed by further back-sliding on the part of the boys. This whole

process even took place a third time. In other words, one can go just so
far with these boys—so long as they need merely buy into the worker's
verbal system—but that last crucial step, a behavior change, is not the
automatic end point. In fact, the threat of the behavior change is often
sufficient to cause a regression in the worker-youth relationship. Then,
as action begets reaction, the worker ends up spinning his wheels and,
sad to say, wasting his time on one boy when he might better turn his
attention elsewhere. In sum, the system does not work.

Although anecdotes can prove nothing, they can bring to life what
may otherwise appear rather dry generalizations of little interest to the
reader. The two reports immediately following were submitted by research observers and help to illustrate what *can* be accomplished when
a worked is not primarily concerned with endangering his rapport with
gang members.

> D. went out to the parking lot where the Operators were sitting
> in D.'s County car. They were quite boisterous and greeted D. with
> "It's about time—we were going to leave without you." D. replied
> (rather mild-manneredly), "I have the keys in my pocket," to which
> the Operators said they were going to hot-wire the car. D. said
> that the worker wanted to speak to Corky and Danny—so to go
> back inside the church. The boys replied loudly and belligerently
> in the negative—D. replied in a quiet but firm manner and opened
> up the rear door beside Danny. The boys started hooting and
> laughing at this and Bruno said "You think you gonna <u>take</u>
> Danny out there?" D. said, "No, I expect him to climb out by
> himself." Danny pulled the door closed and D. opened it again.
> At this Corky opened the door on the other side and got out taking
> off his jacket—Danny did the same—saying they were going to
> deck D.—calling him a mother-fucker, a shit-head—saying they
> were going to beat his ass good! Corky came up and stood about
> five feet away from D. with his hands on his hips—continuing to
> shout profanities and threats. Danny circled around D. to one
> side—doing a sort of dance step from side to side—in a half
> crouch—with his black glove on one hand. He was saying, "Okay,
> Baby, we'll fix you," etc.

> D. stood still—didn't raise his voice and told them, "This shit
> doesn't impress me one bit—just go inside—talk to the man and
> then we can all go home—but we're not going until you go in and
> talk to him." The other Operators stayed in the car but yelled
> encouragement to Danny and Corky. At this point, the two
> Diplomats who had been seated in the other County car got out
> and stood alongside of me (not as prospective combatants—but to
> gain a better vantage point to view the happenings). Rex Adkins
> and Chuck Hastings remained seated in the car; however, Mike

Asbury got out and came up beside me. He said, "You had better step back out of this before they fire on that dude. They may get busted for this but they gonna hurt someone first—if they pull a gun, drop to the deck and don't get up."

Further epithets were thrown by Corky, Danny and the other Operators but Corky seemed to falter—perhaps he hadn't expected D. to stand toe-to-toe with him and not back down. Corky said, "Well, anyway you had better not ever show yourself at the Park again," to which D. replied, "You don't blow any wind my way—I'm going back to the Park again when I have business over there." More names were called but the tension was broken and D. went back in the church followed by Corky and Danny.

This is not the sort of confrontation one urges a worker to undertake. It is doubtful that D. should have allowed himself to be sucked into this situation. But more to the point is that he lost nothing in "rapport points." In the next illustration, a confrontation works out successfuly in the face of absolutely no initial rapport—boy and worker were unknown to each other.

B. had taken a group of El Hunters to see a football game between Manual Arts High and Fremont High . . . . During the game he saw a number of older Centrals gang members in the stands. He talked to them, asked them to play it cool, not to start trouble with the El Hunters.

After the game, B. was leading his group along the cinder track when he noticed a group of younger Centrals approaching. B. had not gotten the word to these kids, and did not know any of them personally. Both groups began making remarks and a fight seemed imminent.

B. noticed the Centrals' leader had his name written on his sweater ("Captain Blood"), pulled out his Probation Department business card, handed it to the boy and said, "Aren't you Captain Blood? Do you remember me, I'm B.—from Probation."

Taken by complete surprise, Blood replied that he did remember B. and the other boys gathered around to read the business card. B. then quickly told the Centrals he wanted them to play it cool because the police were around, asked Blood, "Will you call me at this number Monday?—I'd like to talk with you."

Blood agreed to call him. B. left without incident with the El Hunters.

The above instance reveals a case of almost instantaneous diagnosis and prevention—quick, dramatic, and effective. It was helpful that, as we learned later from a three hour interview with "Captain Blood," the worker had indeed picked out a highly respected, highly status-conscious leader. The action was well suited to the situation. In the following case, failure to take action led to a near tragedy.

> On 2/22 a fight occurred between Ganzia Bolton and Arnold Barber. When Barber ran he was chased by Earl Bolton and Danny Younger, ending up in a liquor store at which point Younger cut Barber in the neck with a roofing knife and was subsequently arrested. A week or two prior to this Younger had used the same roofing knife in threatening student worker R. and two weeks prior to that Younger's knife . . . was used by Earl Bolton in threatening Mr. Brodkin (vice-principal at a high school). On neither of the two prior occasions was an attempt made to get the knife. In the R. incident, R., D., and worker B. all knew of the knife as did the supervisor soon thereafter. Methinks there is a lesson herein.

In the next two instances, the events took place in the weekly "club" meetings of the gangs. In both the question of rapport is involved detrimentally, a failure to build it in the first, a fear of losing it in the second.

> General discussion on getting a better "rep" as social club. Kids almost totally unable to put forth ideas on how to achieve improvement. After 20 to 30 minutes of frustration, the whole group turned to the worker with a heartfelt appeal for ideas and suggestions. He could have served well here, both on rapport and counseling. He parried, again turned question back to group, to fall dead.

> Discussion started on workers as finks. Boy reports statement from member of Operators that B. was reassigned from them to Generals because during a party mess-up he called the police and then led them to individual members' homes. This was a direct accusation—group requested response (remember that previous worker did fink). B. seemed to ask for affirmations of faith from the boys, but never answered the charge nor made a statement of his position. Any thinking gang member must go away from this meeting with serious doubts about B. There is a point at which nondirection becomes destructive!

In sum, then, I have tried to suggest very briefly in this chapter that the theoretical underpinnings of gang intervention processes are very shaky. In the absence of solidly conceptualized rationales and goals, the practice has become the theory and basic assumptions implied in the practice are equally questionable. The result for the detached worker program is clear—the program is the worker; the worker is the program. What he does, what he thinks, what he avoids constitute the form of the intervention. We move on, therefore, to some of the more visible components of the worker's action in the street.

References

1. Irving Spergel, *Street Gang Work: Theory and Practice* (Reading, Mass.: Addison-Wesley, 1966).
2. *Ibid.,* especially Chapter 8.
3. Frank J. Carney, Hans W. Mattick, and John D. Callaway, *Action on the Streets* (New York: Association Press, 1969), pp. 60–66.
4. Saul Bernstein, *Youth on the Streets: Work with Alienated Youth Groups* (New York: Association Press, 1964).
5. Walter B. Miller, "White Gangs," *Trans-action* 6, no. 10 (September, 1969): 11–26.
6. Edwin Powers and Helen Witmer, *An Experiment in the Prevention of Delinquency: The Cambridge-Sommerville Project* (New York: Columbia University Press, 1951); Robert E. Stanfield and Brendan Maher, "Clinical and Actuarial Predictions of Juvenile Delinquency," in Stanton Wheeler (ed)., *Controlling Delinquents* (New York: John Wiley & Sons, 1968).
7. Walter B. Miller, "The Impact of a 'Total-Community' Delinquency Control Project," *Social Problems* 10, no. 2 (Fall, 1962): 168–91.
8. Nathan Caplan, "Treatment Intervention and Reciprocal Interaction Effects," *Journal of Social Issues* 24, no. 1 (January, 1968): 63–88; Carney *et al.* (see reference #3 above).
9. *Ibid.*

Chapter 6: Aspects of Worker Style

Most of the material to follow is taken from the Group Guidance Project. While there was much in that project that seemed to parallel projects in other cities, the Los Angeles situation also had its unique aspects. At the very least, what follows is a description of one program in one city. At the most, it is a demonstration of what probably happens in many cities. To deny the generality of most of our data would seem unnecessarily defensive of the reader and cautious of the writer. To claim high generality would seem unwarranted on both our parts. If we can look at these materials as "what might be," then we can concentrate our attention on "what could be," or how to change detached work programs to meet their ultimate goals.

As noted previously, the Group Guidance Project had numerous goals and subgoals and equally numerous approaches to the achievement of each. Thus the workers found themselves exposed to many categories of both persons and activities.

With gang members, they engaged in individual counseling, group counseling, activity planning, club meetings, outings, and interventions with various social agents such as teachers, police officers, probation and parole officers, juvenile court referees and judges, recreation personnel, employers, tutors, and local business men.

With parents they engaged in individual counseling, group counseling, family counseling, and community organization.

With various societal agents they had to interpret youth behavior, maintain communication, seek permits, gather pertinent information, arrange meetings and events, seek services, offer services, and so on.

They had as their setting the street corner, the central office, police

159

stations, probation offices, schools, playgrounds, hamburger stands, pool halls, homes, Juvenile Hall and the court, and moving autos.

As researchers, we had to categorize these various activities, people, topics, and settings into a few manageable categories to facilitate description, so I hope that the following descriptive data will suffice.

Daily Activities

How did the workers spend their time? A *detached* worker program is so labelled because it is designed to free the worker of the usual agency- and building-centered activities so that his time may be spent with his clients. Accordingly, the popular image of the detached worker is of a young man in informal clothing, standing on the street near a food stand, chatting with half a dozen rough, ill-groomed, slouching teenagers. His posture is relaxed, his countenance earnest, and he is listening to the boys through a haze of cigarette smoke.

This is one of the few romantic images to evolve in recent urban history, and is therefore hard to give up. However, it does not fairly represent the worker—not in Los Angeles, Chicago, Boston, nor New York. The Group Guidance worker in particular would be overlooked if one were seeking for this romantic stereotype. Not only does his "uniform" consist of coat and tie, but the urban sprawl prevents him from spending much time on the street corner—there's not enough action there. He has to seek out his boys, usually by driving. He soon learns at what times of day to be at the school, the playground, the hamburger stand, the home, and the alley.

But even this does not tell the true story. It is still romanticism, not reality. For reality we must look at data, not myth—data such as those presented in Fig. 6-1.

Figure 6-1 presents data over the 19-month period during which workers filled out a daily activities form. One interesting finding is that, for the most part, there is considerable consistency over time. Activity was standard in so far as the allocation of time to major categories is concerned.

But what a surprise is contained in Fig. 6-1! The amount of time spent in the office ranges from 25 per cent to 50 per cent. The average is 38 per cent, or almost two-fifths of the time accounted for by the workers. Nor is this all—most of the activities included in the "Other Time" category are spent alone. They *are* important—traveling, hanging around gathering spots, and so on—but they were nevertheless unpro-

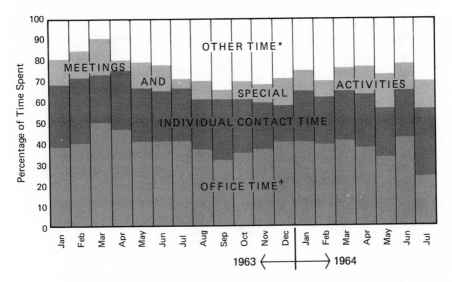

*Other Time includes "hanging around," informal activities before and after meetings, travelling and waiting by oneself, and other uncodeable items.

+Office Time includes staff meetings, supervisory conferences, discussions with other workers, office duties, and writing reports.

**Fig. 6-1: Time spent in four categories of activity,
January 1963-July 1964.**

ductive in any immediate sense. On the average, an additional 25 per cent is accounted for in this fashion.

In other words, almost two-thirds of the average working day is *not* spent with program clients, leaving only slightly more than one-third, or three hours a day, for individual and group contact with the program's target populations. Whether this pattern is typical of gang programs or peculiar to this particular one is not known. It is, nevertheless, surprising. *We are describing a field program which is in the field only 60 per cent of the time, and a "reaching out" program which makes contact only a third of the time.*

Because contact time is thought to be crucial—it is the raison d'etre of detached work programs—we must now determine who is contacted and how much. Figure 6-2 presents the data for individual contact time; that is, time with target populations excluding only formal meetings and outings or other special organized activities.

Once again, the findings are not in accord with generally held stereotypes of detached worker activities. Youth contacts account for

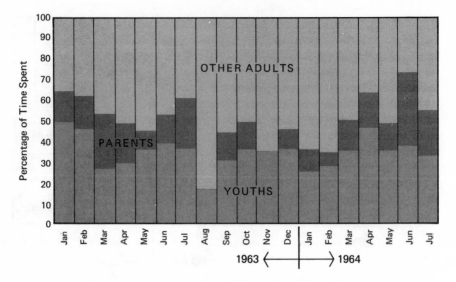

Fig. 6-2: Time spent in contacts with youths, parents,
and other adults, January 1963-July 1964.

an average of 37 per cent of the total contact time, ranging from a low
of 17 per cent to a high of 49 per cent. Parent contacts, the lowest of the
three categories, average 13 per cent with a wide range from zero to
36 per cent. Contacts with other adults are the most numerous of all,
averaging 50 per cent of the total. Again, the range is quite high, from
26 to 83 per cent in different months.

Although these findings may be unexpected, they are not necessarily unjustified. The Group Guidance program traditionally placed
heavy emphasis on dealing with community adults, especially those in
governmental agencies. One cornerstone of program philosophy was
that adults must be included if a genuine rapprochement was to be
achieved between gang members and their community. This was referred to by the workers as "de-isolation." Therefore, the preponderance
of adult contact time illustrated in Fig. 6-2 could be interpreted as a
verification that part of the program philosophy was well implemented.

However, I suggest that this is far too generous a statement (see
Chap. 7). "De-isolation," explicitly and implicitly, was *not* the common
ingredient of worker-adult contacts. This is not to say that it was altogether missing, for we observed many instances of successful "de-
isolation" conversations. But it would be unfair to suggest that the heavy
preponderance of adult contacts was a carefully planned operation.
It was, rather a function of the natural setting of the workers' activities,
their needs in working with the gang members, and their frustrations

derived from the continual failure of many youngsters to respond positively. Adults provided an "escape" from frustration.

Before we leave the data of Figs. 6-1 and 6-2, there is a further
implication which must be drawn out. We noted that meetings and special activities did not account for a heavy proportion of the workers'
time; the average was, in fact, 10 per cent. However, most of this time
was with youths, so we can consider this as youth contact time. Of the
26 per cent of the time devoted to contacts (Figure 6-1), 37 per cent was
spent with youths. Adding 37 per cent of 26 per cent plus 10 per cent
for meetings and special activities, we find that just under 20 per cent of
the worker's total time spent with his primary target population, the
gang member.

Whether one looks at this as an hour and a half a day, a day a week,
or ten weeks out of a year, this is a fascinating piece of information. Gang
workers in this project spent one-fifth of their time with gang members
(and a few siblings, cousins, friends or school mates from time to time).
With 50 to 100 gang members in the neighborhood, and eight hours a
week spent in contact with them, how much impact can reasonably be
expected?

It may be like squeezing blood out of a turnip to think that an
average of five minutes per week per boy could somehow result in a
reduction in delinquent behavior, even if it is matched by half again as
much time with some of the significant adults around him. It may be
foolhardy of the social scientist and the social worker to think that his
five minutes can overcome the forces that have been at work for 10 or
20 years to bring a client to the point at which he can be labelled delinquent, gang member, or criminal. As one of our colleagues succinctly
put it, "Just who the hell do we think we are, what do we think we've got,
to change all this?"

But the situation is not really that desperate, for several reasons.
One of these is that, rather than distributing his time evenly over all the
available boys, the worker tends to separate the wheat from the chaff;
he concenerates his efforts on perhaps two or three dozen boys, depending on the worker. In this way he may in fact have some impact on
specific gang members, but whether this is sufficient to be noticeable in
an analysis of the behavior of a 100 or more boys is a moot point.

A second reason for holding out hope is that group structure can
be used to spread the effect of individual influence. Through influence
on central members of the gang, a worker can hope to have an indirect
influence upon others. In addition, direct group work in "club" meetings
and special activities may have multiple impact from each intervention
(along with the dangers of building gang cohesiveness).

Third, the time spent with parents and other community adults presumably can diminish the alienation thought to cause and reinforce delinquency. If the parents can play a more direct role in their youngsters' lives, and if agency representatives can be brought closer to the everyday dynamics of boys' social adjustment, then some overall impact might be expected.

Thus, despite the relatively low level of contact between gang workers and gang members, there is the distinct possibility that over a long period of time, sufficient change can be introduced to show up in officially recorded delinquent behavior patterns. One must accept such an assumption if programs such as the Group Guidance Project are to have any utility or provide guidelines for future programs. This is a working assumption, a heuristic finger-crossing to justify further examination.*

Club Meetings

One of the cornerstone techniques of the Group Guidance approach was to "transform" gang organization into a prosocial club orientation. Although only 5 per cent of a worker's average week went into the club meeting, it was potentially the most efficient use of his time because he saw from five to several score gang members at a time.

The workers used the weekly club meeting to teach democratic values, procedural mechanisms, activity planning, and to reach the gang members with the program's messages concerning useful attitudes and behavior. From the boys' point of view, the meeting was generally a time for companionship, a place to go, and a way to seek help. At the same time, it probably was a show of strength and a means to reinforce "togetherness."

During periods of inter-gang tension, in particular, the club meeting became the weekly focus of attention. Attendance doubled or tripled. I have seen club meetings of 80 and 90 members on several critical occasions. In these rare instances the drama of gang work reaches its peak: the members are emotionally hopped up, yet seeking some escape from the seeming inevitability of an impending (and frightening) gang fight. At this point the seasoned worker brings to bear all of his resources —counseling, cajoling, manipulating, demonstrating—toward finding and presenting a face-saving device to avoid a clash between gangs.

But this is the unusual situation. Ordinarily the club meeting was a

*Therefore we retain in limbo the question of whether a great deal of contact would be sufficient to produce change. To be necessary is not to be sufficient.

rather humdrum affair, attended by an average of 17 members. Discussions, at least in the project meetings, were often apathetic, disjointed, and disorganized. Topics dealt with the payment of dues or election of officers, plans for outings or sports events, and past gang incidents. Counseling was often at a minimum as these inexperienced boys floundered with the concepts of group organization. Although the phrase "gang meeting" suggests excitement and emotionality, this was seldom the case. More often than not, they were merely caricatures of adolescent gatherings focussed around an adult "sponsor."

Because club meetings represent an efficient means of approaching the gang members, and because in many ways they epitomize a standard approach to gang work, the research team paid special attention to these gatherings. Between January 1963 and June 1965, workers returned forms on 181 male club meetings. Of these, research observers were present at 168. The reported data are taken from these 168 observer reports.

Among aspects of the meetings systematically recorded by the observers were the following:

Number of Topics

As with all other aspects, the number of topics discussed varied widely. The range was from zero (the boys merely gossiped among themselves without any formality) to 15, with an average of 5 topics per meeting.

Content

Topics were divided rather evenly—about 40 per cent business, 40 per cent activity planning, and 20 per cent deliberate counseling. Also, some of the business and activity planning areas were used by the worker for counseling purposes, so that a total of 35 per cent of the topics were coded as having counseling properties. This agrees closely with an overall evaluation of each meeting for its counseling content: the average amount of time devoted to counseling was judged to be just under one-third of the total meeting time.

It was, of course, difficult to make these qualitative judgments about counseling. The workers often said that just about everything they did in the context of the meeting was counseling. We did not feel that viewing counseling in such broad terms would be useful. We therefore decided to limit the designation of counseling to topics in the health, welfare, and educational areas, to deviant behavior, and to those instances in which the observer could be reasonably sure of the worker's intent to counsel. This latter could include a discussion among the boys which was allowed to continue uninterrupted because of its counseling value. Numerous discussions among the observers and the exchange of meeting assignments minimized the possibilities of observer bias, but it is still true that the research team's criteria for coding counseling were uniformly more stringent than those employed by the workers.

With this as background, we can also report the observers' judgments of the degree to which each counseling topic was exploited by the worker for its full value. The average exploitation level was 49 per cent. That is, in the observer's judgments, the workers made about half as much of their counseling opportunities as they, the observers, felt could have been made. Most frequently, this meant that a worker (a) failed to "pick up" on an opportunity, (b) let the topic's value get lost in the discussion, or (c) took a nondirective stance that left exploitation too dependent upon the whims of the boys. Of all aspects of the club meetings, this became the most frustrating to the observers, whose detached role increased their awareness of the potential of the gang meeting for constructive change.

Direction

Observers noted the percentage of time that meetings were conducted by the boys rather than the worker. Program philosophy directed that leadership should slowly but surely pass from the worker to the club officers. In 48 meetings, the workers maintained primary direction; in 60 meetings the primary direction was in the hands of the boys; in 33, direction was shared about equally.

Analysis of pattern changes yielded equivocal results; it could not be established that youth direction increased substantially over time. Rather, a relatively stable pattern quickly developed that depended primarily, not on program philosophy, but on worker style. Generally, the workers preferred to let the boys manage the meetings. No doubt this is one reason for the failure frequently observed in the counseling area.

Disorder

The level of attention or disorder in each meeting was "scored" by the observers according to the scheme below:

According to this scheme, a perfectly ordered meeting would receive a score of 0 while the worst possible score would be 16. Compilation of the data reveals a heavy preponderance of the scores toward the

Table 6-1: Meeting Order Scoring System

Disorder	Portion of Meeting				
	Entire	Over ⅔	⅓-⅔	Under ⅓	None
Severe	16	12	8	4	0
Considerable	12	9	6	3	0
Mild	8	6	4	2	0
None	0	0	0	0	0

lower end of the scale with an overall mean of 4.6. In other words, meetings were typically judged to contain only mild disorder during the bulk of the meeting. Severe disorder was the rare exception, and no disorder was often the observed pattern. Thus, as was noted earlier, the drama of the gang meeting remains more myth than fact; the data reveal the average session to be rather quiet and only mildly disordered by the restlessness and mild inattentiveness of the attenders.

So far, we have reported the meeting data in summary form, ignoring differences between the four clusters and their workers. However, as with many other aspects of their operations, the workers showed quite different patterns when compared with each other. Worker *style* shows up clearly in the way in which club meetings took form. With the exception of the average number of counseling topics, the range of the worker variation was considerable. As example, we can cite the following data:

1. The average level of disorder ranged from 3.29 in the Generals meetings to 7.00 in the Red Raider meetings (1963).*
2. Total number of topics ranged from an average of 2.7 for the Red Raiders (1964) to 5.6 for the Generals.
3. Number of unexploited counseling topics averaged 0.43 for the Generals and 1.50 for the Red Raiders (1963).
4. Average counseling exploitation ranged from 25 per cent in the Operators to 60 per cent in the Generals.

The specifics of these and other similar data are of less importance than simply that such a variety exists. Overall, it appears that the Victor's meetings were typically more highly structured, while the Red Raider meetings (1963) were the least so. More seemed to have been accomplished in the Generals' meetings in terms of number of topics and use made of them. The Operators' meetings were least productive of counseling opportunities.

The interpretation of these data is not easy, nor do I feel very

---

*Years in parentheses indicate that different workers were involved.

confident in attempting one. So far as program philosophy is concerned, pleasure or displeasure with these large differences depends on one's viewpoint. On one hand, their existence can be taken as evidence for the flexibility of the program, allowing each worker to proceed according to his own best estimate of the needs of his group. On the other hand, the observed differences could document a lack of a systematic approach to the handling of group meetings, a failure to adopt a uniform philosophy of intervention (caused partly by poor field supervision). The most appropriate interpretation is not revealed by the data; it can be decided only by an assessment of the requirements of gang intervention programs.

The observers as a group* generally felt that lack of supervision and feedback led to an overly permissive atmosphere in which legitimate and meaningful differences in worker styles and group assessments became unreasonably exaggerated. This feeling was reinforced in those few meetings which were attended by supervisorial personnel. The comments of the supervisor were quite devastating, although they did not lead to much visible change in the structure or function of subsequent club meetings.

Special Activities

Between January of 1963 and June of 1965 the workers reported on 241 events which we have lumped under the category of "special activities." These events were defined as all *planned* group activities other than club meetings. They included:

113 participant sport events (such as baseball, basketball)
 90 outings (such as beach parties, Dodger games, dances, dinners)
 16 service events (such as panel presentations, community projects)
 14 self-help projects (such as charm clinics, sex education films)
  6 truce meetings
  2 money-raising events (car wash)

Not included in the total are attendance at meetings of the Federation of Youth Clubs (two delegates from each gang) or sessions of the tutoring and remedial reading programs.

---

*Nine individuals shared the meeting observation tasks during the two and a half years of data collection.

With 241 activities reported over a two and a half year period, we come up with an average of almost two activities per week, or one every two weeks within each cluster. This shows a rather heavy emphasis on group activity, and along with the club meetings places a very strong group-activity stamp on the program. The average attendance at these events was 11 gang members, based on 162 events for which attendance figures are available.

In contrast to club meeting attendance, special activities attendance did *not* show a decided decline throughout the measurement period. In fact, if anything there seemed to be a slight *inverse* relationship: A decline in meeting activity was counterbalanced by an increase in participation in special activities. Our personal observations and the comments of the workers suggest that when boys lose their interest in club meetings, the workers lean more heavily on special activities, especially sports and outings. For the worker, these events serve the same purpose of providing continuing and multiple contacts with the boys. In addition, one suspects they help the worker retain his self-image as active and busy—fulfilling his role as a group worker. Without such group activities he is left alone in the crowd, without specific focus, without the opportunity for easy access to his group. The worker usually feels isolated as it is, and thus may "push" activities to avoid further contact frustration.

Because the various special activities were so diverse, there is little in our observational data that lends flavor to the description. We judged the degree of planning and organization, on the average, to be medium or high. In other words, the events themselves were generally quite successful *as events.* However, it was clear from our observations that the special activities were seldom used *directly,* as some club meetings were, for delinquency prevention. Access to the boys did not mean direct counseling (with the exception of playing according to the rules); parents were not ordinarily involved; community leaders and agency representatives were not often in attendance. Any major positive impact on delinquency would have to have been indirect, through self-discovered lessons about fair play, the value of prosocial activity, and so on. These potential gains would then have to counterbalance, or even overcome, the dangers inherent in solidifying gang structure through the mechanism of special activities for gang members.

Worker Styles

The next data to be reported are designed to illuminate two major concerns: (1) how uniform the performances of workers were and (2) how consistent the performance of each worker was within his own areas of activity. In the discussion section, we will attempt to delineate some of the major factors that may account for the patterns exhibited in the data. Our major interest is in the support the data might provide for either of two alternatives: that worker performance is primarily a function of each worker's consistent activity level or that it is primarily a function of the demands of the task at hand.

We were brought to this analysis by the startling variability in worker performance revealed by data initially gathered to compare workers in the Group Guidance project with those carrying on "standard" operations. The data revealed that the two sets of workers behaved very much alike *as sets,* but as individuals they exhibited very substantial differences.

During a four-week sample period, one worker reported as few as 34 contacts with his gang members, while another reported 211. Parent contacts ranged from a low of zero for one worker to a high of 47 for another. Among the project workers, police contacts ranged from 1 to 42, probation contacts from 2 to 60. Total time spent in contacts per day averaged 1 hour, 2 minutes for one worker and 4 hours, 33 minutes for another. Among the five project workers alone, we found wide ranges in activity (see Table 6-2).

Table 6-2: Illustrative Activity Ranges, Project Workers

Measure	Most Active Worker	Least Active Worker
Time spent in office duties	2 hrs., 19 min.	4 hrs., 35 min.
Number of youth contacts per day	11.5	3.0
Number of total contacts per day	20.2	6.9
Percentage of contacts in office	9%	41%
Time spent in contacts per day	3 hrs., 59 min.	1 hr., 2 min.

When one studies a field program like this and finds that one worker spends an average of 16 minutes per day with gang members and one minute with their parents while his colleague two miles away spends 94 minutes with his gang members and 53 minutes with their parents, one is forced to ask *why.* Are we faced with lazy workers and conscientious workers, inexperienced and experienced workers, easy neighborhoods and tough neighborhoods, or what? The rather complex analysis which follows was an attempt to answer such questions.

This analysis—and this one only—includes five project workers and five nonproject workers who had similar gang assignments. Because few differences existed between the two sets of workers, their data have been combined here.

The workers included eight men and two women: three Negroes, two Mexican-Americans, four Anglos, and one Oriental. While all were assigned to highly active gang areas, some were working with only one group, others with two or three. The gang members were Negro in the project area and Negro and Mexican-American in the areas served by the "standard operation" workers.

During the late winter and spring of 1964, the workers completed a series of reports on their activities during four one-week periods, each reporting period separated by three weeks (that is, every fourth week for 16 weeks). The *daily activities* form provided for a complete description of the worker's time allocations each day; the *contact report* form provided for a listing of each person contacted by the worker as part of the program. Included in the contact report, in addtition to the name of the contacted person, were precoded categories referring to that person's status, the site of the contact, the initiator and method of initiation, and the five major content areas discussed. Each of the forms was filled out at the end of the day or the following morning, mailed to the university, and checked for inconsistencies, errors, and omissions. In some cases, the workers were asked to revise reports in accordance with their original instructions.

Time Allocation

Time spent on the job (and accounted for on the forms) has been divided into three categories in Table 6-3. *Contact time* is that spent in the actual company of youths, parents, and various community adults in the furtherance of the program. *Organized time* refers to time spent in youth and parent club meetings, planned sports activities and outings, and so forth. *Office time* includes supervisory and staff conferences, talking with other workers, clerical and official reporting duties, and time spent filling out the research forms (this last item averaged 29 minutes per worker per day).

The figures given in Table 6-3 do not necessarily add up to an eight-hour day. Other allocations of time not reported here include travel time, waiting time, and "hanging around" (a common and necessary feature of street work operations). This time will be referred to as "unaccounted time." Also, the researchers were not totally successful in obtaining the full complement of forms from each worker because of vacations, days off, and resistance to or lack of involvement in the research. More than 150 worker days have been reported, 87 per cent of the total possible time. Days off comprise half the missing days.

Aside from these points, two factors of importance stand out in Table 6-3. The first is the high proportion of time spent in office matters —over three hours a day on the average. This confirms the finding on office activity reported earlier in this chapter. As noted there, it does not fit with the usual picture of the detached worker whose street work orientation and job requirements suggest a minimum of office-related duties. One of the supervisors was well aware of the problem: "God damn it, why can't I get to these guys? Why do they have to be reporting late or not going out into the area or not doing the job as they're supposed to be doing?"

A significant feature of this agency could well account for the high office time: The Probation Department exercised much control through supervision and written reports, which required the worker's presence in the office. Once there, it was relatively easy to find additional matters that needed attention. The nature of gang work, including its dangers and the host of frustrating circumstances that face a worker in the field, provides many reasons to spend a maximum amount of time in one's office.*

The second outstanding feature of the data in Table 6-3 is the great variance between workers, especially with respect to field time (contact and organized). Workers 2 and 6 spent approximately four times the amount of time in the field as workers 3 and 10. That the variance is less marked for office time supports the notion that much of this time is organizationally necessary and is thus less a function of worker motivation or the requirements of the field situation. The agency requires a basic minimum of office time of all workers.

What is the origin of this variance in field activity? Is it primarily due to worker motivation, as might be shown by consistent intraworker activity levels, or is it primarily a function of the requirements of the job and the needs of the individual worker's neighborhood?

---

*The workers use the phrase "hiding behind rocks" to suggest the temptations ever present to avoid active time involvement in the field. Examples would include "hanging around" schools and playgrounds known to be used infrequently by gang members, unnecessary visits to agencies or friendly adults, compensated travel time, overlong meal periods, and even visits to the research office. A research observer, assigned to a worker for several days of "cruising," reported the following example:

——— seems at a loss as to what to do on the job. He admitted to me that he knows only 8 or 10 Raiders at this time, meets with them individually or in two's or three's. Monday night he worked on his mileage expense report and then drifted over to (another worker's) parents' meeting. Last night he hung around ——— playground while (another worker) was meeting inside the club house.

It is to the credit of the workers that even more advantage is not taken of these many opportunities.

Table 6-3: Average Time Allocations in Hours and Minutes*

Worker	Contact	Organized	Office	Total
1	1-16 (19)	42 (19)	4-16 (20)	6-14
2	4-33 (19)	53 (19)	2-38 (19)	8-04
3	1-05 (18)	20 (18)	2-59 (18)	4-24
4	1-59 (19)	05 (19)	3-13 (19)	5-17
5*	2-31 (13)	54 (13)	2-51 (14)	6-16
6	3-59 (19)	1-08 (19)	2-19 (19)	7-26
7	2-30 (13)	1-16 (13)	3-22 (8)	7-08
8**	2-32 (15)	26 (15)	4-00 (10)	6-58
9	2-01 (16)	12 (16)	2-54 (19)	5-07
10	1-02 (19)	11 (19)	4-35 (20)	5-48
Average	2-21 (17)	0-35 (17)	3-18 (16)	6-14

*Number of days reported (number of returned forms) is found in parentheses under each column heading. For comparability, number of days used as the baseline for organized time is the same as that for contact time. Actually, of course, meetings and other special activities were not held daily. The numbers given under the heading "contact" refer to hours and minutes respectively (that is, 1-16 means 1 hour, 16 minutes).

**Because of personnel changes, all data for workers 5 and 8 are based on a three-rather than four-week sample.

If the answer lies more in the first alternative—general activity levels—then high positive correlations should exist between the worker's rankings in the various time allocation categories. Rank-order correlations were computed and revealed the following: (1) A significant correlation ($r_s = +67$, $p < .05$) exists between contact time and organized time; (2) field time (contact plus organized) is negatively related to office time ($r_s = -.70$, $p < .05$); (3) unaccounted time (reversed rankings from total accounted time in Table 6-3) is negatively related to field time ($r_s = -.84$, $p < .05$) but unrelated to office time ($r_s = +.33$, n.s.).

The positive relationship between contact and organized time would support both explanations. However, the negative relationship between field and office time supports the job-requirement explanation, not the activity-levels explanation. The third set of correlations shows the same picture. Unaccounted time is clearly related to field time, but not to office time. Assuming that the primary role-required behavior is field time, it should follow that the unmotivated worker in the field would also have a good deal of time unaccounted for. This is not the case. It should also follow that because he compensates for his low field time with greater office time (even though the compensation is not total), he should also compensate with unaccounted time. This would result in a positive relationship between office time and unaccounted time. The obtained correlation of $+.33$ is in the right direction but not statistically significant. This point is further strengthened by the limitation of office time compensation because of the presence of supervisors.

Thus, while the positive relationship between field time and total time initially suggests a distinction between workers based on their overall activity levels, the evidence to date does not support such a distinction. *The most appropriate explanation for the high variance seems to lie in more clearly defined job factors.** If this is true, then administrators of detached worker programs must be highly tolerant of variations in worker activity patterns. This is no place for the application of rigid time controls.

Contacts

Table 6-3 has already shown the considerable variability in average contact time per day. Further data allow us to be more specific about this contact time. Table 6-4 reports the number of contacts for each worker with three categories of people—youths, parents of these youths, and other community adults.

Since number of contacts (Table 6-4) and time spent in contacts (first column, Table 6-3) are highly correlated, the raw data presented in Table 6-4 do not represent an independent corroboration of interworker variability. The interest here is in the percentage columns that report differential contact ratios among the three categories of contact persons. Here again the variability is considerable, although nowhere near so striking as in Table 6-3.

The activity-level hypothesis would lead to a prediction of a positive correlation between primary client (youth and parent) contacts, but a rank-order coefficient of +.15 between youths and parents is not statistically significant. Another variation of this hypothesis would predict a positive correlation between parent and other adult contacts on the basis of consistent worker preferences for working with either youngsters or adults. The rank order correlation between parent and other adult contacts is −.51, and again the hypothesis is not supported.

Consistent with the reasoning and data so far, the correlation between youth and other adult contacts is a highly significant −.88, suggesting that contact allocations *are* primarily a function of the work situation or client preferences, but *not* of generalized activity levels.

---

*In actuality, of course, the two factors are interrelated. Less experienced and less active workers are less likely to be assigned to the "hottest" areas. For example, one of the less experienced workers was for a time assigned responsibility for the development of a new brochure for the agency, while a worker with high field-work motivation was assigned to three active gangs.

Table 6-4: Contracts with Youths, Parents, and Other Adults

Worker	Number of days	Total	Youth Contacts per day	Per Cent	Total	Parents Contacts per day	Per Cent	Total	Other Adults Contacts per day	Per Cent	Total	Total Contacts per day
1	19	40	2.1	53	0	0.0	0	36	1.9	47	76	4.0
2	19	138	7.3	58	47	2.5	20	54	2.8	22	239	12.6
3	18	52	2.9	40	11	0.6	9	66	3.7	51	129	7.2
4	19	74	3.9	55	22	1.2	16	39	2.1	29	135	7.1
5	13	59	4.5	48	22	1.7	18	43	3.3	34	124	9.5
6	19	219	11.5	57	45	2.4	12	119	6.3	31	383	20.2
7	13	68	5.2	47	8	0.6	6	68	5.3	47	144	11.1
8	15	101	6.7	66	3	0.2	2	50	3.3	32	154	10.3
9	16	81	5.1	36	21	1.3	9	121	7.6	55	223	13.9
10	19	57	3.0	44	7	0.4	5	67	3.5	51	131	6.9

Each worker behaves differentially toward these categories of contact people. The data showing average amount of time spent present a similar pattern, although not so supportive of the same hypothesis. (These data are omitted because of space limitations.)

One other source of understanding might come from the relationship between numbers of contacts and amount of time spent in each contact. The correlations present an interesting picture. Number of contacts and average time per contact are unrelated in the youth category ($r = +.16$), almost significantly related in a positive direction among parents ($r = +.51$), and highly significantly related in a negative direction among other adults ($r = -.81$). These contrasted figures certainly do not lend support to the activity-levels hypothesis. Rather, they suggest again that response patterns are a function of personal preferences for different categories of persons, differential responses to the needs of these people and their place in the agency's program, or reactions to the exigencies of the contact situations. Such a broad conclusion is of limited value, but these data do not permit greater specificity.

The final analysis of the quantitative aspects of contacts involves the *method* by which these contacts are initiated. Only 15 per cent of the more than 1,800 contacts reported are made by phone or mail. All the others are face-to-face encounters. In addition, 61 per cent are spontaneous (unplanned), and only 12 per cent are initiated by the other person. Perhaps more than any other data included in this report, these figures characterize a detached-worker program, illustrating their informal, personal, "reaching-out" nature. The raw data are not presented in tabular form because in the case of contact initiation there is relatively little variation.

The only major deviation from the pattern is the case of one worker of whose contacts 69 per cent were spontaneous. The reason for this special case was the heavy use of a particular street corner by the gang to which this worker was assigned. Located halfway between two schools and immediately adjacent to a probation office, this corner provided the worker with easy access to his gang members. He needed only to appear any afternoon between 3:15 and 4:30 to be surrounded by his "clients"; the consequent milling around resulted in numerous spontaneous contacts. Independent validation comes from the fact that the worker next highest in spontaneous contacts was assigned to the female auxiliary of this gang.

This lack of variability in contact initiation and the analysis of a single deviation from the pattern again provide evidence of the preponderant influence of environmental or agency- and job-related factors over worker activity. With the possible exception of time spent per contact, we must conclude that the "press of business" heavily outweighs individual activity levels in explaining work patterns within the Group Guidance operation.

Content of Contacts

The qualitative aspects of contact time—what is talked about during each contact—were recorded through the use of precoded content categories. For each recorded contact, the workers noted on their research forms from one-to-five items of conversation covered in the contact. These were selected from 142 available categories and were divided into four groups for purposes of analysis (Table 6-5).

1. *DA*—Disapproved Acts, comprised of 76 types of behavior for which, by middle-class adult standards, a youngster may be arrested or chastised.*

2. *AA*—32 Approved Acts, consisting primarily of nondelinquent behaviors ordinarily engaged in by members of youth groups, such as sports activities.**

3. *GA*—General Areas, consisting of 33 other areas revealed by an earlier content analysis to be common conversational items used by the workers. Examples include school, employment, finances, home life, enforcement, and judicial and rehabilitative agencies.

Table 6-5: Ranked Use of Content Categories for Each Worker

Worker	GA	DA	AA	Ack
1	1	2	3	4
2	1	2	3	4
3	1	2	3	4
4	1	2	3	4
5	1	3	4	2
6	1	4	3	2
7	1	2	3	4
8	1	3	2	4
9	1	2	4	3
10	1	4	3	2

*These behaviors include all the deviant acts used in Short, *et al.* (chapter reference 2).

**These include the remainder of the 69 items used by Short, *et al.* (reference 2).

4. *Ack*—Acknowledgement, referring to "passing the time in idle conversation," exchange of greetings, the handwave or nod, and the typical street corner gambit, "What's goin' on, man?"

Of the 3,454 conversation items recorded during the four-week study period, 58 per cent fell into the General Areas, 18 per cent were about Disapproved Acts, 14 per cent about Approved Acts, and the remaining 10 per cent were classified as Acknowledgements (of the four content categories, *Ack* was probably most under-reported, and the figures in this category are largely a function of the recording habits of the workers). Interestingly, this overall ranking, *GA > DA > AA > Ack,* held up among youth, parent, and other adult respondent categories (with the exception of a reversal between *AA* and *Ack* among other adults). The consistency of this pattern across contact groups is somewhat surprising in view of the different intents of the program in communicating with each. It suggests that in this area of analysis we may be dealing more with workers' "conversational habits" than with highly discriminating responses to various contact groups.

The remarkable similiarity of patterns, while it disguises considerable variance in terms of absolute figures, indicates that the reported similarity between youths, parents, and other adults is mirrored by a lack of interworker variability. When all factors are combined, as in Table 6-6, a further development can be seen.

The great consistency within each worker's own pattern is far beyond chance expectancy. It must be concluded that workers' conversational patterns—the gross categorization of their verbal interventions—are not highly related to their "audiences." Up to this point in the analysis, the data had supported the general notion that in overall time allocations and in allocation of contacts, the workers were responding to "properties of the field." However, it now appears that this finding does not hold as true *beyond the point of contact.* When it comes to the point of qualitative interaction—what is said to whom—worker interests and verbal habits may take precedence over distinctions emanating from the person contacted. Variance between workers and within categories of a worker's contacts has largely disappeared.

This question can be narrowed down even more by investigating the content of the youth contacts in accordance with Short's five factor findings.[2] The factor analysis of Short, *et al.* revealed five groupings of gang behavior items—Conflict, Stable Corner Activities, Stable Sex Patterns, Retreatist, and Authority Protest. Table 6-7 reports the rankings among the five factors for each worker based on a total of 296 content items.

One significant feature of Table 6-7 is the revelation that sex,

Table 6-6: Ranks of Four Content Categories as Allocated to Youths, Parents, and Other Adults by Each Worker

Worker	Person Contacted	DA	AA	GA	Ack
1	Youths	2	3	1	4
	Parents	.	.	.	.
	Other adults	3	2	1	4
2	Youths	2	3	1	4
	Parents	2	3	1	4
	Other adults	2	3	1	4
3	Youths	2	3	1	4
	Parents	2	3.5	1	3.5
	Other adults	2	3	1	4
4	Youths	2	3	1	4
	Parents	2	3	1	4
	Other adults	2	3	1	4
5	Youths	3	4	1	2
	Parents	2	4	1	3
	Other adults	2	4	1	3
6	Youths	4	3	1	2
	Parents	4	3	1	2
	Other adults	4	3	2	1
7	Youths	2	3	1	4
	Parents	2	3.5	1	3.5
	Other adults	2	3	1	4
8	Youths	3	2	1	4
	Parents	2	3	1	4
	Other adults	3	2	1	4
9	Youths	2	4	1	3
	Parents	3	2	1	4
	Other adults	3	4	1	2
10	Youths	4	3	1	2
	Parents	2	4	1	3
	Other adults	4	3	1	2

Table 6-7: Ranking Per Worker on Five Behavior Factors in Youth Contacts

Worker	Conflict	Stable Corner	Stable Sex	Retreatist	Authority Protest
1	1	2	.	.	.
2	2	1	5	4	3
3	1	2	3	5	4
4	3	1	.	2	4
5	2	1	.	.	.
6	2	1	.	.	.
7	2	1	.	.	.
8	2	1	3	.	.
9	1	.	.	.	.
10	3	1	.	.	2
Overall	2	1	5	4	3

retreatist, and authority protest items are almost totally omitted in conversation between workers and gang members. This obviously cannot
be directly related to gang member behavior, since all the gangs involved
do engage in all five categories of behavior. Rather, it would again seem
that content is more directly related to the interests of the workers. A
previous report indicated that workers found the Stable Sex Activities
factor to be the most common.[3] Yet it is the least commonly mentioned
in conversations with gang members. One final bit of supportive evidence derives from the fact that workers 5 and 8 were assigned to female
groups, yet their conversation patterns cannot be differentiated from
those of the workers assigned to male gangs.

In summary, conversations with gang members—the foundations
of counseling—seem to be responses to something other than just gang
behavior. This opens up a wide area of concern for future research into
agency policies, supervisory techniques, and worker habits, interests,
and values.

Discussion

Three major findings can be drawn from the data: (1) in general,
variability between workers in use of time is very high, (2) individual consistency in various activities is not high and thus cannot be explained
solely by reference to personal characteristics, (3) the above findings
hold for the amount of *time* on different activities and with different persons, but not for the *content* of the interventions with these persons.

The findings were surprising. Our contacts with the workers had
led us to believe that "there are good workers and bad workers." We
thought that the broad range of worker behavior that we observed was
primarily a function of differences first in worker motivation, second in
skills and supervisory practices, and least in characteristics of the field
situation. This opinion has had to be modified considerably, but not
only because of the above data. Our continued observation of the workers in the field and our exposure to the realities documented by supervisory personnel have also eroded our earlier simplistic views.

In addition, the data reported in Chapters 3 and 4 revealed great
variability in gang structures and in the cohesiveness of some of the
gangs involved. These differences between gangs necessitate different
approaches, and the differences in worker style reflect this necessity.

All this is not to deny the importance of motivation and habit in
explaining the work styles of these or similar workers. However, in this

area individual factors are not so pervasive in their effects as to override situational variables. As to the present data, several of these situational variables seem paramount.

1. Group Guidance policy and supervisory practice emphasized *flexibility* in field work style in response to each field situation. This policy did not apply to office time, however, because a large bureaucratic structure and the requirements of a governmental agency necessitated a good deal of paper work and other routine practices. This accounts for the lower variance and high allocations in office time reported in Table 6-3.

2. Gang structure and cohesiveness play a part, especially when they are clearly known to the worker and his supervisor. This matter depends greatly, of course, on the evidence about structure and cohesiveness available to worker and supervisor. When evidence is abundant, worker style is directly related to the nature of the gang. When evidence is minimal, as in the first months of service or when an inexperienced worker is not well "tuned in," worker style may be far less rationally related to properties of the field.

3. Community interest in youth affairs and community response to agency programs is also a partial determinant of worker style. When adult response is high, adult contacts take more time. That is, agencies respond to the situation and the initial response in the community, rather than developing community aspects of their program to elicit the sort of response required by their primary task. (This slight overstatement is deliberately inserted to force the reader's consideration of this reversal of agency goals as ordinarily stated.)

In contrast, the *qualitative* nature of the interaction between workers and their contacts does not seem to be related (or sufficiently related) to the characteristics of the contacted individuals. Why this should be the case requires some explanation.

1. Appropriateness of verbal interventions (especially individual counseling) is a function of diagnostic and prescriptive skills in conjunction with tight, on-the-spot supervision. These were generally lacking in the Group Guidance program as we observed it.

2. The nature of gang work generally leads to the recruitment of individuals who are resistant to close supervision and insist on being given a relatively free hand.

3. If these first two statements have some validity, it would then follow that personality-determined work styles would be most in evi-

dence when visibility of work is lowest. That is, work style will be highly responsive to policy and supervisory practice when there is a good measure of direct accountability. But individual contacts are not generally visible, and their nature is communicated only through the "filter" of the worker's perception and memory. The nature of the contact is seldom observed by supervisors (or researchers) so that cues to possible modification are minimal.

This is not a situation peculiar to gang work, of course. It is true of any organization or service in which either the product or the process of service is not highly visible or is not easily subjected to objective criteria. The problem is common to many areas in health, education, and welfare fields and in work consisting primarily of interpersonal relations.

Finally, a few obvious points for agency administrators: First, because gang work depends so much on the field situation, the first task of any detached worker and his supervisor should be to make a comprehensive analysis of community structure, gang structure, and gang cohesiveness. *Second*, the agency must build into its structure and program a tolerance for variability in worker styles. *Third*, far more attention must be paid to diagnostic and prescriptive skills in individual relationships, especially with respect to active intervention into delinquency patterns. *Fourth*, means must be found to increase field supervision—on-the-spot observation, analysis, and modification of field performance—and to reward worker and supervisor alike on the basis of field activity.

Supervision

As some of the comments above must make obvious, the role of the supervisor in detached worker operations can be crucial. Since this became clear to the research team just as the variations in worker style were emerging and capturing our attention, perhaps this is the appropriate place to consider this matter of supervision in some detail.

In his recent book, *Street Gang Work: Theory and Practice*,[4] Irving Spergel devotes a full chapter to the importance and the problems of supervision in detached worker programs. Citing three major functions of this supervision as administration, teaching, and support, he notes that

> . . . It assumes very great importance because of the complexity and demands of street work techniques, the lack of fully qualified workers, and especially the low visibility of agency structure, e.g., the absence of a building facility, office, or program routine, and the <u>ad hoc</u> nature of the supervision. Particularly under the area

approach, supervision in the street work setting has unique characteristics, with attention centered on that level of supervision most closely related to direct practice.[5]

It is this last phrase, "supervision most closely related to direct practice," that interests us most. It refers to *field* supervision, that is, supervision *in* the field, not *about* the field. Consider the phrases which have been adopted to characterize gang work—street work, detached work, extension work, and so on. These phrases or labels have been chosen by gang work agencies to emphasize the "reaching out" aspect of the operation. Gang workers are sent out to the streets, the playgrounds, the homes, and the hangouts of gang members precisely because these boys, more than any others, are reluctant to come inside the physical and normative confines of an agency. Without belaboring the point, it must be clear that the gang worker has to be out in the community "where the action is"; his impact on individual boys, groups, and adults in the community will be roughly proportional to the amount of time he spends with them on their home grounds.

If you want to know what a gang worker does, don't ask him—go with him: cruise with him, make the rounds, hang on the corner, watch him attempt to manipulate a gang meeting, and be prepared to give up your treasured nights at home. It's not an easy life, despite the freedom and flexibility inherent in this macabre routine. It is frustrating, at the least; at its extreme it is both potentially dangerous and conducive to emotional breakdowns. And by the same token, to be followed and understood, detached work must be supervised when and where it takes place. To be effective, *supervision must take place in the field.*

An information sieve exists between every two levels in a bureaucratic hierarchy. This sieve acts as a filter for information being processed both upward and downward between adjacent levels, and it serves the purposes of both levels involved. When line workers are *physically* separated from their supervisors, as in the case of a gang work program, the holes in the sieve become exceedingly fine. They are diminished by physical separation, by status and ego-satisfaction needs, by perceived threats to independent role enactment, and by a host of other factors that lead to the withholding of information. If the holes are to be widened and more information shared, line worker and supervisor must be permitted and encouraged to view situations together at first hand. Only good field observation can make this possible. I am talking, then, about common knowledge, not about close scrutiny; I am talking about collaboration in planning and action, not about one-way directives.

Supervision in the Group Guidance project tended to follow the pattern set by Probation Department norms, rather than by the exigencies of the field situation. With some variation between them, the three Directors of Group Guidance during the project period were quite office bound, tending administrative concerns, interdepartmental liaisons, and interagency connections. Their knowledge of the gang populations, the nature of the test area, and indications of progress and stalemates came primarily through the project supervisor and meetings with the workers: The sieve was constantly in position.*

By the same token, the line supervisors (there were two during the project period) were often confined to their desks by an abundance of rationally devised paper work of doubtful utility. Analysis of supervision time-allotment data during the last year and a half of the project revealed that the supervisors during that period spent less than 30 minutes per worker per week in direct field supervision and observation. Most of this time occurred at formal program events, such as the remedial reading program, so that little direct observation of street action occurred. One supervisor recognized this problem, felt strongly that his opportunity to be in the field was very inadequate, and constantly planned to increase his field time:

> Field time—had we started with some kind of precedents and had I had the time to do it, I would have liked to have been out every day for four hours at least, but there were other demands made of me at work.... I think I would have enjoyed being out there and I think some of the staff would have been benefitted by it, by my being out in the street more because they were looking for something to lean on..., when I first came they were looking for someone to lean on very, very bad.

But, somehow, it never happened.

The reader may feel that we are stressing this matter unduly, but after several years of field observation which allowed research observers to compare their information with that known to the supervisor, I find this matter of filtered information crucial. Let's cite a few examples.

Parent Groups

It was understood that a part of each worker's assignment was the development of a parents' group associated with each cluster. With the

---

*When, in the context of a project review meeting, it was mentioned that the research observers had noted the presence of the Director in the field only once during the prior year, the Director countered this datum indignantly, saying, "That's funny, I saw you three times." Of 168 club meetings observed by the research team, supervisory personnel were present in only nine. They attended only 5 of 49 special activities at which observers were present.

possible exception of one cluster, the time spent, techniques employed, and attitudes toward parental involvement among workers clearly militated *against* a successful parent program. Research observers became aware of the situation long before the supervisory personnel, but their differences in perception led the latter to reject the research team's suggestions for modification of parent programming. The following worker quotes are indicative of their attitudes:

> As for the parents' clubs, I'm on the fence. I don't think they should be used as pressure groups in the community, but we may have something in them if they're turned to discussing the kids' behavior and how the family unit operates. Parents should exchange experiences, become aware that they all have common problems—that their problems aren't unique—and share whatever solutions they might have found. But their main value might be in getting the parents to have more understanding of their kids' behavior. As I say, I haven't made up my mind on that yet.

> Mrs. Jourard* called to ask me my business in the area. I explained .... She thought this was good. She explained that she allowed the boys to meet at her home regularly. They played cards and kidded around with her daughters. She said she felt she did her bit in keeping the boys off the street. She also stated that I could count on her for help in dinners and so on.

> I called his Dad up and I (laugh), I just put the phone on the desk for about ten minutes, and when he got through runnin' off his mouth I picked it up and said, 'I gotta go, you see, and I'll be over to talk' and hung up.

> Parents' groups are no good. They're just social groups. You can't get them to be effective in the neighborhood.

> Two weeks ago I sent out 75 letters to parents. I told 'em the whole bit would fold up unless they showed they wanted to support the program by coming to the next meeting. Two parents showed up.

Counseling Opportunities

Although there was always *some* confusion over the official Group Guidance policies concerning counseling and other direct intervention procedures, it existed more because of lack of examples than because of any lack in stated policy. Because the workers seldom had the opportunity to observe others at work, and seldom received on-the-spot feedback from field supervision, they were left to their own devices (or lack of them). In club meetings, in particular, research observers became

---

*All names are pseudonyms.

highly frustrated time and again as they saw good counseling opportunities go by the board. Nor was this simply a matter of unrealistically high expectations, for note what happens when the supervisor *is* present:

2/17/65:   Worker indicates that since the pullout from official group
            qua group activities with the group, he has also avoided
            counseling situations with them, claiming that he felt
            uncertain as to whether he was to continue even individual
            contacts. Supervisor is certain this is just an excuse.
            El Taco has long been known as a major hangout for the
            group. Asked how often he had been in El Taco, worker
            replied "once." Asked why, he said he could not think of a
            legitimate reason to enter it.
                          (Research Observer notes, supervisory conference)

5/19/65:   Worker was questioned about any possible counseling on
            relationships with girls. He said that he deliberately avoids
            all questioning and counseling on boy-girl relations for
            several reasons: he feels it is inappropriate for him to probe
            in such a private area; that it is not his business; that he
            is not there to counsel on sex relations. The only time he
            will do this is if the boy himself opens the door and seeks
            advice. In addition, he feels that he will lose rapport if he
            dabbles in 'such a sensitive area' and might even be seen
            as attempting to cut in on a good thing.
                          (Research Observer's notes, supervisory conference)

10/16/65:   Supervisor has been doubtful of worker's ability at
            counseling kids and dealing with adults, but after attending
            ... meeting last week he also has some doubts re worker's
            sincerity with kids. Supervisor noted that the kids don't
            seem to respect worker, don't look at him when they talk
            to him, don't seem to listen to him when he speaks.
                          (Research Observer's notes, conversation with supervisor)

In each of these instances, the supervisor became aware of the situation from the three-way discussion between worker, researcher, and himself, and took immediate steps to advise the worker and help him handle these problems more effectively.

Numerous further examples could be cited, but only at the risk of too much negativism. The point here is that, in the absence of supervisory observation in the field, any worker is likely to take the easy road, or the road most likely to lead to a *comfortable* response rather than a *confrontive* response. When the supervisor is on top of the field situation, however, the workers have a greater opportunity to demonstrate their skills, experiment with untried techniques and learn new approaches.

Psychiatric Counseling

An example of what can happen when a supervisor is *not* sympathetic to an idea is cited below.

2/15/65:   Occasion: meeting between supervisor, four workers, and Dr. R., Psychiatrist at the Central City Community Mental Health Center. The meeting was arranged by the community organizer to look into the possibilities of group therapy for kids in the program.

Unless there is considerable follow up, the whole thing will be a bust for the following reasons:

1. Late arrival due to wrong address given by supervisor in spite of his being advised of the correct address at several points.

2. Organizer's inadequate explanation of the program and kids to Drs. C. and R.; for example: all the kids are on probation and therefore could be ordered into groups; for example: that these are regular probation officers, not street workers; for example: since the kids are on probation the County could pay for the therapy.

3. Supervisor put the damper on the theory early in the meeting obviously not wanting to get involved in a new program development, but using money angle as an excuse. It was the observer who reminded the participants of the $2,000 available for these purposes. Supervisor did not think of it; organizer did not remember it.

4. The inflexible psychiatrist, Dr. R., who wants $5.00 per kid per session for the Clinic, constant attendance, deeply disturbed and therapy-motivated kids. He seems unwilling to change any aspect of his program for this special venture.

5. The workers', and especially supervisor's unwillingness to solve the transportation and money problems. (Dr. R. says the groups must be run at the church.)

6. The session would have lasted only 30 minutes had the observer not directly intervened (tch, tch) to express his surprise that all concerned were going to turn down the

program so quickly. This had the effect of triggering (worker) who definitely wanted to take advantage of the program and resulted in another 30 minutes of hopeful sounding discussion.

Follow through by supervisor, any one worker, organizer or the psychiatrist could lead to a useful activity. The question is, is anyone going to follow through?

Note: Organizer is leaving the program at the end of this week.   (From Research Observer's notes)

As the observer feared, no follow-up took place and the opportunity to explore avenues toward therapeutic consultation was lost. The blame lies only in part on the level of commitment of the personnel involved. For the most part, an inappropriate bureaucratic structure is to blame—a structure ill-suited to a flexible field program and unable to adjust to the supervisory practices called for by a street work program.

Gang programs should not be run from an office, nor burdened with reporting procedures that have nothing directly to do with the understanding of and accountability for field practice. The supervisor *must* be on the street. In the Chicago Youth Development Project, the workers knew that at any time, any place, they were likely to come upon the program director. In the YMCA gang program in Chicago, supervisors were asked to carry a small group of their own in order to ensure constant contact with field problems. While this latter system may be so extreme as to be dysfunctional, it does emphasize the importance of the entire matter. This is a case in which familiarity breeds, not contempt, but effective collaborative action.*

Worker Attitudes and Programming

Field supervision in the Group Guidance Project was minimal. This meant that, to a greater extent than is normally the case in gang programs, the level and nature of programming was very often determined by the workers themselves. Their decisions were based upon their esti-

---

*The problem addressed here is not unique to Group Guidance. In his study of the New York City Youth Board, Gannon states, "These findings do not coincide with the concept of supervision we get from Youth Board publications. If workers eventually feel certain ambiguities in their roles, one wonders how much of this could be avoided by more careful and purposeful supervision. . . ."[6]

mates of need, upon response to their activities, and upon their own attitudes toward various alternative activities. Because there was seldom enough time in the field to do everything, each worker had to set priorities within the policy guidelines of the Group Guidance program—and occasionally without reference to these guidelines.*

Given something less than a highly structured policy, and given a minimum of field supervision, it is clear that an adequate description of the test area program cannot be made without reference to the workers' own predispositions. The *de facto* program must be considered, not the program one might read in a brochure. Now that we have considered the actual field behavior of the workers, we can increase our understanding of this behavior by viewing some of the supposedly critical program components as the *workers* viewed them. This provides a somewhat different perspective on the problems they faced, including those they surmounted and those they did not.

An illustration of the "anti–Group Guidance" sentiment often found in the community is provided below to set the stage for the following discussion. The Group Guidance Director reported the following excerpts from a phone conversation on 2/28/63 with a volunteer coach at H. Playground, chairman of the Managers and Coaches Association:

> All Group Guidance does is entertain hoodlums—takes them on treats, trips to the mountains, beach, Pacific Ocean Park, puts on dances, etc.—Period. Ain't nobody doing anything like that for decent kids in the community.

> Kids tell me, "I can go to the beach with Group Guidance." Also they tell me, "Those Group Guidance men are dumb fools; they take us places, man, and buy us cokes and hot dogs, take us to shows and put on dances for us—and we don't have to do nothin' for it."

> These kids need to be straightened out. They need discipline; they need training. What is Group Guidance doing to learn 'em a trade? Nothin'—not a damn thing. Just dances, games, sports, beaches, <u>treating</u> them—and 5 years later they're still hoodlums. Only thing is they've killed a few decent people—beat up a few decent kids, raped a few women.

> Group Guidance should have some retraining schools where these kids could be sent. Send 'em away for a while until they learn how to behave. Train 'em in a useful trade.

---

*Gannon (reference 6) writes cogently about this problem: "One gets the feeling that the workers are rather confused about the limits of their jobs." See pp. 54–55 and 59–61.

They come around the playground and right away they take over. . . . No decent kid will come to the playground any more. Why should we let those hoods take over a good playground so decent kids can't use it?

Up at the school, B. and G. are sponsoring a dance tonight. I talked to Sgt. S. of the LAPD, they don't like it; he said he'd go over and see what is going on over there.

I've watched these kids and I don't see no change. I'm not against rehabilitation but what has Group Guidance got to show for 20 years of work? Can you name one Negro kid who has changed for the better under the Group Guidance program? I asked C. that last year and he couldn't name one. See what I mean? I'd like to see some results, period.

Now what are you going to do about it? Are you going to put some teeth in it or are you going to let them continue to cater to these hoods and coddle them and treat them like kings and do things for them that nobody's doing for the decent kids in the community? If we'd get together and plan a good program we could straighten 'em out. Now in the army we had some of those guys and we didn't take any thing off of them. We put 'em to work and gave 'em a little discipline. That's what your hoods need—discipline!

Your Group Guidance men organize 'em and protect them and put 'em in the community and let them terrorize women and children, bust up decent programs—and do nothin' to retrain them and make good citizens out of them. It's worse than a waste of tax money—I do believe the Group Guidance people are promoting gangs so as to perpetuate their jobs. Now that's a hell of a thing to do. People like that ought to be fired! Period.*

Employment

There is no question but that the employment and training opportunities in and around the project area were limited. The war on poverty had not yet made significant progress, and there were no major industries in the area. In employment, these youngsters already had four strikes against them: they were Negro, they were untrained, they were young, and they were gang members.

Q: What's your feeling about the availability of jobs in the area?

A: Practically nil, that's what I think. There are just so many car washes, you know.

---

*This quote was slightly edited for readability.

A: None. My own advice is "Well, see the employment people."
      I'll take kids to go see about it if they've got a specific
      address. I don't go off wandering to some undisclosed
      destination. I've taken some kids to various locations, but
      they never got the jobs.

A: Well, something between ten and fifteen jobs have come
      my way; but I've never seen a kid employed because of this.

A: Frisco got his job through the employment office—first time
      I ever heard of a guy getting a job from an employment office.

These quotes describe a rather frustrating situation—frustrating to
the boys, to the workers, and to the community at large. But some jobs
were found, and a few training opportunities did develop. The Group
Guidance Research Committee assigned to one of its members the
responsibility of looking into such larger situations as MDTA and OMAT,
but no consistent follow-up was undertaken.

However, we would be remiss were we to mention only one side
of the story—the lack of opportunity. We noted earlier that the workers
had to fix informal priorities on their various alternative activities. Rather
uniformly, they gave surprisingly low priority to employment—or at least,
to *direct* involvement in seeking job openings.

Well, a lot of them just go walking the streets. I usually try to give
them some direction, like a look in the paper every morning . . . .
Usually I don't get so much involved in taking the kids looking
for a job as to telling them how to go about looking, because I find
that you can waste a lot of time that way. Because a lot of times
you push a kid to get a job and he don't really want one.

Well, I'd ask individuals, you know, about a job or hear that
they're using kids in training and this kind of thing. It's been no
specific job-finding kind of program. (Have you any idea, when
you make these referrals, how many of these kids actually get
a job?) No, I don't have any idea.

I got jobs for only two members. Lots of others wanted jobs, but I
didn't know of jobs around 'cause I had no resources.

This has been the kind of counseling—"You gotta get up and go."
Because if you take a kid and he doesn't want to really go he
hasn't really done anything anyway; and you may set up a job
and a man is waiting for a boy and he's just not ready. But I think
that when he begins to initiate the contact he's showing quite a
bit of interest and . . . there's a possibility of his being just a little
more ready than he would be if you were taking him. So this is
what I depend on more than anything else.

My belief has always been one of "Well, if you're looking for a job, why don't you try over there. If you want to, if you don't, well that's all right." You always end up in a bind if you tell a kid specifically that he can get hired here, and it doesn't work out he comes to you. If a guy gets hired and he fucks up, his employer comes to you. I don't need that.

The other pattern—the worker who gives high priority to employment only to run up against a blank wall—is equally devastating:

Lucius. There's been a lousy, miserable failure with Lucius. He's so believing and trusting in me I get embarrassed and ashamed. Outside of a little penny-ante job that I got . . . for he and Herbie, you know, one shot—that kind of thing—outside of my personally paying them for doing yard work for me, our relationship has been a counseling one. I've counseled the living daylights out of him so he's ready, so he's motivated—so I don't have anything.

Schools

If the employment situation is complex, it is but a simple anagram compared to the jigsaw puzzle of the school situation. Most gang members are either behind in school or are dropouts. They tend to receive little educational support in the home, nor do they win any popularity contests with their teachers. Vice principals are seen as "junior cops" and they in turn view the gang member not as a student but as an unwelcome disrupter of the daily routine.

Under the circumstances, should workers strive to return dropouts to school? Should they seek transfers to other schools? Is the frustration of the school experience worth the unlikely possibility that the boy can "make it" and receive his diploma? With some exceptions among the workers, the answer to each question was a qualified *no*. The sentiments below may express valid attitudes, but by and large the *actions* of the workers were in opposition to these statements.

I convinced five kids to go back to school—night school. I don't push education on the kids, if they're not for it themselves. But I do stress vocational training a little more.

You know, you don't punish them by kicking them out . . . . These guys are all messing up so that they can be suspended from school legally. They can lay around the park that way.

You have to realize you're not dealing with future doctors, lawyers, engineers. What's so great about getting a kid back in school, if he really doesn't belong there? You're doing both the kid and the school a disservice.

Here indeed is a case in which action speaks louder than words, for a youngster who brought a school problem to a worker was more likely than not to receive help.

> She had been suspended for excessive absences ... so I spoke to (the vice principal) about her. She accepted the girl back in. She'd had a baby and the baby was sick.

> Mr. Blaylock was reminded of the earlier agreement some months ago that if Benny completed the summer school program elsewhere and successfully, Benny would be allowed to re-enroll .... Mr. Blaylock reviewed the boy's report card and informed Benny that he could re-enroll this week.

Many similar instances could be cited to demonstrate that intervention on behalf of particular individuals was rather consistently undertaken *when the youngster indicated the need.* On the other hand, relatively little attempt was made to intervene in the abstract, that is, to develop a collaborative program or procedure for dealing with gang members with school problems. As data will show in Chapter 7, the workers tended to rely on personal relationships, selling themselves but not their program.

> I felt real happy around that school. I'm always welcome and always called on to come over. ... It's fun to go to a school where they recognize you and they want you.

> He has on several occasions called me instead of the police when (group members) are involved. We have handled problems without need for court adjudication.

But the problems are often too large, too complex to be handled in this fashion. They require a more coordinated effort, a collaboration between agencies as well as between agents.

> Only 40 per cent of the Generals are currently attending school, and of this figure approximately 50 per cent are attending special behavior schools.

> Mr. Lawrence and Mrs. Hatch gave surface acceptance to the program, although Mr. Lawrence stated that he would not attend a parent-youth banquet to which he had been invited because "I don't want people to think I am either for Group Guidance or for the police."

The schools have no identity. This influx of Negroes is incompre-
hensible to them. Their techniques no longer work—they're the
very things the kids are rebelling against. The schools' attitude
is not rational, it's emotional. They're scared.

The sorts of problems to which these last quotations refer are
organizational or community problems. They cannot be satisfactorily
dealt with on the level of individual relationships. They require *departmental* involvement of a sort not developed during the project. Consequently, the workers were thrown back on their own resources and on
their own experiences and attitudes, shifting ground in their interventions
in an attempt to meet the varied approaches of each boy, each teacher,
each vice principal, and each school. It was a "seat of the pants"
approach to school problems, rather than an approach based on a
coordinated policy.

Gang Families

Imagine the plight of the physician in a medical specialty who finds
that drugs and medicines have little effect on the incidence of a widespread disease. As a result of his clinical experience, he decides that
the only way to treat his patients successfully is to deal with the infectious
agent at its source.

This is the position of the worker who feels that his actions can
only hold the line against gang activity. To decrease it he must go to its
roots, and very often he sees these roots in the home, in the network of
family relations that has spawned the young gang member. The worker
can identify the roots of the problem, but he can have little or no impact
on them.

Earlier in this book we documented the family situation with statistics on broken homes, family income, and so on. And there is no
question but that low incomes and disrupted families are prevalent
enough in the neighborhood to constitute a norm. A youngster from a
poor home situation knows full well that his situation is similar to that
of many of his friends. But that's not much comfort either to him or to
the worker. To both, the family situation is the source of constant frustration. The workers have described some of these difficulties:

It's very difficult for parents to discuss their children's problems. . . .
Just because you're the sponsor of their kids, doesn't mean that
they'll tell you all their problems.

See, Donny's father's interested but he's working night and
day . . . . Harry, his mother's on the East side of town, his father
on the other and neither one is real interested in getting
involved . . . . So you've got a real problem.

I would much rather work with kids shooting at each other than
with the parent who you have to drag out and convince that she's
in danger of something or other. I say she because the fathers,
they always stay home or they aren't home.

Long talks with Mr. Law, Midget's father, and mother and they're
very much concerned and all that, but they get out of work late,
eight or nine o'clock in the evening, and they haven't got the
time left to do anything.

I came by the house, and saw the boys with a car, and I told the
boys "Well, the police know all about this car, they got the license
plate numbers." My impression, my point was to shake the boys
up regarding proper driving, stop and go violations, you're
known in the community. She heard this and right away she
sided with the boys immediately. She'd had a few—she had a
can of beer as she came out talking—and pretty soon she went
into a tirade about, "Well, this car is paid for and nobody's gonna
bother us," and this kind of thing. So I terminated the discussion.
The boys left, so I went back in the house and I said "You know,
Mrs. Simmons, I had asked you several weeks or months before,
are you going to help us, are you with me, and you said yes. And
I'm out here talking to the boys about the car and right away
you sided with them. You aren't helping me."

Given such a situation as indicated here, it is little surprise that
only one of four parent groups was successfully maintained in the program. Missing or uninterested parents are ruinous to active programming. On the other hand, the experience of the one more or less stable
group suggests that just as important as the parents' availability and
motivation are the workers' skills, motivation, and persistence. The
absence of continuing parent groups in all but the General's cluster
cannot be blamed solely on parental apathy. The seeds of parent concern needed the fertile ground of worker and supervisory energy, but
the seeds were definitely there:

In the beginning I didn't approach parents . . . . They came to me.
Let's use Mrs. Arlen as an example. She came around and she
says, "You guys are really something—you really try to help a
kid." And you know, it's there.

Eloise Carver's mother has been a strong, positive influence not
only to her own daughter but to most of the youth in the area who
frequent her house. She has become an active member of the
local parents' group and was recently elected to an office in the
Federation of Parents Club.

The parents' group has progressed greatly and has had regular
meetings twice a month with approximately 15 parents in regular

attendance. Special occasions, such as guest speakers, have
brought out more parents. The parents have shown great interest
and are now ready to act as a civic group.

Why weren't these seeds cultivated? One reason, as always, is
the limited amount of time available to the workers. A second, as we
noted, was their pessimism about the success of parent work, or their
own discomfort in dealing with parents. For example:

> To some degree I don't really believe in having a parents
> group .... I couldn't think of how I could entertain them ....
> I always wonder why confront one parent with another person's
> problems, and back and forth. It just seems to be a black morass
> of problems and you can't solve any of them, really: airing them
> and talking about them forever and it still doesn't solve a damn
> thing.

But a third reason, and equally valid to the line worker, is that so
many of the family situations present seemingly unsolvable problems.
The workers are not trained family counselors, and they are not backed
up by adequate community or professional resources. Faced almost
daily with variations on standard themes of family disruption and poverty,
yet feeling that within the family are the basic secrets to rehabilitation,
they are placed in an intolerable position. As a result, they often react
by withdrawing from the family arena, or by handling family problems in
the fashion of detached observers who merely document the problems
that exist.

> It's unusual. You should see the interior of that home. The interior
> is magnificent ... wood paneling, that kind of thing (laugh).
> Fantastic range, fantastic difference of two blocks in the same
> community ....
>
> I'm always struck by the few united homes I've been in ... there's
> just no communication between boys and the parents.
>
> ... She's been bleeped up with public assistance funds for so
> long that she has no more initiative.
>
> I met the grandmother .... The father lives in the rear of the
> house. I understand him to have a broken back or something,
> that he's completely incapacitated. (And the mother isn't there?)
> I don't think so. I think she remarried and is living in the South
> somewhere.
>
> The father could be characterized as a "week-end father," who
> doles out instructions on Friday or Saturday and expects the boys
> to carry out his orders throughout the week.

I never met the man—never. I guess a lot of these boys have
de facto fathers.

... the family situation is not really clear. The father is in jail
for narcotics.

Robert's mother is cohabitating with a man who is not her legal
husband. The man gives Robert spending money.

The mother ... left with an overnight bag and from the orders
she left with Sandra ... I gathered that the mother would return
sometime the next day. Sandra stated that she was used to it.

All the male members of the family have been Operator gang
members. The mother calls it their way of life.

Community Facilities

To different people, the concept of community resources may mean
different things. To the "dedicated delinquent" it may refer to opportunities for criminal engagement:

... right there at the corner, anything you need you can get ...
Whatever kind of narcotics or women or anything ... if you're
hungry you can go get it right there.

They've got their home life, and they've got their park life, and
they've got their life on the streets ... Lot of them aren't moving
out of the community and they find everything they need, or
which they think they need, right there.

Though the park staff may make the rounds, they are not police
nor are they able to effectively control what goes on. There have
been several gang bangs, as well as drinking, drunk rolling,
fighting, and gambling at the same time that sports activities or
socials have been going on.

But to the worker these things soon become ordinary and accepted,
so much so on occasion that they don't bother to comment on them to
the boys.* Of more interest to the worker are the attitudes of the park

---

*Occasionally this pattern became clear to the supervisor:

"This is why you're being kicked out of one playground and another because
you don't ... talk about this car stealing and these problem things. Talk about
them. Talk about them. *Kids want to talk about them,* and if you don't talk
about them, then they don't want you. Hell, we've got recreation directors all
over the place. They want somebody to come over there and talk problem to
them. .... It's not being done in the home, it's not being done in the school.
Someone has to do it."

managers and coaches, the settlement house staff, the managers of
the Taco stands, and the members of various inter-agency committees.
These people can open doors to gang members or close them pretty
much on their own initiative and with impugnity. Since gang members
more often represent trouble than involvement, the doors generally seem
closed.

> Trouble with this job is you're an outcast in the community, and
> you don't have the backing of responsible people.

In addition, collaboration on gang problems requires some mutual
agreement that the gang is a part of a community and that the community
is responsible for its members.

> What community are we talking about? People who live in this
> area don't think of themselves belonging to a community . . . .
> How can you have pride in your community if you don't know
> what your community is, where it starts and stops . . . .

The result, then, was to "test out" the various community agents.
If they were sympathetic they were worked with. If they were not sympathetic, little attempt was made to effect a change. In other words, this
is a description of an insecure program dependent on the "soft sell"
approach to collaboration.

> They let them in to play pool and they're under 18. Couple of
> guys (are) selling pills. (How do you know?) I don't go inquir-
> ing . . . . They haven't invited me to come in and I'm not about
> to make myself unpopular with anybody that's running the place.
> We held a dance at the playground under a phony name—a boys
> club—'cause (the director) didn't want his supervisor to know he
> let the gang use the playground for a dance.
> It's not an honest relationship.

With only one community center located near the project area and
few if any churches committed to delinquency prevention with activity
programs specifically aimed at the adjudicated delinquent, the workers
were thrown back on two resources: community coordinating councils
and playgrounds. Their attitudes toward the former ranged from skep-
tical to negative, and with good reason.

> These community councils—they're good material to work with,
> but you have to have a planned program ready-made when
> you approach them, not try to plan along with them. They're
> very hard to work with.

... was disappointed to observe that members of this council tend to discourage deep discussion of problems of youth in the area and take no positive action toward the control or prevention of youth problems. The group appears to be more of a social gathering . . . .

Sparsely scattered though they were in the project area, the playgrounds were left as the major community facility to which the workers could turn. Every playground in the area was used by the workers and their youngsters; the loose structure of the park or playground seemed far more acceptable both to worker and boy than any other form of community facility. Many of the workers were former recreation workers and successful college athletes who felt at home in the playground setting. They communicated well with the playground staff.

They've got a guy named Al Marshall, who's my buddy.

And yet there were problems. Gang members are a threat (regardless of their actual activities) to the normal programming on a playground. They hang around, occasionally take over an activity or an area, frighten younger boys, make parents nervous, and present more than their share of problems to the staff. Some playgrounds tolerate them, some kick them out, some seek departmental policies to legitimate exclusion policies.

The Directors . . . remain quite friendly . . . even though the playgrounds are not available to the . . . program. One has flatly refused to grant a permit to the program to use the facility. The other will not okay a permit, but has been cooperative in letting the program use the facility without a permit.

Mr. Richards informed (me) that he had received the permit and that it said, "Absolutely no, permission denied."

Unlike most playgrounds whose staff keep out undesirables, (this one) allows them to hang around. They may use all the outside facilities, but not the indoor rooms. This is the only restriction. The staff will tell you that the moment they are allowed inside they become vandals. Let them destroy the outside, but not the inside.

With the exception of one Group Guidance worker ("If I could, I'd drop recreation activities"), the ambivalence was almost totally on the part of the playground staffs and their departmental supervisors. Where the workers differed—drastically—was in their approach to *levels* of programming in recreation. They spanned the extremes from no recreational activity to team practice and league play several times a week. To some recreation was a delinquency prevention process because of both physical involvement and inculcation of democratic values. To others it was a crutch, a way of establishing or maintaining rapport as well as putting in one's time.

The worker who spends little time in recreational activities may be reprimanded by his superiors for his seeming inactivity. The one who programs heavily is seen as highly active and expects to be rewarded. Yet here is a paradox, for as our data have already indicated, heavy programming may in fact work *against* program goals. It may increase gang cohesiveness without the compensating change in attitudes and values expected of it. Perhaps—and admittedly this may be hard to swallow—the refusal to permit gang members to participate in playground activities actually works to the gang members' own benefit. It is not beyond reason that being "kicked out" of the park will help them to keep *out* of trouble. The point is worth considering.

> ... we got into this basketball league which I thought would be a good strengthening point for the group—kind of a hold on something and "see, we are doing something." But it didn't quite work out this way .... The league turned into a winning type thing and what happened was we recruited more and more the older boys. ..."

The Younger Boys

One final comment before I conclude this material on worker styles. In considering the data on increased offense behavior among younger gang members, I mentioned that this might relate to "recruitment"—the process by which the gang perpetuates itself by appealing to the younger age levels in the neighborhood. This process is a "natural" one in that it occurs in the absence of adult interventions. Our observations suggest as well, however, that the process can be reinforced by the worker who *needs* groups in order to maintain his work style. I offer this suggestion as an interpretation rather than as a fact and the following description as an illustration rather than as proof.

In the winter of 1963–64, a number of the Baby Generals returned to their area from probation camp and Youth Authority facilities and rejoined their fellow club members. Ordinarily, the sudden influx of returnees is a source of anxiety to a worker because he knows little about what to expect under such circumstances.

But in this case there was a reason for optimism. It soon became obvious to the worker (and thereafter to the research observers attending Baby Generals meetings) that the returnees were a "set up" for positive programming. They seemed surprisingly mature, serious about club affairs, and even appeared to be serving successfully as positive role models for the other members.

11/6/63:   Good meeting, quite a bit of interaction. Youth appear quite receptive to the Group Guidance approach to program. Group is "ready" for work.   (Worker meeting report)

11/13/63:   Very responsive to D.P.O. and suggestions. Seem to be making progress.   (Worker meeting report)

11/27/63:   Youths in this meeting appear to be moving in a positive and constructive manner. There is need for more improvement, however, the group seem quite positive and receptive to counseling or suggestion.   (Worker meeting report)

The behavior of the members also seemed to give the worker a second wind. His morale rose, he interacted more in meetings, and began to search actively for new ways of meeting youth needs.

11/6/63:   (worker) did a fine job of presenting his role, setting limits, getting kids to state positive goals and attitudes, etc. . . . This is a "new" and potentially very effective worker—a beautiful example of . . . worker style. These kids know just where he stands and what the basic ground rules must be!   (Observer meeting report)

When this situation was brought to the attention of the supervisor, the latter mentioned the Beverly Hills Executive Club* to whom he had spoken some months earlier. Although the socio-economic and cultural disparity between the Baby Generals and the Executive Club was enormous, he decided to investigate the possibilities of sponsorship.

Over a period of several months, the arrangements took shape. Members of the Baby Generals** attended Executive Club luncheons, and Executive Club members attended Baby Generals meetings to explain their role and the advantages of sponsorship. Baby Generals

---

*A pseudonym for a nationally affiliated businessmen's group which includes the sponsoring of youth groups in its charter.

**The reader should not be misled by the name—the "Babies" were 16 and 17 years of age.

learned to recite the long "credo" of the Executives Club (this would be analogous to the Chinese "Red Guard" reciting the Bill of Rights). The Executives learned to refer to the area as a "set" where "all the dudes are."

But it all came to naught. Just as the time arrived to formalize matters with an installation dinner and the other trappings of formal investiture, school ended, meetings ended, and the natural looseness of summer life on the streets asserted its habitual reign. Furthermore, at the end of the summer the Baby Generals showed no desire to reconvene their meetings nor, with some notable exceptions, were they so visible on the street corner as they had been. Evidence began to mount that as an organized gang they were beginning to dissolve. It is interesting to speculate—and the worker considers it more fact than speculation—that the prospects of formal incorporation into a middle-class club structure such as the Executive Club may have served as a symbol of graduation out of gang status. This is not to say that the introduction of·the Executive Club notion *caused* the disintegration of the Baby Generals, but rather that it may well have legitimated a change that was already under way.

In any case, this notion was not prevalent when summer ended, for in fact an attempt *was* made to reorganize the Baby Generals under the Executives' banner. This time the leadership within the Executives delayed matters, and not until January 1965 did the program start up again. By that time it was clear that the Baby Generals were no longer interested, so attention was turned to the Diplomats, a younger group in the Generals' cluster who averaged 15 years of age.

At this point, it was only the Diplomats and their "sister club" the Diplomettes who were meeting formally. The response of these younger boys was encouraging and so they became the Beverly Hills Diplomats Junior Executive Club. It is impossible to document significant changes among the Diplomats during the six months between their sponsorship by the Executives Club and the end of the project. But we do have attendance data for 17 weekly club meetings from which some measure of club response can be deduced.

The first meeting was attended by nine boys, of whom five participated more or less consistently throughout all 17 meetings. Twenty-one additional boys attended one or more of the remaining meetings, for a total of 30 attenders. Eight acknowledged members of the Diplomats never participated in the sponsored program. Eight of the attenders ceased their participation after just a few sessions.

The attendance picture, then, is a mixed one, just as with the tutoring and remedial reading programs. Part of the difficulty in this case

what are the dynamics of delinquency proneness

can be attributed to the large cultural gap between the boys and representatives of the Executives Club. As anecdotal evidence, consider the
example of the Executive who pushed the boys for several weeks to learn
about the famous naturalist, John Muir. He brought books written by
Muir, showed slides of Yosemite and Sequoia National Parks, and generally emphasized *his* area of interest rather than seeking out the boys'
interests. The reaction was summed up neatly by one boy who noted
in an aside to the research observer: "Aw, he ain't nothin' but a naitcha
lovah!"

The Executives Club program was intended (although not with
unanimity among the members) to deal with the potentially hard-core
members of the Diplomats as a means of cutting off at its source the
perpetuation of the Generals cluster. If the delinquency-prone Diplomats
could be steered into positive streams of interest and activity, it was
felt that the Generals cluster might cease to exist as a highly visible
negative force in the community. But the Diplomats who responded to
the program did not constitute the more delinquent sector of the group.
The average prior offense record of the 21 higher attenders was 0.48
offenses. For those eight who ceased attending the figure was 3.50 and
for six who never participated the figure was 4.33.* The average age
of the first group was six months lower, hardly enough to account for
the large difference in offense accumulations, but enough to illustrate
the recruiting process.

This finding is consistent with findings from the tutoring and remedial reading programs. It is the less delinquent boys who respond to
these programs, and yet it is the more delinquent boys that the detached
worker approach is designed to reach. The "out" is, of course, the contention that involving less delinquent members in community-based
programs frees the workers' time for more concentration on the hard-
core members. But why should a worker beat his head against the wall
by reaching out to those very boys who are most likely to rebuff him, to
frustrate his aims, and to make his career basically unrewarding? If
there *are* workers who thrive under these conditions, they must be a
highly select group—self-selected—and probably very atypical of the
role models which most theorists would recommend for hard-core delinquents. There are many paradoxes in gang work, and this is one of
the most prominent. To be fully accepted by "hard-core" gang members, most workers feel that they must not be seen as the embodiment
of middle-class values. In fact, to be accepted by these boys the worker

---

*The offense records of three boys were unobtainable because sufficient iden-
tifying information was not available.

may have to be so similar to them in values and levels of maturity that his ability—or even desire—to transform the boys into socially acceptable youngsters is very low.

References

1. Hans W. Mattick and Nathan S. Caplan, "Stake Animals, Loud-Talking and Leadership in Do-Nothing and Do-Something Situations" in Malcolm W. Klein (ed.), *Juvenile Gangs in Context: Theory, Research, and Action* (Englewood Cliffs, N.J.: Prentice-Hall, Inc., 1967), pp. 106–19.
2. James F. Short, Jr., Ray A. Tennyson, and Kenneth I. Howard, "Behavior Dimensions of Gang Delinquency," *American Sociological Review* 28, no. 3 (June, 1963): 411–28.
3. Malcolm W. Klein, Wiley P. Mangum, and Herbert Aarons, "Study of Delinquent Gangs in Los Angeles: First Report" (Los Angeles: Youth Studies Center, University of Southern California, 1963) (Mimeo).
4. Irving Spergel, *Street Gang Work: Theory and Practice,* (Reading, Mass.: Addison-Wesley Publishing Co., 1966).
5. *Ibid.,* p. 191.
6. Thomas M. Gannon, S. J., *The Changing Role of the Street Worker in the Council of Social and Athletic Clubs,* New York City Youth Board, Nov. 1965, p. 48 (mimeo).

Chapter 7

The Community
Response

It is well nigh impossible to describe a detached worker program without reference to the relations between the workers and their agency to other workers and other agencies in the community. Gang workers are supposed to interact with—and, in any case, cannot totally avoid—police, probation, parole, school, welfare, and recreational personnel along with various businessmen and other lay members of the community. These interactions can be critical. In the Group Guidance Project, the police controversy indirectly led to the most significant changes in the whole program. A similar controversy in New York led to what many welfare workers considered an emasculation of the New York City Youth Board's gang program. On a broader level, Miller concluded that the community agencies themselves constituted the greatest impediment to delinquency prevention during the Roxbury Project!

The Group Guidance Project provided two opportunities to concentrate our attention on the matter of community response. The pivotal police controversy was one of these, but before analyzing that situation, we can establish a useful context from a survey taken during the last summer of the project.

The Community Survey

In 1963, the seven Group Guidance workers involved in the project during that year reported the names of 702 community adults (other than parents of gang members) with whom they had had contact. Of these

205

702 people, 234 were named by the workers as crucial or potentially crucial to their work.

Of the 234 "crucials," a 25 per cent stratified random sample was selected for interviewing, with a final list of 56 persons resulting. Of these 56, one refused to be interviewed. Two others could not be located because of faulty information (the workers were unable to recall who they were, thus suggesting that the designation "crucial" should not be taken literally in all cases). What follows is a summary of the responses of the remaining 53 people interviewed during the summer of 1964.

The Sample

The following is known about the sample:

1. sex—33 were male, 20 were female
2. race—23 were Negro, 23 Anglo, 5 Mexican-American, and 2 Oriental
3. residence—11 lived in the test area, 12 lived outside the test area but in the same general section of the city, and 30 lived far-removed from the test area
4. job tenure—34 had been in their positions for three years or less, 19 for over three years
5. affiliation—12 were in the Probation Department, 12 in the Police Department, 9 in the City School System, 5 in the city or county Recreation Department, and 15 were noted as contacted because of other, often unofficial, affiliations
6. contacts—as recorded in the workers' reports, the respondents were seen from one to 38 times each during 1963. The averages per person for each affiliation category were: Police—13, probation — 8, schools — 5, recreation — 8, and other community adults—6. However, of the 53 respondents, 10 had been contacted only once during that year, and 12 only twice. On the average, respondents were contacted by the workers about eight times during the year. These figures seem surprisingly low, since we are dealing with a sample of worker-designated, "crucial" individuals

Public Relations

Almost half of the respondents had been *unaware* of the project's existence until receiving interview correspondence from the research team. Eight of the remaining 28 people, or 33 altogether, had not heard about the project from anyone in Group Guidance or Probation. Probation and school officials were least aware of the research project, whereas the police were most aware of it—especially of its location in the city. Probation and police officers were most "in the know" about Group Guidance, the police being most familiar with the operations and probation with the personnel. Neither the project, nor Group Guidance generally, was very successfully publicized, even with people thought to be important to the success of the program. The respondents' knowledge of pertinent matters was lower than would be expected. As a result, it is a likely assumption that their reactions to and evaluations of the program were less a function of factual information than of individual values, reactions to particular workers, and so forth.

Program Reactions

A series of questions in the interview requested the respondents' reactions to the program as they envisioned it. Probation officers and other community adults were most prevalent among those who saw the program as helpful to them. The school and police officials were *least* able to cite *actual* benefits of the program, and only the police were able to cite specific harmful events in any number.

Reactions to Workers

Police officers in particular felt that they had not been contacted sufficiently by the workers, and that the workers were at times less cooperative than was desired. Along with school officials, they also were more likely to feel that they had been of little help to the workers.

Summary

From this brief review, what overall picture do we find? This sample of crucial adults was not heavily contacted—in fact two fifths of the respondents were reportedly seen only once or twice during the year in question, 1963. Considering this basic fact, some of the other findings are not surprising. The respondents knew relatively little about the project, nor had they heard what they did know from Group Guidance or the Probation Department. "De-isolation," the guiding principle behind the Group Guidance program, was practically unknown among these crucial respondents. Half of the respondents felt that the project had had no effect on their jobs. These findings all hold together—*low contact, low impact.*

And yet the respondents' reactions to the individual workers were generally warm and positive. There was a "flavor" running through a majority of the interviews that suggested a lukewarm (at best) reaction to the program, yet a positive response to the program agents—the workers—as individuals. Here, perhaps, is the most important point of all: like many welfare personnel, the workers successfully sold themselves, but not their agency or program. This was an act of omission: that is, the workers attempted to use their good personal relationships for their job needs; *they did not act as agency or special project representatives.* The almost total lack of contact between the respondents and Group Guidance supervisory personnel added to this overall picture.

Significantly, although analyses were done on the basis of the respondents' ethnic status, orientation toward gang work, and level of contact with the project, the factor of the respondents' agency affiliation was the most important (in the sense that knowing the person's affiliation leads to the best predictions of his responses). Probation officers and "other community adults" were most sympathetic to the program in contrast to police and school officials. Police stood out as most knowledgeable about the program, and school officials as the least. The police, more than any other group in the community, emerged from the survey as the most concerned, the most knowledgeable about the program, and the *most antagonistic* toward it. This antagonism was mutual in many instances.

The Workers' View of the Police

Of all adult groups with whom gang workers have important relationships, the police are the most challenging because of their enforcement role. The police officer sees little good in the gang member; he sees him as a threat to law and order and to the values the police officer treasures most. But to be successful, the gang worker must "infiltrate" this threatening group to the point of honest acceptance by them. How then can police and gang workers get along? "Not well," is usually the answer.

This is not the place for a treatise on the roles and values of these two agents of society, but I would like to indicate some of the workers' feelings in their own words. Had we access to comparable police interviews, we could easily flip the coin and document the opposing position. It would be equally fascinating, equally intransigent, and equally ambivalent (if this is not a contradiction).

Legitimacy of the Police Role. Several dominant themes come to light from the workers' comments about the police. The first emphasizes the legitimacy of the police role.

> You got to understand the police have a specific job to do . . . .
> They're not in the rehabilitation business, they're not social
> workers.

Unequal Relations. The second theme might be termed the *unequal relations* theme. Here, the complaint is that attempts to collaborate with the police are seldom reciprocated, or that reciprocation is only a surface appearance designed to ferret out confidential information.

> (Did they ever volunteer any information to you about boys . . . ?)
> I think they were doing this at one time, but it was done in order
> to receive information, and when they didn't receive this kind of
> information that was wanted, it was no longer done.

Least-stress Accommodation. The third theme, more common than the first two, stresses accommodation on a least-stress basis. The goal here is to avoid conflict between the agency representatives by avoiding situations which might lead to conflict.

> I've never had difficulty because I don't believe in making a lot
> of police contacts . . . .
>
> We have a friendly relationship that goes a little beyond
> diplomacy, no action. But it's difficult at that. I don't frequent
> that place much.
>
> —— Station of the LAPD has had very little contact with the Group
> Guidance Program. In return (I) have not frequented the —— Station.

Rousting. A fourth major theme stresses the harm that police practices do in solidifying the feelings of gang members. Such practices include rousting or harassment, false arrests, downgrading the program in the community, and expressing the "once-a-hood, always-a-hood" syndrome. But, perhaps mirroring the feelings of the boys, it is the rousting complaint that appears most often.

> Almost daily these youth would meet at the back gate of school
> and proceed homeward. Almost daily they were stopped in
> front of other peers, searched, questioned, and released. Out of
> the 27 times I witnessed these incidents, only four times were
> arrests made. Two of these arrests ended by releasing the youths

within the hour. Officer M. commented . . . that harassment was
a successful deterrent to this group's delinquent behavior.

With the increase of (police) surveillance, the group's notoriety
increased in the eyes of the adult community, and popularity in
the eyes of the youth. Girls and younger youths idolized the
Victors and I witnessed as many as 100 youths following the
members of the Victors home with high anticipation that they
would do something "adventurous." The relationship between
police and Victors appeared to be a game of "cops and robbers."

Many parents still won't let their kids come to club meetings
because of this police pressure we've been getting.

Without a separate study of police-community relations, it would
be almost impossible to state how accurately these statements approximate police practice. Throughout the study—and much to the disgruntle-
ment of some of the workers—the research team approached reports of
police brutality, harassment, and discourtesy as in a rumor study. As
with rumors, these reports in most cases proved impossible to validate.
But the *feelings* of the workers cannot be disputed, for they existed and
they affected interagency practices.

The Police Perspective

Our interviews and conversations with individual police officers and
their superiors revealed an equally one-sided approach, with these
differences:

1. The legitimacy of the gang worker's role was always questioned
   and seldom accepted
2. The unequal-relations theme was more specific, being limited
   to information on likely suspects and total gang rosters
3. The counterpart to the workers' harassment theme was the
   police officers' complaint about workers' protecting and cod-
   dling gang members

As only the researcher, the middle man in the operation, can testify,
feelings were such that neutrality was the greatest sin of all. The research team was constantly under the gun to take sides, to be "with"
the police or "with" Group Guidance. The distinterested observer presented both sides with a common "enemy" or, more accurately, a common target for influence attempts. The uncommitted stance of the
researchers made few friends for social science.

The Police Controversy

During the period from March 8 to March 16, 1963, a series of gang-related incidents took place in the vicinity of the test area, involving principally the Red Raiders and the Generals. During this period, the Los Angeles Police Department recorded 13 "crimes of violence" including several shootings, beatings, a stabbing and a small pitched battle between the warring factions. These incidents brought to a head the long-standing disagreement between Police and Probation Departments concerning the proper means of dealing with delinquent gangs, and resulted in a public airing of the issue as well as a temporary suspension of the activities of the Group Guidance Section including those of the project staff. The chronological listing of events is as follows:

3/8–
3/16: A series of incidents involving Red Raiders, Generals, and Victors.

3/18: Truce meeting supervised by Group Guidance staff, and attended by about 60 boys, 13 community adults, news reporters and a television crew. A truce was agreed upon.

3/27: County Supervisor Kenneth Hahn, after receiving strong complaints from Chief of Police William H. Parker, ordered an investigation of the Chief's charges that supervised gangs accounted for 3½ to 4 times as many crimes as unsupervised gangs, that the program provided "official recognition, status and a cohesiveness" to the gangs and their leaders, and that "what happens is that they go to the meetings for two hours, leave and generally beat somebody up."
(Los Angeles Times, March 28, 1963)

3/28: County Sheriff Peter Pitchess supported the police position, stating, "The Group Guidance Program in Los Angeles County, rather than solving the problem has only served to accentuate it.... The program causes more crime than it solves. The idea may have been noble; the results have been disastrous." (Herald Examiner, March 28, 1963)

3/29: County Supervisor Ernest E. Debs, with the concurrence of the Chief Probation Officer, suspended the program pending the completion of the investigation. In addition to the police charges, the suspension announcement stressed the necessity for cooperation between agencies concerned if the program was to continue effectively.

4/1:   A detailed report and documentation of charges was submitted by the police to Chief Probation Officer Leland C. Carter.

4/1–   Conversations between the principals in the controversy
4/17:   took place, positions were clarified, and it appeared likely that a new modus vivendi would be developed. In this period, also, individuals and groups in the Los Angeles community spoke out, released statements, picketed in front of the Hall of Administration, sent letters and wires to local and state officials, and generally made it clear that the controversy was highly meaningful and important to them. The bulk of community support seemed clearly to be for the Probation position.

4/15:   First draft of the Probation Department's investigation report (response to police charges) was submitted to Probation Officer Carter. This 58-page confidential draft, by and large, either refuted or cast considerable doubt on the validity of major police charges.

4/18:   An "Agreement between Law Enforcement and the Probation Department for the Operation of the Group Guidance Section of the Probation Department" (see Appendix C) was released. This statement was primarily the work of the Director of Group Guidance, Inspector Collins (LAPD) and Inspector Stallings (Sheriff's Department). Basically, the "Agreement" was a restatement and slight modification of Group Guidance policy with an emphasis on points particularly desired by enforcement agents.

4/22:   The program was resumed by order of the Board of Super-visors, with the understanding that at the end of the next year (July, 1964) further investigation might be undertaken to determine whether the program should be permanently terminated.

6/18:   The Board of Supervisors approved Probation Officer Carter's report dated 6/3/63, a pro forma statement responding in brief to the spirit of the police charges and recommending confirmation of program resumption, support of the research project, and commendation of the officials who hammered out the "Agreement" of 4/18.

Upon resumption of the program, the situation had all the earmarks of a "truce." Both sides, by policy, avoided further public statements, both went about their activities in a more or less normal fashion, and, at least at the "line" level, both seemed to be stockpiling defensive weapons for a possible future conflict, that is, carefully gathering information about interagency contacts so as to be prepared with a strong defense should this become necessary. More than one person noted the similarity between this situation and a truce between rival delinquent gangs. Because the research staff was not involved in the negotiations during or after the period of the controversy, it is difficult to document the degree to which this "truce" was genuine in spirit at the line level. However, our impression was that this was an "armed truce" in which each side put forth an occasional cooperative effort more for practical, political purposes than because of a genuine rapprochement in philosophy and values.

Another interesting point about this controversy concerns the change of focus which took place between the first and last rounds. The initial police charges were concerned with delinquency rates, gang encouragement, and "official recognition" of gang status. As negotiations progressed, it became apparent that these matters were less crucial to finding a mode of resolution than were particular "grievances" on the part of enforcement agencies. One of the early demands made was that all members of the test area staff be removed. Others had to do with Group Guidance officers "recruiting" new gang members, solidifying the leadership status of "gang psychopaths," and withholding gang rosters from the police*; with recruiting older gang members to work with younger ones; with interfering in proper enforcement and adjudication procedures by withholding information from the police and appearing in court on behalf of gang members; and with a number of similar concerns. In other words, the negotiations and the "Agreement" had less to do with whether or not Group Guidance fomented gang activity than the *modus operandi* of Group Guidance workers. Thus the controversy was really based, not on effect, but on philosophies of intervention.

The effect of the controversy on the morale of the Group Guidance workers was quite marked. Two members of the test area staff (the target group in the controversy) requested and received transfers out of the program. Many others felt themselves to be under personal attack and were greatly discouraged by what they considered minimal support from their own department. In many respects, they felt very much on the defensive, and there is reason to believe that some of this feeling was transferred to the gang youths.

---

*"Sergeant Hawkins reviewed a Victor list presented to him, and checked off those youths who have gang packages . . . He was able to check off about 10 youngsters out of a list of 130 names." (Worker interview, 1964)

The police saw the controversy as strengthening their position, although they did, I believe, act and speak with greater caution after the resolution. The workers understandably became more antagonistic toward the police, although they too were forced to mind their p's and q's. Nor were they necessarily of one mind about police officers, as the following interview quotes demonstrate:

Q: Who do you feel least comfortable working with?

A: I can't really say categorically, but of all kinds of people, I'd say the police are the hardest.

A: Aside from the kids, I feel most comfortable with the police. It's cut and dried with them—it's on paper—you know where you stand. The schools are wishy-washy. They just pass the buck. Parents aren't willing to take responsibility. At least the police take a stand, and you know what it is.

A: When you and I call the police we get protection by the police. I feel that many of these kids' life styles are such, they need protection from the police. I mean, to call the police for help would be one of the last things to do.

A: I'd like to say that they have called me to give me information, but when they call me to give me information, then I do believe it's with the hopes of filling them in further. I believe they try to use me. They give me as little as possible in return.

A: Ah, he just had the boys in there and he talked to them; he told them what he would like to see them do, and I know of an occasion when he told a boy, "if you don't report to school regularly, well next time you gotta go," and requested that the boy show him the report card.

Q: In your point of view is this a good thing?

A: Yes.

Q: No interference with your job?

A: No, it's an aid. It's a definite assist.

A: I go into the police station in an area once and introduce myself and then stay away . . . They've been brainwashed. They either can't or are afraid to deviate from the norm. Their attitude is, once a guy commits a crime, he's a crook.

I might add here that, in their zeal to show support for their workers, I often heard supervisory personnel in Group Guidance make clear antipolice statements—"Once a cop, always a cop," "They're out to wreck us if they can," and so on. I have heard equally vehement anti–Group Guidance sentiments in the police station—"They're no better than the hoods they work with, that they protect." Small wonder, then, that genuine collaborative efforts between such agencies seldom get translated from paper to policy, to say nothing of practice.

Controversies about Intervention

Instances like the foregoing are seldom marked by any total resolution of value differences—nor should one expect such a total resolution. Indeed, they may in time become nothing more than models of conflict between enforcement and detached-worker agencies. But they do allow us to specify some of the major differences in assumptions underlying the two positions in these conflicts and to suggest that for most of the assumptions there are data presently available or obtainable that can be used to test them. When two agencies can look at one set of data and draw diametrically opposite findings, then obviously the argument is less over the nature of reality than over philosophies of gang intervention. In fact, the nature of the interagency conflicts suggests that *both* sides to these controversies may be working more from myth than from fact.[2]

Listed below are some, but by no means all, of the questions about which arguments between enforcement and detached-work agencies seem to revolve. In each case, the underlying assumptions could be tested with data at hand or data that are not difficult to collect. Perhaps a brief specification of these underlying assumptions and some suggestions about sources of data will motivate one or more research workers to determine their validity.

1. *Do "sponsored" gangs create more trouble than "unsponsored" gangs?* A "sponsored" gang—and this is evidently not a very useful term—is one to which a detached worker has been assigned. The statement is often made by police officials that the effect of worker supervision is in the long run an increase in the number of gang fights, gang incidents, and individual delinquencies associated with the gang. In Los Angeles the police reported figures suggesting that supervised gangs accounted for three and a half to four times as many gang incidents as unsupervised gangs.

The Group Guidance personnel retorted that this *should* be true because workers are assigned to the most troublesome gangs just as more firemen are assigned to the worst fires and fire areas. Moreover, the fact that a worker is assigned to a gang means that more is known about it and naturally its activities are more likely to come to light than those of gangs that are not clearly identified or followed.

Obviously there are many questions about this set of arguments. For instance, what was the pattern of gang incidents before supervision was begun? What has it been since the advent of supervision, and for what period of time? (Detached workers will often say that it takes them one to three years to have a significant effect on some gangs.) In order to evaluate changes in gang incidents, one must consider the age of the youngsters. In American cities, delinquency generally reaches its peak at around the age of 16 or 17. One expects it to rise before this age is reached and then to decrease. This fact must be separated from any analysis which attempts to pinpoint the effectiveness of a detached worker.

Which boys are the target of supervision? Does the detached worker concentrate his time on the core members or on the fringe members in an attempt to move them away from gang membership? How intensive is supervision? Does the worker spend five days a week with the boys or only one or two? Does he have a significant effect on arrest records, or also on the number of court appearances and the disposition of cases? One must also distinguish between minor and major delinquent activities.

The point here is simply that the question of an increase or decrease of delinquent activity in the presence of detached workers is one that can be and in part now has been answered with data. It need not be merely a subject of speculation or untested assumptions.

2. *Does supervision of gangs lead to increased status?* This question became particularly important in Los Angeles because the detached workers were probation officers. It was the position of the police that this fact alone tended to give official sanction and status to gang membership. Elsewhere, too, it is often believed that the assignment of a worker to a gang gives public recognition to that gang's "toughness." It has been reported by gang workers and researchers across the country, for instance, that neighboring gangs not being served often tend to increase their activity with the explicit purpose of obtaining a worker; that is, they seem to be saying, "Man, we're so tough that they have to assign a worker to us." This matter of status increase associated with the assignment of a worker can be more than a mere assumption. It is a hypothesis that can be tested through the use of data.

For instance, one could, in a carefully constructed interview, attempt to ascertain from the boys themselves whether the assignment of a worker has increased their feelings of status within the general community and within the delinquent subculture. One could question community adults in the same manner. Since the assignment of the worker, have adults been more aware of the existence of the gang? If so, has this awareness come about merely because of the worker's prominence or because gang activities have increased or become more visible? If awareness of status increases after assignment of a worker, which gang members and which kinds of people in the community become more aware of the gang?

Even more important is the underlying assumption that an increase in status—for the gang or for individuals—leads to an increase in delinquency. Do the boys who feel an increase in status also seem to be getting into more difficulty? Are they being arrested more? Are they being arrested for more serious acts than before? How do they view this increase in status if and when it takes place? Is it a positive or a negative sort of status? Does it have to do with them as individuals or as members of the given group? Is it status as club members, or is it status as delinquents?

One of the subunits of the Operators cluster separated "club" status and "gang" status; rather than just belonging to a gang the boys saw themselves as belonging both to a gang and to a club, as supervised by their detached worker. Do gang members really make a genuine distinction between these two kinds of status? Which one is more important to them? Is the worker successful in getting them to attach more importance to their *club* status than to their *gang* status? Each of the above is a question that can be answered by careful research and need not be left to speculation alone.

3. *Does supervision lead to greater cohesion within the gang?* Both enforcement agencies and detached workers and their administrative directors generally agree that a more cohesive gang is likely to be a more delinquent gang. They also suspect that the more cohesive group tends to be the more conflict-oriented group. At this point, we know that data from detached workers alone—even without going to the boys for information—can be collected which clearly distinguish between more cohesive and less cohesive gangs. It then remains to follow the pattern of cohesiveness over a period of two or three years and to follow the pattern of delinquency during this same period.

In dealing with cohesiveness, it is also important to make a distinction between the early and later stages of assignment by gang workers. It is possible that cohesiveness is initially increased by the presence of the detached worker. He offers activities, and perhaps status, but certainly a focal point around which organization can take place. Under such circumstances an increase in cohesiveness can be expected. But as the group's cohesiveness increases, can the worker at the same time

begin to weaken cohesion before a troublesome increase in gang delinquency occurs? Here is the focal point of the argument. The impression
from the Los Angeles data is that cohesion does indeed increase in
the beginning, but that later it may decrease. It may be that the decrease
can be achieved faster by removal of the worker from the gang even
before he feels that the gang is ready for termination of service.

4. *Is gang leadership psychopathic?* Yablonsky[3] and many enforcement officials have indicated that gang leaders are by and large
psychopathic, sociopathic, or, in some other sense, clearly sick individuals. No doubt some boys in gangs are genuinely sick and do have
the potential to influence certain other members of the gangs in a destructive direction. But to what extent do they possess general leadership of their groups? To find out, one could undertake an analysis of
the kinds of activities influenced by the "psychopathic" members as
opposed to those influenced by relatively "healthy" gang leaders, persons who also very clearly exist in gang structures.

One of the first tasks for any gang worker is to attempt to replace
negative leadership with so-called "positive" leadership. To what extent
this can actually be done is still problematic, but it is the stated goal of
gang work insofar as leadership is concerned. Both observational and
sociometric analysis of gang leadership can provide many answers to
this question of whether the gang, *ipso facto*, is psychopathically led.
My own personal observations and those of my research colleagues
do *not* support the notion of any extensive psychopathic leadership.

5. *Are truce meetings between rival gangs helpful or harmful?* A
number of detached-worker programs hold truce meetings between
gangs or get-togethers between gang leaders when "rumbles" or "hassles" are under way or threatened. Obviously, bringing together the
leaders of two rival gangs in which feelings are strong is a delicate
matter. The truce meeting may lead to some resolution of the differences, but it may also lead to a heightening of hostilities. A number of
police officials maintain that the net effect of truce meetings is to let
the members of each rival gang know exactly whom to pounce on next
time. One means of looking at this—granted, it would be hard to get an
agency to agree to such an approach—would be to hold truce meetings
in half of those instances in which they seem to be indicated and to
avoid such meetings in the other half of such cases. After a sufficient
period of time perhaps a large enough number of cases could be logged
to attempt some answer to the question of the effectiveness of truce
meetings.

Other data are also needed. For instance, suppose that a truce
meeting is followed by certain acts of a delinquent nature. Are these acts
in any way related to the matters brought up during the truce meeting?

For instance, if a truce meeting deals with intergang hostilities and if after the truce meeting several of the boys go out and commit statutory rape, is it then legitimate to consider their act a *result* of the truce meeting? Second, if delinquent acts do take place following a truce meeting, who participated in them? Were the participants gang leaders or fringe members of the gangs? Were they members of one gang acting against its rival, or were the acts committed against persons or property unrelated to the rival gang? To what extent did the boys at the truce meeting manage to pass the word along to other gang members to "cool it"? One must ask and answer questions such as these before achieving any genuine evaluation of the effectiveness of truce meetings.

6. *Do gang workers increase antipolice feelings among gang members?* The police, perhaps because they are aware of the value differences between the detached workers and themselves, believe that gang members increase their hostility to police when they receive supervision by detached workers. Detached workers, of course, maintain that this is not their intent, and they add that they counsel gang members about the nature of the legitimate and necessary role of the police officer. On the other hand, there have been instances in which activities or statements by detached workers have been used by boys to justify their own hostile feelings toward the police.

This is a matter to be investigated through careful research. Attitudes can be measured. More specifically, attitudes toward the police can be measured both before and after the assignment of a worker to an area. Because gang members are a highly heterogeneous lot of youngsters, it could well be assumed that feelings toward police will be more a function of the boy himself than of the detached worker. That is, no matter what he says about the police, the detached worker may have a positive effect on the attitudes of some boys and a negative effect on the attitudes of others (and perhaps no effect on the majority). Research could delve into this problem and attempt to distinguish between these differences and also attempt to determine what types of statements by detached workers lead to attitude changes. How do the boys differentially view the statements made by detached workers (or by anyone else, for that matter)?

Each of the above instances is an example of questions which can be studied empirically. Although this list could be extended, these questions are adequate to establish the point of this discussion, that many of the assumptions underlying the controversies between police and detached workers are nothing more than that—assumptions, beliefs, convictions—and that data can be collected to validate or invalidate the assumptions in whole or in part.

There are, of course, other problems in such controversies. For instance, there is some disagreement on the importance of the collaboration between the police and detached workers. All agencies officially say that cooperation and collaboration are highly important. In fact, they often say that no detached worker program can be effective unless it has the cooperation of local enforcement agencies. However, a number of detached workers (not agencies) believe that they can work independently of the police, and some police officers prefer to work with juveniles without contact with detached workers to whom these juveniles are known.

Another source of controversy revolves around "finking," that is, providing police with information about the boys. The detached worker position, stated in its extreme, is that if the worker does "fink," the boys will inevitably know it and the worker will have lost his chance to establish rapport. Once the boys have any substantial reason to accuse the worker of being a fink, the worker can no longer have any effect on the boys. On the other hand, the police position is that withholding information about serious delinquent acts is tantamount to defying law and order; every citizen has a duty to make illegal infractions known to the duly constituted authorities. Furthermore, refusal to provide such information suggests to the police that the worker is on the side of the boys, rather than on the side of society. The most crucial case concerns firearms. While most detached work programs state as official policy that firearms are to be turned over to the police, the fact remains that many individual workers ignore the policy, either because their rapport with the boys is tenuous, or because they fear losing rapport.

Rosters pose another critical example. Very often gang workers develop rosters of gang members. Very often the police request these rosters, since their intelligence role requires them to gather as much information as possible on actual or potential criminals and delinquents. When refused access to rosters, as they often are, police understandably come to feel that the worker is working against them, rather than with them. On at least one occasion in Los Angeles gang members themselves were so concerned about "finking" that they refused to give the worker their names for fear that they would then be open to increased "harassment" by the police.

In summary, it is time for police and detached worker agencies to stop arguing about what delinquents are like, about what is or is not appropriate intervention policy, about whose right it is to intervene. Both police and detached workers know what the respective positions are, and those who have been involved with both of them also know these positions. Responsible enforcement and social work administrators must come together and consider dispassionately what sorts of data are helpful in understanding the differences and in resolving the problems. Once requests for data have been made, there can be great strides in the development of empirically based programs for the handling of juvenile gangs.

References

1. Walter B. Miller, "Inter-Institutional Conflict as a Major Impediment to De-linquency Prevention," *Human Organization* 17, no. 3 (Fall, 1958): 20–23.
2. Mary E. Blake, "Youth Workers and the Police," *Children* 8 (September-October 1961): 170–74; William Dienstein, "Conflicts of Beliefs about Causes of Delinquency," *Crime and Delinquency* 6 (July 1960): 287–93.
3. Lewis Yablonsky, *The Violent Gang* (New York: The Macmillan Company, 1963).

Part III

THE
LADINO
HILLS
PROJECT

Chapter 8: The Context

Parts I and II of this book have combined two approaches which I trust have been somewhat complementary to each other; that is, a review of knowledge about gangs and a description of various findings from the Los Angeles experience. Ordinarily, such a book might well stop right here. However, past experience and knowledge should, ideally, produce a search for new experience and new knowledge. And for me such a quest was made possible and was undertaken. Part III reports the rationale and the results as seen in The Ladino Hills Project—an attempt to use both action and research to learn more about the delinquent gang or, better, to test our newly derived notions about gang delinquency and cohesiveness.

Part III, then, has three contexts, separable but by no means independent of each other. One is the context of gang work as a method of social intervention with delinquent youth groups. The Ladino Hills Project, within this context, was an experiment in gang intervention through "detached work" procedures.

The second context is that of delinquency theory and research. The Ladino Hills Project was based upon empirical data from which were derived a theoretical *model* of gang intervention and a series of experimental and evaluative *procedures*. Within this context, the project was designed as a test of a major hypothesis concerning the relationship between gang cohesiveness and delinquent behavior.

The third context is perhaps more personal. My colleagues and I spent several years evaluating the Group Guidance approach to gang intervention. The findings of that evaluation were quite negative, indicating that the experimental program had in fact *increased* delinquency among the groups involved. In analyzing the reasons for this failure (and

225

in making them public) we found ourselves in a "put up or shut up" position. We decided to *put up*. In this final context, then, the Ladino Hills Project represented a professional gamble that we could mount an empirically based, theoretically guided gang intervention program that would have positive impact on gang delinquency. Thus the project represented not only an exercise in theory and practice, but a test of professional competence. Needless to say, this led to a high level of ego involvement which may have been as important to the project's execution as were its empirical foundations. This is but one of the many paradoxes of action research.

Action Research

Now, what do we mean by *action* research? I am not very comfortable with past definitions I have seen,[1] but neither have I been able to evolve a satisfactory alternative. Instead, so that we may share at least a global notion, let me attempt to characterize action research in terms of its general goals and approach. And let it be clear that my focus will be on the research end of things.

If we assume that basic research is directed primarily at building knowledge for scientific disciplines, and that applied research is directed primarily at the solution or amelioration of the problems of work, then obviously action research falls between these two poles. It does so either because it attempts to serve both purposes simultaneously, or because it accepts some goal intermediate between the two extremes. And it does so in a nonlaboratory setting.

The criterion of polarity would seem to be a function of who will use the data, and for what purposes. In some ways, we might even say that the pivotal question is how one looks at the impact of the researcher on the impact of the program that provides the context. In *basic* research, we try to eliminate the impact of the researcher on the outcome. In *applied* research, we couldn't care less. Unfortunately, however, the matter is far more complicated than this, as witnessed by the following list of goals which have been associated with action research:

1. scientific knowledge building, exploratory or theory testing.
2. evaluation of impact
3. evaluation of process
4. program improvement, often via "feedback"
5. documentation of obstacles to the program
6. experimentation with new approaches

7. training of practitioners in research
8. training of researchers in practice
9. filling the requirements of significant audiences, such as funding agencies, politicians, and professional peers.

Given so many goals and the lack of agreed upon criteria for setting priorities among them, what can one say definitely about action research? Perhaps only that action research is an ill-understood process in which researchers and practitioners work toward diverse ends in common, sharing information which each believes the other should desire.

Research Seduction

To illustrate some of the foregoing, I'll ask you to go back with me to the fall of 1962. At that time I was asked to take over the research direction of the Group Guidance Project which had already been under way for over a year. Since the first few days on the job made it painfully clear that the research and action teams were working almost without reference to each other and that the collaboration level resembled that between Galileo and the Inquisition, naturally I called for a series of meetings between both staffs. I asked the researchers what their mandate was and what they hoped to get out of the project. Well, they hadn't quite thought that through yet—"We're collecting data that may be useful." The action team, however, had a very firm notion of the researchers' mandate—"You're supposed to document all the obstacles in the community that keep us from doing our job!"

Extended and somewhat painful discussions* brought some of these difficulties out into the open where the discrepant views of the two groups could be analyzed and dealt with openly. Change took place almost immediately: acute deterioration set in.

To take advantage of this deterioration, I presented my situation to a university seminar, knowing that an academic discussion was surely the quickest way to resolve dilemmas and find the righteous path. For that seminar we prepared the illustration shown in Figure 8-1. The consensus among my colleagues was that we should forget about the problems of collaboration and just evaluate the Group Guidance Project as it existed—the message was, "Don't make waves." But if we didn't make waves, we might have been in a position of evaluating a program with

---

*The word "unprofessional" emerged as the most common epithet.

Research Purity		Action Seduction	
a.	scientific training	e.	rapport establishment
b.	scientific reference groups	f.	open access to data
c.	scientific dogma	g.	practitioner reference groups
d.	academic reward system	h.	practitioner reward system
j.	action staff apathy	i.	requests from action staff
n.	professional retrenchment	k.	feedback mandate
		l.	field knowledge requirements
		m.	program catalyst requirements
		o.	ego-involvement in program
		p.	social conscience

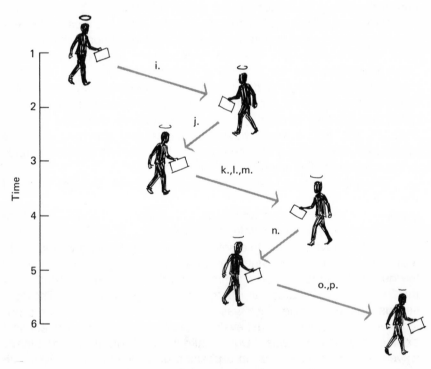

Fig. 8-1: Sequential steps from research purity
to action seduction.

little or no chance of having impact, thus depriving ourselves of some very important data. Figure 8-1 illustrates this quandary by focusing on what I have called the Seduction of the Researcher.

Time 1: We start with the researcher oriented toward research purity. This comes about through his training and indoctrination, his choice of reference groups, the reward systems of academia, and his scientific dogmas concerning objectivity and replicability of data-gathering events. But at the same time, he is propelled toward the action pole by the necessities of rapport establishment, maintenance of open access to data sources, and practitioner reference groups and reward systems available to him. Even at the outset, then, the researcher in the action setting cannot remain totally aloof, totally uninvolved in the action world. The seduction process has started.

Time 2: Soon after the involvement process starts, the researcher receives requests from the practitioner. This very fact moves him over toward the action pole, the degree of movement being further determined by the nature of the request, his response, the reaction to his response, and his research accommodations to that reaction. Examples of such requests in our own projects included:

a. being asked for the arrest records of gang members
b. being asked to help develop a work program for gang members
c. being asked for information on workers' performance which could be used as negative personnel evaluations
d. being asked to exclude from the evaluation certain administrative matters that reflected on the agency's mode of implementing its program
e. being asked for preliminary data of questionable validity during the police controversy over the program's effectiveness.

If it helps the reader to gauge our position, I can report that we acceded to the first, second, and fifth requests, but not to the third and fourth. In any case, it is clear that requests, of whatever nature, cannot simply be ignored if the research is to continue. The way in which the requests are handled sets the style of future collaboration and clearly seduces the researcher away from his pure position.

Time 3: However, for every action there may be an equal and opposite reaction. The action people tend to ask for "data" that are not very reliable, and not of much interest to the researcher. When the researcher in turn provides feedback in matters *he* considers interesting and important, the response is seldom enthusiastic. He interprets these disparities variously as apathy, disinterest, lack of professional values, or just plain stupidity on the part of the practitioner. Consequently, he pulls back toward the ivory tower, preferring to avoid these frustrations of the action setting. He is welcomed with open arms by his academic colleagues.

Time 4: Other factors now come into play. The feedback mandate of the action researcher requires that he remain involved with his practitioner colleagues. But even more important, it becomes increasingly obvious to him that to do a professionally competent job of feedback and evaluation, he simply must be conversant with what is happening in the action program. He can't do that adequately while sitting behind his desk calculator. And, he must be certain that there is enough of a program going on out there to *be* evaluated, to provide the data he needs. He becomes, however grudgingly, a program catalyst, growling and beating his chest to make the natives restless.

Time 5: If he is successful in his chest beating, the researcher can once again reduce his action involvement. He says, in essence, "Okay, you guys, I've gotten you back on the track, so now you're on your own. Keep in touch." By now, of course, the researcher knows the jig is up and he has lost his purity. He has invested himself in the action program, if only to guarantee that his research will have some theoretical payoff.

Time 6: If we look closely at this point, we may find now that all of this oscillation has had a telling effect on our poor researcher. He's become involved in more ways than one. Perhaps he has reached that critical point when he says to himself, and sometimes out loud, "If only I could run this whole show." We can cite several reasons for this. The researcher is not without a social conscience, and short-run problem-solving becomes a salve for his conscience. He has an ego investment in his own feedback. And finally, he comes to realize that, whether justifiably or not, program failure will reflect on *his* prestige. Halo effects work both positively and negatively. How often do we hire researchers whose past projects have failed to have impact on their client populations? For all his purity, the researcher would rather be associated with a successful project.

Now obviously, the foregoing has been a caricature of a real situation. Things are seldom so black and white as pictured here, nor is there such temporal regularity as I have implied. Still, the Group Guidance Project was in many ways the epitome of this process, and in all honesty, I must suggest that the frustrations of that experience may have played a part in the launching of the Ladino Hills Project equal to that of scientific curiosity or the "publish or perish" dictum of academia. But lest we dwell too long on the irrational, let's look briefly at some of the major issues raised by action research projects.

Central Issues

1. First, there is the issue of *control*. Who shall be responsible for the overall program? Should there be an action director and a research director? The issue is partly theoretical, partly practical, partly uncontrollable in any case. But if we are speaking of the ideal situation—ideal in the sense of maximizing the payoff for rational, data-based social planning—experience currently points to the preferability of single control in the hands of research-oriented personnel.

Mattick's Chicago Youth Development Project[2] started with a separation of powers, but evolved of necessity into a research-controlled operation. Our Los Angeles projects, the first bipartisan and the second a research oligarchy, leave little doubt in my mind about which system leads to greater long-run payoff for science *and* for practice. Some of the reasons for this have been pungently stated by Freeman and Sherwood in the following two comments:[3]

> But unless the social science researcher participates, indeed leads the dialogue and bargaining required for the development of an impact model—including the identification of the goals, the description of input-output variables, and the elaboration of a rationale that specifies the relationship between input variables and goals—these tasks are likely to remain undone. Once the impact model is formulated, the researcher must continue to remain within the environment, like a snarling watchdog ready to oppose alterations in program and procedures that could render his evaluation efforts useless. (p. 16)

> The researcher has three choices: he can ... try to guess the intermediate and overall goals, and later be told that the ones he selected were not relevant at all; he can insist that program persons provide them in which case he should bring lots of novels to the office to read while he waits, or he can participate or even take a major responsibility for the development of the action framework. (p. 17)

Just one example from the Los Angeles projects was the question of "targeting in" on critical youngsters among a gang membership of perhaps 100. In the Group Guidance Project, the research team tried to recommend concentration on boys who could be connected with some nongang activity—jobs, remedial training, and so on. The action supervisors alternately recommended concentration on gang leaders or "hard-core" delinquents. With no agreement on strategy, and no one in a position to resolve the issue, the workers usually made their own decisions based on their own individual styles. The result was randomness or chaos, depending on one's viewpoint, and a tragic inefficiency in the use of program resources.

In the Ladino Hills Project, the opposite occurred. Intervention targets were selected according to a clear and consistent model based on the relationship between each boy and the group. No significant deviations were permitted. At the risk of blowing our own horn, I believe this was a major reason for our success in Ladino Hills.

2. A second issue, referred to in the quotes from Freeman and Sherwood, is the complex matter of *evaluative criteria* and expectation levels. This subject merits separate treatment, so for present purposes I will only indicate the seriousness of the problem because it deals with both the rational and irrational relations between researchers and practitioners.

Experience suggests that the presence of an evaluation team, because it can easily be seen as "snooping," often exacerbates the practitioner-researcher gap. This is especially true because of the difficulty of obtaining agreement on acceptable criteria. In this vein, Rodman and Kolodny indicated that "he [the practitioner] may view the researcher's persistent request for 'evidence' rather than 'impressions' as carping and quibbling."[4]

Worse yet, the researchers' criteria often imply to the practitioner that his own type of evidence is useless or phoney. Consequently, the practitioner withdraws from evaluative opportunities and we are left in the quandary posed by Rodman and Grams, ". . . We are in the curious position of having to conclude that the most successful programs are those that have not been carefully evaluated."[5]

3. The third issue is that of the *use of the data* generated in an action-research project. Short epitomizes the extreme academic viewpoint when he maintains, forcefully and convincingly, that the most important contribution of the researcher in these programs is the contribution to knowledge.[6] But this is not totally realistic, for if there is too great a ratio of data taken to data given, we'll soon run out of practitioners willing to collaborate with us. There ain't many of those around to spare.

On the other hand, those who state that the primary use of the data should be program improvement or development must deal with the indisputable truth of Freeman and Sherwood's observation: "Certainly it is difficult to point to many instances in which programs actually have been modified, expanded or terminated because of evaluation findings."[7] Sometimes this is because of the equivocality of the findings or the logical and methodological errors in their derivation. More often, however, it is because major program decisions are based on a different kind of data, those having to do with power, influence, politics, financing, and the like.

Two months after the end of the Group Guidance Project, the entire Group Guidance operation ceased to exist as a gang intervention program. Our data had indicated that the program significantly *increased* the level of gang delinquency, especially among the younger boys, especially with respect to high-companionship offenses, and especially in those gangs which had been worked with longest by the same worker. But these data, devastating as they may seem, had nothing to do with the demise of Group Guidance. It died as a gang program for political reasons arising from the aftermath of the Watts riots. Had there been no riots, I seriously question what impact our data would have had.

The Ladino Hills Project was designed in full accord with the director of our new collaborating agency, to be replicated and expanded should it prove successful. It did prove successful, with reductions in gang cohesiveness and delinquency approaching 30 to 40 per cent. But when it was over and a new director had taken over the agency, our worker was the only full-time gang worker left on the agency staff. Any possibility of employing the project model had fallen before the onslaught of new agency policies which were, in turn, reactions to the new social and political realities of 1967 Los Angeles.

4. A fourth issue is that of *experimental control*. The poles here are well represented by Freeman and Sherwood on one side, and by Short on the other. Freeman and Sherwood forcefully maintain that proper program evaluation depends on the application of the laboratory model of research to the field setting, with control groups, assignment of subjects to experimental and control conditions on strict sampling bases, and so on. Short, on the other hand, sees this approach as almost totally unrealistic, since our usual dependent variables, such as delinquency, are subject to uncontrolled contamination by noninduced factors and are replete with inherent measurement problems. Our own experience has demonstrated, I believe, that the lack of experimental controls can be partially overcome and that the problems raised by Short are not totally debilitating to impact assessment.

5. A similar issue is that of *replicability*. Here, the questions raised are: Can programs of demonstrated effectiveness be replicated (without their evaluative component) and *will* they be replicated? I have already

mentioned our two negative experiences. Miller feels that the maintenance of the *status quo* is so crucial to agencies that ". . . for the great
majority of organized institutions which maintain programs directed at
juvenile delinquency, the adoption of operating procedures and philosophies which would be effective in reducing juvenile crime would, in fact,
pose severe threats to the viability of the institution."[8]

Yet so many programs of *unproven* value are adopted that I must
conclude that Miller's statement is more descriptive than predictive.
What is needed, perhaps, is an engineering component of action-
research programs which would develop techniques for the incorporation of validly tested programs into existing institutions. An analysis of
factors impeding such incorporations in the past would be a most worth-
while initial step.

6. The sixth issue has to do with the *theoretical basis* for the best
project payoff. Miller has made very clear his position that the major
impediment to progress resides in the official and lay community agencies dealing with delinquency. He would have us start there. Others,
especially those trained in the psychological and casework traditions,
would concentrate on the individual delinquents, basing counseling
techniques on concepts of individual dynamics and change. Group
workers obviously have their chosen target, typically applying techniques
designed to capitalize on group properties to bring about a change in
shared group norms and values.

Our own accumulated experiences in Los Angeles lead us to urge
that the target be group *dissolution* through counteracting those factors
which bring about group cohesiveness. The juvenile gang, I hasten to
add, is one of the very few social problem aggregates for which such an
approach is appropriate. We have found individual counseling to be
relatively fruitless. The same is true of efforts at community organization or the modification of agency policies. The target should be group
dissolution by discouraging group activities as such and by identification
and provision of a variety of nongang alternatives.

7. The final issue to be raised here concerns the level of evaluation to be undertaken. This is not the place to go into a detailed analysis
of all the complexities of evaluation in action-research projects. However, it has been my experience that the reactions of practitioners to a
research team are highly dependent upon the major thrust of the research effort. If research emphasizes the *feasibility* of a project, then
the professionally oriented practitioner is most threatened, for it is the
professional field which is under scrutiny.

If research emphasizes the *implementation* of the project, then the
supervisory staff comes under the gun as those responsible for translat-

ing a programmatic statement into a field operation. Here, the handling of the feedback process is crucial because it may undermine the supervisor's authority with the field staff and lay bare his level of competence before the agency administrator.

If, finally, the research concentrates on *outcome measures*, then it is the *agency administrator* who is most unnerved. Presumably, he must assume ultimate responsibility, credit or blame, for the outcome of the project. It would be well for the researcher to consider these matters carefully prior to project initiation and plan some collaborative strategy. In the Group Guidance Project this was not done. We chose to evaluate on all three levels, and I have the bruises to document the inherent dangers of such a comprehensive approach. To judge by his writings, so does Walter Miller, while Short, eschewing the evaluative route, seems unmarked.

The answers, in terms of the researcher's health, may lie in the assumption of project direction by the researcher. I don't say this facetiously at all; if researchers are to continue in this strange enterprise called action research, some thought must be given to their protection and nurture. There aren't many good ones to spare.

The Gang Setting

Is there anything about gangs or gang programs that makes action research in that setting different from action research in other settings? Probably not, in a qualitative sense, but there may be some quantitative differences worth considering. I will mention just a few.

First, the action is in the street. This means that the practitioner is in essentially alien territory and requires an appropriate set of strategies. These strategies have not been well conceptualized. In addition, action in the street scene means, almost inevitably, lower levels of line supervision than is commonly present in action programs. For the researcher, this supervisorial gap poses serious problems of data validity, discrepant views of the action, feedback mechanics, and proper implementation of program or special experimental procedures. In a word, there is little *control*, and certainly less than is found in most action-research settings. Let me cite just one example from the Group Guidance Project.

In the last year of the project, it became obvious—at least to us—that the increasing cohesiveness of one gang cluster was a function of the increased programming the detached worker was arranging with the gang members: a weekly club meeting, two and even three ball games a week, and so on—group work with a vengeance. With the complete support of his supervisor, we asked the worker to suspend all organized activity for at least a month in order to see whether this would (a) halt the increase in cohesiveness and (b) start a decline in illegal activities, which had also been climbing at a precipitous rate.

The results of our little experiment were, at best, equivocal because of the lack of control over what happens in the field setting. Not only did the worker cease all organized activity, but he dropped by about two thirds his individual contacts with the gang members. Later conversations made it clear that we had taken away his crutch; he could not justify the change to "his boys," he didn't know how to face them, and so he literally turned his back on them. In fact, for the next month his field contacts were so low that we couldn't get a reliable measure of cohesiveness from his field data.

A second issue that is particularly crucial in the gang setting and brought into perhaps exaggerated focus is the conception of the intervention target as an *individual* versus a *group* phenomenon. Detached worker programs exist in their present form because *gangs* exist; what is not yet clear is that the gang phenomenon *requires* a group work approach, at least in the standard sense. Our own experience suggests very strongly that standard group work procedures, because they tend to maintain or reinforce group structure, merely exacerbate the problem. We believe that the detached worker, if he is to continue in existence, should strive to put himself out of existence as a group worker. This is the lesson of our research, but it is not one which endears us to the practitioner.

Finally, there is the question whether it is even necessary to do gang work. Delinquency in the United States tends to peak at age 16. Gang affiliation similarly peaks at around age 16 or 17. Maturational, cultural, and social forces all combine to bring about a decline in delinquent and gang activity after that time. Shouldn't we be satisfied with this, and put our efforts into areas in which such natural declines do not take place?

Most gang programs—at least those with a research component—have failed to document success in delinquency reduction. Some have had an adverse effect. But, of course, we don't have all the answers yet; good, conceptually justified and carefully implemented programs have not tested the full limits of intervention efforts. Were I in a position to do so, I would immediately eliminate *all* gang programs except those few— if they exist—which are truly experimental in the scientific sense of that word. The rest represent a waste of manpower and an affront to the evaluations which have taken place in recent years.

References

1. Edward A. Suchman, *Evaluative Research: Principles and Practice in Public Service and Social Action Programs* (New York: Russell Sage Foundation, 1967).
2. Hans W. Mattick and Nathan S. Caplan, *The Chicago Youth Development Project* (Ann Arbor: Institute for Social Research, University of Michigan, 1964).
3. Howard E. Freeman and Clarence C. Sherwood, "Research in Large-Scale Intervention Programs," *The Journal of Social Issues* 21, no. 1 (January, 1965): 11–28.
4. Hyman Rodman and Ralph L. Kolodny, "Organizational Strains in the Researcher-Practitioner Relationship" in Alvin W. Gouldner and S. M. Miller (eds.), *Applied Sociology* (New York: The Free Press, 1965), p. 96.
5. Hyman Rodman and Paul Grams, "Juvenile Delinquency and the Family: A Review and Discussion" in *Task Force Report: Juvenile Delinquency and Youth Crime* (Washington, D.C.: The President's Commission on Law Enforcement and Administration of Justice, 1967), p. 208.
6. James F. Short, Jr., "Action-Research Collaboration and Sociological Evaluation," *The Pacific Sociological Review* 10, no. 2 (Fall, 1967): 47–53.
7. Freeman and Sherwood, *op. cit.,* p. 13.
8. Walter B. Miller, "Inter-Institutional Conflict as a Major Impediment to Delinquency Prevention," *Human Organization* 17, no. 3 (Fall, 1958): 20–23.

Chapter 9: The Ladino Hills Model and Implementation

The Model

One of the difficulties encountered by many past programs stems from the enormous complexity of the gang problem. It has been assumed that a problem deriving its existence from a multitude of sources (family, community, economic deprivation, individual deficiencies, etc.) must be dealt with on all levels. Yet most gang programs have been of the "detached-worker" variety, a form of intervention for which this multilevel approach is inefficient at best, and in reality almost impossible. Detached workers can have relatively little impact on individual character disorders or psychological deficiencies, family relationships, poverty, educational and employment disadvantages, community disorganization and apathy, and so on. These factors are not highly manipulatable by individual workers for the most part. On those occasions when workers have been able to intervene in these matters, it has generally been on behalf of an individual gang member with little or no spread of effect to other members.

There is, however, one area in which gang workers can have a significant impact which maximizes the efficiency of their operation. *Gang structure and cohesiveness* constitute the one set of factors peculiarly open to the detached worker but to few others. **The Ladino Hills project employed a gang intervention model based primarily, but not exclusively, on considerations related to gang structure and cohesiveness.**

The model implicitly employed by most gang programs attempts to reduce delinquency through transforming the acting-out group into a

238

social club, with the attendant transformation of norms and values. However, our model attempted this through dissipation of the gang by undermining its sources of cohesiveness. The model rested, in part, on the following assumptions.

1. *A certain, currently unspecifiable, portion of the delinquent acts committed by gang members would not have occurred if no gang existed.* Some of these are the result of the direct influence and companionship of members; some are the result in part of the acceptance, or even approval, of group peers. A recent conference of gang research experts from across the nation[1] revealed that all accepted this assumption as valid. Many writings by both practitioners and theoreticians make this assumption explicit. Significantly, no one has as yet definitively investigated the point empirically, so fundamental and obvious does it seem.

2. *The gang reinforces both deviant values and deviant behavior.* Empirical verification of this assumption has been supplied by Gordon *et al.,*[2] and is commonly observed by practitioners and researchers alike.

3. *Formalized structuring and adult "sponsorship" of gangs tend to reinforce individual deviant behavior within the gang.* We can support this assumption with several sets of evidence.

   a. Two large gang clusters from the Group Guidance Project, the Victors and the Red Raiders, were observed by the research team, the detached workers, and the police before and after the workers were removed from the clusters. All agreed that, following worker transfer, both clusters broke up and member offenses decreased.

   b. One group failed to maintain its unity when its worker backed one faction (a losing one) during an intragang struggle for leadership.

   c. Two cluster subgroups declined in delinquency involvement immediately following the cessation of formal gang meetings.

4. *The rate of delinquency, especially of certain delinquent patterns, is a function of the status conferred on these patterns by group members.* This assumption, like the first above, is widely accepted and supported by anecdotal data.[3] It has not been empirically tested.

5. *The cohesiveness of delinquent gangs derives largely from reactions to extragroup factors, rather than from common intragroup factors such as common goals and norms.* Further, it is assumed that a significant number of these factors, both extra- and intragang, can be manipulated to decrease cohesiveness. This assumption, though unsupported

by data comparing gangs to other peer groups, is in accord with observations of Yablonsky[4] and of Gordon.[5] It is consistent with our own observations in Los Angeles, and is indeed a cornerstone of our entire approach to gang work.

6. *The majority of gang members, given the opportunity, will cooperate with adult efforts to provide alternative (extragang) sources of satisfaction and growth.* This has been amply demonstrated by the Boy's Club program in Chicago,[6] the consultant program of the Metropolitan YMCA in Chicago,[7] and numerous other instances including the tutoring, remedial reading, and employment components of the Group Guidance Project.

Other assumptions of this nature might be listed, but these are sufficient to indicate our belief that gang dissolution is both possible and necessary, and that it can be accomplished at a faster pace than gang workers generally believe. Taken together, these assumptions led us to the following propositions. They lay at the base of our approach, and served as checks upon each act of intervention:

1. The ultimate group work goal is to dissolve the gang. Any act, verbal or behavioral, that serves this end and is morally acceptable as well as practicable should be implemented as consistent with the model.

2. Gang dissolution can best be accomplished through decreasing the sources of cohesiveness.

3. Individual member activities which decrease gang participation or identification, or serve as positive examples for other members, should be encouraged. Activities having the opposite effects should not be encouraged.

The action base for eventual gang dissipation rested primarily on four pillars:

    a. *the structure* of traditional gangs in Los Angeles
    b. a *typology* of gang membership patterns
    c. the manipulation of *sources of cohesiveness*
    d. the utilization of *alternative community resources.*

These four major foci were woven together in the action model with data and observations derived primarily from our previous experience with the Group Guidance Project. The action model which resulted was the product of both inductive and deductive reasoning; it incorporated a number of findings directly related to the four foci as well as directly related to the processes of working with gangs. Figure 9-1 summarizes the model.

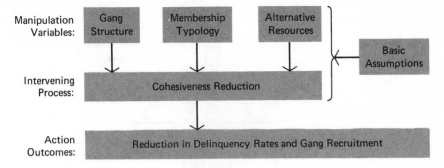

Fig. 9-1: The action model.

As Fig. 9-1 indicates, the action model was a three-step affair. In step one, gang structure, a membership typology, and alternative resources were to be manipulated by the staff in order to bring about step two. Step two, the reduction of cohesiveness, was the intervening process through which we hoped to achieve step three, the reduction of delinquency. In the parlance of the experimental scientist, the model involved manipulating three *independent variables* whose effects would be mediated through one *intervening variable* to change two measures of the *dependent variable.*

In addition, evaluation of the model was to be facilitated by two forms of experimental control. The first was to be a simple comparison of its outcome with the results of the Group Guidance Project. The second was to derive from the collection and comparison of group size and delinquency data from other comparable traditional gangs being served by staff members of the Los Angeles County Commission on Human Relations. Arrangements had been made with the Commission staff to collect the data on these "control gangs," but changes in Commission policies and procedures made this impossible. Within a few months of the project's initiation, standard detached-work services were abandoned and the Ladino Hills Project became the sole standardized detached-worker program with traditional gangs in the entire county of Los Angeles. As a result, we found ourselves with an uncontrolled field experiment.

Gang Structure

The Group Guidance Project yielded very comprehensive data on the structure of the four gang clusters with which it dealt. Although there were variations across the four clusters, the general pattern emerged as shown in Fig. 9-2 and Fig. 9-3. The distinctive features of the traditional

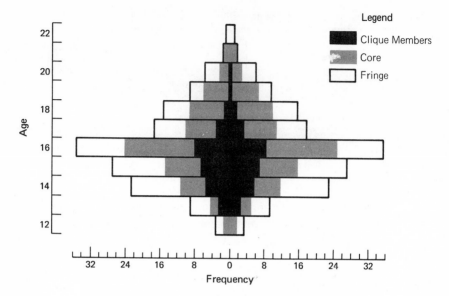

Fig. 9-2. Generalized gang structure by age.

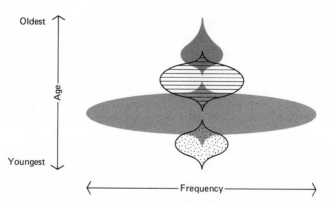

Fig. 9-3: Pattern of subgroups in cluster.

gang are the age range (from about 12 to the early 20's), the number of boys involved (upwards of 150 to 200 over a four-year period), and three levels of involvement (clique members, other core members, and fringe members).

    Figure 9-3 illustrates one other distinctive feature of the gang cluster—the existence of age-graded strata or subgroups within the cluster. Often, each age stratum will adopt a subgroup name while still identifying itself with the overall cluster. Also, there will often be one or two girls groups attached symbiotically to the cluster (not illustrated).

The importance of gang structure to gang intervention lies in the nature of the subgroups and their ties to each other; the age range; the clique, core, and fringe involvement levels; and the roles of the girls' groups. A successful intervention program will treat these dimensions and distinctions differentially and will judge its impact, in part, by the nature of the structural changes it can effect.

The Membership Typology

In an analysis reported in Chapter 3, we determined that core and fringe membership was related to two major independent factors, which we labelled the Deficient-Aggressive factor and the Group Involvement factor. The first factor described individual characteristics of the gang member; the second described the level of his involvement with gang peers. A boy who was high on either factor, as scored by his detached worker, was also independently labelled a core member.

Because other data showed that core members were far more delinquent than fringe members, we combined these three dimensions to yield the eight-celled Table 9-1.

Table 9-1: The Typology

Deficient-Aggressive	Group Involvement	Offense Record	
		High	Low
High	High	Mess-ups	Luckies
High	Low	Crazies	Shadows
Low	High	Social Delinquents	Cool-heads
Low	Low	Racketeers	Nobodies

Each cell of the table was assumed to represent a somewhat different type of boy, especially as he related to his gang peers and to gang activity. The labels in each cell came either from the boys' own terminology or from our guesses about significant characteristics. The purpose of the typology was to allow the staff to move away from random or intuitively based interventions. Each type of boy was to receive differential "treatment" as suggested in the following excerpt from the original project proposal.

Mess-ups: These boys score high on the D-A and GI factors, and have accumulated relatively high offense records. They are the most difficult to wean away from the group. They require hard-core group counseling.

Luckies: Seemingly similar to the Mess-ups, these boys have managed to avoid serious police and court involvement. Analysis of factors differentiating them from the Mess-ups may lead to treatment suggestions. Prior to this, they represent a hard nut to crack, but in hard-core group counseling can be used as role models for the Mess-ups, at least with respect to offense patterns.*

Crazies: These boys have high Deficient-Aggressive and delinquency scores, but relatively low Group Involvement scores. They approach the concept of "loners" whose delinquency may be more individually- than group-determined. They might be expected to "graduate" to retreatist behaviors and other individual offense patterns which serve more to fulfill psychological rather than economic needs. Individual therapy and counseling seem most appropriate to this group. Also, resource development would be highly desirable, since the pull of the group would be less likely to cause recidivism or leaving jobs and school than in the case of the Mess-ups and Social Delinquents.

Shadows: These boys resemble the Crazies except that they have avoided official attention. If one can assume that the high offense rates of the Crazies represent to some extent an acting out of their individual problems, then an important difference between Crazies and Shadows may be that Shadows have found alternative need expressions that do not lead them to official trouble. We believe this may take many forms—hanging around with the gang, attaching themselves to sympathetic adults (such as detached workers), developing hobbies or special school interests, and so on. If this is correct—and we know a number of gang members who fit this picture very well—then a primary treatment approach would involve developing such interests and seeking resources for their activation. This would not only help wean these boys away from the group, but could also be used as a model for the Crazies. Possible pairings of Crazies and Shadows in "extracurricular" activities should be attempted.

Social Delinquents: High group involvement and offense rates but low deficiency scores suggest that these boys have gotten into trouble primarily through their gang involvement. One would expect their offense patterns to show a disproportionate number

---

*Throughout this discussion, it is assumed that the most convenient role models for high-offense boys are low-offense boys with similar factor profiles. They are expected to be compatible for counseling purposes.

of charges such as gang activity, curfew violations, group assaults, etc. They would be good candidates for introduction to other recreational and social youth groups and to hard counseling on the dangers of following the deviant patterns of others.

Cool Heads: In many ways, this is the most interesting of the subgroups in the typology. We have come to know a number of these boys, as they respond more easily to adults and represent a core of boys who show promise as subprofessional aides. Seemingly secure and confident, they have a strong group commitment and seem capable of responding to guidance, even to the point of taking responsibility for effecting change in the group. Their low offense rates make them more commonly available to the worker. We propose to use these boys as primary role models, to the point of paying some of them to work as worker aides. In particular, we would hope to have them serve as primary avenues of influence to the younger members, emphasizing their "cool" approach ("Hold your cool, and you'll make it, man").

Racketeers: These boys have low scores on both the Deficient-Aggressive and Group-Involvement scores, and are labeled as fringe members by the workers. Yet, they have relatively serious offense records. One possible explanation for this situation is that these boys have become involved, directly or indirectly, in the adult criminal world, following one pattern always available in high crime districts. If so, we might expect to find them charged with a disproportionate number of thefts, possession of stolen goods, pimping, pushing drugs, forgery, numbers involvement, etc. Thus, it may well be that the project's main goal with respect to these boys would be to isolate them from the rest of the group to avoid influence and recruitment.

Nobodies: This category accounts for a large number of fringe members who seem to have no great need for gang involvement. Many are easily discouraged from participation by a competent worker after they have had a taste of the gang world. They are the best candidates for ordinary public and private agencies whose interests lie in serving neighborhood youth who do not disrupt their programs. They must be actively discouraged from aligning themselves with core members of the gang.

It will be obvious that these are capsule, stereotypic descriptions with no allowance for overlapping of categories. Thus, there is an aspect of artificiality to the scheme. However, to the extent that it provides suitable guidelines to differential treatment procedures, the model stands as a pragmatic device around which the project may take form.

The model has several drawbacks that should be made explicit. First, it can be applied only to those boys for whom scores on each factor can be obtained through the workers' knowledge.* Second, it does not apply in full to the youngest boys whose delinquent careers do not as yet permit dichotomization into high and low delinquency seriousness. In these cases, the basic assumptions earlier stated, and our approach to sources of cohesiveness, take on added importance in providing directions for intervention.

Even with these minor drawbacks, this membership typology promises to be a significant advance over the simple distinction between core and fringe members. The core-fringe distinction is commonly recognized by gang workers, and on occasion is indeed employed as a conceptual anchoring point for differential treatment procedures. However, the three-dimensional typology to which our data have led us represents a meaningful refinement in understanding some of the important bases for gang membership status. It allows the worker to move from mere labeling (core or fringe) to an initial grasp of membership dynamics, which in turn should lead to more appropriate and effective treatment decisions.

Alternative Resources

The commission of delinquent acts by delinquent gangs, like any other social problem, could be resolved by the simple elimination of all persons who pose the problem. But, in a society which places high value on human life and welfare (particularly that of youth), this solution is unacceptable. By the same token, any other proposal for decreasing the number of delinquent acts by juvenile gangs must prove that, in the process of reducing the problem, the individuals involved are not destroyed, either literally or figuratively, but are benefited.

Thus, the positive appeal of any scheme for the reduction of gang delinquency must be bound to this social context. Consideration should be given to achieving a balance of concentration and effort between the assumptions and techniques involved in dissolving a delinquent gang and the alternative activities which will be available to members as the gang becomes more inaccessible.

The experience of the Group Guidance Project demonstrated clearly that the level of resource development required, along with the desired follow-up on youth placements, could not be achieved by a detached worker. He had neither the time, nor, in some instances, the

_____

*See page 73.

inclination. We learned also that the community organization approach is relatively inefficient and seldom produces specific placements or help for specific boys.

Accordingly, the alternative resources would have to be managed by a staff member hired for that specific purpose. A *team* must be developed—the traditional gang is too much for one man alone. The job of this "resources worker" would be to provide the alternatives to gang participation, in line with the considerations deriving from gang structure, the typology, and the assumptions listed earlier. Employment would be the resource worker's major responsibility, but he would also be involved with the schools, recreational facilities, health and welfare facilities, and so on. In addition to finding the resources, he would be responsible for all follow-up procedures, reinforcing the youth placements. He would leave the detached worker free to concentrate on individual, group, and family counseling.

Once more, the emphasis would be placed on gang structure and each boy's place within it. The fact that youth A wanted a job was to be secondary to his position in the structure of the gang and his placement in the typology, the latter also being based on structural elements. The decision of the resources worker was determined by the available data.

Tests of Success or Failure

As an exercise in action research, the Ladino Hills Project must be evaluated on several levels. One of these, its contribution to the scientific literature, can only be assessed by the reader on the basis of the overall report and the data included therein. The other levels, however, are the responsibility of the project team; self-evaluation is risky, but is nonetheless an integral component of the concept of action-research. In our particular case, three categories of questions or areas of evaluation seemed most appropriate:

Implementation: To test the cohesiveness/delinquency hypothesis, it was first necessary to take certain action steps to implement the action model. The first test, then, must be of the staff's success in launching and carrying through those procedures which were designed to reduce gang cohesiveness. Here one would be interested in gauging the effectiveness of staffing, community contacts, resource development, using the membership typology, maximizing the feedback of data into the action procedures, and so on. This is the test of staff ability.

Cohesiveness: If action implementation was successful, the second test arises—did the action procedures lead to a reduction in gang cohesiveness? This is a conceptual test, one which asks whether the notions about gang structure could lead to differences in cohesiveness. Given successful implementation, negative or negligible impact on cohesiveness would invalidate the conceptual model. A positive impact would lend strong support to the model's validity as far as factors related to cohesiveness are concerned.

Delinquency: The final test depends on the first two. If the action model was successfully implemented and if this led to a reduction in gang cohesiveness, is there a corresponding reduction in gang delinquency? This is the test of the major hypothesis that cohesiveness is related to delinquency in a causal fashion, such that cohesiveness reduction will lead to delinquency reduction. A failure to find a reduction in delinquency would invalidate the hypothesis, as herein tested. Finding such a reduction would support the hypothesis, especially if the data show some *direct* relationship between the two variables.

Implementation

We come now to that aspect of the project that is the most difficult to describe, because to describe the methods of the project is to describe our own actions. To be truly objective about oneself is seldom easy; to be objective about one's involvement in a project personally conceived, designed, and carried out may be impossible. Two years of one's professional career, with all the personal and professional stakes involved, are not lightly regarded. The defense of self produces formidable weapons.

To guard against convenient lapses of memory and to prevent omissions in reporting, a daily Project Log was maintained by the research staff. This log reports in detail every step taken, its rationales, and its results, both good and bad. Included were the intrastaff relationships as well as behavior of the gang members. As a final check the field observer, who was closer to the field action than anyone else, reviewed and amended the Log in accordance with his own perceptions of what took place during the project. Much of this chapter is based in part on Log entries.

The Latin gang itself has been in continuing existence for over 30 years. The name derives from Latin Street, a location earlier at the center of the lowest-income Mexican-American population, but now largely industrialized. A "gang area analysis" completed in March of 1961[8] identified five subgroups within the Latin gang cluster, named Jesters, Los Locos, Little Jokers, Latin Midgets and Cutdowns, and Jokers (Eastside Latin). This report identified 123 cluster members, and an additional 17 who were believed ready for membership. Of the 123 members, 108 were or had been on probation or parole, 10 had no record, and 5 had unknown statuses. Latin members outnumbered the members of 53 other known gangs in 1960 probation camp attendance.

As a result of the above survey, the Latin groups were assigned a detached worker by the Group Guidance section of the County Probation Department. Prior to the project, that worker had been concentrating his efforts on the Jokers, Little Jokers, and Jokerettes (a girls' auxiliary). Little progress seemed to have been made in the face of the many obstacles the worker had to face. Gang recruitment, gang delinquency, and intergang raiding were still occurring.

Structure

At the outset (May, 1966), we expected to find the structure with which we had become familiar through the Group Guidance Project; two or three age-graded subgroups of boys with a girls' group attached to them. In addition, we expected a total *active* roster of perhaps 75 boys and 20 girls, with another 50 boys and 20 girls in various inactive statuses. This would have allowed us to start planning for differential subgroup treatment based on age and sex.

Our expectations were largely fulfilled, but several critical differences became obvious. There were two male subgroups and one female group. The female group was more tightly involved in the "club structure" than we had expected, as a result of worker Jack Snell's style. A female student worker was obtained through the County Commission on Human Relations and assigned to the girls' group.

The larger boys' subgroup consisted primarily of 16- and 17-year-olds and clearly constituted the active core of the Latins. However, the smaller subgroup was an unusual combination of 15- and 16-year-olds on the one hand, and 18- to 20-year-old "veteranos" on the other. The connecting link was provided by sibling and cousin relationships, of which the Latins had far more than the Negro gangs we had studied.

Finally, while there were some younger boys hanging around, they had not as yet coalesced into a visible subgroup. Had we come upon a unique gang cluster, or was this typical of the Mexican gang, or had we come on the scene just at a transitional point in the Latins' structural evolution? We found in talking to other workers that this missing subgroup was *not* the typical situation, and were told by worker Snell that Latin was not unique, that the younger group could be expected to coalesce at any time. Thus, we concluded that fortune had smiled upon us—one of the few times she would in the next year and a half—and our first major structural guideline was determined, to prevent, if possible, the formation of the youngest subgroups. The specific procedures will be detailed later.

Evidence that the Latins were similar in other respects to the Negro gangs in the Group Guidance Project is available from the probation records. Both gang populations (Negro and Mexican-American) had 72 per cent of their members on probation by the end of the respective project periods. Family median income levels were almost identical ($4,500 and $4,600); median parental educational levels were similar (tenth grade and ninth grade), although 13 per cent of the Negro parents had had some college experience as opposed to 1 per cent of the Latins' parents; the percentage of boys living with both natural parents was very close (28 per cent vs. 29 per cent), although more Negro boys had stepparents (42 per cent vs. 26 per cent); family size was similar (4 children vs. 3.5 children; five persons in the average home of each group); median intelligence test scores for both populations were similar (84 and 80).

The major difference between the two sets of backgrounds was in residence patterns. Five per cent of the Negro parents were born in Los Angeles County, as opposed to 20 per cent of the Latins' parents. On the other hand, one third of the Latins' parents were foreign born (Mexico). By the same token, fewer Negro boys were born in Los Angeles (45 per cent vs. 64 per cent) and those born outside the county had moved in more recently (in-county residence of 8.4 years vs. 11.7 years prior to respective project starting dates).

In summary, then, the Negro and Mexican-American gang populations were found to be very similar on most background characteristics available from their probation files, and equally represented in that data source. This increases our chances of generalizing from the findings of this new project to other traditional gang settings.

As to the "strange" subgroup of boys ranging in age from 15 to 20, our first thought was to attempt a separation of the younger from the older boys. However, we were dissuaded from this strategy by two sets of data. First, as I already mentioned, the connection was based on family relations and therefore not very amenable to outside manipulation Second, a check of offense records showed that, without exception, the older boys in this clique were relatively "clean": they had been in very little trouble with the law. In terms of the gang membership typology, they were "Cool Heads" (see Table 9-1) and thus good role models for the younger clique members. One of them, an older brother of a younger clique member, was already on the payroll as an assistant to the worker. In this situation, then, efficiency demanded that we turn our attention to more serious problems than this particular clique represented.

In addition to the subgroups already mentioned, there was a subgroup called the "Cutdowns," the 19- to 21-year-old boys who had been the most active group several years earlier but had now dissolved into small dyads and triads—seen fairly often but not committed as a group to gang life. Our primary objective with them was to reinforce their outward movement, especially those who seemed attracted to and were admired by their younger compatriots.

In summary, our first glance at the structure of Latin suggested the following guidelines:

1. Concentrate on the major active clique (subgroup name, the "Jokers")
2. More or less ignore the mixed age group (and cross our fingers)
3. Reinforce the dissolution of the "Cutdowns"
4. Attempt to prevent the coalescence of the youngest boys into a new subgroup
5. Assign a female worker to the girls' group to (a) wean them away and (b) use their influence in a positive manner with respect to intergang rivalries

Two other surprises met us when we took to field, both having to do with worker Snell's approach to Latin. The first had to do with group size. Entries in the Log tell the story:

3/29/66: Big problem . . . Snell says entire co-ed group has 27 members. Considers them core. Can't tell if this is total, or he's out of touch with fringe and younger and older (Cutdowns) groups. Is gang already dissolved?

4/21/66: Received roster from Snell—25 boys and 12 girls—all listed as core. Obviously, we have a problem here in . . . definition of gang membership. Jack's thinking is primarily in terms of "club."

4/25/66: M.K. started working on Snell's old reports—problem of gang size . . . is disappearing—found an additional 40 boys' names and 14 girls' names—mostly older kids. Haven't looked at some '65 and '66 reports yet.

4/28/66: Now have additional 68 male and 20 female names from Snell's reports as possible members!

Thus, despite our first fears, it became clear that Latin had not dissolved, and field observation commencing in the first week of May, 1966 confirmed the existence of a full-fledged gang cluster as described earlier. The difference lay in the worker's reporting and perceptual style —he had come to think of his group in fairly narrow terms as consisting of those who regularly attended his weekly club meetings.

The last initial surprise of this nature concerned core and fringe membership. In the Group Guidance Project, the workers rather uniformly labeled their members core and fringe on a 50/50 basis, but never exceeding a 60/40 ratio. But as indicated in the Log excerpts above, the Latins' worker did not follow this pattern. All active club members, we were told, were core members of the gang. We investigated this further with the worker on the first day of the project, with the following results:

5/2/66:   Snell's definition of "core": level of participation, especially but not only, in club affairs. Obtained core-fringe [designations] on 94 boys and 32 girls.

	core	fringe	unlabeled
boys:	70	14	10
girls:	25	1	6

Obviously, Snell's response bias differs from our previous workers. This put more importance on the factor judgments.

If the worker sees most gang members as core members, the utility of the terminology is greatly diminished. Thus, the factor judgments, the basis for the membership typology, became even more important to the determination of differential treatment procedures. Hopefully, these factor judgments would undercut the poor core-fringe dichotomy but, at this point, we were admittedly becoming nervous that the worker's unusual perceptual approach would also affect the validity of the factor judgments. As will be seen in a moment, our fears were justified; but the results were, if anything, to strengthen the structural foundation of the intervention model.

Membership Typology—Targeting

Reviewing briefly, the eight-category typology was derived by separating boys into the upper and lower scores on three dimensions. One of these, "level of delinquency involvement," was taken from official delinquency files. The other two dimensions, the "deficient-aggressive" factor and the "group-involvement" factor, were derived from the worker's assignment of item scores to each boy. These two factors were independent: A boy could be judged high on both, low on both, or high on one and low on the other. This independence is of course crucial, or we could not validly speak of two factors rather than one.

As soon as we had satisfied ourselves that we had a fairly adequate roster of Latin members, a rating form for each was given to the worker. Each form contained 25 items comprising the deficient-aggressive and the group-involvement factors and required that for each boy, on each item, the worker make a judgment about the boy's rating as compared with the average gang member. For example,

item 8: As compared with the average member of this group, to what extent does he look at the group as his primary world?
( ) more ( ) less

item 24: As compared with the average member of this group, how much control does he have over his own impulses?
( ) more ( ) less

The results of this exercise can be followed in these Log entries:

6/3/66: Internal reliability on 85 returned Group Involvement scales equals .88 for the five-item scale, .96 for the eleven-item scale!

6/6/66: Continuing analysis of the factor judgments now makes it painfully obvious that, as used by Snell, the two sets of factor scores are highly correlated. This means telescoping the typology into just four cells, with resultant changes in treatment rationale. Stay tuned for further bulletins.

The completed analysis revealed that, like the group involvement scale, the deficient-aggressive scale was highly reliable ($r_{tt} = .94$). But the correlation between scores on the two factors was +.85. In other words, the worker did *not* use the factors independently but, as with his core-fringe judgments, adopted a single, global approach to the criteria for levels of gang involvement.

Our eight-fold category system now had collapsed to four, which was little more than the old core-fringe distinction combined with high and low delinquency involvement. Worse still, the worker's dichotomization was such as to label most boys as core members and to give them high factor scores. In other words, the data told us to abandon the typology, even though it was one of the principal components of the model.

Before taking this step, we embarked on a tortuous conceptual journey to see if we could salvage the typology. Since the problem seemed to lie with the worker's conceptual system, an attempt was made to re-orient the scheme to his approach, but we could find no solution which did not do irreparable damage to the notion of a *data-based* intervention model. We reluctantly dropped the typology and turned our attention in other directions.

The direction to take was determined by our attempt to salvage the typology. This attempt forced the staff to return to the original rationale for it: *to employ structural data (variations of group membership) toward the most efficient use of intervention practices.* Faced with 100 or more gang members, and limited by personnel and resources, it is necessary to "target in" on certain boys on the basis of their relationship to the gang.

After a series of trial and error attempts and much intrastaff discussion, we chose four *structural criteria* for selecting target gang members, those on whom we would concentrate.

Clique Leaders: The research observer collected data daily on the companionship patterns of Latin members. These data, covered in more detail in the next chapter, revealed membership cliques and clique "leaders," the boys seen most commonly in the company of others. Figure 9-4 depicts the "Joker" clique of May and June, 1966, the first two months of the project.

Using numbered circles to represent the boys, and connecting lines to represent the most frequent companionship patterns, it is clear that boy 5 was pivotal; for whatever reason, he was a clique leader—at least in terms of popularity. Thus, he became a primary intervention target on the assumption that positive impact on him might have a "spread of effect" to others—more so than would be the case with any of the other boys.

Cohesiveness Builders: Since our major intervening variable was cohesiveness, it followed that boys who served to build or reinforce cohesiveness worked against the aims of the project. Any boy who stood out *behaviorally* as building gang cohesiveness became an intervention target. Clique leaders are of course an obvious example, but there are other ways to build cohesiveness:

a. gang talking and recalling old gang exploits
b. attempting to instigate intergang raids and fights
c. being a "supplier" (money, drugs, alcohol)

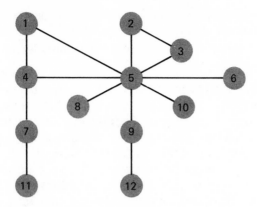

Fig. 9-4: Original "Joker" clique.*

    d. cruising—cars are sure-fire popularity builders
    e. activity planning—"Let's hold a dance, man," or "How about takin' us to the beach once a week?"

Recruits: Any boy who started to hang around with gang members or expressed an interest in joining was watched very closely. A boy who had existed on the fringe but then began to participate more heavily was also "suspect." All such boys became target members, with the exception of those who showed up after being "on vacation," a euphemism for incarceration.

    "Best Bets": These were the boys whom the *companionship data* indicated were least tied to the group—loners, fringe members. Our thought here was simply that the boy with weak group ties could most easily be weaned away.

    These four categories of boys—clique leaders, cohesiveness builders, recruits, and "best bets"—replaced the categories of the original typology. Whenever a staff decision was made that a boy was to be targeted for one or more of the above reasons, a "target card" was made out for him and inserted in the "Target Board" on my office wall. This board had five columns into one of which each card was placed. The column headings were:

    1. Employed
    2. Out of the area (moved or placed by the court)
    3. In custody

4. Other (usually low participation, but might refer to therapy, parental restrictions, and so on)

5. Current target (those requiring maximum intervention)

Progress or retrogression of each boy was followed on a daily basis, with each change in target status entered on the target card. Some boys had only one entry in one and a half years; at the other extreme, one boy ("Richard"—see Chapter 3, p. 86–89) had 26 entries as he went through ten jobs, five arrest detentions, and one residence move out of the area. He is currently in prison for murder.

Originally, the target board contained only a dozen names, but as some moved out of current target status, others moved in, and with the continual shifting of status and changes in membership and membership patterns 64 boys eventually ended up on the target board. On the last day of the project, the board showed 26 employed, 6 out of the area, 10 in custody, 8 in the "other" category (7 for low participation, 1 killed in a gang fight), and 14 current targets. One could summarize this as 40 successes and 24 failures in intervention, but these status patterns shift so often that I am loathe to adopt such an approach to evaluation. The board was not meant to evaluate the project, but to keep up to date on the status of the boys as we worked with them. This, in turn, kept the staff on its toes as it necessitated constant feedback and checking on where to concentrate effort, and how. Selected excerpts from the Log may illustrate the process.

5/31/66:   Completion of clique analysis from first four weeks' observations reveals Mario Olivas* at center of group including Pachecho, Bustamante, Harper, Felix Romero, Inzunza. Mario looks like our first good bet for removal from group since he's already shined on two jobs; maybe placement is the answer. He's a noted runaway problem— what about Spanish-American Institute? Job Corps?

6/2/66:   Snell cites Freddie Romero, "Patsy" Suarez, Eddie Acosta, "Go Go," George Morales as the younger mess-ups moving into core behavior and status. M.K. told R. to get to know these kids very well. Also Popeye Castillo's younger brother.

8/15/66:   Discussed targeting "Nando" and George on basis of July clique structure findings. R. to seek more background information on both.

---

*All names are pseudonyms. The initials M., K., R., L. and others generally refer to project staff members.

8/29/66: As a target, Aguilar is rough. He's working at the car wash, and increasing his involvement primarily because of residence (same court as Lorenzo and Clarios).

9/14/66: Gringo's job ceased 1½ weeks ago. Note that his contacts have jumped up since then. R. says he is actively recruiting for the Cutdowns. Better target in on Gringo.

10/6/66: September clique structure shows 2 Joker subgroups linked by several, but especially Manny. He becomes prime target. Also target on new visibles: Humpty, Eddie Vargas, Jimmy Alaya.

Six month target list summary:

18	employed
2	out of area
6	in custody
4	other
11	current targets

11/3/66: Analysis of clique structure and companions/appearance ratio for the first six months adds the following to the target list: Torres (best bet); Mantilla (best bet); Sanchez (clique leader); Sanhueza (increasing participation); Zarate (increasing participation).

11/4/66: October clique structure shows augmentation of the two Joker cliques, with Georgie and Nando central in one, Chico and "Casanova" central in the other. . . . Chico is added to the target list.

12/6/66: November clique structure analysis reveals continuing breakup into smaller segments, and no new targets except Ralph Gomez who already goes to school and works.

2/20/67: Addition to target list: Dave Dominquez—upswing in visibility; Ralph Gomez and "Taco" Herrera—returned to gang.

2/22/67: Joseph Dominquez' job placement is the seventh in a week, and all of a sudden we're in good shape again. Target board shows, of 57 targeted members,

21	(37%)	are employed,
6	(11%)	are out of the area,
8	(14%)	are in custody,
14	(25%)	are exhibiting low appearance levels,
8	(14%)	remain as current primary targets.

4/5/67:   ... there is no important growth in clique size, nor return of
            the older members. It's all Jokers, but we have to watch
            out for Arnold Gutierrez, Alfredo Mehias, and Corrales
            (all those, I believe, are in school). Summary: we're just
            about holding the line—pray for the next six months, add
            Alfredo to the target list.

5/2/67:   Biggest increased participation is from George, Tiger, Billy,
            and Freddy Aponte. On the other hand, Frank Moran,
            Eddie, Jesus Romero, and Taco Herrera are now low enough
            to be pulled from "current target" column.

5/10/67:   Humpty lost fight with Diaz on 5/10, was seen "chesting"*
            three other times today. Confirms R.'s observation that
            Humpty is actively seeking group status—appeared at the
            church** for the first time since September.

6/6/67:   Of greatest significance is the gathering status by Humpty
            who emerges now as a center of attraction for three of the
            high school attenders ... plus Corrales and Joseph
            Dominquez. His attempt to move in via Chico and Mario
            is resulting in the formation of a new subgroup. Therefore,
            he becomes Target #1. Participation levels have increased
            for Tiger (back to current target) and Banuelas and
            Saldivar (two new target board entries).

6/7/67:   Looking at "best bets" for May, we get Galan, Ralph Gomez,
            "Patsy," Dave Dominquez, Jesus Romero, Gus Bueno,
            Teddy Dominquez, "Birdman," and Eddie. All of them are
            already on the board.

7/6/67:   Recruits Luna, Lenny Guerro, and Corrales go on the target
            board—the latter has risen in participation, the first two
            have now been around over a month. Eddie, Ernie Orduno,
            and Sanchez are increasing their participation, so they
            also move to current target status.

6/28/67:   Georgie told R., "I gotta get a job—Nando's been working so
            long now." Then got job with Woodchuck at $1.60 (How's
            that for verification of clique leader approach?). With
            Nando, Chico, Ruben, and now Georgie working, and with
            continued peer pressure from them plus Lucy kidding him
            and making fun of his half-hearted approach to job seeking,

---

          *"Chesting" is play fighting with no head blows—a "safe" test of fighting ability
and courage.
          **Official club gathering spot on Wednesday nights.

Mario is judged by R. to be ready for job placement again. Decided to make him first priority to "get him while he's ripe."

7/12/67:   Mario got job with uncle on 7/7 at Plasticard Corp.

Alternative Resources

From the preceding discussion and illustrations of the targeting procedures, the importance of developing resources as alternatives to gang involvement becomes clear. Equally clear is the intimate relationship between these two components of the intervention model. Targeting without resources for the chosen boys is a waste of time. Resource development without careful selection of boys to use the resources is highly inefficient, at best.

All workers, of course, make implicit—and sometimes explicit—judgments about which boy is "ready" for, or will benefit most from, new opportunities opened up to him. The difference, and a crucial one, between the usual approach and that of the Ladino Hills Project is in the criteria for selecting boys. Need, "readiness," and personal benefit were secondary in our case to the *nature of the boy's group involvement.* We wished to have impact on a group, not a collection of individuals, and thus placed our bets on the individual/group connection. This was done in a far more systematic fashion than in any other program with which I am familiar.

Unfortunately, we were not able to be so systematic in the area of resource development. In this area, it was necessary to move away from the "safety" of our own data and into the subchaotic world of community opportunities. The experience of the Group Guidance Project dictated the hiring of a separate individual to act as "resources worker," leaving the detached worker free for individual, group, and family counseling.

Therefore, the proposal called for the services of a community resources worker whose primary functions were to seek out, develop, and activate community resources as alternatives to gang participation. His domain was to be unrestricted, but the emphasis was expected to be upon employment and educational opportunities for older gang members and upon avocational and recreational activities for the younger members.

Matching of youth to opportunity was to be worked out with the detached worker, following the dictates of the typology (later, the target board system). Each "assignment" of a boy to a resource opportunity was to serve not only to aid the boy and decrease his gang identification, but also to provide a model for others in the group to whom the boy was related by typological characteristics and clique structure. Putting this another way, the selection of one boy from others was to be determined in part by the potential "spread of effect" within the gang.

During the Group Guidance Project, we observed the activities of four community specialists assigned to the project. These observations and systematic data collection on their role enactments provide some useful guidelines for the Ladino Hills Project, as follows:

1. Considerable emphasis in the earlier project was placed on community organization *per se.* In sum, there was literally no payoff from these efforts for the project. Los Angeles communities are highly *unorganized*, and no single individual can expect to have much impact in this area. On the other hand, workers who concentrated their efforts on attaching *particular* gang members to *particular* employment, school, or training openings had considerable success. We proposed to follow this second path in the new project.

2. One of the significant findings of Short and his colleagues in Chicago[9] has been verified by the experiences of the Los Angeles workers, namely that gang members suffer from a paucity of adult contacts.* Combining this datum with the *typological* factors suggested a very specific guideline for the resources worker. It will be recalled that one group of boys was high on the Deficient-Aggressive factor but low on the Group Involvement factor (these boys were labeled "Crazies" and "Shadows)." It was our belief, especially with respect to the "Shadows," that they are most susceptible to adult contacts as alternatives to gang involvement; that is, the needs brought about by their heightened interpersonal or personal deficiencies could be met through providing sympathetic adult "sponsors." This is a need fulfilled in part by the detached worker, but the worker is divided many ways and cannot adequately relate to a few individuals among scores of their fellow members. The loss of the typology early in the Ladino Hills Project did not invalidate the reasoning here—it merely necessitated different selection procedures.

The Human Relations Commission had inaugurated a program called "Friends Unlimited," a community-based big brother approach in which indigenous adults were to be recruited for "sponsoring" individual youngsters who exhibited the need for this type of relationship. We had the youngsters with well-documented needs. The resources worker was to be responsible for pairing them off with the appropriate adult males and for providing follow-through on the developing relationships.

---

*This is no doubt one of those many instances in which social scientists have "discovered" what has been obvious to practitioners for many years.

3. The previous community workers took on responsibilities that were not related to the project, and in highly individualistic fashions. This, plus the lack of focus and supervision provided them, led to ineffective "targeting" of their activities. None spent more than 40 per cent of their time in active contact work, averaging in fact only two "contact situations" per work day and 4½ individuals contacted per day. Community meetings, travel time, and paper work accounted for an inordinate amount of their time. Time spent in all three of these categories was considerably reduced in the Ladino Hills Project.

We must emphasize again that the resources worker was to be the "back up man" for the detached worker. As the latter prepared youngsters for activities and assignments alternative to gang identification, the resources worker would supply these extragang alternatives through his community contacts. The essence of a team approach is the coordination of *complementary but separate roles*, and this was the aim here. By the same token, the resources worker was not to engage in more traditional community organization functions except when these held promise for providing contacts of direct benefit to Latin members. Without this latter restriction, the approach being demonstrated here would no longer have been clearly of the detached worker variety, pinpointed to *gang* intervention *per se.*

Cohesiveness

The preceding exposition of the intervention model and procedures covers much of what might be discussed about gang cohesiveness. But in addition to the above, a few other guidelines were employed.

For instance, there was good evidence from the Group Guidance Project that an emphasis on programming—dances, sports, activities, outings, club meetings, and so on—had the inadvertent effect of reinforcing or even increasing gang cohesiveness. Accordingly, we made a determined attempt to discourage and prevent such activities in the Ladino Hills Project. An exception was made for instances in which two or three Latin members were to participate in non-Latin events. Such participation is a form of opportunity or resource development rather than gang activity as such.

A similar guideline was employed in the event of serious gang fights. Rather than make impending fights legitimate through formal truce meetings or react as a staff as if an emergency were on hand, we planned instead to "pooh-pooh" these incidents, to act as if they were minor and not worthy of organized response. However, events were to prove that this is more easily said than done. A gang killing leads almost automatically to emergency response.

10/16/66:   Learned from R. on 10/16 that Manny had been shot and
             killed by the High Riders (rival gang) at 5:00 the previous
             night. Snell in Mexico. L. got T.'s number and (a) we got
             T. into area at 4:00 accompanied by R.N., (b) M.K. in area
             at 1:00, (c) S.E. in area by 4:00 after checking location of
             girls and pulling three out of the area, (d) M.K. to police
             station to arrange for heavy patrolling of Latin and High
             Rider areas. Rest of Sunday spent by all in cruising,
             talking with Latin boys, and generally being as visible
             as possible.

Another decision had to do with relations with the police. Because
of our position that gang cohesiveness is more a function of extragang
rather than internal variables (that is, the gang differs from most enduring
groups in that the reinforcing variables are primarily environmental),
relationships with the police were planned to minimize field contact. The
interaction between police officer and gang member, given their mutual
distaste for each other, is ordinarily conducive to increasing the sense
of gang identification. If the Ladino Hills Project staff were to make a
"special deal" with local police officers, the effect would be the same,
to increase the salience of gang identification as such. Therefore, except
in the most unusual situations, staff/police relations were confined to the
management level through the central Juvenile Division of the city police
department. This liaison had been well established for several years
prior to the project and although the Juvenile Division command was
doubtful about the project's likely success, it was supportive of the effort.

The major, summary point about cohesiveness as a variable to be
"managed" by the staff is simply that every decision and every action
was subject to the same test: would it more likely serve to increase or to
decrease gang cohesiveness? In weekly staff meetings, in phone calls,
in street contacts, and in meetings with community agencies, the staff
was required (though not always successfully) to consider their suggestions and their actions in the light of this one overwhelming consideration
—what will it do for cohesiveness? It was in answering this question,
more than in perhaps any other aspect of the project, that we did in fact
rely upon our accumulated experience, knowledge, and intuition.

References

1. Lois Wille, "Streets: Research Discussion Conference," a report prepared
   for the STREETS Project and distributed by the Metropolitan YMCA of
   Chicago, 1968 (mimeo).

2. Robert A. Gordon, James F. Short, Jr., Desmond S. Cartwright and Fred L. Strodtbeck, "Values and Delinquency: A Study of Street Corner Groups," *American Journal of Sociology* 69, 2 (Sept. 1963): 109–28.

3. Richard A. Cloward and Lloyd E. Ohlin, *Delinquency and Opportunity: A Theory of Delinquent Gangs* (Glencoe, Ill.: The Free Press, 1960); Albert K. Cohen, *Delinquent Boys: The Culture of the Gang* (Glencoe, Ill.: The Free Press, 1955); Walter B. Miller, "Lower Class Culture as a Generating Milieu of Gang Delinquency," *Journal of Social Issues* 14, no. 3 (Summer, 1958): 5–19; James F. Short, Jr. and Fred L. Strodtbeck, *Group Process and Gang Delinquency* (Chicago: University of Chicago Press, 1965); Frederic M. Thrasher, *The Gang: A Study of 1,313 Gangs in Chicago,* abridged and with a new introduction by James F. Short, Jr., (Chicago: University of Chicago Press, 1963); William F. Whyte, *Street Corner Society* (Chicago: University of Chicago Press, 1943).

4. Lewis Yablonsky, *The Violent Gang* (New York: The Macmillan Co., 1963).

5. Robert A. Gordon, "Social Level, Social Disability, and Gang Interaction," *American Journal of Sociology* 73, no. 1 (July, 1967): 42–62.

6. Hans W. Mattick and Nathan S. Caplan, *The Chicago Youth Development Project,* (Ann Arbor: Institute for Social Research, University of Michigan, 1964).

7. YMCA of Metropolitan Chicago, "Youth Consultant Project," developmental report for October, 1961 to January, 1963 (mimeo).

8. Raul Nunez, "Area Gang Activity Analysis: Community of Ladino Hills," Los Angeles County Probation Department, March, 1961 (mimeo).

9. James F. Short, Jr., Ramon Rivera, and Harvey Marshall, "Adult-Adolescent Relations and Gang Delinquency," *The Pacific Sociological Review* 7 no. 2 (Fall, 1964): 59–65.

Chapter 10: Assessing the Impact

It was stated earlier that the project should properly be subject to three tests: how well the intervention model was implemented, how much impact on gang cohesiveness resulted from the intervention, and what effect there was on gang delinquency. While these three levels are not totally independent either conceptually or functionally, I will treat them in this chapter as if they were.

Implementation

It is impossible to summarize, as comprehensively as the participants would like, the many major and minor occurrences of an 18-month project. Only the project Log would fulfill that function, and it is 400 pages long. Therefore, we must abstract from the 18 months those project components that were (a) most highly emphasized, (b) most important to the outcome of the project, and (c) hopefully the most illustrative of both the ups and downs of the intervention process. The feeling of the staff was that implementation was successfully achieved in the main, but that there were several failures which prevented total euphoria.

Staffing

The project employed two "sets" of staff, research and field. It is the field staff that is of primary interest here, although the project was greatly benefited by the competence of the research assistants who remained within the confines of the university.

The field staff consisted, at the beginning, of the detached worker, the resources worker, a female student worker assigned by the Human Relations Commission, and a research observer. The detached worker and resources worker functions have already been described.

The student worker, a young female college graduate, was assigned to the detached worker to assist with the girls' affiliate of Latin. Her success with this group was quite considerable in a short period of time as most of the girls lowered or totally ceased their gang participation. However, the student worker wished to work independently and without regard to the intervention model or in concert with other members of the team. Some staff dissension resulted, and she left the group after six months.

The research observer's primary function was to collect daily observational data on gang cohesiveness. To accomplish this, he cruised the Ladino Hills area 40 hours a week noting all appearances of Latin members. The companionship data thus collected will be described later.

To make his role legitimate in the eyes of the gang members, he introduced himself to them as a student worker, a role with which they were already familiar because of the past history of gang sponsorship. Being of Mexican-American background himself and only a few years older than the boys, he was quickly accepted. His instructions were to be helpful to the detached worker whenever doing so kept him in good observational position. However, trips out of the area or long sojourns at any particular site were ruled out as interfering with his primary observational task. His hours and routines were standardized as much as possible to be sure that changes in the boys' grouping data would reflect *their* behavioral changes, rather than his. All this was not an easy task, but various statistical and observational checks revealed a generally consistent and always conscientious approach being pursued. As a result, we have on hand full data on gang member companionship for a full 18 months, vacation time excepted.

Teamwork was of the essence in the project, and a good deal of time was spent in orienting staff to the spirit of the intervention model and the importance of collaborating in accordance with its dictates. For the most part this was achieved, but the detached worker became an exception; at times he seriously threatened staff morale and on too many occasions actually hampered the project. He came to resent the project and the role of the project director, resisting the model and for a while deliberately avoiding contact with everyone but the resources worker and the research observer. This in turn put these two people in a very uncomfortable situation, acting as go-betweens and caught in the midst of interpersonal conflicts.

Morale problems of this sort generally have many roots, including personality clashes, role conflicts, ideological differences, and personal incidents. In our particular case, at least three of these roots became evident. The first was the worker's personal style, the second the past frustrations of the job, and the third the conflict between these and the requirements of the intervention model.

With respect to past frustrations, two points are important. First, the worker had been dealing with gangs for a number of years. The rewards of such work are few and far between, and the experienced worker typically loses heart and withdraws from innovative activities which expose him to further disappointments. Second, our worker had witnessed the killing of one of his Latin boys at the hands of a rival gang during a club gathering the year prior to the project. This tragic event had a long-lasting effect on his reactions to high-tension periods and led him to withdraw from active involvement in certain situations. These two factors in turn led to a style of work which can be illustrated by Log excerpts:

7/5/66:   Snell seems to have given up on individual interventions unless a kid comes to him; e.g., Gil quitting Job Corps, Spade pushing pot, Felix' medical problem....

7/27/66:   After meeting, "Narco" came in and rounded up boys to "throw blows"—intend to cruise rival areas.... Nando, Ruben, Gonzales, Pedro, Popeye, Benny Garjel, Casanova among those involved. It took at least 20 minutes of hanging around and moving back and forth from car to church before they got started. Snell did nothing to intervene except remind Nando he was already in trouble. Group caught three High Riders on Broadway and chased them and beat them.

8/15/66:   Snell late to beach party—went to (probation) camp... because Frank Moran was adjusting poorly. Then left early because Sally Maya was having neighbor trouble. This is clearly the cornerstone of Snell's style, responding to calls for help of any kind, rather than reaching out before something breaks.

6/7/67:   It looked like old times... 19 boys and 7 girls showed up... some talk of a High Riders threat, anxiety.... Luna was initiated in (five against one) . . . the new boys provided much of the focus. With a lot of beer being consumed, it all took on the appearance of a celebration. With all the drinking, loud noise, and initiating going on in the parking lot, one would expect Jack to intervene, but he didn't. He seems to have given up any possibility of having an effect on ongoing group activity.

6/7/67:   Staff meeting: Concentrated on the meeting situation last Wednesday. . . . Jack . . . maintained, as predicted, that you can't stop something like that. The fact is that he isn't sure enough of himself or his relations with the kids to test this out.

6/14/67:   Quite a night! The wake was not as big an affair as previous one. . . . Still, it served to mobilize the forces. Between 20 and 25 were seen at the church, and two High Rider cars were cruising. . . . Because of the High Riders, Jack closed out the church and left the area, hardly the rational way to handle things. Soon after he left, we cruised and found 20 kids gathered at the Courts. Stopped, chatted just long enough to remind them of our presence. R. stayed until at least 10:30 when we left. The group at the Courts reportedly had guns. Dissolved by 10:30.

The difficulty in all this comes when this style—reacting only when sought out and withdrawing from situations of high group tension—conflicts with the intervention model, as it did on numerous occasions. Had the worker been more flexible in his approach (beyond that already indicated by voluntary involvement in the project) we could have fitted his style into the model without undue strain. But sufficient flexibility was missing and the worker was never fully able to accept the model as providing guidelines for him, personally.

7/27/66:   Mr. R. from Job Corps showed up to make a pitch, but because Jack again stalled the meeting, he had to leave (and Gil was there and could have given a personal testament).

8/4/66:   Val Ramirez, the new recruit, is from Church Street gang and with Pedro in the Elysian Park killing—wants to stay clean. Jack says he won't discourage Val's participation because he's been cut off by S.S.G. (another detached worker organization).

8/4/66:   Tuesday, Jack went to the beach with Val, Pedro, Gus,
          Tiger, Sam, and Eddie. Sam and Eddie shouldn't have
          gone. Jack was told this about Eddie after the last beach
          affair. He's not listening, or he doesn't care enough. He
          says he wants to include Eddie in all activities because he
          feels sorry for him.

8/9/66:   Staff meeting: It may be difficult for Jack to comply with
          the model requirements of active discouragement/
          participation in group activities by some boys unless
          alternative, easily accessible activities are developed—
          most especially, recreational ones.

3/27/67: Staff meeting: Drew blanks from all, especially Jack Snell,
          on (a) how to discourage potential recruits from Junior
          High School and (b) how to prevent additional Latin
          involvement in Lobo Villa hassling. Jack sees the problem
          with Lorenzo perfectly well, but does not consider the
          problem of "contagion."

6/27/67: Call from R.: Jack seeking personal favors for younger
          brothers of Terry Montez; campership for one, job with
          project money for the other. Jack relayed message, but
          won't talk to us about money matters—it's the old sugar
          daddy approach of last year. L. to investigate camp
          possibilities, but the job notion is totally inappropriate—the
          kid has no Latin connections, and is no different from all
          the other needy boys in the area. Jack refuses to understand,
          or accept, the notion of project money being granted for
          specific purposes.

8/7/67:   Jack reports: He will take 6 to 9 boys camping for three days.
          Boys to be selected sans model, age, core-fringe, school,
          work, or other references.

It must be emphasized again that the approach exhibited by the
worker in these selected excerpts is under normal circumstances quite
common and typical of detached worker operations. Only the existence
of the special project and its requirements—imposed by others—makes
this worker's approach inappropriate. Among ten workers from whom
we had collected activity data in 1964 (see Chapter 6), this man stood
out as the *most active;* more time spent in contacts with youths and their
parents, and more time spent in the field, than any of the other workers.
He was the worker we most wanted for the Ladino Hills Project. Thus
these Log excerpts illustrate, not fault or blame, but the nature of the

conflict and some of its consequences. These latter, developing at times into genuine staff dissension, are illustrated next.

7/8/66:   M.K. <u>attacked</u> by Snell tonight—manifest issues were:

        a. red tape for out-of-pocket expenses.

        b. office space wasted money—should give it to the kids.

        c. insufficient money for camping.

        d. all the money goes to salaries—should go to kids.

The meeting was half an hour late getting started because Jack simply sat around—the kids were wandering all around, waiting, but Jack was in a bad mood and seemed determined <u>not</u> to start the ball rolling.

7/11/66:   1:00 staff meeting: Snell lowered the boom on us! "Forget it," "Go back and start all over again"; "You had a five-year project and didn't learn a damn thing"; "Why didn't you ask me what I wanted," etc. Jack wants a sugar daddy, buckets of money for the boys (and some for him). Project just an extra burden, and so on. Then R.M. attacked Snell, and so on around the table. L. moved in as mediator/interpreter and did beautiful job moving toward resolution.

Decisions:

        a. Check with Washington and look at Ford budget re flexibility of money for paying kids.

        b. L. to move in full-scale on program implementation in the field—work with R., locate resources, including money for camperships.

Couple of more sessions like this could be very healthy, especially if we can show Jack by our <u>actions</u> that we can produce. . . .

From this point on, for the next nine months, staff morale was on the upswing and the research and action components acted more and more as a team.

10/3/66:   Snell's attitude far better now—sees impact of project on member visibility, now goes along with suggestions by M.K. and L.

Then in late spring of 1967, for reasons unknown, but not connected with the project (which seemed then to be achieving its objectives), the pendulum swung back.

1/28/67:   At church: 13 boys, 10 girls. Snell not only avoiding M.K. and L. but also the kids—clearly in a depressed state.

6/29/67:   As another indication of Jack's current "black mood," he has not returned any of the time forms for the last sample week.

7/5/67:   Snell still avoiding me, and paying little attention to the boys. This is the longest period of depression during the whole project. Focus of his beef with me is County's failure to reimburse him for the first two months' expenses. He knows I've promised to get the money to him, but he'll believe it when he sees it. Meanwhile, I seem to represent a convenient whipping boy, which would be O.K. except that, in the process, his work is suffering—no staff coordination, low visibility at the church, etc. He has not filled out the final sample week of contact forms—a direct attack on me.

7/7/67:   Call from T. (Jack's supervisor) to set meeting with Jack on Monday. T. volunteered that Jack has been avoiding him also—makes me feel less paranoid.

7/24/67:   Again Jack failed to appear for staff meeting. After 45 minutes he called R., but refused to speak with me. Even R., as close to Jack as he is, referred to this behavior as "childish".... Jack is not only being childish, he is deliberately failing to perform job tasks. He puts R. and F. in a very uneasy position, using them as go-betweens. If necessary, we can finish this job without Jack and if it comes to a showdown, I'll recommend his transfer. The financial problems he seems so concerned about have been solved, but his sheer physical absence makes it impossible even to communicate this. God only knows what kind of feeling he's communicating to kids and adults in Ladino Hills.

9/18/67:   Staff meeting: Snell failed to appear—just have to work around him for the remaining month and a half.

9/20/67:   At the church: 11 boys and 5 girls showed up. Very quiet, pleasant gathering. Jack was there ... tried three conversational gambits with him, with a remarkable lack of success. He's just going to pretend I don't exist.

Yet even this is not the end of the story. The worker's attitude did not lead to serious reduction of effort by other staff members. He was left alone in his resistance. Then, as the end of the project neared, and perhaps because of this, the pendulum swung back once again.

9/27/67:   At the church: 9 boys, 4 girls in a very relaxed atmosphere. Jack showed, and was actually quite friendly this time.

10/6/67:   R. in: says Jack may return to our staff meetings! Has softened his critical attitude and shown slight interest in meeting with us on Mondays.

10/9/67:   Staff meeting: R. gets a gold star for prediction—Jack showed up and joined in the general conversation.

10/23/67:   Staff meeting: Jack returned ... and again in a very pleasant mood. He cites the following as major accomplishments of the project:

   a. so many boys with jobs, bringing home pay checks.

   b. decrease in size of group gatherings—used to be 20 or 30, now unusual to find a dozen together.

10/25/67:   Church gathering: last one of the project. Twelve boys, four girls. Jack again in fine mood, collaborative.

10/30/67:   Last field staff meeting: Gave bottles of imported champagne to R. and Jack—hope they hold their liquor better than the Latin boys! *

To satisfy a request from the Office of Juvenile Delinquency and Youth Development, the worker was asked to fill out "contact forms" for four sample weeks. These same forms had been used in the Group Guidance Project and by the worker during that time. They permit an analysis of the nature of his field contacts—with whom, where, for how long, about what, and so on. Unfortunately, the morale problems covered above led to the completion of only 12 days' worth of forms—not what was desired, but enough for analysis purposes.

A comparison between the 1967 data and the 1963 data for the worker revealed that during the Ladino Hills Project he spent less time in programming (group activities), and increased the number of contacts

---

*In considering these Log entries, the research observer summarized his view of the difficulties as being attributable to three factors: (a) The worker's lack of respect for the project director on the basis of differences in personal background and the worker's minor role in formulating the project design and procedures; (b) The worker's peers, former Group Guidance officers, whose experiences with the Group Guidance Project led to some negative evaluations of the research director; (c) Value differences between the practitioner and the researcher.

per day by 25 per cent. These were precisely the directions desired
and worked toward in the design of the project.*

Three other aspects of staffing should be mentioned here. Supervision was revealed by the Group Guidance Project experience to be
crucial, especially *field* supervision. In the Ladino Hills Project, supervision was approached from a functional viewpoint, with the aim of
having (a) full staff knowledge of all staff activities, (b) constant correc-
tive feedback, and (c) continuing feedback of changes (progress or
retrogression) in gang member behavior and project goal attainment.

These functions were served through weekly field staff meetings,
the presence of the research director and his research associate at all
gang meetings and activities, continuing contacts between these research personnel and community agencies, and the installation of a
telephone and answering service through which the university and field
offices were in daily contact. Except during the detached worker's
"black periods," there was little happening that was not known to all
concerned.

Feedback, the second additional point of interest, was not only a
matter of full staff communication about field events. It also meant ongoing data analyses of gang structure, offense behavior, and changes
of "target status" among the boys. These analyses were carried out
by the research team and reported to the field staff as quickly as they
were completed. This was especially critical with respect to the boys'
target status, since the resource worker's activities were highly dependent on this. Both field and telephone contacts between staff
members were constantly taking place (with the aforementioned exceptions) so that there was seldom any question about the state of
progress achieved or the action steps required for the future. This very
fact, so different from the case of the Group Guidance Project, was one
of the strongest sources of staff cohesiveness and undoubtedly played
a major part in the overall impact of the project.

Finally, it should be noted that the project had the services of a
consultant psychiatrist for a number of months. Although our aim was
to develop therapeutic resources for the boys, he defined his role as a
consultant on staff matters. He was available during the "smooth"
periods, but not during the summer periods when staff morale was
endangered. Thus, although his insight into the behavior of particular
boys was often helpful to staff members, his impact on the project was

---

*The presence of the resources worker was undoubtedly the major factor here in
bringing about this more focused activity, but in addition, all paper work was discarded
by agreement with the Human Relations Commission, formal group activities were discouraged, and a field office was provided which reduced unnecessary travel time.

less than both he and we would have liked. His involvement was a good experiment of limited utility.

In summary, then, we might characterize implementation of staffing matters as follows:

1. Staffing design was complete, with the exception of the female student worker who left and could not be replaced.

2. Teamwork, supervision, and feedback procedures were accomplished for the staff as a whole, with the notable exception of several extended periods of alienation involving the detached worker. This latter problem was probably more detrimental to staff morale than to program implementation, as the staff learned how to "work around" its disaffected compatriot.

Community Contacts

In the Group Guidance Project, the workers were given to understand that they were to be "all things to all people," to be generalist workers responsible not only for youth and parent work but also for community organization procedures. It proved to be an impossible and therefore unimplemented role prescription. Even the addition of a full-time community organization specialist did not substantially change the situation.

In the Ladino Hills Project, several modifications were made. No attempt at community organization was undertaken. No community contacts were undertaken unless they served useful public relations purposes or had direct relationships to realistic resources development.*
Formal public relations contacts were restricted to the research director or his research associate to leave field staff free to devote their time to their primary clients. Most of the adult contacts can be grouped into the following seven categories:

Public Relations. Project visibility and image were promulgated *formally* by several methods. A small brochure was printed and distributed throughout the community by the staff as well as by agency personnel contacted by staff. The project director gave speeches about the project before various community groups. The local newspaper carried several front page stories about the project. Finally, a list of potentially important lay and professional people in the community was obtained and each was contacted individually. These were the only

---

*Of course, one man's realism is another man's pipe dream, as a discussion of our "adult sponsor" program will indicate on the following pages.

predetermined and formal procedures undertaken. They seemed sufficient to open most of the right doors, and sufficient to permit informal follow-up by individual staff members. For the most part, and in the broadest sense of the term, we had a "good press."

Schools. Most of the Latin members were out of school—dropouts, kickouts, or truants. At no time were there more than 15 Latin members enrolled and attending school, including the girls. Staff contacts with school personnel were primarily with the vice-principals or the employment coordinators. Usually these were staff-initiated contacts for the purpose of reenrollment, transfer, or job development within the schools' Neighborhood Youth Corps. Occasionally, staff was asked to respond to behavior problems or gang tensions within the schools. In some cases, the intervention model suggested that reentry into school would be unwise and staff discouraged these boys from considering school—at least day school—as a realistic action step.*

7/6/66:   All six school enrollees . . . are in danger of quitting
            or being kicked out . . . .

9/7/66:   R. and L. talked with Welfare and Attendance Officer
            regarding aid in getting readmittance to school for
            several youths . . . highly cooperative, promised to begin
            steps to assure assignments by 1st day of semester.

9/12/66:   M.K. and R. talked with vice-principal at Ladino Hills High:

            a. Ruben can enroll direct.

            b. Galan can enroll direct.

            c. Casanova can enroll through Counselor.

            d. Popeye can enroll if his (transfer) record is
               acceptable.

6/19/67:   Sam Bueno will be joined at graduation by Saldivar
            and Ralph Gomez—3 gradua es, by God!

---

*On a strictly observational basis, we have found a considerable difference between Mexican and Negro gang members with respect to school attendance. The dropout rate was much higher among the Mexicans, started at earlier age levels, and was more often tacitly or explicitly condoned by parents. The Mexican girls were more often required to stay home and tend the house and siblings, while the boys reported more pressure to look for jobs. Forty per cent of 10th-graders at Ladino Hills High School failed to graduate. Among Latin boys and girls whose school status was known at the end of the project, 97 were dropouts, 15 were enrolled in school and 4 were high school graduates.

Recreation. Several recreational facilities were available in the Ladino Hills area. However, one playground was off limits to Latin because of a shooting in 1965, and at another their presence was actively discouraged (although they used it after hours for "pot" parties). This left only the Teen Post, a one-and-a-half room facility with minimal equipment, and the Boys' Club, a large, very well equipped and staffed facility.

Soon after the project began, we were told by various Latin members that they didn't use the local Teen Post at all, that there was nothing there. The detached worker echoed their sentiments, characterizing the facility as a "Mickey Mouse outfit." There was the additional fact that administration of the Teen Post was placed under an Episcopal priest whom the worker did not respect at all (we learned later that the feeling was mutual).

However, when it later became apparent that recreational facilities in the area were so limited, we decided to look into the possibilities of the Teen Post.

> 7/14/66. M.K. and L. visit Ladino Hills Teen Post and talked with Director and Father L. Turns out Mario, Dicky, Eddie and maybe others have been using it (saying they have cut away from Latin!). Frank's sister (a member of the girls' group) works there.

As we became more familiar with the situation we learned that a number of Latin members used the Teen Post on occasion, but "on the sly." Rather than risk a reversal of this informal policy, we kept in touch with the Director on an informal basis, and encouraged the Latin attenders only when other Latin members were absent. Since the Teen Post was never identified with Latin *per se* and because Father L. was a social activist whose concerns were with the entire community, the Teen Post represented an *alternative* resource, rather than a locus of Latin gang activity. Our efforts were directed toward a continuation of this state of affairs which remained relatively stable throughout the project period. One outcome was the hiring of several Latin members to work at the Teen Post or an affiliated program administered by Father L.'s church.

However, the most significant recreational enterprise was the project's affiliation with the Boys' Club. Despite the Club's stated and traditional policy not to work with supervised gangs,* discussions be-

---

*This policy had been adopted primarily as a reaction to negative experiences with the Group Guidance program.

tween project staff and Club personnel led to an agreement to work collaboratively with Latin. Thus, the Boys' Club became a popular gathering spot for Latin boys who played pool or ping pong, became the site for remedial tutoring for several members, and—with several notable exceptions—was accepted by Latin members as a "demilitarized zone." For the most part, their behavior in the Club was surprisingly orderly.

This relationship was not an easy one for either staff and, at several points, joint special meetings were called to deal with the anxieties of Club staff over Latin behavior or possible gang fights on the grounds. The critical incident occurred in the twelfth month of the project.

4/21/67:   At luncheon meeting, Boys' Club staff announced its firm
           decision to close out Latin, permanently and without
           exception. No specific incident, but the year's accumulation.
           They feel presence of Latin discourages other boys from
           coming, and have found themselves unable to
           influence Latin.

           This decision was not up for discussion (except for the
           date of its implementation). In fact, both N. and J. said that
           it hadn't occurred to them to discuss it with us—they
           clearly don't want to entertain notions of compromise, just
           a clean amputation. N. will come to the church Wednesday
           to explain to the boys (and lots o' luck, Charlie!).
           Wednesday was agreed on as the last day.

           This sort of close-out, being gang-related rather than
           based on individual behaviors, is just the sort of thing that
           reinforces cohesiveness. We'll do our best to turn it to
           our advantage through counseling, but the chances are
           against us. There's no honest denying of its meaning:
           the last and only decent youth facility is turning its back
           on Latin—the reasons are perfectly good ones, but try
           and tell that to the Nandos, Chicos, and Popeyes.

4/26/67:   M.K. and L. meet with N. and J. to test out their Latin
           close-out. Hit them with:

               a. test cases, e.g. Eddie, Art, Teddy, girls

               b. guilt by association

               c. staff responsibility (Boys' Club) for failing to
                  enforce their own rules and limits

               d. poor psychology of their approach.

THE BOYS' CLUB'S POSITION
RELATIVE TO THE
LATIN GANG

For a number of years the Boys' Club has worked with youngsters who call themselves "Latin." We have attempted everything from working with the gang as a group to allowing them to participate as individual members.

During these many years:

1. Too many youngsters have stopped coming to the Boys' Club rather than come in contact with the gang.

2. The presence of gang members has negatively affected attendance in the Senior Games Room. Attendance decreases throughout the building as gang member attendance increases.

3. Constructive influence of the Boys' Club staff upon the gang group is difficult, if not impossible to detect.

4. At times the Senior Games Room has the aura of a gang's hideout. Many Boys' Club members as well as parents and staff have indicated this to the club administration.

Therefore we have reluctantly decided to exclude Latin from membership in the Boys' Club.

The cutoff date is to be decided at a joint meeting of the administrations of the Ladino Hills Project and the Boys' Club.

4/21/67

J. in turn hit us with questions of mutual cooperation.
Outcome very favorable:

   a. No close-out announcement will be made
   b. B.C. to develop written rules and criteria
   c. Kickouts will be on individual basis, dependent
      solely upon behavior <u>within</u> B.C. walls.

After this series of events, matters returned to normal and the Boys' Club has remained open to Latin members ever since. It goes without saying that maintaining this facility depended upon a considerable amount of counseling with the boys as well as continued contact work with Boys' Club staff. The sensitivity of gang members to house rules and the threat and inconvenience to staff members of continued gang presence required that we spend much energy in these directions. The openmindedness of the Boys' Club administrators made it all possible.

Criminal Justice Agencies. Under this heading we include the police, the courts, and probation and parole agencies. Field contacts with local patrol officers were deliberately kept low to avoid problems of stigmatization and group identification, but higher contact was maintained with the Juvenile Division to handle emergencies and maintain cooperative liaisons.

The juvenile court judges and referees heard a special presentation about the project in a seminar setting and were sympathetic to *any* project which offered such alternatives to incarceration. On several occasions, project staff offered such alternatives, while in others they recommended institutional placement for boys who were "cohesiveness builders" within Latin.

Probation and parole contacts were the primary responsibility of the detached worker, a former probation officer himself who had many personal friends in these agencies. The recommendations of these agencies for court dispositions were made in most cases after consultation with the detached worker. This in turn generally followed discussion by project staff in an attempt to coordinate the needs of the individual boy with project designs based on his relationship to the group. This entire area of concern was handled informally, and there is no way to know how often staff interventions affected treatment plans for individual gang members. However, there was seldom an instance in which project design was hurt by agency decisions (other than unavoidable ones such as releases of cohesiveness builders following incarceration, or reductions of charges).

Employment. It may be recalled that the resources worker was to ferret out, expand, and stimulate resources for the Latin members which would serve as alternatives to gang activity. His realm was to be unlimited, including employment, recreation, education, welfare, and so on. However, as time wore on it became increasingly evident that employment would be his major endeavor.

There were several reasons for this. First, he enjoyed job solicitation and felt personally that this was the most important need for alienated youngsters. Second, the job situation in the area held some promise since there was a good deal of light industry within a radius of a few miles. Third, the relative lack of recreational facilities and the low educational aspiration level in the community served to increase the salience of employment as a viable alternative. Finally, the Mexican-American culture emphasized the "duty" of the son to contribute to the family income.

At the beginning of the project, 16 of the 64 boys who would eventually become "target" members were working on a part- or full-time basis. Only one of these retained his job throughout the project. The other 15 retained these initial jobs for an average of four and a half months. Thus, the resources worker's job was cut out for him.

He went about his task in several ways. He contacted all the relevant agencies, including those funded under the War on Poverty. He followed up on membership lists from local businessmen's organizations to whom the project director had made formal presentations. And, most effectively of all, he walked the streets, brochure in hand, knocking on the door of every store, factory, shop, gas station, and other establishment within reach.

The results in the employment area can be summarized briefly as follows. During the 18-month project period:

1. Ninety establishments were contacted which yielded at least the promise of some help; an untold number of others were contacted only once

2. These contacts yielded 108 job placements shared by 46 Latin members (including several girls)

3. These job placements yielded $36,443 in gross income to the members, or an average of $792 per member (average job tenure was 53 days)

4. An additional 38 members found jobs on their own. These jobs lasted longer; self-initiated job placements yielded an average of $1,431 per member (average job tenure was 104 days)

A later section of this chapter will report on the relationship between employment and cohesiveness. Here, let me illustrate some of the processes involved, since they were alternately sources of great satisfaction and great frustration. Some days, for instance, were very good job days:

5/25/66:   Sam Bueno got job through R. at plastics company. R. just walked in and asked. 36 hours a week at $1.50 per hour after school and weekends. The owner donates $5,000 a year to L.A. Trade Technical School. If Sam hangs in, owner will pull scholarship for him at Trade Tech. Others might follow, so R. will follow Sam closely.

6/17/66:   Note well: Mario Olvivas had a job last week, and was observed on the street only once—alone!

9/28/66:   Call from R.: He has placed Pedro Ramirez at $1.85 an hour through the private agency. He has placed Georgie and Johnny at a clothing plant at $1.50, through R.'s brother. Eddie . . . puts in ten hours a week working on lawns.

2/2/67:   Call from R.: (1) "Birdman" hired at May Company. (2) Contact at May Co. set up meeting for R. with west coast manager who has federally funded training program. Spent two hours together, will take several of our boys into their operation. Bravo, R.!

2/10/67:   Miguel Martine hired—punch press operator at $2.19 via R., "Birdman" hired at auto supply shop at $1.50 via R. and State Service Center. "Spade" hired for five days at clothing store.

2/15/67:   From R.: "Spade" will be held on at clothing store for a while. "Gringo" and Johnny were hired there today with strict orders to keep apart. We don't like having three at one spot like this, especially when "Spade" is one of them, but until the job situation gets better it's the lesser of two evils.

2/17/67:   Call from R.: Plastics company will hire Joseph Dominguez on Monday at $1.60 with training possibilities. Woolen mill may take 2 stock boys and 2 night maintenance boys. It's opening up again!

2/22/67:   Dominguez' job placement is the seventh in a week, and all of a sudden we're in good shape again.

4/28/67:   Nando (via R.) to start at printing shop at $1.60. Owner
           also may take on sponsor role if he and Nando hit it off
           well—owner is a tenth-grade dropout, deliberately asked
           for a dropout boy.

These were some of the good days in employment, and fortunately
they outnumbered the bad ones. But the bad ones were equally important, as each meant a lost opportunity to decrease Latin cohesiveness.

5/13/66:   R. reports on 3 N.Y.C. (Neighborhood Youth Corps) job
           prospects: Dicky Inzunza took it, is working. Mario Olvivas
           quit on second day—too hard. Georgie Pachecho didn't
           show up.

5/16/66:   R. says Dicky Inzunza failed to show for work Friday.

10/10/66: Georgie quit work, not in school, stayed away from home
           several nights last week. Pedro quit. Mario quit.
           "Cornflakes" tried the Air Force today—not acceptable
           because of his record.

11/21/66: Felix Rivera, Tiger, Cornflakes, and Robert Chavez all
           laid off this past week. Also, Miguel Martine and Pedro quit,
           so R. has his work cut out for him. Gringo and Harper
           are on the ropes as well.

12/27/66: M.K. visited Boys' Club: Staff reports no problems, but two
           N.Y.C. jobs filled by non-Latin. This may be failure
           on our part.

1/9/67:   R. describes job openings situation as miserable. Last
           week's cohesiveness was up; this week's certainly will be—
           there are no jobs, etc. So right now we're clearly in a
           bad period.

1/17/67:   Call from R.: Clothing plant has opening now, but the boss
           says only Cornflakes is acceptable—and he's in jail.
           Nando mouthed off at bosses, Johnny was suspected of theft,
           Tiger has been fired. It's Cornflakes or no one.
           We try and cry!

2/7/67:   Call from R.: Has a $2.60 job for boy 18 or over. Gave him
           four names from target list who might have transportation.
           Second call from R.: (a) Birdman had fight with mother,
           has left home for San Bernardino and can't be located.
           (b) Joseph Dominguez won't take it without brother

David ... , (c) Same with David Dominguez, (d) Art Mantilla
says it's too far away. ... Ho hum! Now R. will try
Gringo, who lives within two bus transfers of the place.
Third call from R.: Gringo can't take the job—no
transportation. That finishes off the eligible target members,
so now we'll try Sam Bueno who might be scared enough
now to be weaned away. If Sam says no, move to Lucy's
boyfriend who has just been released.

2/24/67:   Returned call from Mr. G.—he had two spots for us in the
foundry, but R.'s absence this week killed it. He hired
two other boys. Will keep us in mind for the future.

4/25/67:   Call from R.: has two job openings. First requires 18-year-old
with driver's license, second requires 18-year-old, husky,
with math ability. We can't fit either slot, damnit!

These excerpts illustrate some of the sources of satisfaction and
frustration in the project, and occasionally show how the target list was
employed to concentrate efforts on particular boys. There is one sequence of Log entries which illustrates the most interesting use of
targeting, concentration on a clique leader in the hopes that any success
with him will spread to his immediate companions.

The case in point is Nando, a 16-year-old, hyperactive, and verbal
clique leader. He was a high school dropout who had practically no
work experience, nor any desire for employment. After a considerable
amount of counseling, he accepted a job in August, 1966, in a soap
factory where two other boys had already been hired. Within three weeks
he had started missing work. Through staff intervention, he was allowed
to return and remained on the job another month before quitting. A
month later, in November, he was given a job by the staff at a clothing
plant at $1.50 an hour, but was laid off after a month.

It then took four months before Nando talked seriously of working,
as a result both of counseling and of seeing others bring home the
"bread." In addition, his girl friend was urging him to find a job. Our
narrative starts at the point of the next job, and indicates the "spread
of effect" that occurred on several occasions. Nando's final placement
occurred at a one-man print shop (see excerpt for 4/28/67, p. 281).

5/3/67:   Nando very pleased with his job situation as a trade
potential and with his boss as a possible personal friend—
"he's too nice, man." Looks like a built-in sponsor.

5/15/67:   R. reports boys now call Nando "Sweetie" (his girlfriend's
term for him), laying it on about his square behavior and

lower participation. We will reinforce him. Among other
things, this confirms his crucial position and the potential
he represents for us.

Georgie told R., "I gotta get a job—Nando's workin' so
long now." Then he got himself a job at $1.60.

career?

In short order, almost every member of Nando's clique had a job.
Those who didn't became the subject of much joking and derision in
group settings and the acceptance of jobs in the boys' value orientation
was assured. Nor did the process stop here, as the following excerpt
illustrates.

L. broached night school to Nando and George Morales.
Interesting demonstration of personal influence and peer
pressure followed. Nando very willing to attend if he could
learn offset printing; George noncommittal with negative
overtones. Gil (standing near) was then asked if he wanted
to take any classes—finally decided, if upholstery and
math were available. George: "I want math, too." At this
point Mario Olivas chided Nando with, "You'll never
stay in school." Nando, "That's what you said about my
job, too—remember?" Nando then suggested asking Ruben
and did the selling to Ruben. Mario capitulated and said
he wanted offset printing if Nando took it, but added (more
enthusiastically) that it would help him get promotions
in his job (furniture mfg.) if he also took woodworking.
Viva el Nando!

In summary, the employment aspects of the project were perhaps
the critical factor in achieving the results to be described later. Employment interventions with gang members are extremely difficult, yet if a
significant breakthrough can be made, the result can be most satisfying.
One successful job experience is worth months of intensive counseling.
The two together, even with all the firings, layoffs, quittings, and work
anxieties one encounters, can indeed change the path of gang delinquency. If nothing else, the comparison between the employment
achievements of the Group Guidance and Ladino Hills Projects drives
this point home.

Adult Sponsors. The County Human Relations Commission had
planned to launch a program called "Friends Unlimited" in the minority
group areas of Los Angeles. This program was designed to enroll

indigenous adults from these areas to work with younger fringe members of juvenile gangs and with younger brothers of gang members. This was to be a "Big Brother" type of program specifically designed for gang neighborhoods. The Ladino Hills Project was to be tied to this program in a joint effort. However, the Commission was unable to get Friends Unlimited off the ground, and as a result project staff were forced to develop an adult sponsor program of their own. With a few exceptions, the attempt was not successful.

Staff members sought out people who lived or worked in Ladino Hills who were willing to spend time in one-to-one relationships with Latin members, usually younger or fringe members of the gang. A dozen such people were found, meetings with them were held, and mechanisms for pairing off sponsor and boy developed. Several of these pairings showed promise:

1. A city fireman paired off with two brothers
2. A school teacher paired off with the youngest brother of three gang members
3. A college student paired off with a young fringe member who desired and responded to a tutoring relationship

None of these three pairings developed into a lasting relationship, although the original connections were solidly established. No other useful pairings developed. The reasons are several.

First, gang boys are highly suspicious of adults who take an interest in them, figuring that there must be a "catch" to it.

Second, the adults who volunteered for the program were, with few exceptions, Anglo, middle-class people whose backgrounds did not fit well with that of the boys.

Third, successful mechanisms for starting the relationships were hard to come by—both boy and sponsor felt uneasy about the "legitimacy" of the arrangement.

Fourth, project field staff were sometimes unable and often unwilling to devote sufficent time to the sponsor program. As a group, they felt it was unlikely to work. They were uneasy about the values and abilities of the sponsors, and were hesitant to "turn over" a boy to an unknown adult. Staff reticence resulted in relatively poor and unenthusiastic initial and follow-up relationships with the potential sponsors.

All in all, the number of man hours that went into the adult sponsor program probably were not justified by the results. Had more time been put in by people more committed to the rationale of the program, the payoff might have been well worth the effort.

Programming. One of the strongest hints in the data from the Group Guidance Project was that formal group programming tended to increase or reinforce gang cohesiveness. Thus a consistent effort was made throughout the duration of the Ladino Hills Project to discourage and avoid special outings, ballgames, dances, truce meetings, and weekly club meetings. When the project started, these kinds of activities were a part of the gang tradition, since the group had already had a worker for over two years.

During the project period, only three small outings and one dance were organized. Formal club meetings were discontinued after the first six months to be replaced by informal Wednesday night gatherings. This change, which led to a 21 per cent reduction in average attendance, represents a compromise between the detached worker's standard procedure and the suggestion in the intervention model that all such gatherings be disbanded. As it turned out, much useful research data were gathered on Wednesday nights as the boys became accustomed to confiding to staff in this setting their latest escapades, arrests, job status, and so on.

Although one cannot empirically demonstrate it, we believe this drastic reduction in programming was instrumental in the reduction in gang size and recruitment to be described later. As time went on Latin became less *visible,* as an organized group, to those who might desire gang membership, and had less to offer these potential recruits by way of passing the idle hours.

Interestingly, the reduction of formal group activity never led to serious pressures from the gang members for the resumption of activity. They often asked about beach trips or dances, but there developed little of the negative reaction that was anticipated. Our suspicion was to this extent confirmed, that group programming is more important to the worker than to the gang member.

Other Interventions. The preceding discussions cover the major procedures and activities of the project staff, but of course much is left out. No systematic analysis was undertaken of the informal counseling done with gang members and their parents, but this was of course an ongoing, daily process. Similarly, many contacts with adults in the community, both lay and professional, were as unrecorded as they were numerous.

For instance, quite a bit of effort was spent in finding clinical help for boys whom we felt could benefit from some form of psychotherapy. Since the project had no funds with which to pay fees, volunteers were sought among psychiatrists, clinical psychologists, and psychiatric social workers in the Los Angeles area. It is with great sadness that I report the results.

Only one clinical psychologist volunteered free time, but after one session with a gang member, he found he could not deal effectively with this kind of youngster. We never heard from him again. A similar experience occurred with a psychiatrist attached to a "crisis clinic."

For almost a year, the services of a resident in community psychiatry at the county hospital were available to the staff, but unfortunately (a) he wished only to consult with the staff, rather than to work with individual gang members, and (b) he was not available during the periods of staff dissension mentioned earlier. When available, he was the source of some very useful insights and suggestions. However, what the project needed most was a resource for the boys whose own emotional difficulties affected those around them.

By way of summary, it seems fair to say that the intervention model, as modified by the targeting approach, was successfully implemented in most areas, but not in all. Staffing matters worked out well overall, but there were periods of overt dissension which occasionally hampered the effectiveness of the action team. The collection and use of empirical data both in the design and implementation of the action efforts was accomplished in a relatively consistent and effective manner. The employment area, although marked by many individual reversals, was more successful than had been anticipated. Efforts at developing other resources met with varied success: recreational and educational aspects were satisfactory, if not exemplary, while the adult sponsor and therapy aspects represented failures in implementation. Now the question is whether program implementation reduced gang cohesiveness, for this was the intermediate step toward delinquency reduction.

Cohesiveness

Before describing the measures of gang cohesiveness and the findings with respect to Latin, there are two issues that must be discussed because of their moral or ethical implications. Some practitioners have suggested that one does not have the right to "break up" a gang (a) because it is a *natural* group and (b) because youngsters, especially those in disadvantaged areas, have a strong need to belong to groups. For those who have raised these questions, the following responses might be considered.

1. The gang is not a "natural" group; that is, it is neither necessary nor common. It derives its being not only from the needs of its members,

but also from the pressures and deprivations of slum neighborhoods. Are these pressures and deprivations "natural" and therefore not the proper realm of the practitioner? We doubt the acceptance of such a view.

2. The traditional gang is, statistically, a most "unnatural" group. It consists of anywhere from 50 to 200 members while attempting to maintain the interpersonal ties associated with smaller, more intimate groups. It is a *caricature* of most youth groups—the result more of pressure than of desire. The Ladino Hills Project was not designed to dissolve Latin into over 100 separate individuals, but rather to change the situation enough to break the pressure-based ties and permit more "natural" affiliations to exist.

3. There are no data to support the notion of a "group need." There *are* data to support an affiliative need among both youth and adults, and groups are one form of such need satisfaction. The project did not reduce the opportunities for the satisfaction of the affiliative need. It may, in fact, have made possible forms of companionship even more conducive to affiliative need satisfaction.

4. If our hypothesis is correct, that a reduction in gang cohesiveness leads to a reduction in gang delinquency, then one must balance any dangers of cohesiveness reduction against the gains to both the gang members and society from the reduction in delinquency levels. Each member of the project staff considered this balance—it was discussed explicitly in staff meetings—and each was convinced that the balance clearly favored testing of the hypothesis which the project represented.

A second ethical issue, raised specifically by the federal funding agency, was that of the informational responsibility of the project to its clients, the gang members. The members knew why we were there and were told everything about the project *with one exception:* and this is where the ethical issue arises. They were *not* told about cohesiveness reduction, for the obvious reason that knowledge of this aspect of the intervention model might have defeated any possibility of success. We could not afford the response, "Nobody's going to break up my group!"

Whether we were correct in anticipating this response is not the point of the argument here; the issue is, rather, whether we had the right *not* to discuss this point with the members of Latin. Ordinarily, professional ethics dictate informing the subjects of an experiment about their role in it or, when this would invalidate the experiment, informing them afterwards about the nature of the materials withheld from them. We did neither. Rather, we took a position that has been clearly stated in a report by the Panel on Privacy and Behavioral Research appointed by the President's Office of Science and Technology. The panel concluded in part,

> Participation by subjects must be voluntary and based on informed consent to the extent that this is consistent with the objectives of the research. It is fully consistent with the protection of privacy that, in the absence of full information, consent be based on trust in the qualified investigator and the integrity of his institution.[1]

Because the project was to have a six-month follow-up period, revelation of the cohesiveness reduction design was not possible after the 18-month project period. Further, because data analyses suggested that the project's aims *were* being achieved and that they were being maintained in the follow-up period as well, no attempt was made to "tell all," on the grounds that we had no desire to endanger this happy state of affairs. I feel comfortable with these decisions, but I recognize that the ethical issue has not been resolved, merely considered. With these points in mind, we are now ready to consider the findings on cohesiveness.

Group Guidance Measures

Preliminary analyses of possible measures of cohesiveness developed during the Group Guidance Project revealed that the recording of contacts between gang members by an observer—a detached worker, in that case—yelded data that successfully distinguished between more cohesive and less cohesive gang clusters, as well as between subgroups within the same cluster. We were encouraged, therefore, to adopt a similar approach in the Ladino Hills Project. This is the reason for a full-time research observer on the project staff.

Preliminary Analyses of Project Data

The progress report submitted to the funding agency after the first six months of the project included a preliminary analysis of cohesiveness measures. Six measures were employed:*

a. Number of boys contacted
b. Number of appearances (number of boys times the number of contacts for each)

---

*Each measure was collected on a weekly basis.

   c. Number of solo contacts (one boy seen by himself)

   d. Number of mutual contacts (for each contact situation, $n(n-1)$)

   e. Number of solo plus mutual contacts divided by number of appearances

   f. Number of appearances divided by number of contact situations

Analysis of the intercorrelations between these six indices revealed two factors, one involving sheer numbers (a, b, and c) and the other involving grouping of boys (d, e, and f). Since our approach to cohesiveness is strictly empirical in the absence of satisfactory *a priori* nominal definitions, this suggested that there were two significant kinds of group behavior to follow as indicators of cohesiveness. The sheer number of gang members visible to the observer during standard time periods was taken as one such indicator. The extent to which visible members appear *together* was the second.

Measures of Cohesiveness

In the analysis undertaken for the progress report, number of boys and number of mutual contacts were found to be the indices with the greatest amount of common variance within their own factors, so it is these two measures that were selected for final use. The data for both measures come from the research observer's reports.

Number of Boys refers merely to the number of male gang members observed at least once during each week. However, an analysis of the observer's cruising patterns revealed, not surprisingly, that when many boys were visible he cruised less than when fewer boys were visible. The correlation between number of boys seen and the observer's mileage was $+.74$. To control for this factor, the index employed was the number of boys observed *per mile* (mileage was available from the observer's expense reports).

Gang Recruitment was also followed as an indirect measure of cohesiveness related directly to the number of boys observed. When and if recruitment stops, or even slows to a point insufficient to overcome natural attrition in gang membership, this will of course affect the number of boys observed. But more important, gang recruitment relates directly to gang size and therefore was expected to affect one of the measures of delinquency to be described later. The entire field staff, therefore, kept eyes open for new gang members for both action *and* research considerations.

Mutual Contacts were similarly related to the observer's cruising mileage, but the number of mutual contacts *per contact situation* was not. Number of mutual contacts is defined as $n(n-1)$ in each contact situation. Thus, if three boys are observed together (each being in contact with two others), the number of mutual contacts equals 3×2 or 6. If five boys are observed together, the number of mutual contacts is 20. The total index for each week is obtained by summing all the mutual contacts and dividing by the number of contact situations (or observations) for that week.

Clique Membership emerged from the Group Guidance Project as significantly related to cohesiveness of gang clusters. It was not the number of cliques, but the number of boys in cliques which differed between high and low cohesive clusters. Thus, in Ladino Hills, we followed the change in *size* of clique membership as well as the clique *structure.*

Reactions to Threat seemed to distinguish, in the earlier project, between clusters which were dying out and those which remained strong. Specifically, it seemed that the cluster whose cohesiveness was decreasing often failed to respond to serious raids by rival gangs. The ability or will to mobilize counter actions was taken as a qualitative measure of cohesiveness.

Anecdotal Impressions

To follow gang cohesiveness over time on the basis of personal observations has proven to be a fascinating exercise in wishful thinking. Cohesiveness, if followed on a weekly basis, does not vary along a smooth line, slowly rising or falling in ordered fashion. It wavers, jumps up, collapses in seemingly irrational or even perverse fashion to bedevil the hopeful observer.

Then, one grasps at straws: Fewer boys come to consecutive club meetings; the girls seem less evident on the street; several clique leaders are not seen for a number of days; potential recruits stop hanging around the taco stand; a threatened retaliation against a rival gang fails to materialize; several boys make comments about leaving the gang or about "putting down that kid stuff." Each such instance raises the hopes until an accumulation of disappointments finally teaches its lesson: cohesiveness reduction can be *seen* only over a lengthy period of time and cannot be judged by individual incidents.

By the end of the project, however, the individual incidents had mounted up. We had seen cliques dissolve, the core group of girls disappear, recruitment cease, large group gatherings occur less often, club gatherings diminish in size, fewer boys appearing on the streets and—when seen—appearing more often by themselves. The detached worker remarked on the change, noting that whereas group gatherings used to include 20 to 30 members, now it was unusual to find a dozen together. The research observer also commented about the change:

10/2/67: In chatting about cohesiveness and differences between last year and this, R. confirms some of my own feelings with the following:

1. The groupings last for a shorter time;

2. In the groupings, there is more in and out movement, with many just dropping by to check things out but not staying;

3. Content of the conversations is much lower on gang rivals, weed, and alcohol, higher on jobs, school, and past exploits and incidents related to individuals rather than to groups;

4. Tension level is much lower—they seem less nervous, more secure;

5. In answer to my query, he says he has heard nothing about size of group, new boys, etc. that would indicate any concern over cohesiveness or recruitment matters.

Still, these are only personal observations, subject to the frailties of human perception and desire. The agreement of all staff on what had happened could be taken as verification, or merely as a measure of common delusion resulting from *staff* cohesiveness. The answer lies in the companionship data to be reported next.

Empirical Findings on Cohesiveness

The data on cohesiveness show a rather consistent trend, verifying the observations that the cohesiveness of the Latin gang cluster decreased over the 18-month project period. However, the five measures do not yield the same amount of measured reduction. We can offer no *a priori* criteria for selecting among these measures—the reader must make his own choice.

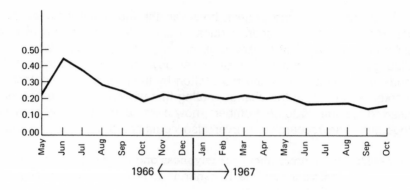

Fig. 10-1: Number of boys seen per mile of cruising.*

Number of boys. Figure 10-1 (reproduced from Chapter 4) reports the monthly averages for number of gang members seen per mile of the observer's cruising.

The initial month, May of 1966, was the period during which the research observer was getting to know the boys on sight. His reports for this first month, especially during the early weeks, mention sightings of "unknown boys" which were not included in the data. We can be reasonably certain, then, that the rise in the graph from the first to the second month is *primarily* because of this artifact of the observational process. Some of it may also be the result of the impact on the boys of a larger group of interested adults than they were accustomed to seeing; in other words, the project may initially have acted as a secondary source of cohesiveness.

However, the most important aspect of Fig. 10-1 is the steady decline in the number of boys observed. If we compare the first six months with the last six months, *the resultant reduction equals 40 per cent.* This 40-per-cent reduction is even more significant than it sounds because the maximum possible reduction of 100 per cent is a physical impossibility which could be achieved only by a mass emigration from Ladino Hills. Boys residing in a neighborhood are going to be observed regardless of any group affiliation.

Another point of interest in Fig. 10-1 is the *rate* of reduction, which is greatest during the first six months. It may well be that one reaches a significant point of diminishing returns early in the game in a project like this, with the remainder of the action period serving more to reinforce than to effectuate major changes. This does not mitigate the importance of continued work, but it may suggest some changes in strategy.

Gang Recruitment. By gang recruitment—a common but unfortunate term—we mean the addition to the gang structure of any boy not previously associated with the group. In most cases, a boy is not actively recruited by active members in a formal or planned fashion, although this does occur on occasion. Gang recruitment usually differs little in process from the formation of youthful nongang associations.

We judged a boy to be a *potential* recruit if he started to "hang around" with gang members. He became an *actual* recruit if he continued this pattern for a month or more *and* was treated by the members as an accepted companion. While these criteria may sound a bit hazy, we discovered in practice that they worked very well. In Ladino Hills, in any case, a boy's decision to continue with his new gang affiliation was made soon and with surprisingly little equivocation.

Figure 10-2 summarizes the recruitment data for the project period. It distinguishes between those who became *visible* as recruits but soon disappeared, and those who *retained gang identification.*

In its gross aspects, the data in Fig. 10-2 resemble the data in Fig. 10-1 concerning number of boys observed. After the initial period, there is a sharp decline followed by a general leveling off. Slightly more than half of the potential recruits retained affiliation with Latin (24 out of 42). *There were no new members after the first year (May, 1967).*

These data suggest that the reduction noted in Fig. 10-1 occurred in part because older members left the gang and were not replaced from the available reservoir of neighborhood boys. The normal recruitment

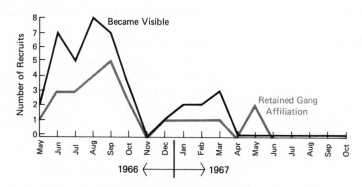

Fig. 10-2: Recruitment.

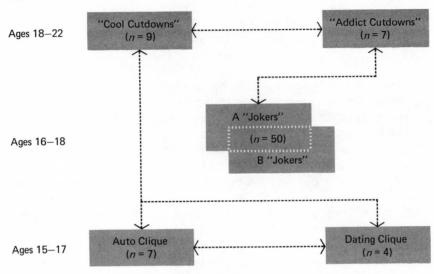

Fig. 10-3: Number of mutual contacts per
contact situation.

pattern was interrupted, and no juvenile gang can maintain its size without "new blood." In a group the size of Latin, one would ordinarily
expect an average monthly recruitment of about three boys. On this
basis alone, Fig. 10-2 suggests that Latin was—at least temporarily—a
dying organization.

    This is particularly true when one considers the age levels of the
recruits who did appear. None were below the age of 15, and most were
in the 17- to 18-year-old age group. A younger subgroup, the *sine qua
non* of the perpetuation of the traditional gang, never developed in Latin
during the project period. The formation of such a subgroup was our
greatest fear and we worked hard to prevent it from occurring, for the
lesson of the Group Guidance Project was very clear on this point.

    Mutual Contacts. The number of mutual contacts per contact situa-
tion is summarized in Fig. 10-3 (also reproduced from Chapter 4) and,
as can be seen, a rather different pattern emerges. Because the graph is
so irregular, a dotted "best fit" line has been inserted to demonstrate the
slight downward trend which the high variance in the data obscures.
The reduction from the first six months to the last six months equals
11 per cent, far less than that shown in Figs. 10-1 and 10-2.

    A comparison of these latest figures with the preceding ones sup-
plies some interesting suggestions about gang cohesiveness. First, the
mutual contacts measure is much more sensitive to changes in the
environment—a distinct advantage over measures based solely on num-

bers of boys. The rises in the graph in June and September of each year are directly related to the beginning and end of school vacations. Weekly measures, not shown here, emphasize this relationship; they also show smaller changes associated with each significant break in the school routine—Thanksgiving, Christmas, mid-semester, and Easter. Because so few of the boys were enrolled in school, we can conclude that gang cohesiveness is directly affected by those aspects of the societal and neighborhood structure and culture that relate to periodic school attendance cycles. Of additional interest is that the rise takes place just *prior* to the school break; it is an anticipatory reaction.

Similarly, the rises in cohesiveness in October of 1966 and in January and October of 1967 are directly associated with intergang fights. In October 1966, a Latin member ("Manny"—Chapter 3, p. 84) was killed by a rival gang in the climax of a week of mounting tension. In January 1967, Latin retaliation for the killing resulted in four assaults and seven arrests. In October 1967, on the anniversary day of the first killing, a Latin member killed an elderly man while on a retaliatory raid (see the case of "Richard," Chapter 3).

These three instances and other less dramatic ones have revealed an interesting pattern in the delinquency-cohesiveness relationship. In periods of intergang tension (which also involves the fear of a police crackdown) fewer boys are visible, but those who are tend to group together more. Thus, the two measures of cohesiveness, number of boys and number of mutual contacts, would at such times yield conflicting results.

In addition to these explanations of peaks in the cohesiveness graph, the comparison between the two types of measures yields another and most important suggestion. Comparing the 40 per cent reduction in number of boys with the 11 per cent reduction in grouping, one can tentatively conclude that programs aimed directly at gang cohesiveness are more likely to affect gang size than gang grouping patterns. This was certainly one of the findings of the Group Guidance Project: the "successes" had primarily to do with group size, recruitment, and the interruption of the "natural" development of younger subgroups.

Nor need one limit the implications of these findings to cohesiveness. If there is a partial causal relationship between cohesiveness and delinquency, then it may be that different conceptions of the former will be related to specific forms of delinquency levels. This is a question to be investigated later in this chapter.

Clique Membership. One of the indices which distinguished between the more cohesive and less cohesive gang clusters in the Group Guidance Project was the proportion of members belonging to identifiable cliques. The proportion was much higher in the more cohesive clusters. In the Ladino Hills Project, a boy was arbitrarily listed as a clique member if he had five or more appearances with any other member during a monthly period. Table 10-1 reports the relevant monthly data for clique membership in the Latin gang cluster.

Table 10-1: Clique Membership, Numbers and
Proportions (Boys Only)

	Clique Members	Available Gang Members	Proportion in Cliques
May 1966*			
June*	28	81	.35
July	22	90	.24
August	26	98	.27
September	25	105	.24
October	30	108	.28
November	24	108	.22
December**	—	—	—
January 1967	22	111	.20
February	17	113	.15
March	20	116	.17
April	20	116	.17
May	26	118	.22
June	25	118	.21
July**	—	—	—
August	26	118	.22
September	27	118	.23
October	23	118	.19

*Combined data for the first seven weeks when the observer was unfamiliar with some members.
**Insufficient data during observer vacations.

It can be seen in Table 10-1 that the absolute size of clique membership remained rather stable over the project period, but that the proportion of boys achieving clique membership followed the pattern of previous data, declining rapidly at first and then leveling off. This is, of course, a function of gang size and recruitment. The significant fact seems to be that as new boys became *available* for clique membership, there was nevertheless no growth in clique size. During the first six months, any new clique members acted as "replacements" for those who were pulling away from the cliques. Beyond that initial period, stabilization of clique membership accompanied increasing member "availability," thus yielding lower clique proportions. Another way of saying this is that as time wore on the proportion of fringe-to-core membership *increased*—precisely what one would desire in this type of gang project.

Aside from the matter of proportions, some interesting qualitative changes took place with regard to the clique structure of Latin. Figure 10-4 describes the overall clique structure if the data for all 18 months are combined.

The largest number of boys, the active "club" members, called themselves the Jokers. There were approximately 50 members in the two sections of this group, a number of these being fringe members. The older Cutdowns had split into two smaller cliques of nine and seven members at the beginning of the project, while two younger cliques of seven and four members had emerged as potential inheritors of the gang tradition. About 30 additional boys did not align themselves clearly with any particular clique.

Major changes took place during the first six months. Both Cutdown cliques dissolved. The Jokers began to separate into the two sections— illustrated in Figure 10-4 with the B Jokers (the group most closely tied to the project staff) generally increasing in size, while the more delinquently oriented A Jokers remained constant in size. The two younger cliques lowered their general participation levels and shifted affiliations until the last few months of the project, at which point they began to coalesce while the Jokers split apart.

Although it seemed at the end that this youngest group might indeed provide the nucleus for gang perpetuation, there were several hopeful

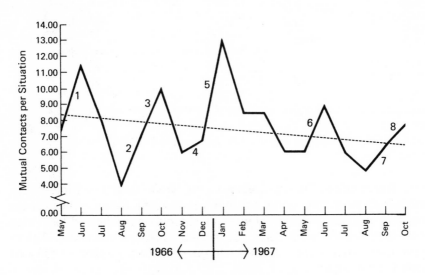

Fig. 10-4: Overall clique structure, 18 months.

signs. First, they did not recruit any new members. Second, they were a comparatively nondelinquent group whose interests lay primarily with automobiles rather than with gang activities. Finally, none of them was classified as a "cohesiveness builder."

By the end of the project, the Cutdowns had become a matter of past history. The Jokers were splitting up and reducing their clique membership. The auto clique had shown no signs, in their solidification, of replacing their predecessors either as a hard core delinquent group or as the focus for new gang membership. Thus, all the signs pointed toward the clear demise of Latin. How permanent a demise this might be was anyone's guess, although data from the six-month follow-up period (to be reported later) left hope for the future.

The general change in clique affiliations is summarized in Table 10-2 which indicates, on a quarterly basis, the number of clique members appearing sufficiently often to be considered active participants. For the purpose of this analysis, inclusion in the table requires at least five appearances during a quarterly period.

Table 10-2: Quarterly Appearances of Clique Members

| | | Quarterly Periods | | | | | |
		1st	2nd	3rd	4th	5th	6th
	Addict Cutdowns	0	6	2	0	0	0
	Cool Cutdowns	4	5	4	0	1	3
Clique	A Jokers	9	12	8	9	11	7
Members	B Jokers	9	17	15	21	22	22
	Auto Clique	5	4	4	3	5	6
	Dating Clique	3	2	3	2	2	3

Reactions to Threat. Data from the Group Guidance Project suggested strongly that gang clusters which were losing cohesiveness became involved in fewer intergang incidents and retaliated less often for "raids" into their territory or assaults against their members. Therefore, every known and rumored intergang incident involving Latin was noted in the project Log.

Unfortunately, a review of this material makes it clear that no conclusions can be drawn about reactions to threats because so much of the information was only rumor. In addition, the tangle of events involved in intergang tensions is so complex that one cannot empirically or conceptually differentiate between original threats and retaliations. Each raid on a rival gang's territory is "explained" by the boys as a retaliation, but is in fact merely a continuation of a string of mutual counter attacks. Carney *et al.* refer to the same pattern in Chicago: "Gang fights can involve as few as three boys: two members of one group who 'jump' a member of another group. The latter then goes to get his allies and the process can begin. Strictly speaking, this is a typical precipitating incident which is usually based on an alleged or real previous incident and so on, backwards, *ad infinitum*."[2]

Every gang I have seen refers to itself as a "defensive club" which retaliates but never initiates. Since intergang contacts are so often the results of preceding contacts, such a statement actually comes close to the truth. If there were enough *dramatic* attacks on one gang during a specified time period—18 months in our case—one could analyze the reactions to these. But such incidents are rare. During the project period we logged a total of 111 actual and rumored incidents of assaults, threats, and raids between Latin and other gangs, but only two of these resulted in homicides. Most of the others were accepted by the boys as a normal component of gang affiliation not calling for organized response. Thus, reactions to threat, as an index of cohesiveness, proved useless in this project.

Employment and Cohesiveness. With so many things happening in the field, only a few of which are caused by deliberate project intervention, it is obviously impossible to *prove* that project activities were responsible for the observed decrease in gang cohesiveness. However, one project activity does permit us to do more than guess. Because of the emphasis on employment, 49 boys had periods of both employment and unemployment during the project.

By comparing each boy's field activity during his working and nonworking periods, it should be possible to suggest the nature of the relationship between employment and cohesiveness; i.e., between a particular project intervention and the level of involvement of the boys with their peers. Once again, the field observer's data provide the measure of involvement.

During working periods, the average number of appearances per day was .25, as opposed to an average of .36 during nonworking periods.* In other words, the observer spotted these boys during his

*This difference yields a t of 2.87 significant beyond the .01 level.

normal cruising routine 30 per cent less often when they were employed. Considering that some of the jobs were part time, and that many of the boys were on shifts that did not coincide with the observer's cruising schedule (early afternoon to late evening), this 30 per cent difference is quite striking.

In addition, the number of mutual contacts per contact situation was 9 per cent lower during working periods.* This reduction is obviously less striking in size, but nonetheless quite meaningful, for it suggests that the boys seek out each other's company less when they are employed.

So far as companionship or cohesiveness is concerned, then, it seems clear that the employment program, in addition to any monetary and training advantages it supplied, did help to reduce Latin group activity among those who were directly involved. Whether it had any tangential effect on other Latin members would be purely conjectural, but not an unreasonable supposition.

Summary. Fifty-two members of the Latins were siblings. Another 14 were related in some other way, usually as first cousins. Most lived within walking distance or a short drive, had gone to the same schools, and many had been arrested together before the project began. I mention these facts to suggest why, as a project staff, we are more than satisfied with the amount of cohesiveness reduction during the project. One might hope for even more, but what the practical limits might be is impossible to gauge.

It is clear that the first six months of the project were the most effective, but that a general decline continued throughout the 18 months. Number of boys observed decreased by 40 per cent. Recruitment was completely halted. Grouping, as measured by the number of mutual contacts per contact situation, was reduced by 11 per cent. Clique membership showed a proportional though not an absolute decline, and major cliques were observed to be slowly disintegrating.

While grouping showed some decline, the major change was related to the *size* of Latin. This would strongly suggest that programs aimed at grouping phenomena can expect less success than those

---

*This difference yields a *t* of 2.25, significant beyond the .05 level. The two measures of activity, number of appearances and number of mutual contacts per contact situation, are statistically unrelated to each other in this analysis (Chi Square = .38, n. s.). These reductions were not related to number of days worked or overall activity levels of the boys involved. The 9 per cent reduction was not related to age, but the 30 per cent reduction in appearances took place primarily among the younger and older boys. Those in the middle (ages 16 and 17 at the beginning of the project) showed less variation between work and nonwork periods.

aimed at reducing gang size. The reduction in gang size achieved in the Ladino Hills Project can most properly be attributed to a few major factors:

1. The cessation of planned group activity
2. The active discouraging of new memberships
3. The many small attempts to treat the members as individuals rather than as a group
4. The placement of members in alternative settings, most particularly employment situations

By the same token, we can list the following as factors limiting cohesiveness reduction:

1. Common residence and school patterns
2. Family ties
3. Seasonal (school-related) spurs to group activity
4. The presence of unserviced rival gangs
5. Various community forces not under project control which reinforce gang identification and cohesiveness.

Delinquency

The original analysis plan called for a comparison of delinquency among the Latins with that among other traditional gangs being serviced by the Group Guidance agency. However, soon after our project started, service to these other groups was abandoned by the agency, leaving us with no basis for comparison. Accordingly, the only *comparative* statements that can now be made are between project and preproject periods involving Latin only.

There are the usual problems with this sort of comparison. The two 18-month periods may not be strictly comparable with respect to police, probation, and court practices. Changes in the Ladino Hills community might mask or accentuate differences in the level of gang delinquency. Figure 10-5 reports the number of delinquency arrests for the two 18-month periods (preproject and project) in the two police divisions covering the Ladino Hills community.

There is no discernible trend in these data—a general rise or decline—over the three-year period. The average monthly arrests figure is 207 in the preproject period and 201 in the project period, an insignificant difference. The only fairly consistent pattern in these data is the

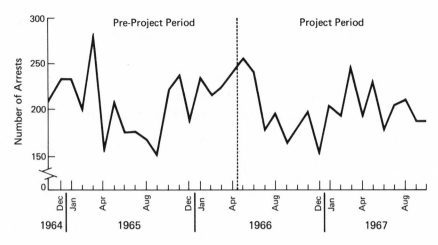

Fig. 10-5: Juvenile arrests (delinquency and
predelinquency) in two police divisions
serving Ladino Hills area.

seasonal cycle, which shows a peak in the early spring and a low point in
the fall of each year. On the basis of the data in Fig. 10-5, we can have at
least some confidence in the following comparisons between the preproject and project periods.

Delinquency Rates

Reduction in gang delinquency can be measured in two ways. One
of these is the *rate* at which members commit offenses and the other is
the absolute *number* of offenses committed. The two are independent
because of the age limit (18 years) necessitated by the legal separation
between juvenile and adult offenses. Youngsters under the age of 18 are
processed in a very different fashion by the various agencies of the
criminal justice system, and the offense recording systems reflect this
differential handling. Rates and absolute numbers of juvenile offenses
would yield identical findings if we were dealing with a constant population. However, the project's emphasis on reducing gang recruitment and
size calls for two separate analyses which might well yield different
results.

Looking first at delinquency *rates,* we find that the project had
no discernible effect. The analysis procedure, identical to that employed
in the Group Guidance Project, combines the number of offenses for
both periods, assigns an *expected* rate on the basis of monthly age

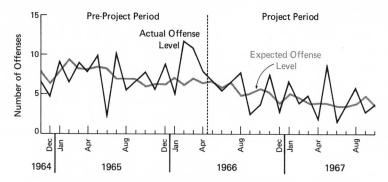

Fig. 10-6: Monthly expected and actual offenses,
preproject and project periods.

quotients, and compares this rate with that actually observed. Project impact on delinquency rates would be indicated by comparing the discrepancies between expected and actual figures during the preproject period with the discrepancies during the project period. If the actual number of offenses were greater than the expected number during the preproject period while the reverse were true during the project period, it would indicate success—a reduction in rates during the project. The opposite pattern would indicate failure, as happened in the Group Guidance Project. Figure 10-6 reports the results of this analysis.

Comparing the preproject period to the project period reveals no difference in the degree to which actual offense levels vary from the expected levels. Nor is there any discernible pattern within the project period alone. The actual monthly offenses vary in a strictly random fashion around the expected offense levels. Whatever the variables were that led to the actual offense rates, project intervention was not one of them. In the absence of data on comparable gangs during the same period, we cannot go beyond this equivocal statement. However, in comparing these findings with those of the Group Guidance Project, one can at least take heart that the dramatic increase in delinquency rates during the earlier project was not repeated in the Ladino Hills Project.

Number of Offenses

As clearly as Fig. 10-6 shows no change in delinquency *rates,* it shows just as clearly that the absolute *number* of offenses decreased significantly during the project. There were 139 offenses charged against juvenile (under 18) members of Latin during the preproject period, compared with 91 during the project period. This is a reduction of 35 per cent.

That such a large reduction is possible despite the failure to reduce delinquency rates should not cause confusion. The rates are a statement of summated individual arrests in relation to age-related expectancies. The 35 per cent reduction in total numbers is caused by a combination of two factors: (a) the fact that many boys achieved and passed the upper age limit of 18 years during the project period, and (b) (most important) the fact that gang recruitment ceased completely during the project. Thus, *as boys grew older and contributed less to juvenile arrests, they were not replaced by younger members joining Latin in sufficient numbers to maintain the original group level of offenses.* This, then, is where cohesiveness reduction seems most obviously related to delinquency reduction. In particular, it means that the effect on gang membership, rather than gang grouping, was related in the project to the effect on total number of juvenile offenses committed by Latin.

This relationship can be dramatically illustrated by Fig. 10-7 which reports the actual number of offenses (as in Fig. 10-6) but collapses the data into two-month periods to provide greater stability. The important point about Fig. 10-7 is that the major delinquency reduction takes place during the first six months of the project, the same period during which the number of boys observed showed the greatest decrease and during which the recruitment reduction was taking place.

This coincidence in timing does not *prove* that the observed reduction in delinquency was caused by the observed reduction in cohesiveness, but it does constitute good supportive evidence. Further supportive evidence can be derived from the employment data. Because the earlier comparison of working vs. nonworking periods related to cohesiveness was found to be unrelated to age, we can undertake a direct comparison of offenses committed by the 49 boys who had periods of both employment and nonemployment. A total of 42 offenses were committed during 6,330 working days, as compared with 61 offenses committed during 4,851 nonworking days. In other words, there were approximately four working days for every three nonworking days, yet the ratio of offenses was approximately four to six in the reverse direction. There were almost twice as many offenses per day during nonworking periods,* and once again the project's employment program stands out as a crucial factor in the level of success that was achieved.

---

*Chi-Square, basing expected frequencies on the ratio of the two sets of days, equals 10.10, $p < .01$. In this analysis, offenses committed beyond the age of 18 *are* included.

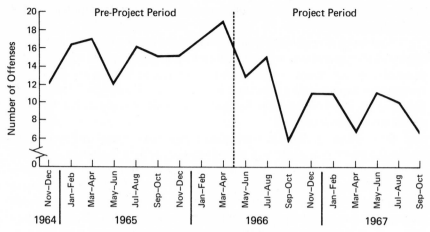

Fig. 10-7: Actual offenses, preproject and project
periods, in two-month segments.

Qualitative Differences

From our comparison of the Ladino Hills Project to the Group Guidance Project and our claim of more success for the one than the other, the reader might wonder whether the Latin gang was not an "easier nut to crack" than the gangs in the earlier project. The answer is clearly "no"; in fact, just the opposite.

At the outset of the two projects, Latin was considerably more cohesive than the Negro gangs were. Latin was a "family related" gang, in that over half the members were siblings or first cousins as opposed to an estimated 15 to 20 per cent in the Negro groups.

Prior to the project, the groups were about equal in the proportion on probation, but Latin members had committed almost twice as many offenses: 6.49 vs. 3.31 per boy with a record. Qualitatively, the Negro and Mexican-American boys were charged with similar types of offenses with the exception of minor thefts (higher in Negro gangs) and drug and alcohol offenses (higher in Latin).

The final comparison of importance has to do with intergang rivalry. The gangs in the Group Guidance Project had very few traditional rivals, typically only one or two. Latin, on the other hand, was "surrounded" by four rival gangs with whom they had been fighting literally for decades. Three of these were very active during the project period and periodically became embroiled in gang "hassles" with Latin.

In the gang world, there is no greater cohesiveness builder than an active rival gang.

There was no substantial difference in the kinds of offenses charged against Latin members in the preproject and project periods. Proportionately, minor thefts and robberies increased and auto thefts decreased. However, other findings in the Group Guidance Project were reversed in the Ladino Hills Project—reversals for which we have no adequate explanation.

One of the findings in the earlier project—a crucial one to our formulations about programming, cohesiveness, and delinquency—was that high-companionship offenses were significantly increased by the program while low-companionship offenses were relatively unaffected. In the Ladino Hills Project, there was no significant difference between changes in high and low companionship offense rates (Chi Square = 2.40, $p > .10$). However, whereas the Group Guidance Project had no differential effect on more versus less serious offenses, the Ladino Hills Project manifested a significant differential (Chi Square = 5.83, $p < .02$) with proportionately more serious offenses being committed during the project period.

The first finding is not displeasing, as it again suggests that we were more successful on the cohesiveness dimension than were the workers in the Group Guidance Project. It is disappointing that we could not actually reverse the trend, but to do so would probably have required greater success than the 11 per cent reduction in grouping actually achieved.

However, the reversal on the seriousness dimension *is* displeasing. It would seem natural to blame this on the higher proportion of older boys as the project proceeded, but earlier analyses revealed very little relationship between age and offense seriousness, at least as measured here. It may be that the sorts of interventions practiced in the project (such as the employment programs) have their effects primarily on the less serious kinds of offenses, with the more serious behaviors being more impervious to project efforts. However, this is more of a description than an explanation of the finding. We do not have the data to suggest anything further.

Summary

The project *did* successfully and substantially reduce the amount of delinquency associated with the Latin gang cluster. It reduced the amount, but not the rate per boy under 18 years of age. As compared with the Group Guidance Project, it fared better with respect to high companionship offenses, but not with respect to more serious offenses. The employment program seemed to have a very beneficial effect on offense behavior, but the almost total absence of any such program in the Group Guidance Project prohibits comparison.

Combining the delinquency data with the cohesiveness data summarized earlier, it seems reasonable to suggest that reduction in gang size accounts for the bulk of the delinquency decrease. The 11 per cent reduction in grouping was not sufficient to affect delinquency rates; and the hypothesis that the grouping phenomenon in the gang is a partial determinant of the rate of gang delinquency remains untested. Only a project even more successful in affecting grouping can provide such a test.

The Follow-up Period

Predictions

What happens to a large gang cluster when it is deprived of a team of helping adults after a year and a half (or more) of service? Some might suggest that it would be forced to fall back in upon itself to compensate for the loss. If so, one would predict an increase in cohesiveness, at least as measured by the extent of grouping. Compensation might also be achieved by recruiting new members to provide the illusion of strength and continued existence as a viable force in the gang subculture. Such predictions as these would presumably be based on an anxiety rationale: The loss of adult support heightens collective anxiety, which in turn calls forth responses to relieve this anxiety.

A second prediction, also anxiety-based but supported by the conception of the adult staff as a damper on gang activity, would suggest an increase, probably a dramatic one, in acting-out behavior. Both as a petulant reaction to the adult withdrawal and as a means of reasserting common bonds, such acting-out behaviors as "testing" rival gangs, vandalism, and "authority-protest" behaviors (such as auto theft or runaway) might be expected to increase.[3]

A third prediction, based on the conceptions of Cloward and Ohlin,[4] would be that retreatist activities would increase, principally liquor and drug use. This increase would occur because of the reduction of access to legitimate opportunities occasioned by the removal of facilitating adults, but only if criminal and conflict reactions were for some reason relatively futile. In the absence of delinquency data this latter prediction could be tested among the Latins by watching for the emergence of a new addict clique or the reemergence or amplification of the old Addict Cutdown clique (see Fig. 10-4).

In contrast to these predictions, all of which suggest a deterioration in the situation immediately following adult withdrawal, the overall experience and data of the Group Guidance Project suggested a *diminishing* of both cohesiveness and delinquency. In that project, worker transfers and programming reductions were generally followed by a decrease in general gang activity. We found no support for Jansyn's proposition[5] that cohesiveness reduction is followed by an upswing in gang activity.

Staff Changes

Fortunately, we are in a position to present pertinent evidence for some of the above predictions. When the staff withdrew from Ladino Hills at the end of the 18-month project period, arrangements were made for the field observer to continue his observations on a half-time basis. He put in a regular eight-hour day every other day for a full six months following the end of the project. Because he maintained his ordinary cruising procedures, we have companionship data for these six months which are perfectly comparable to those already reported.

We do not, however, have any official delinquency data. To collect it would have taxed our resources; but even more important, it could not have been very conclusive. A projection from the rates during the project period, considering the continuing age changes, suggested that only about 20 additional juvenile charges could be expected to be filed during the six-month follow-up period. This number would have been insufficient for analysis purposes and not worth the effort required in searching the records.*

To assess what happened in Ladino Hills after the project ended requires first a description of the change in staffing. On the first day of November, 1967 (the first day of the follow-up period), all research personnel including the project director left the area and did not return. The field office was closed, the answering service discontinued. The resources worker also departed and was henceforth unavailable to the Latins.

In addition to the field observer who was present on a half-time basis, this left only the detached worker. Originally, the Human Relations Commission had planned to reassign him to another area in East Los

---

*During the project period, the field observer learned of 63 out of 91 official juvenile charges from the boys themselves. During the follow-up period, he was told of 15 juvenile offenses. Using the 63:91 ratio, this suggests that the projection of 20 charges was probably not out of line with reality.

Angeles. However, rather extensive work by project staff had led to a minor flood of letters from various agencies and individuals requesting that the worker be retained for at least six months while project data were being analyzed. Then these agencies, through the Regional Welfare Planning Council, were to suggest approaches for reinforcing the assumed success of the project. The Planning Council never did follow through on these plans, with the result that Ladino Heights is still a disorganized community, but at least they were successful in keeping the worker in the area for an additional six months.

What the worker did during this final period has been assessed by the field observer as "minimal service." He continued to meet with a few members on Wednesday nights, and made a few job connections for them, using the employer list compiled by the resources worker. Beyond this, his presence in the field was not very evident. To all intents and purposes, the services available to Latin during the follow-up period were quite similar to those prior to the project, except that the absence of group programming typifying the project period was continued.

Cohesiveness

Figure 10-8 repeats the project period data for number of boys observed per cruising mile, but adds the data for the follow-up period. The latter are reported in three two-month segments to adjust for the observer's cruising on a half-time basis.

Figure 10-8 indicates that the reduction in member visibility achieved during the project continued during the follow-up period. The withdrawal of the staff led to no appreciable change in the trend. Fur-

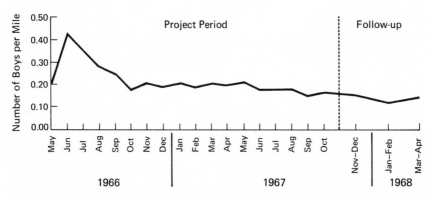

Fig. 10-8: Number of boys per mile, project and follow-up periods.

thermore, no recruitment took place during these last six months. The observer saw no new faces among the old. Although several younger brothers of Latin members verbalized an interest in being "sponsored" by the detached worker, the observer noted, "... there was no new group or new generation of Latin that had coalesced into an even minimally structured group." In the same field report, the observer said,

> In terms of the older existing groups of Latin it appears none of the Jokers or Cutdowns are at all interested in these younger boys. I have never observed any of the older boys giving any kind of leadership to these younger boys nor showing any special interest in getting them to become 'new' Latin.

Of course, the seeds of a rejuvenated Latin gang are always present. The younger brothers are the obvious potential inheritors of the Latin tradition and sibling relations have been a constant source of gang continuation. One cannot say that Latin is dead, only that it has shown few signs of recovery from its depleted condition.

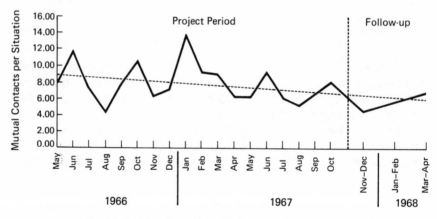

Fig. 10-9: Number of mutual contacts per contact
situation, project and follow-up periods.

Figure 10-9 reports the grouping data as before with the addition of the follow-up data. The overall trend noted earlier is continued, despite the rise starting in January of 1968. Again, evidence to support any of the anxiety-based predictions is lacking.

However, the rise in grouping toward the end of the follow-up period is probably not a chance phenomenon. During those last few months, both the High Riders and the Gaylords renewed their rivalry with Latin. Numerous raids, minor assaults, and "fair fights" took place. In addition, Tiger, a very popular member of the Joker clique, was killed by an old member of a farther-removed gang in the aftermath of a New Year's eve barroom brawl. Fifty-six Latin members attended his wake.

Earlier, all of this activity would have sent the grouping index shooting upward, as it did in October of 1966 and January of 1967. The very gradual and minimal rise shown in the follow-up data confirm the belief that Latin was somewhat of a shadow of its former self. Latin was still there, and still active, but it was not a serious threat to community peace.

Even the employment program seemed to be continuing in the absence of the project. The observer learned of 15 hirings as opposed to seven instances of quitting, being fired, or being laid off. Although these numbers are considerably lower than the rate established during the project, the ratio of job-gaining to job-losing was excellent. Three additional boys went off to the Job Corps.

Finally, significant changes in clique structure took place following staff withdrawal. During the project, six fairly distinct clique formations comprised most of the core membership of the Latins. As illustrated in Fig. 10-4, these were labeled the Addict Cutdowns, the Cool Cutdowns, the A Jokers, the B Jokers, the Auto Clique, and the Dating Clique.

By the end of the project, both Cutdown cliques had effectively dispersed. The B Jokers had remained as the largest subgroup, centering around Chico Santiago, who was on the project payroll. The A Jokers constituted a fairly constant group which was more delinquently oriented than the B Jokers, and oriented somewhat toward the Addict Cutdowns. The younger Auto and Dating cliques, manifesting fairly nondelinquent orientations, had remained small and relatively independent.

After the project, significant changes took place. The B Jokers, the largest and most visible group, broke up dramatically. The A Jokers expanded their membership by incorporating remaining B members and clearly became the core of Latin. The Auto and Dating cliques coalesced as the former expanded to form the presumed base for the continuation of Latin. The most hopeful sign in this latter development was, of course, the orientation of this younger clique toward "fun and games" rather than conflict. The way in which the original six cliques dissolved into two is illustrated in Fig. 10-10. The additional dyads pictured in Fig. 10-10 show the pairing off that accompanies clique dissolution.

Perhaps most striking of all is that the younger clique averaged 18 years old during the follow-up period, with the youngest boy being 16. With recruitment of younger neighborhood boys being held in check for a year and a half, Latin became a "young adult" gang. Any perpetuation of Latin would have to take place as a new phenomenon, an almost spontaneous generation of a new gang of young teenagers rather than a downward extension from existing cliques.

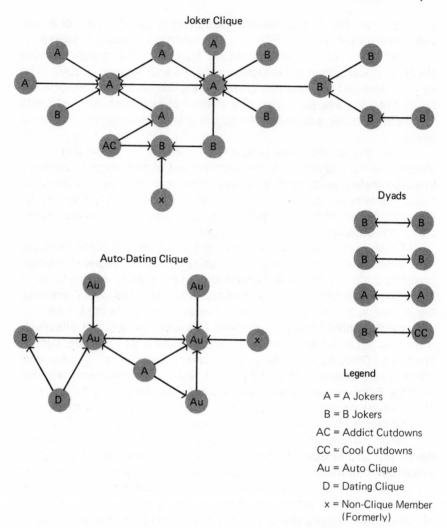

Fig. 10-10: Cliques in the follow-up period.

No such development has taken place in the two and a half years between the end of the follow-up period and the date of this writing, or 33 months since the termination of the action period. A conversation with the director of the Boys' Club in February, 1970, yielded the opinion that Latin was almost totally inactive, with very few of the known members being visible and no younger subgroups in existence. Similarly, the juvenile officers in the two involved police jurisdictions and the "Gang Detail" of the police department reported that Latin had not been active as a gang and that criminal activities had been relatively few and on an individual basis. The police put the age range of Latin members at 17 to 25 years.

A generation gap of such magnitude existed, then, that the normal self-perpetuation dynamics of the traditional gang cluster had been interrupted. Herein, perhaps, lies the best hope for youngsters in Ladino Hills, if one assumes that affiliation with a delinquent gang is, on balance, harmful to the individual youngster (to say nothing of his family and his community). In this, I directly oppose Walter Miller's position[6] that gang membership within the lower class urban setting is "normal" and functional to the adjustment of the youngster.

Summary

This section began with the enunciation of several alternative predictions as to the probable outcomes of staff withdrawal after an intensive 18-month gang intervention project. The withdrawal was immediate and drastic, but the data concerning both cohesiveness and delinquency failed to confirm predictions of increased activity, whatever their conceptual base.

The patterns we observed merely continued those of the past. Cohesiveness remained low except in the face of intergang conflict. Recruitment failed to reappear. Older cliques continued to dissolve in the absence of new clique generation. The dissolution of the large B Jokers' clique in particular seemed to repeat the empirical findings of the Group Guidance Project, since this was the clique most closely involved with the positive intervention efforts of the project staff. Two of its core members were on the project payroll and were employed as role models for their compatriots. When we left, so did these two boys to all intents and purposes. As in the Group Guidance Project, it seems reasonable to suggest that staff members themselves became important sources of cohesiveness.

The difference in Ladino Hills was that staff withdrawal meant less of a change for the boys. In the Group Guidance Project it had meant an end to heavy group programming, but this had already been accomplished with the Latins. The major impact on Latin had been accomplished in the first six months by design, rather than inadvertently by worker transfer. The follow-up period in Ladino Hills may therefore be viewed as a *reinforcement* of already existing patterns—there was little room left for the more dramatic results of staff withdrawal that occurred in the Group Guidance Project.

References

1. "Privacy and Behavioral Research: Preliminary Summary of the Report of the Panel on Privacy and Behavioral Research," *American Psychologist* 22, no. 5 (May, 1967): 345–49.
2. Frank J. Carney, Hans W. Mattick, and John D. Callaway, *Action on the Streets* (New York: Association Press, 1969), p. 60.
3. James F. Short, Jr. and Fred L. Strodtbeck, *Group Process and Gang Delinquency* (Chicago: University of Chicago Press, 1965), especially Chapter 5.
4. Richard A. Cloward and Lloyd E. Ohlin, *Delinquency and Opportunity* Glencoe, Ill.: The Free Press, 1960).
5. Leon R. Jansyn, "Solidarity and Delinquency in a Street Corner Group," *American Sociological Review* 31, no. 5 (October, 1966): 600–614.
6. Walter B. Miller, "Lower Class Culture as a Generating Milieu of Gang Delinquency," *Journal of Social Issues* 14, no. 3 (Summer, 1958): 5–19.

Appendix A:

Tabular Data

Table A-1: 54 Item Contents Employed in Core-Fringe Comparison Interviews

Item Contents	x^2	p	Selected for Factor Analysis
1. Familiarity to worker	5.7	$<.02$	yes
2. Loyalty to group**	19.4	$<.001$	yes
3. Total contribution to group*	14.7	$<.001$	yes
4. Level of participation in spontaneous group activities**	7.9	$<.01$	no[+]
5. Length of residence in area	10.9	$<.01$	yes
6. Readily available money	1.6	.20	yes
7. Willingness to fight other groups*	28.5	$<.001$	yes
8. Level of *recorded* offense behavior	17.7	$<.001$	yes
9. Adoption of "posture"	13.4	$<.001$	yes
10. Ability to fight**	9.7	$<.01$	yes
11. Level of participation in planned group activities**	1.3	n.s.	no
12. Duration of membership*	22.4	$<.001$	yes
13. Frequency of participation in planned activities**	0.9	n.s.	no
14. Involvement in nongang interests*	4.0	$<.05$	yes
15. Frequency of participation in spontaneous activities**	11.5	$<.001$	yes
16. Inappropriateness of behavior or opinions	0.6	n.s.	no
17. Level of *undetected* offense behavior	17.5	$<.001$	no[+]
18. General social abilities	1.4	n.s.	no
19. Popularity with girls	0.1	n.s.	no

315

Item Contents	x^2	p	Selected for Factor Analysis
20. Acceptance by core members*	8.9	<.01	yes
21. Verbal ability**	0.4	n.s.	no
22. Involvement in clique within gang	7.1	<.01	yes
23. Physical and athletic abilities**	1.3	n.s.	no
24. Adequacy of school work	10.6	<.01	yes
25. Emotional dependence on group*	7.5	<.01	yes
26. Frequency of class cuts and truancy	17.1	<.001	yes
27. Preference for follower roles	0.8	n.s.	no
28. Group-related ideational creativity	0.0	n.s.	no
29. Level of respect by others for fighting prowess	9.1	<.01	no[+]
30. Level of worker-member rapport	2.3	<.20	no[+]
31. Ability to remain calm during high tension periods	4.4	<.05	no[+]
32. Desire for leadership**	10.9	<.001	yes
33. Intelligence	3.6	<.10	yes
34. Level of heterosexual activity	1.6	n.s	no
35. Presence of core member sibling	9.4	<.01	yes
36. Use of home as member hangout	8.9	<.01	yes
37. Use of home for parties	0.0	n.s.	no
38. Ability to drive a car	3.5	<.10	yes
39. Avoidance of implicating others**	11.5	<.001	yes
40. Tendency to play stereotyped group role (e.g., clown)	1.0	n.s.	no
41. Access to car	0.0	n.s.	no
42. Pronounced psycho- or sociopathic tendencies	13.5	<.001	yes
43. Residence central to gang territory	0.0	n.s.	no
44. Known for protecting others from detection**	8.1	<.01	no[+]
45. Age*	0.1	n.s.	no
46. Level of worker liking for member	0.0	n.s.	no
47. Difficulty of working with member	4.2	<.05	yes
48. Level of impulse control	3.4	<.10	yes
49. Desire for rehabilitation	8.5	<.01	yes
50. Degree member seeks help	2.6	<.20	yes
51. Degree member feels environmentally "trapped"	9.5	<.10	yes
52. Worker expectations of member progress	1.8	<.20	no[+]
53. Frequency of "money in the pocket"	5.7	<.02	no[+]
54. Worker estimate of member's need for help	7.9	<.01	yes

*Taken directly from prior worker interviews.

**Transformed from items taken from worker interviews.

[+]Employed as reliability check on another item; therefore eliminated from factor analysis.

Table A-2: Factors and Factor Loadings of 30-Item Analysis: Core and Fringe Members

	Original Item #	I	II	III	IV	V	VI	VII	VIII	IX	Communalities
						Factors					
I	7	58	−48	−09	−23	−23	−06	−06	−13	18	74
	8	80	−07	−21	05	−26	−02	08	−12	09	79
	14	61	−03	06	−23	00	−16	−03	−36	−11	60
	24	86	07	−08	−15	02	−17	−07	15	−04	83
	25	65	−41	02	−14	22	−10	−06	06	39	82
	26	79	−01	−24	−09	−04	−18	02	20	23	82
	33	83	11	−11	09	04	−30	−12	−24	−23	93
	39	80	−30	06	−04	−07	−10	13	−06	34	88
	42	76	−21	08	−34	−01	08	−08	−25	25	88
	48	81	−12	06	−31	03	−03	−13	−10	06	79
	49	77	−14	00	39	−05	−06	−09	−22	09	84
	54	70	−15	−06	−55	−17	−18	07	−04	12	90
II	3	03	−60	−37	00	−17	−03	−32	−02	−12	65
	15	13	−78	−12	−14	07	−08	−13	03	−12	70
	20	−01	−48	−26	−01	−42	−16	−43	−07	−23	74
	22	14	−76	20	12	−24	−04	−12	−14	29	82
	32	22	−52	−26	−42	−11	08	07	12	37	74
III	1	02	−09	−88	01	−06	−18	−04	−04	01	82
	2	07	−42	−69	−11	12	12	−27	−02	22	83
	36	33	08	−63	−08	−29	01	−19	−02	50	88
IV	51	29	−10	−04	−83	−03	−07	−03	−18	20	87
V	10	11	−42	−22	−06	−66	09	03	−05	−05	69
	38	03	02	08	−02	−79	−14	−27	05	17	76
VI	47	46	−22	06	−08	05	−74	04	−06	09	84
	50	21	01	−17	−03	−13	−84	−11	−09	09	83
VII	5	03	−12	−07	06	00	−08	−88	−04	08	81
	12	09	−25	−17	−09	−32	02	−79	00	11	85
VIII	6	23	−04	−07	−11	01	−11	−04	−92	14	96
IX	9	40	−13	−04	−11	−27	−02	03	−21	64	72
	35	03	10	−25	−23	08	−25	−25	−04	63	65

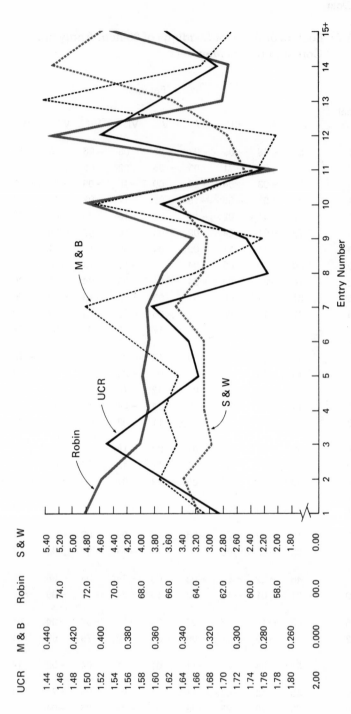

UCR	M & B	Robin	S & W
1.44	0.440		5.40
1.46	0.420	74.0	5.20
1.48		72.0	5.00
1.50	0.400		4.80
1.52		70.0	4.60
1.54	0.380		4.40
1.56			4.20
1.58	0.360	68.0	4.00
1.60			3.80
1.62		66.0	3.60
1.64	0.340		3.40
1.66	0.320	64.0	3.20
1.68			3.00
1.70	0.300	62.0	2.80
1.72			2.60
1.74		60.0	2.40
1.76	0.280		2.20
1.78		58.0	2.00
1.80	0.260		1.80
2.00	0.000	00.0	0.00

Fig. A-1: Comparison of average seriousness score per offense
(core and fringe combined).

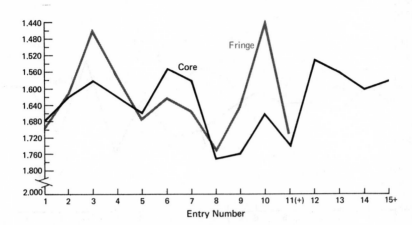

Fig. A-2: Average seriousness scores, core vs.
fringe—Uniform Crime Reports.

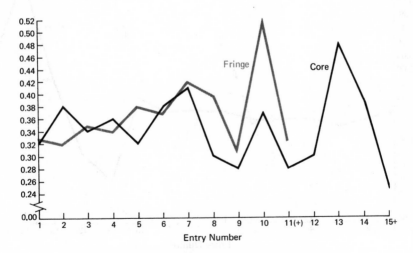

Fig. A-3: Average seriousness scores, core vs.
fringe—McEachern and Bauzer.

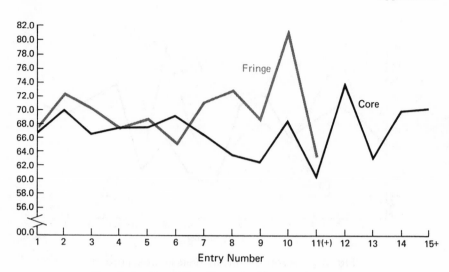

Fig. A-4: Average seriousness scores, core vs.
fringe—Robin.

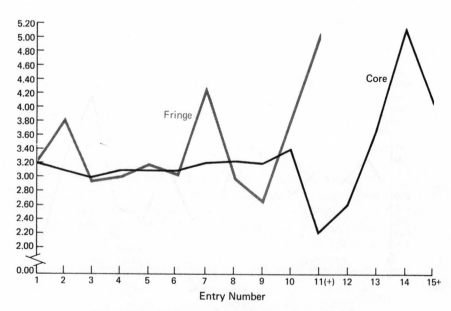

Fig. A-5: Average seriousness scores, core vs.
fringe—Sellin and Wolfgang.

Appendix B:

Analysis
Procedures, G.G.P.

The Delinquency Criterion

In all program evaluations, there will be differences of opinion concerning the most appropriate criteria to be used for judging levels of success. Our workers stressed one criterion over all others—the change in gang member attitudes and values in a "positive" direction. Conversations with workers in other cities confirm the generality of this approach which is certainly an understandable one. But in the Group Guidance Project, we relied heavily on the criteria of gang recruitment and delinquency involvement for the following reasons.

First, the expressed purpose of the Group Guidance operation, from its inception in the early 1940's, had been to control gang formation, fighting, and delinquency. This was also the major emphasis of the Ford Foundation grant upon which the research is based.

Second, the expectations of the community, both lay and professional, are that gang workers will achieve a decrease in gang problems. It is the deviant *behavior* rather than the deviant attitudes which is of concern to the police, the school and recreation officials, and the residents of gang neighborhoods.

Third, the availability of official records makes the collection of "hard data" on delinquency more feasible and pertinent to agency programming than would be the case with interview and questionnaire data. These latter forms of data are particularly suspect within a gang member population, and the possibilities of surveying the entire membership population or even a representative sample are remote.

Three record sources were potentially available for use in the project: police records, a Central Juvenile Index (CJI) which is a repository for all enforcement agencies, and probation records. Legal restrictions prevented use of police records, but an independent study of a sample of gang member records revealed that CJI had a 31 per cent and probation a 10 per cent loss of police records. The correlations of number of offenses per boys were in the .80's between the three sources. Since the vast majority of gang members did become probationers, the probation records were chosen as the most feasible source of delinquency data. Analysis revealed no systematic bias in types of offenses when police and probation records were compared.

The Delinquency Measure

Measurement of three characteristics of the delinquency data were considered: analysis by seriousness of offenses, by categories of offenses, and by sheer numbers of offenses. As indicated in Part I, seriousness was empirically determined to be a poor discriminator between groups, at least for the gangs in this study. It was also mentioned that categories of offenses did not emerge from a factor analysis of all recorded offenses. Thus, we were left in the seemingly awkward position of saying that the best choice among the three criterion measures was the simplest and the most gross of all—number of offenses. Since probation records were more comprehensive than CJI records in terms of number of boys and number of offenses, the choice of these records as our data source was reinforced.

Analysis Procedure

There were no comparable Negro gangs, with known and complete membership rosters, that could serve as control groups for the project gangs. Similarly, while there were comparable geographic areas, these were not gang territories of sufficient intensity to provide good comparisons with the project's test area. Additionally, the contributions of gang member offenses to overall delinquency rates for given geographic areas are not sufficient for a change in gang offense levels to be reliably revealed in area rates.

In the absence of acceptable control groups and useful area rates, the only comparison left is with a preproject period, using the gang members as their own controls. We can seek to determine whether the gang member offenses increased or decreased during the project period as against an equal four-year period immediately preceding the project. This is the choice we made, although this approach also implies some difficulties.

To make this comparison, one must assume that the test area did not undergo substantial change during the two relevant four-year periods. Analysis of available data from the census and the Welfare Planning Council suggests that this is a reasonable assumption. One must also assume that the data recording systems (probation records) were used in substantially the same fashion during the two periods. Conversations with the relevant agency officials indicates that this was the case. Still, the matter remains as an untested assumption, and due caution is in order.

The major problem, however, is to institute proper age controls. Delinquency is not randomly distributed across age groups, but tends to peak around the 16-year age level. Our gang members were four years older during the project period than during the prior four-year period. These two facts necessitated the development of a more complex analysis procedure.

If the project had no impact, the number of delinquent acts charged against 12-year-old gang members should be equal during the project period and during an equal period just prior to the project. The same would apply to every age level. If the project were successful (positive impact), offenses committed by boys of a given age level would be fewer (per boy) than those by the same aged boys in the prior period. The converse would be true if the project were detrimental (negative impact). The analysis procedure was carried out with specific age controls in a variation of a cohort analysis designed to produce an *expected* number of charges per month against which the actual number of charges could be compared.

The steps for deriving such an expected number of charges are as follows:

1. Over the entire eight-year period, determine the number of offenses charged against all boys when they were 12 years, 0 months of age. Do the same for 12 years, 1 month, and so on up to 17 years, 11 months. The 12 years, 0 months limit represents the lowest age of gang involvement, while the upper limit of 17 years, 11 months is the last month of status as a juvenile under the California court system. After this latter age, recording and disposition of cases are on an adult basis and not at all comparable to the recording and disposition of juvenile cases.

2. Divide the total number of offenses at each year and month of age by the number of boys who had attained that age during the eight-

year period. For example, if 22 offenses were attributed to boys at the age of 15 years, 6 months and 440 boys had attained that age during the control and project periods, then the expected number of offenses per boy of 15 years, 6 months of age would be 22/440 or .05. Judging by performance over the entire eight-year period, a gang member of this age stands 5 chances in 100 of being charged with an offense *at that age.** Since we are including in this analysis the ages 12,0 through 17,11 or an age span of six years, it follows that six times 12 (or 72) such quotients were determined.

3. The control period fell between July of 1957 and June of 1961, while the project period extended from July of 1961 through June of 1965. There are thus 96 monthly periods. For each of these monthly periods, determine the number of boys at each age level by year and month. For example, in July of 1957 how many boys were of the age 12 years, 0 months; 12 years, 1 month; and so on up to 17 years, 11 months.

4. Within each monthly period, multiply each age-level *quotient* by the *number* of boys of that age, and summate. This step yields the number of offenses to be expected during each month solely on the basis of the empirical relationship between age and offense record. Graphing each monthly sum then yields an expected level of offense behavior through the control and project periods.

5. Finally, subtract the *actual* monthly offense frequencies from the *expected* monthly offense frequencies. This will produce a graph, as in Fig. B-1, expressing the relative increase or decrease from expectations during the preproject ("control") and project periods. In this analysis, it is important to remember that the gang members serve as their own controls. The numbers of actual, obtained offenses are statistically meaningless in and of themselves; they take on meaning only as their distribution over time is compared with the age-derived expected offense frequencies.**

---

*This figure is purely illustrative.

**The final procedure also controlled for each boy's periods of incarceration.

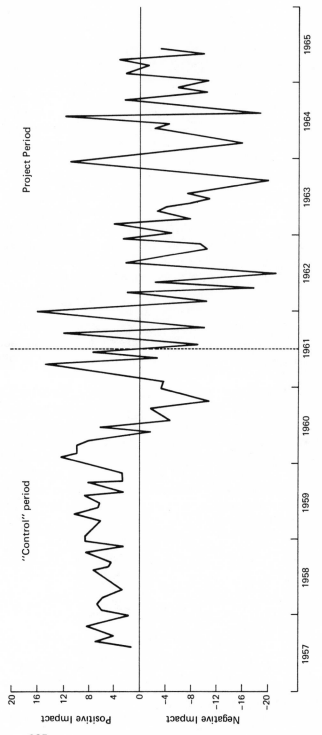

Fig. B-1: Expected minus actual offense frequencies.

325

Appendix C:

AGREEMENT BETWEEN LAW ENFORCEMENT AND
THE PROBATION DEPARTMENT FOR THE OPERATION OF
THE GROUP GUIDANCE SECTION OF THE PROBATION DEPARTMENT

April 18, 1963

"Group Guidance" is a delinquency prevention and control program
for youth in Los Angeles County. Under authorization of the Juvenile
Court Law (Welfare and Institutions Code Sections 516, 536, and 580);
Section 1203.13 of the California Penal Code, and by order of the
Board of Supervisors of Los Angeles County, the Los Angeles County
Probation Department has allocated staff to fulfill the purposes set
forth in the foregoing code sections.

Group Guidance services are provided for the purpose of preventing
and reducing delinquency, particularly destructive gang activity,
affecting youth in Los Angeles County.

The objectives of Group Guidance are achieved through the medium of
activity programs, individual and group counseling, and the promotion
of understanding between the youth and the community.

It is the policy of Group Guidance and law enforcement to cooperate
and to share information when the public safety is affected.

Regular meetings between representatives of law enforcement and
Group Guidance staff should be held for discussion of operating
problems of mutual concern. Insofar as possible these meetings should
be held monthly.

Group Guidance workers are concerned primarily with the prevention
of delinquency; the interests of minors are represented in Court by field
deputy probation officers. Group Guidance Sr. DPO's appear in Court
only as needed and only with the approval of the Supervisor and the
Director of Group Guidance.

Student workers, student professional workers, and group members are used as assistants to the Sr. DPO's, but only under supervision of a Sr. DPO and with the approval of the Supervisor and the Director of Group Guidance.

The intent and purpose of Group Guidance in working with predelinquent segments of gang groups is to encourage these youth to become active in recreational and/or counseling programs where these are available to the youth and when the agency is able to accept the youth.

Group Guidance will give emphasis to youth between the ages of 13 and 17 inclusive, but recognize that older youth have potential for disrupting the program and often require attention. Youths who prove to be not amenable to the program should, insofar as is possible, be removed from the program.

Names of groups and titles of officers which cause community concern, designation of areas of private domain, recruiting of members, wearing of unacceptable gang insignia, are all symptomatic of the gang psychology and are regarded as undesirable. However, these are so well integrated into the thinking, gang lore and patterns of some groups that they are relinquished with great reluctance. It is the aim of Group Guidance to guide groups toward socially acceptable names, titles, and activities as rapidly as possible.

Group Guidance staff attempt to become acquainted with, and to exert influence upon, both core members and fringe members of established gang groups and their parents for the purpose of becoming a link between the gang members and the community's opportunity system of learning, recreation, employment, and citizenship. In this role the Group Guidance staff lead gang members to become disengaged from gang conflict and identified with socially acceptable goals. Group Guidance staff do not engage in gang recruitment efforts.

Group Guidance staff are assigned to work in areas or with specific groups in response to requests from responsible groups or agencies in the area. Insofar as Group Guidance staffing permits, female Sr. DPO's are assigned to work with female or coed groups. Male student workers are assigned to assist with boys' groups when such workers are available to the Group Guidance Section.

Group Guidance staff members work an evening shift of 8 hours between 1 p.m. and 10 p.m.; therefore, regular group meetings will usually be ended by 9:30 p.m.

Such programs as Group Guidance provides can be successful only with sincere cooperation, mutual helpfulness and support between agencies; therefore, it shall be the purpose of Group Guidance, Los Angeles Police Department, and Los Angeles County Sheriff's Department to strive for cooperation and understanding to the end that the best interest of the community is served.

Index

Though the author demonstrates his honesty in "having it" with gangs, his introduction should have also led him to serious question the validity of writing this book. Instead, the amount of fresh material offered here could have easily been presented in an article format.